THE POSSIBILITY OF PHILOSOPHY

Northwestern University
Studies in Phenomenology
and
Existential Philosophy

General Editor Anthony J. Steinbock

THE POSSIBILITY OF PHILOSOPHY

Course Notes from the Collège de France, 1959–1961

Maurice Merleau-Ponty

Edited by Stéphanie Ménasé
Foreword by Claude Lefort

Translated from the French by Keith Whitmoyer

Northwestern University Press
Evanston, Illinois

Northwestern University Press
www.nupress.northwestern.edu

Printed in the United States of America

10   9   8   7   6   5   4   3   2   1

Library of Congress Cataloging-in-Publication Data

Names: Merleau–Ponty, Maurice, 1908–1961, author. | Ménasé, Stéphanie,
    editor. | Whitmoyer, Keith, translator. | Lefort, Claude, writer of foreword.
Title: The possibility of philosophy : course notes from the Collège de France,
    1959–1961 / Maurice Merleau–Ponty ; edited by Stéphanie Ménasé ; foreword
    by Claude Lefort ; translated from the French by Keith Whitmoyer.
Other titles: Notes des cours au Collège de France, 1958–1959 et 1960–1961.
    English | Studies in phenomenology and existential philosophy.
Description: Evanston, Illinois : Northwestern University Press, 2022. | Series:
    Studies in phenomenology and existential philosophy | "Originally published
    in French under the title Notes de Cours: 1959 –1961. Copyright Editions
    Gallimard, Paris, 1996." | Includes bibliographical references and index. |
Identifiers: LCCN 2021039792 | ISBN 9780810144538 (paperback) | ISBN
    9780810144545 (cloth) | ISBN 9780810144552 (ebook)
Subjects: LCSH: Philosophy. | Ontology. | Philosophy, Modern—19th cen-
    tury. | Philosophy, Modern—20th century.
Classification: LCC B2430.M3763 N6813 2022 | DDC 194—dc23
LC record available at https://lccn.loc.gov/2021039792

Contents

Appendixes

Translator's Preface

Keith Whitmoyer

I was very happy to have the opportunity to make the text of these courses and the appendixes available to an English-speaking audience after what has been a protracted lapse from the publication of the French edition, *Notes de cours: 1959–1961*, by Gallimard in 1996. The notes for these courses, as Claude Lefort indicates, while elliptical and at times obtuse, nonetheless shed a great deal of light on Merleau-Ponty's thinking at the end of his life. They represent, as it were, a reservoir of philosophical and textual references as well as the faint traces of a thought in action, a thought that managed to coalesce in the polished essay known to us as "Eye and Mind" but which only partially expressed itself in *The Visible and the Invisible*. Merleau-Ponty began working on the former in the summer of 1960,[1] leading into what would be his last courses at the Collège de France, "Cartesian Ontology and Ontology Today" and "Philosophy and Nonphilosophy since Hegel." In reading these courses, especially the section of the "Cartesian Ontology" course called "Fundamental Thought in Art," one gets a more detailed and fine-grained picture of the constellation of artistic and philosophical anxieties that motivated Merleau-Ponty's final published work. As for the latter, we know that Merleau-Ponty began drafting the text we now know as *The Visible and the Invisible* in 1959,[2] the same year as "The Possibility of Philosophy Today" course, and he continued working on the text until his sudden death. In this respect, all three courses presented here can be read as a kind of cipher for that unfinished work. For example, in reading the working notes for *The Visible and the Invisible* that deal with Descartes and the "tacit cogito" in conjunction with the course on "Cartesian Ontology and Ontology Today," what may sometimes appear in the working notes as vague or elliptical is articulated in more detail in the course notes (and vice versa). In this way, these courses are essential for truly understanding the scope, intent, and content of Merleau-Ponty's late thought.

I want to take a moment to specify how these courses fit in with some of Merleau-Ponty's other courses at the Collège de France. Of the entire series, from his first course in 1952 until those presented here, some have been published in French, some have also been translated into English, and some have been either not published (at all) or not translated (yet). Since Merleau-Ponty expressly said that "The Possibility of Philosophy Today" ought to be read in conjunction with the courses on nature, I will begin with those, listed by academic year:

1956–1957
I. Study of the Variations of the Concept of Nature
II. Modern Science and Nature

1957–1958
I. Animality, the Human Body, and the Passage to Culture[3]

1958–1959
I. The Possibility of Philosophy Today

1959–1960
I. Husserl at the Limits of Phenomenology[4]
II. Nature and Logos: the Human Body

1960–1961
I. Cartesian Ontology and Ontology Today
II. Philosophy and Nonphilosophy since Hegel

We can see that the first course presented in this book, "The Possibility of Philosophy Today," has a peculiar place in this series. On one hand, it sits in the middle of the courses on nature, and as Merleau-Ponty himself stresses, it ought to be read in continuity with them rather than as marking a departure, hiatus, or "parenthesis." In addition to the discussion of "nonphilosophy" in the form of art, literature, and music that makes up the first part of the course, we find here sustained and detailed discussions of Husserl and Heidegger in the course's second part. In fact, the discussion of Heidegger is the most rigorous, detailed, and explicit engagement with his work that we find anywhere in Merleau-Ponty's oeuvre. The discussion of Husserl is also very interesting because Merleau-Ponty would pick up where he left off here the next year in his course "Husserl at the Limits of Phenomenology," where he develops and expands the discussion of Husserl's "The Origin of Geometry" and "Ur-Arch" essay begun in "The Possibility of Philosophy Today." No doubt there are more crossings and intersections to be found reading the notes to these courses in series and in conjunction with "Eye and Mind" and *The Visible and the Invisible*. With the publication of this translation, English-language readers now have the privilege of getting a more complete picture of Merleau-Ponty's late thought.

As for the translation itself of *Notes de cours: 1959–1961*, I have made a deliberate effort to err on the side of being "too literal," so there are likely to be occasions when the syntax may sound a bit French to native English ears. English is a flexible and versatile language, however, and in fact many of the structures that are idiomatic in French are quite possible in English (if not sonorous). So in an effort to communicate Merleau-Ponty's effort as transparently as possible (a doomed effort to be sure), I have attempted to preserve, as much as possible, the syntax and phraseology while still trying to make this communicable to an English-speaking audience. I feel that this is especially important in the context of lecture notes such as these, where we find more often than not incomplete sentences, phrases jotted down, and sometimes only a single word. I have tried, for the most part, to follow other translations in word-choice, with a few exceptions. I translate *dévoiler* as "disclose" but sometimes as "unconceal," since Merleau-Ponty uses this word to render Heidegger's *unverborgen*. Merleau-Ponty will typically use *être* to translate Heidegger's *Sein* (Being) and *étant* (and sometimes *être-été*) to translate *Seiendes* (beings). English doesn't have the same resources as German and French to designate Heidegger's ontological difference, so I have attempted to mark these instances consistently with Merleau-Ponty's chosen French term and have otherwise followed the standard procedure of writing "Being" and "beings." To add another level of complication, we have Gilbert Kahn's neologism, adopted by Merleau-Ponty, *ester*, which Kahn used to render Heidegger's *Wesen* in his French translation of the *Introduction to Metaphysics*. Merleau-Ponty was happy to adopt this term, it seems, since it helps emphasize the verbal sense of *Wesen* that he insists upon, rather than its nounal sense. Rather than use a cumbersome (and somewhat dizzying) rendering like "is-ing" or "to is" (or "essence-ing" or "to essence"), I've opted to leave *ester* untranslated, following Alphonso Lingis's decision in its appearances in *The Visible and the Invisible*. Finally, an important point where I have deviated from standard English translations is *empiétement*, which is almost always rendered as "encroachment." For the most part I render this as "overlapping" instead, a term that appears in English on more than one occasion over the course of the lectures. Similarly, *en gigogne* I render as "trundled" and *emboîtement* as "nesting," all of which indicate Merleau-Ponty's attempt to imagine and communicate what he finds in the German term *Ineinander*: "one inside the other," the curious "image of thought" which seems to have preoccupied the author at the end of his life; this denotes a being in *mélange*, where "inside" and "outside" no longer have the same sense and meaning. Hegel and Nietzsche's *aufheben* is translated into French as *dépasser*, which I render as "overcome." *L'interrogation* and *interroger* I for the most part render as "interrogation" and "to interrogate" in conformity to Lingis and the text of *The Visible and *the Invisible,* only using "question" when deemed necessary. The French *sol* I have rendered as "soil," its English cognate, using "ground" only when *sol* is used to translate the German *Grund.*

I have attempted to retain and render Stéphanie Ménasé's careful marking and annotation as faithfully and as much as possible. Notes are labeled [Ed.] for Ménasé's (or in the case of the "Philosophy and Nonphilosophy" course, Lefort's) editorial notes, [M.-P.] for Merleau-Ponty's notes, and [Trans.] for translator's notes. Unmarked notes are textual citations. References to French translations and texts were added by Ménasé. I have substituted these with their English equivalents where available. Asterisks within a note indicate a citation to text quoted within the note, where the citation is included in brackets. The French text includes text in square brackets, which I've retained and marked as necessary.

The pagination for the French text, *Notes de cours: 1959–1961,* is given in brackets, e.g., [1]. Merleau-Ponty will often refer to his own pagination, which is given in brackets and in bold, e.g., **[1]**. Over the course of the lectures, Merleau-Ponty frequently quotes texts in other languages. In these cases, I've used standard English translations of these texts where available. Merleau-Ponty will occasionally translate German texts into French. Again, in these cases I've endeavored to use the standard English translation where available, amending or modifying it as necessary to convey certain decisions made by Merleau-Ponty. I've retained Merleau-Ponty's capitalization as far as possible. And I've made an effort to insert headings from the course outlines in the main text as signposts for the reader, where these were missing. Sometimes there was no precise indication of where these ought to appear, so these are approximations. Headings are bracketed if they were not written by Merleau-Ponty.

I would like to thank Trevor Perri, Anne Gendler, Faye Thaxton at Classic City Composition, and the staff at Northwestern University Press for their assistance and help during this process, as well as Leonard Lawlor and Duane Davis for their encouragement and advice. Any and all errors are my own.

Foreword

Claude Lefort

Maurice Merleau-Ponty was reading and perhaps correcting the notes written for the course he was supposed to give the next day at the Collège de France when, late in the evening of Wednesday, May 3, 1961, he suddenly suffered a heart attack. On his desk, near the couch where he had settled with his papers, awaiting a visit from a loved one, a book was wide open: Descartes's *Dioptrique.*

The course he was working on was called "Cartesian Ontology and Ontology Today." His notes for that course constitute part of the present volume. Stéphanie Ménasé has deciphered them with great care and provided many valuable references to facilitate reading them. Merleau-Ponty's teaching duties in 1961, like in the preceding years (with the exception of 1959), included two sets of classes. The first, the principal course just mentioned, was on Thursdays, and the second course was on Mondays. The second course, largely consisting of textual commentary, was on "Philosophy and Nonphilosophy since Hegel." I transcribed the notes for this second course and published them in *Textures,* a low-circulation journal, in 1966. They are also included in this volume. At the time, in spite of the success that his books had during his lifetime, Merleau-Ponty's work was of interest to a fairly small audience. The philosophers who were then well-known ignored the turn he took in phenomenology and the access to a new kind of ontology that he opened—"indirect," according to his [8] formulation—by linking together the problems of philosophy, psychology, psychoanalysis, the natural sciences, art and literature, and politics within a single question. In recent years, as if it had to undergo a period of latency, Merleau-Ponty's work has become more and more widely recognized, both within and outside of France. It is thus very fortunate that Éditions Gallimard, on the initiative of Marc de Launay, published his notes for his two final courses at the Collège de France. Readers of his philosophy previously had access to his teaching only through the *Résumés,* written for the Annuaire du Collége until 1960 (and published by Gallimard under the title *Résumés de cours* in 1968), but with this new publication, we have a more complete documentation of these courses.[1] In addition, Stéphanie Ménasé has had the auspicious idea of including the 1959 course ("The Possibility of Philosophy Today") along with the 1960–61 courses. As we will see, this course, which Merleau-Ponty presents in his summary as a parenthesis to his study of the concept of nature—a study that had occupied him for the two previous years and with which he intended to reconnect the following year—inaugurates a line of questioning that he would pursue to the letter, though following different paths, in 1961. The three sets of course notes published here form an ensemble that is all the more interesting since they give us a better glimpse of his incomplete book, *The Visible and the Invisible.*

Needless to say, the notes Merleau-Ponty wrote for his classes only provided him with support. All those who heard him lecture remember that he did not read but only glanced at his notes, evidently relying more on the flow of his speech. In addition, there is a striking contrast between the expertly composed, elegant *Résumés*, which mobilize his literary artistry, and the notes, thrown down on paper, heedless of syntax, with their discontinuities, which are sometimes elliptical to the point of making their meaning questionable. As it is, they nevertheless testify to the free pursuit of a new ontology, which when written down, rigorously governed, does not give us the entire idea. In order to be convinced, it is sufficient to compare the summary of "The Possibility of Philosophy Today" with the abundant notes that far surpass its purpose. [9]

The Possibility of Philosophy Today

The course of 1959, "The Possibility of Philosophy Today," is preceded by an outline that Merleau-Ponty followed. The first part of the course is about "Our State of Nonphilosophy;" and the second part is about Husserl and Heidegger, who "come to define philosophy by questioning its very sense and possibility." In fact, in this second part, it is a matter of restoring their itinerary in order to highlight a displacement of the problems in both thinkers: problems that take place under the effect of an internal requirement and which cannot, therefore, be conceived in terms of rupture, still less in terms of denial. Even more than the exploration of Husserl, to whom Merleau-Ponty was repeatedly indebted, that of Heidegger is precious insofar as Merleau-Ponty is concerned both to defend him against false interpretations and to be firm in criticizing—though indeed briefly—a direct ontology, whose danger would be to lead the philosopher into silence; whereas it is through contact with the world of life, and through art and the adventures of science, that the philosopher can seek the "indirect expression" of Being.

When reading "The Possibility of Philosophy Today," we should perhaps question the reasons why Merleau-Ponty refrains from showing the distance he has taken up from Husserl and Heidegger more clearly. The construction of the course, it seems to me, both reveals and obscures this distance. It is, I said, the present state of nonphilosophy that turns out to be the origin for an interrogation of philosophy, its sense and its possibility. In affinity with the two philosophers, I believe, Merleau-Ponty formulates a radical alternative: one or the other, either the death of the thought that, even at the price of misguidance, achieved the heights of philosophy, or its rebirth, thanks to remembering its origin and to abandoning the idea that it could define itself as "detached thought." However, from the first part of the course, Merleau-Ponty not only seizes upon the signs of the volatility (*emportément*) characteristic of an extreme naturalism and artificialism within nonphilosophy. He certainly indicates them, in particular when he mentions those latest technological developments that go so far as to make the threat of humanity's annihilation credible. Enthusiasm for this in fiction, however, is already visibly denounced: "These manners of thinking [10] are almost oneiric, museum of horrors." There is no doubt about Merleau-Ponty's resistance to the temptation of catastrophism. Thus he notes that if modern science is, from its beginnings, elaborated through contradiction, believing itself to be "dealing only with *constructa* inseparable from humanity" and postulating a nature in itself, this contradiction always remained concealed by recourse to divine reason. "On the contrary, science today cannot claim such a foundation: it is manifestly human and yet the circle man-nature is obvious." We understand that, regardless of attempts to escape into one positivism or another, the circle has been nonetheless recognized. While this language does not suggest that Merleau-Ponty espouses the idea of a radical alternative, we should also not forget his statement: "My thesis: this decadence of philosophy is inessential."

In the passage I just cited he adds, preserving all the emphasis: "what is a situation of crisis for our thinking could be a point of departure for a deepening: the energies that emerge from the framework of the constituted world reveal contingency. But this awareness of a *Boden*, of a sedimentation, could be rediscovered from nature (on the condition that one does not conceive this nature as the one described by objectivist science and as universal cause in itself), rediscovery of a nature-for-us as the soil [*sol*] of our culture, and in particular, where our creative activity is enrooted, which is thus not unconditioned, which has to maintain culture in contact with brute being, to confront culture with brute being."

Merleau-Ponty's thought wants to anchor itself in the present. At the very beginning of his course, ruling out the idea of "justifying (ontological research) through a history of philosophy," he announces his intention: "rather, to transport oneself to the present, to characterize ontological research through the philosophical void where we are and which is linked to our entire history." He is not postulating, he immediately specifies, the "identity history-philosophy, punctual parallelism of [a] philosophical and sociohistorical position . . . but the question is given—the calling into question of philosophy is given by our time." Either way, this remark is as much a rejoinder to Heidegger's philosophy as it is to Husserl's, with this reservation: that Merleau-Ponty wants to detect within the present, within social life, [11] within the transformation of the historical configuration, a new proof for *contingency,* that of another relationship to the *soil where our creative activity enroots itself.* The present is thus not this moment, which detaches itself from history, and from which the great alternative that went without being thought would emerge: it is thick, opaque. If we can name it, it is what the sign of nonphilosophy precisely designates. However, what must be understood by "nonphilosophy" is not only the nullification of philosophy; it includes modes of activity, as well as knowledge foreign to philosophy; in addition, it includes all that attests, outside the field instituted by philosophy, to a new regime of thought, and far from making us lose sight of the philosophical requirement, nonphilosophy relaunches it. So literature, painting, and contemporary music can help us understand the full extent of the question posed: *What is philosophy?*

In one of the texts written to serve as a preface for the studies gathered in *Les Philosophes célèbres* (Mazenod, 1956), Merleau-Ponty wrote: "A concrete philosophy is not a happy one. It must stick close to experience, and yet not limit itself to the empirical but restore to each experience the ontological cipher which marks it internally . . . Much can be expected of an age which no longer believes in philosophy triumphant but is, through its difficulties, a permanent appeal to rigor."[2] These lines clarify the scope of the analyses we mentioned. The division between "our state of nonphilosophy" and "the problems of philosophy" that Merleau-Ponty announces in his plan conceals the division that is in fact operating in the examination of the present time, the division between what is a sign of ignorance, or the rejection of philosophy, and what is a sign of *fundamental thought* (a term introduced in the course "Cartesian Ontology and Ontology Today"). Now, this thought lives within literature and contemporary art as much as it lives, although differently, within Husserl's or Heidegger's philosophy. Nevertheless, I remind you, Merleau-Ponty is silent on the meaning of a project that puts him in opposition to Heidegger. This was still Heidegger's project, even at the end of his life, as he indicated in the interview in *Spiegel.* When asked about his condemnation of modern art, which he had judged [12] to be "destructive," Heidegger answers: "All right, cross the word out. I would like to observe, however, that I do not see anything about modern art that points out a way [for us]. Moreover, it remains obscure as to how art sees the specific character of art, or at least looks for it."[3] However, Merleau-Ponty precisely does not think that there would be a place for art. Let us say more: what characterizes present literature and art is, to understand it, the examination they make of their indetermination in the paths they open. We owe this power in part to the attempts of writers, poets and novelists, painters and musicians—the gift of the question that the present gives us, the power that "much can be expected of an age which no longer believes in philosophy triumphant," the gift of a time where one advances in darkness.

Regardless of which domain Merleau-Ponty turns toward, the same image comes back: that of a "shifting soil" (*ébranlement du sol*) upon which the writer or the artist once believed themselves to be established. In fact, they do not produce analyses; they only indicate rather varied landmarks in order to convince us, following paths independent of each other, that a search is emerging. Some lines, sometimes just a few words are sufficient for suggesting the direction: in Mallarmé it is a matter of "language . . . made into a sort of mutism, cut off from the positivity of the world"; in Rimbaud, of an "upheaval of relationships between sign and signification," not by turning away from the positivity of the world but by entering without reservation into its pre-logical unity; in surrealism, in Breton in particular, of a will to "give voice to the undivided life," to the "clots of signification" of the unconscious . . . , and then of a "reconquest of profound speech"; in the American novel, of a disarticulation of the narrative that defies the categories of subjective and objective. We can better understand the kinship Merleau-Ponty wants to establish between literary research and his own when he notes: "After Proust, Joyce, the Americans, the mode of signification is indirect: myself-other, the world, are deliberately mixed, implicated in each other, expressed by each other in a lateral relationship." Or (with respect to Proust): "time, at the same time absence, dispossession, and, through the same possession, each human being sits upon a pyramid of time that is [13] theirs" (the "pyramid of time" was already mentioned in *Phenomenology of Perception* in the chapter on the "Cogito").[4] Likewise, there are references to Cézanne and Renoir, of which we know the place he gave them in his works, but also to Masson, to Bazaine, to the painters of the École de Paris, to Klee and Michaux, who present the idea of a slippage of the painter's soil in a flash. Merleau-Ponty pulls this judgment from the commentary on Klee, which seems to have pushed the reflection on painting in our time farther: "thus the painting [is] a kind of philosophy: grasping its genesis, philosophy entirely in action." The considerations of music are more succinct but have the same sense:

"the abandonment of privileged forms of tonality" implies the loss of the soil upon which musical communication was founded. Henceforth, "the soil turns out to be a contingent historical or cultural formation, music comes into itself." The notes are doubtless allusive. In what concerns painting especially, as well as the invocation of Klee, Merleau-Ponty's essay "Eye and Mind" remains a work of incomparable richness. However, in this first part of the course, where, remember, the manifestations of "nonphilosophy" are scrutinized, one finds a concern not encountered elsewhere: namely, to discern the threat that weighs upon literature and art, since freedom makes either pure experimentation or a direct seizing upon Being into a pure fantasy. After having said that "music comes into itself," Merleau-Ponty adds: "This does not cover, does not justify all 'generalized' music; there remains the mysterious problem of knowing what it is to truly be a musician in this freedom (like truly being a painter or being Mondrian)—i.e., not to inventory the abstract possibilities (the other as new, arbitrary other, combinatorial, blind combination)." A little later, after having extensively cited a beautiful text by Michaux ("A Certain Phenomenon One Calls Music," in *Passages*), Merleau-Ponty remarks: "danger: narcissistic musical signification, oneiric (possible illusion: does folk music make its true sense legible in eight minutes?) ('Illusion of a crossing from being to being')."

In the section on painting, after having put the accent on the fecundity of contemporary works, Merleau-Ponty likewise issues [14] a reservation: "Question of non-figuratives: wouldn't the picture be even more free to give the essence if all links were cut? Painting of the being? In reality, it can happen that it then falls back onto itself precisely as a thing: again it resembles things, bacteria, awkward biological forms. One is limited to rendering (moving besides) more general physical structures: a torn-down wall where only the colored thing or even matter in general neither vibrates nor dreams." Observing the increased multiplication of webs presented under the sign of a vindication of the abstract—of the painting of Being or of Nothingness—one can appreciate Merleau-Ponty's wisdom. In this part on nonphilosophy, where he discerns the germs of a new ontology, he also perceives what carries the mark of its misery.

Cartesian Ontology and Ontology Today

The course "Cartesian Ontology and Ontology Today" maintains a manifest kinship with "The Possibility of Philosophy Today." Doubtless, at first sight, the objective does seem different. It looks like a return to the history of philosophy. Merleau-Ponty expressly challenges this movement, how-ever. He opens his first class by declaring: "This is not history of philos-ophy but the past invoked in order to understand what we think." Then he (twice) goes on to underline this: "We do not know what we think." This does not simply mean that we live in ignorance but that we are incapable of elevating what is happening in current research to the level of reflection. In his introduction, after having mentioned Gueroult's severe criticism of commentators on Descartes, he indicates the "aim" of his course, which "is to seek a philosophical formulation of our ontology, which remains implicit, in the air (and to do so by contrast with Cartesian ontology)." Merleau-Ponty did not conceive of this project suddenly. He was inter-ested in the book he had in preparation (published posthumously as *The Visible and the Invisible*). One finds his project formulated not only in the few outlines he had drawn up, but already in an introductory note from January 1959 for the work he was still calling *The Origin of Truth* (*Origine de la verité*) at that time, and which became *The Visible and the Invisible*.[5] This note indicates in the first place: "Our state of nonphilosophy—the crisis has never been so radical" [15] and ends with: "Reflection on the ontologies of Descartes—the 'strabism' of Western ontology." Descartes, among all the philosophers to whom Merleau-Ponty referred, occupies, as we know, a privileged place in his work. (One already finds analyses which anticipate those of his final course in *Phenomenology of Perception*, in its first chapter, "Attention," and in one of the last, "The Cogito.")

When he approaches Cartesian ontology in the second part of the course (titled "Descartes"), Merleau-Ponty takes care to specify that it is not a matter of restoring "what Descartes has said in response to his prob-lems in the order where he has said it." Such was, he points out elsewhere, Gueroult's intention, which he opposes, since it would lead to omitting a whole part of Descartes's trajectory. Such an omission amounts, in the first place, to not asking what is singular in the decision to circumscribe an "order of reasons" while declaring oneself resolved to respect the use of life, to the point even of inviting his readers not to follow him and to make philosophy an exercise that is valid only for a few hours a year. However, it is also not a matter of posing "our problems" to Descartes. In short, the problems that Descartes formulates do not necessarily give us the sense of his enterprise because he first dealt with them in a move-ment of thought that we have yet to understand: delimiting what is only accessible to pure understanding. In a note that is not part of the course, Merleau-Ponty's design is formulated better: "Study the pre-methodic Descartes, the *spontaneae fruges*, that natural thought 'which always precedes the acquired thought'—and the post-methodic Descartes, that of after the Sixth Meditation, who lives in the world after having methodically explored it—the 'vertical' Descartes soul and body, and not that of the *intuitus mentis*—And the way he chooses his models ('light,' etc.) and the way that, in the end, he goes beyond them, the Descartes of before and after the order of reasons, the Descartes of the Cogito before the Cogito, who always knew that he thought, with a knowing that is ultimate and has no need of elucidation—ask what the evidence of this spontaneous thought consists of, *sui ipsius contemplatio reflexa*, what this refusal to constitute the Psyche means, this knowing more clear than [16] all constitution and which he counts on."[6] Now, the very reason that forbids us from relying on Descartes's methodological approach alone (or, according to a formulation from the course, "from taking him at his word") prevents us from believing that, failing to submit to the order of his thought, we can only grasp it by introducing our own problems into it. The junction between Descartes and ourselves, between ourselves and Descartes, takes place naturally because his problems and our problems have the same origin: despite the centuries that separate us, it is always a question of time, of space, of things, and of these bodies that are and are not things, of what one calls thought, feeling, desire, and communication. Merleau-Ponty declares, it is true, that he seeks a formulation for our implicit ontology through a contrast with Cartesian ontology, but this statement must not conceal the fact that the contrast that it was intended to establish is not given.

So Merleau-Ponty describes a circular course. On the basis of rapid considerations that lead one to doubt the possibility of understanding Descartes through the order of reasons, he highlights some significant aspects of contemporary painting in the first part of the course, "Fundamental Thought in Art," in order to ask: what new thing happens in the work of the painter? What about depth, the line, movement, color, light? Finally, what is the picture, the icon, which is neither thing in itself, nor reflection, nor trompe-l'oeil? What knowledge of vision does it hold, and what knowledge of our manner of dwelling within being? Along the way, the search of modern painters shows itself to be anticipated by Leonardo: "it rediscovers the Renaissance above Descartes." These pages, which bear the imprint of the meditation from "Eye and Mind" (section 4), the essay having been written the previous summer (most of the references and examples are identical), conclude with two questions: What did Descartes say about the same subjects? Does the aim of what literature seeks have an aim that is "so different"?

In fact, Merleau-Ponty initiates, in the second part of "Fundamental Thought in Art," a study of the *Dioptrique* which first of all deals with Descartes's "treatment of light through models." A little later, he notes, commenting on Leonardo: "To see is not to have a *quale*, but to have access to a figure of Being that is in principle the absolute image (Chastel), the *proportionalita in instanti*—simultaneity is openness to what we [17] are not, fission of being from what we are and which is not a property of vision—'window onto the soul.' Light is what one sees and that by which one sees, which in a sense, 'sees.' Vision [is] something entirely different from projection, is not anamorphosis, fixed point of view. It happens everywhere as well. It is *ek-stase*; it is natural vision—(spherical, Leonardo)." In his essay "Eye and Mind," where Merleau-Ponty makes reference to the *Dioptrique*, following a path that is also very close to that of the course, he writes: "Descartes does not say much about painting, and one might think it unfair on our part to make so much of a few pages on engravings. Yet the very fact that he speaks of painting only in passing is itself significant. Painting for him is not a central operation contributing to the definition of our access to being; it is a mode or a variant of thinking, where thinking is canonically defined as intellectual possession and self-evidence."[7] Perhaps the notes for the course make the movement of Merleau-Ponty's thought better known, as they are oriented in terms of elucidating our ontology. The examination of the *Dioptrique* is justified, really, by the exploration of contemporary painting because this contains, in the absence of a concrete discourse and philosophical elaboration, a new idea of *seeing* (*la voyance*): a new idea of feeling the painter's inherence within the visible, things that solicit the gaze, *of making seen* (*se font voir*). Descartes thus attracts our questioning at the point where he does not lend himself to it, where it is necessary, as if those questions were resolved. Descartes wants to reduce light to rays that enter the eye, to discern its action and the means which we have to act in response to it, to make light an obstacle, to deflect it, to reflect it. He forges this model in the service of artificial organs and of the manipulation of light. But the philosopher is not interested in light as such. "There is no need," he had written, "for me to say what its true nature is." So Descartes deliberately ignores the phenomenon of vision at a distance, as he does that of the immersion of the seer in the visible, and instead he compares the operation of vision to that of touching (the blind person who touches bodies with a cane). Let us not dwell on the conclusions that Merleau-Ponty draws from Cartesian analysis in order to highlight the definition of the picture as an artificial product [18], elaborated thanks to the application of a code that permits optical illusion. Let us rather turn again to the rigorous separation, introduced by Descartes, between the operation of thought and the body's employment. Now, this separation, we are told, leaves something in its shadow: the contingency of the sign. How is the sign given to thought? The answer seems to be this: for Descartes, "the sign [is] the occasion adequate to the thinking of the signified." Everything happens "as if our body had been instituted by such a thought." So there would be a "reconstitution, in the order of thinking, of the divine thought that gave us this body."

Later, in the second part of the course ("Descartes"), this is what will make Merleau-Ponty fully reveal the sense of "construction through models," of the reduction of light to rays that affect the eye and of the reduction of vision to thought: "The Cartesian Beginning—vision of the eyes and vision of the mind. Vision modeled on the eyes: Descartes [is] aware of what is new in speaking of [the] vision of the mind [reference is made to the *Regulae*]. He deliberately, expressly constructs the *intuitus mentis* upon vision of the eyes . . . ; it is necessary, like a craftsman, to direct the gaze according to a *singula puncta*." There is no need, therefore, for a definition of vision by way of comparison with touch, although it does not lose its validity. To truly see is to fix upon the detail, isolate the figure, identify it through the operation that makes it irreducible to any other, that makes it present insofar as it is clear; that is, it contains nothing of the obscurity given to it by its insertion in a field, by its promiscuity with other visible relatives. What is distinct, clear, and present, is the *simple*. Far from confining himself to contesting that vision of the eyes is reducible to thought of seeing, Merleau-Ponty goes so far as to affirm that it is "thanks to the analysis of vision of the eyes, as vision of figures defined by vision of the mind, that most of the problems of the philosophers are revoked in doubt in the name of an all or nothing intellect." Let us again refer to an earlier working note, where he makes reference to the *Dioptrique*. As in the course, in *The Visible and the Invisible*, Merleau-Ponty emphasizes Descartes's wisdom when he criticizes the objectivist theory of [19] projection: "*who* will see the image painted in the eyes or in the brain? Therefore finally a *thought* of this image is needed—Descartes already sees that we always put a little man in man, that our objectifying view of our own body always obliges us to seek *still farther inside* that *seeing man* we thought we had under our eyes."[8] However, what is ignored, Merleau-Ponty remarks, is that this notion, the "thought of seeing," does not deliver us from this illusion: "This thought, this disclosure of being which finally is *for* someone, is still the little man inside man, but this time contracted into a metaphysical point."[9] These lines show quite well why Merleau-Ponty is so interested in the *Dioptrique* and the *Regulae*. He finds within them what he calls a "positivism of the vision of the Mind" that contrasts with the experience painters have of space which makes them challenge the separation of an inside from an outside.

In the next section of "Fundamental Thought in Art," to which I now turn, Merleau-Ponty defers drawing conclusions from the Cartesian analysis of vision; in effect, he wants to immediately show that the theory of the legibility of signs by thought discredits linguistic creation as much as it discredits pictorial creation. Drawing on a letter to Mersenne, in which the project of a universal language is examined, Merleau-Ponty recalls that, if Descartes judges this unrealizable, he considers it possible in principle: "Idea of a universal language where signs would have their meanings circumscribed exactly—this is equivalent to the theory of perspective." In other words, there is nothing in the sayable, just as in the visible, that is not possible to decompose in order to reach the simple element, and is not possible to order for the sake of accounting for the complex. So the true philosophy would consist in "enumerating all the thoughts of man" and conceiving of a perfectly clear language.

It is thus by taking up the theme of light again in a new way that Merleau-Ponty begins a third section of "Fundamental Thought in Art," one dedicated to the work of modern writers. His purpose is to "search within literature for the attestation of the writer writing 'under the dictate of that which is thought, of what is articulated in him,' and which retains the very essence of the visible." This *seeing* (*voyance*), which Descartes expelled from vision in vain, [20] conceived as an operation of thought, now returns in writing. In the passages that I have already recalled, where he announced the search for an ontology at work in the spirit of our time, Merleau-Ponty specified that he wished to present examples of fundamental thought. He takes this term, "fundamental thought," up again. These are simple examples that he wants to produce in the absence of stylized analyses. Even though he mentions other writers (no doubt in particular due to his sensitivity to Valéry and later to Michaux), there are three with whom he recognizes his own orientation to be in contact: Proust, Paul Claudel, and Claude Simon. The intimacy Merleau-Ponty maintains with the work of Proust is so old and so constant that one might rightly wonder whether he has not drawn as much inspiration from him as he had from the other philosophers in whose footsteps he followed. The reader will observe that, in the first place, he cites a long passage from Proust as an example (evoking the emotion of Swann listening to Vinteuil's sonata), a passage so well known and so often celebrated that one would think that one had nothing new left to learn about it. But Merleau-Ponty restores to it, without the commentary losing any of its charm, a power of meditation whose scope is measured by way of contrast with Descartes (remember that the same passage from the *Recherché* is mentioned in *The Visible and the Invisible*).[10] He brings out the words or sentences from Proust's text that bear the mark of an experience of Being from which classical philosophy had turned away. Nothing in this really allows for the recognition of musical ideas, which are "veiled in darkness," unknown, "impenetrable to the intelligence," distinct but not disjoined, a life of the soul in its "night";

the musical idea is a light in sensible space, where we cannot doubt that it emerges, a presence of the past in us that defies the ordinary notions of actual vision and memory, a fecundity of thought, such that these ideas in principle turn out to be *uncountable*; finally, a work of writing is only capable of opening access to our inner domain, of making us read what was imprinted on us by our frequentation of the world. Now, in following Proust, Merleau-Ponty detects, beneath musical ideas, that which already is the mystery of visibility, *notions without equivalent*, "light, sound, relief, pleasure," [21] which initiates us into the world and from whence we derive intelligible ideas.

The same investigation is continued thanks to an incursion into the works of Claudel, without focusing more specifically on a text. Under the title "Simultaneity," Merleau-Ponty immediately underlines the themes that assume importance in *The Visible and the Invisible*, what affinity they maintain with the notion of the *flesh*. Moreover, Claudel is cited several times in that book (and in his previous works). He finds especially in Claudel the notion of a "cohesion of being" which defies any representation of space as extension and of time as a succession of moments, and which implies an idea of being not as above but beneath us (as Claudel said elsewhere more faithfully with respect to God): the idea of a participation of all in all that does not signify indistinction but the "union of incompossibles."

The notes on Claude Simon are particularly eye-catching.[11] Although they are even more elliptical than the preceding ones, they indicate a new breakthrough in Merleau-Ponty's exploration. Without being able to fix the date at which he became acquainted with Simon's novels *Le Vent, L'Herbe*, or *La Route des Flandres*, I remember that Merleau-Ponty told me almost immediately of his impression of having made a discovery comparable to the one he had had in reading Proust. The images introduced a little earlier return: those of overlapping (*empiètement*), nesting (*emboîtement*), and the superposition of beings. Nevertheless, he wants to open up a new entry point into literature—a passage, if I may say so, to a nonfigurative writing, the attempt to render quasi-sensible, beyond things, characters, settings, moments, which are objects of perception, of knowledge or memory, from the place where we are, the "magma" of which they as well as ourselves are a part. "Generally valid: Claude Simon: his profound newness, no longer rendering what is outside space, time, men according to their figure as 'figures,' exterior contours in transparency, but as 'a thing which exists totally' [Simon's expression, [22] taken from an interview], a thing from which each experience that we have is taken, the totality always showing through as a sort of encompassing of the magma." Proust, certainly, has broken with the conventional model of narration; however, while he makes way for the emergence of time, defying the order of succession and obeying no other law than that of a revealing creation, he still delivers portraits, describes situations, whose sense each time depends on the position of the narrator in a space-time, but whose fragmentary views are finally connected in "figures." In addition, this is a search that Proust takes up and which, coming back to itself, reveals the story of the work's genesis at its completion. This is finally a sequence of speech such that we never cease being in contact with its movement. By contrast, in Claude Simon, Merleau-Ponty discovers a new type of narrative, where the articulations that Proust made in the service of the recomposition of a space and of a time conquered against understanding fade. Commenting on this or that extract from one of Simon's novels, Merleau-Ponty notes: "the years are one upon another," or "the places are nested [*s'emboitent*], one within the other," or "bodies are overprinted, one upon the other," or in a still more striking fashion: "there is a sort of overlapping of bodies, one upon the other, and what happens to one, its life and its death, metamorphosizes the duration, the age of the other." Merleau-Ponty speaks of a "vegetative space," as well as an "elemental time." In his language, in his frequent erasure of punctuation, in his usage of "undivided phrases," Claude Simon makes us recognize a concern for the non-separation of the said and what is given to see or to hear, which goes hand in hand with the non-separation of what is thought and what is said. Citing a statement Simon made in the course of an interview: "I do not believe that I think," [Merleau-Ponty] makes this comment: "He thinks like Cézanne 'thought in painting'" (a formulation of painting that has been often recalled), and adds: "this type of disclosure of the world, without *separated thought* [Claude Lefort's emphasis], is precisely modern ontology."

The place that Merleau-Ponty gives to literature and painting before taking up his study of Descartes is remarkable. To the observer, we are reminded of a [23] formulation from a working note that accompanies *The Visible and the Invisible*: "Being is *what requires creation of us* for us to experience it."[12] It is followed by this injunction: "Make an analysis of literature in this sense: as *inscription* of Being."[13]

In the second part of the course, Merleau-Ponty returns to Descartes, as I have already suggested when I mentioned his critique of the vision of the mind conceived on the model of vision of the eyes, though there is not space to enter into the details of his analysis. Merleau-Ponty's purpose is not to refute Descartes's arguments. Rather, he wants to show that the questions which are taking shape in our time were not foreign to Descartes, that they are reflected in the displacements to which he is constrained by maintaining his thought in the direction of a new ontology.

Descartes's design is to subtract philosophy from what would be nonphilosophy, but one leads to the other. In order to understand his steps, it is necessary to not stop at the exposition of his method but to restore a path that, in contrast to the search of modern literature, "goes from knowledge to being" and nevertheless is not "that of someone to whom our idea of an experience of being no longer applies." More precisely, we have to discover a movement that takes place in two reversals: the first, which returns to the *Cogito* after the confused apprehension of the world through its application in life; and the second, which, from the certainty in which the conjunction of thought and being is attested, returns "to the existing world, to the union." Now, if this is Descartes's philosophy, which does not coincide with what Descartes circumscribed as philosophy—and if these two reversals are not contradictory—then "it must contain . . . an ambiguous relation of light and feeling, of the invisible and the visible, of the positive and negative. It is this relationship or mixture that we should seek." This is really the task that Merleau-Ponty gives himself. From the *Regulae* to the *Meditations*, he shows the passage from the idea of a natural light that falls under a positivism of the vision of the mind to a natural light that [24] is given in the certainty of the "*I think, I am*," thanks to a crossing of the "night of doubt" and the hypothesis of an all-powerful and deceitful Evil Demon. However, that doubt must dissolve in the certainty of the *I think*, and the fact that the idea of an Evil Demon turns out to be unsustainable is not reduced to a positive thought; the operation of the negative is not effaced; thought is only reconquered as thought in suspense, which welcomes everything under the title of *cogitationes*—that which is felt, dreamed, imagined, like that which is perceived—"without repressing anything in the name of distinction." The *I think, I am* remains a "shimmering of doubt and certainty," in the sense that it is confused with an "it seems to me that" without there being the reestablishment of an object-being. Existence is given as what has resisted the attempt of negating all being at the same time as the presence to self of all vision, as that which is solely mine. So the discovery of the *Cogito* changes the significance of the natural light. If it doesn't bring us out of time, since it only procures certainty at this instant, then this certainty is of an order other than that of mathematical truths; it is that of "inner testimony, of non-thetic 'inner consciousness,' of the *non-dissimulation* of myself to myself and of all things to myself." The moment the natural light "is purified," it illuminates everything that is indistinctly presented and, at the same time, illuminates its own "mixture with obscurity." Finally, Descartes is delivered from the double objection that the *Cogito* does not take us out of time and that it could derive from our natural constitution only by the idea of God, from a Being without restriction. But this

God passes the limits of understanding; it is both "immense light" and at the same time supreme incomprehensibility, creator of eternal truths and "God-abyss."

Philosophy and Nonphilosophy since Hegel

In the introduction to the 1959 course, Merleau-Ponty pushed aside the idea of interrogating our state of nonphilosophy through an examination of Kierkegaard, Nietzsche, and Marx. This would, he said, lead to the observation that metaphysics comes to an end with Hegel, and he only wonders if the three thinkers who broke away from him have truly broken [24] with metaphysics and to what extent they announce the problems of our time. He preferred to go straight to these problems. Nevertheless, his second course of 1961 reopens the path that he seemed to have abandoned. It is true that its title, "Philosophy and Nonphilosophy since Hegel," is partly misleading. Kierkegaard is barely mentioned, and Nietzsche is the object of only brief reflections inspired by a long extract from the "Preface" to *The Gay Science* (1886 edition). The classes focus essentially on Hegel himself and on Marx. (In certain respects, the course provides a follow-up to the analyses developed in the 1956 course "Dialectical Philosophy," of which we know the *Résumé*.)

Hegel

Everything in this part of the course happens as if, after having decided to scrutinize the ambiguities of the great critiques of Hegelianism, Merleau-Ponty has yielded to the attraction that the author of the *Phenomenology of Spirit* exerted on him and wants to show that the questions which matter to him so much—those of the relationship between philosophy and nonphilosophy—were already at the center of Hegel's work and, therefore, that the thesis of the fulfillment of metaphysics ignored the most lively part of Hegel. Anyway, this part of his course is principally dedicated to a commentary on the last four pages of a fragment of the *Phenomenology of Spirit* we know under the name of "Introduction" but whose function was not originally fixed. It is a matter of a text, therefore, where one can wonder whether it does not testify to a hesitation that touches upon the very nature of the work: phenomenology, in one sense, having to be sufficient in itself, and in another, arousing the need for a speech that opens its field to it and gives it its justification.

Remarkably, Heidegger had already given, under the title of "Hegel's

Concept of Experience," a long commentary on Hegel's "Introduction" that was included in *Holzwege*.[14] More remarkable still, it is through this essay (at the time untranslated) that Merleau-Ponty reads Hegel's text, where it was reproduced. If he proceeds in this way, it is not in order to be spared the trouble of consulting the *Phenomenology*: he directs himself both to Hegel and to the great philosopher who, since Hegel, has thought philosophy and nonphilosophy.

In the entire first part of the course notes dedicated to [26] Hegel, we see that the accent is placed on a critique of Descartes closest to the one that Merleau-Ponty himself formulates in "Cartesian Ontology and Ontology Today." The critique of a conceptualization that begins from knowledge is the same, with the exception that Hegel makes constant use of the concept of the Absolute, while Merleau-Ponty prefers to speak of Being. Furthermore, Merleau-Ponty suggests that Hegel opens his path to phenomenology when he writes: "It is necessary that the relation to the absolute is prior to the *Erkennen* by other means, that the absolute is *schon bei uns*, that it is the light itself that un-conceals." The theme of light, so important in "Cartesian Ontology and Ontology Today," emerges later in the examination of the Hegelian dialectic. Merleau-Ponty notes: "a new idea of light: the true is for itself *zweideutig*, because it must be *Wesen* or *Ansich* and can only be by being *für das Bewusstsein des Ansich* . . . The *Veildeutigkeit* is not a shadow to be eliminated by the true light." Previously, after having shown the inability to separate knowledge from the Absolute, Merleau-Ponty signaled the Hegelian critique of Descartes's "false radicalism." In a general way, Merleau-Ponty's concern is to accompany Hegel as far as possible in the thought of an experience that excludes any overhanging position in and any separation between "measuring" and "measured"—consciousness and the object alternately turn out to be each other. Insisting on the Hegelian idea of a dialectical exchange between consciousness and the object, he writes: "Experience, i.e., the effective assumption of a being, is alone capable of giving rise to a dialectic because it alone is the opening onto something that can be unconcealed, that has depths, a latency, that thus can give rise to the *ek-stase* from whence a *new* truth will come." Merleau-Ponty's language, as it is recognized in his use of the terms "chiasm," reciprocal envelopment," "frame," and "*Gestalt*," lends itself so naturally to the interpretation of Hegel's text that we come to wonder, in approaching the last class while aware of Merleau-Ponty's thought, how he will come to detach himself from Hegel before denouncing the conversion of phenomenology into a logic. In fact, there are many signs in the commentary which suggest the conclusion that Hegel's blindness to his own approach, the [27] reference to consciousness, is what makes all exteriority come to be reabsorbed in knowledge.

Merleau-Ponty is working to detect the tension between the two needs that order Hegelian thought all throughout the *Phenomenology*. On one hand, it is a matter of reconceiving the dialectic as immanent to experience, as a "movement of the content." The dialectic is neither accomplished by consciousness nor objective. Far from being "a property of consciousness, it is rather consciousness that is a property of the dialectic." In this sense, while recognizing that the transformation of one object into another occurs in the relationship of consciousness with itself, we must agree that this consciousness is opaque, grasped in experience. So it seems vain, as Hegel is the first to emphasize, to want to put the dialectic back on its feet. On the other hand, the dialectic implies a disjunction between consciousness understood as included within experience and consciousness understood as knowledge of experience; and the restitution of the successive figures of consciousness is of such a kind that the moment must be reached when it ceases to be presented as a consciousness bound to the world that appears to it, consciousness of what is given to it as outside, where it therefore ceases to be mystified, partially ignorant of its own movement, and where it becomes fully consciousness of itself, where it attains knowledge of its genesis and is entirely one, "equal to its outside." At this moment, Merleau-Ponty notes, experience is metamorphosized into absolute knowledge. At the same time, philosophy is separated from nonphilosophy. What makes Merleau-Ponty's interpretation interesting is that he discovers, in Hegel's attempts, something other than a ruse, that is, the construction of an experience that would immediately hold its signification in order to make us believe in the necessity of the order of the world that it conceives in the present. Merleau-Ponty expresses his own idea of a circularity between experience and knowledge of experience. He only specifies that this circularity is without end, but in this way he provides the sense of his rupture with Hegel. He does not reproach Hegel's ambiguity but rather the passage from a good to a bad ambiguity. In his penultimate class, recalling in passing that by deciding to put the fragment examined at the beginning of his work, "Hegel himself no longer sees that there is no Introduction to the phenomenology of Spirit that *is* the presence of the absolute," Merleau-Ponty notes: "There is a relationship of *Ineinander*, a concentric situation, a reciprocal envelopment, in 1807, which gives way then to enveloping thought of the 'positively rational'—or of the speculative." The critique is expressed in this happy formulation: "It is 'the identity of identity and non-identity' that finally subordinates *difference*." As it is indicated some lines farther on, the Absolute changes its sense: "[it] empties itself, becomes *indifference*, and pure conservation."[15] We understand that Hegel allows himself to justify everything. Finally, in the last class, referring to the constant reference to consciousness, Merleau-Ponty will convey how much his interpretation of Hegel is linked to his own conception of phenomenology and will provide the extent of his filiation and of his rupture. Stressing that the Hegelian Absolute "is neither on the side of the In Itself nor on the side of For Itself, as they present themselves at the level of *Bewußtsein*," he will say of the Absolute, "it is only in the milieu of experience, it is the frame, it is the figure. . . . In the movement of experience that understands itself, we touch the absolute, which is not something behind it or under it, which is filigreed in it and only exists in filigree."

The philosopher who comments on Hegel here is indeed the same who commented on Proust, Claudel, and Claude Simon.

Marx

Marx, we observe, similarly to Hegel, was already the object of the 1956 course "Dialectical Philosophy," which itself bore the mark of Merleau-Ponty's earlier book *Adventures of the Dialectic.* The texts studied in this part of the 1961 course support Merleau-Ponty's earlier analyses, and are principally taken from Marx's *Critique of Hegel's Philosophy of Right* and from the *Manuscripts of 1844.* The aim in this part of the course is to show that Marx, despite his intentions, remained Hegelian "from one end to the other"—Hegelian in the best sense of the term, when he conceives a dialectic that is the movement of content and does not allow for the separation of philosophy and nonphilosophy, but still Hegelian when he gives in to the temptation of an [29] entirely positive knowledge, and finally, when he elaborates, in *Capital,* a system that is the equivalent to that of Hegel's *Logic.* I leave the argumentation aside, which is easy to follow and which recognizes the central function that exercises negativity in Marx's thought, in contrast with that of Feuerbach, and the effort to liberate the immediately equivocal relationship between consciousness and the object from the limits he imposed on it, as in Hegel. What seems to me to deserve to be underlined is Merleau-Ponty's concern to reunite, as he is already working on doing in his examination of Hegel, what is new there and what is more fecund in Marx's attempt. "The philosophy sketched by Marx is essentially dialectic, i.e., nature, humanity, and history are understood not as substances definable through a principal attribute, but as movements without locatable discontinuity where the other is always involved—No cleavage of material-idea, object-subject, nature-humanity, in itself-for itself, but a single Being where negativity works." From the entanglement of the human being and the nature from which humanity emerges, the human being is neither the subject nor a fragment, not external but in principle sensible; from this entanglement, it is implied that history is the very *flesh* of the human being.[16] Merleau-Ponty quotes from a long passage in the *1844 Manuscripts* which has become famous, but is commented on closely by him, and his conclusion is that history "is the true natural history of the human being," that the inspiration of Feuerbach is close, and that of Hegel no less, with the difference that the latter's "negativity" descends into the *flesh* of the world. (I emphasize again the term that we know illuminates his own conception of ontology.) The section in which Merleau-Ponty formulates this subject is entitled, moreover, "Sketch of a Marxist *Seinsgeschichte*." One is right to judge that Merleau-Ponty discerns the direction that he himself will follow on a segment of Marx's route. One can even believe that Marx opens, in his eyes, a path that seems barred. But this path turns out to be again without continuation. In effect, if Marx maintains, against Feuerbach, the idea of a "negation of negation," it is finally in order to circumscribe it within the time that prepares for the advent of a reconciliation of the human being with nature. Marx imagines a [30] movement through which history overcomes itself or comes to realize itself in the true essence of humanity. But whereas Marx had known how to discern Hegel's positivism (as Merleau-Ponty had recalled before) in order to show that his description of the process of humanity's exteriorization in religion, law, or politics ended, once absolute knowledge was reached, in a conservation of anterior modes of consciousness and led to the conclusion that "reason is at home in un-reason as un-reason"; this itself turns out to fall back into positivism, reduces the negation of negation to dis-alienation, and conceives an end to history or to what he calls "pre-history." The work of the negative, after having been reconquered by the idea of an itinerary of consciousness, turns out to be strictly enclosed within the borders of a humanity that is discovered to be natural after being delivered from its divisions.

Philosophy and nonphilosophy? From one course to another, Merleau-Ponty persuades us of the impossibility of separating them and of confusing them.

Editor's Note

Stéphanie Ménasé

This book gathers Maurice Merleau-Ponty's last courses at the Collège de France, which relate to the possibility of philosophy. For the course of 1958–59, which was in fact begun in January 1959, Merleau-Ponty wrote a summary, later published by Gallimard in the *Résumés de cours* (1968), under the title of "The Possibility of Philosophy."[1] It is the only course which he gave that year. While this course interrupts the classes on nature,[2] "The Possibility of Philosophy" does not mark a parenthesis. This type of interrogation is taken up again on a new path in the principal course of 1960–61,[3] "Cartesian Ontology and Ontology Today," and in the course on "Philosophy and Nonphilosophy since Hegel." It seemed important to include the notes for this third course in this edition. The courses of 1960–61 were not completed because of Merleau-Ponty's death on May 3, 1961, so we do not have the summaries of their subject matter. The notes for the course on "Cartesian Ontology and Ontology Today," presented in this edition, are published here for the first time. The preparatory notes for "Philosophy and Nonphilosophy since Hegel" were transcribed and edited by Claude Lefort in *Textures*, a low-circulation journal, in 1974.[4]

In addition, I thought it would be appropriate to publish a draft corresponding to the chapter "Interrogation and Intuition" of *The Visible and the Invisible* in the appendixes.[5] This "rough draft" has never been taken into account. As Lefort indicated in his editorial note to *The Visible and the Invisible*, he left it out since Merleau-Ponty had abandoned it in favor of a new draft, the one published. From the fact that this "rough draft" is related to the theme of the courses and since it is interesting in itself, I have made it figure in this edition, despite its somewhat lacunary form towards the end. [32]

Out of concern for readability, I have transcribed these course notes and given all the references that seemed necessary. Certain articles, as well as certain words that correspond to the signs =, ≠, →, have been reestablished between brackets when these seemed necessary. The punctuation has occasionally been modified. Illegible words are indicated by [?]. The author's pagination of the manuscripts is reproduced in the text (in bold). We have reconstituted outlines for the courses from the titles of different sections throughout the text.

Motivated by the search for his way of working within philosophy and especially his relationship to art practice, I undertook my study of Merleau-Ponty's manuscripts at the Bibliothèque Nationale de France. I have carefully carried out the transcription of these documents, a difficult and demanding process, where small and lively handwriting was difficult to decipher. Like all other researchers who have looked at these handwritten pages, there was a lot of emotion when the breath of reading, at first hesitant, then more and more regular, gave life to these signs.

I warmly thank Suzanne Merleau-Ponty, who has authorized and facilitated the publication of this edition, and Claude Lefort, who has supported this project and has made it possible by editing Merleau-Ponty's posthumous work, a project of which he was the initiator. I thank Marc de Launay for correcting the transcription of the German texts, and overall, for his warm encouragement. I thank Marc Jimenez for the precious advice and lessons he has lavished on me over the years. I thank Jacques Neefs, who in his interest in Merleau-Ponty's manuscripts, was able to share his experience of the handwritten manuscripts with me and who has enriched my own research method. My thanks also go to Florence de Lussy, conservationist at the department of manuscripts of the Bibliothèque Nationale, and responsible for the Merleau-Ponty archive, who has responded to the needs of my research with efficiency and benevolence.

Course Notes from the
Collège de France, 1959

The Possibility of Philosophy Today[1]

[Course Outline]

Overview

I. Our state of nonphilosophy.
    1) Crisis of rationality in relations between human beings.
    2) Crisis of rationality in our relations with nature.
    3) [Modern science—world and truth].
    4) [Cultural symptoms and the possibility of philosophy].
        a) Literature.
        b) Painting.
        c) [Music].
        d) [Psychoanalysis].

II. Philosophy in opposition to this nonphilosophy.
    [A.] Husserl: philosophy as a problem.
        I.   The period of the *Logical Investigations*.
        II. From the *Ideas* to the *Cartesian Meditations*.
        III. The last period.
             Husserl. End.

    [B.] Heidegger: philosophy as a problem.
        I.   From the analytic of *Dasein* to the *Seinsfrage*.
             1) From *Dasein* to *Seyn*.
             2) Truth, *Offenheit, Verborgenheit* and *Unverborgenheit*. [36]

        II. *Seyn* or ~~*Sein*~~
             1) The Heideggerian notion of Being.
                 a) being [*l'être*], beings [*l'étant*], essence.
                 b) Being and *Grund*.
                 c) [What can one say about *Sein?*]
                 d) But, is it necessary to positively say what it is?
                 e) "Activity" of being that "*is*" [*este*], "mysticism" of being.
             2) About the passage from *Dasein* to *Sein*.
                 a) "Passive" and "mystical" language.
                 b) Are all these thoughts *mystical?*

III. Being and speech.
1) The problem of language, speech, the cardinal problem of philosophy.
2) It is necessary to recover operative speech as the pre-imaginary myth.
3) What does the *sense* of this *Sage* consist of?
4) Hence the relation of language to being and to man.

IV. *Zeit und Sein.*
1) *Zeit* [is the] *Vorname* for *Sein.*
2) The *Seinsgeschichte* [is] seen from [the] philosophy of history.
3) [The history of philosophy and philosophy].
4) Relations of philosophy and history.

Conclusion.

[Supplements:]
[d] Psychoanalysis.
II. Philosophy in opposition to this nonphilosophy.

[Overview]

[37] Place of this year's course together [with the others]. Constituting part of the course on Nature:[2] we have looked at Physics and φύσις, we have looked at animality—The study of the human body as the root of symbolism, [and] covered the junction φύσις-λόγος. Because our aim is φύσις-λόγος-History, it is even more generally ontology (in the modern sense), i.e., consideration of the all [*du tout*] and its articulations beyond categories of substance, subject-object, cause, i.e., metaphysics in the classical sense.

Disclosure [*dévoilement*] of a type of being different from these, where what are called "matter," "spirit" [*esprit*], "reason" reside. We are in contact with this type of being through our science and through our private and public life. But it does not have official existence: when it is not silent, our "philosophical" thought remains spiritualist, materialist, rationalist or irrationalist, idealist or realist. Sense of Revel's pamphlet:[3] one feels that there has been a philosophy, one feels that there are valid things in psychoanalysis, ethnology, etc. But, between philosophy in the classical sense, based on the above categories, and the concrete research too quickly identified with science—one does not see a place for a philosophy as interrogative ontology, even though we are satisfied neither with classical philosophy nor with scientism.

[38] First lectures: I would like, in the first lectures, to underline the sense of this ontological research before returning to Nature.[4] One might want to justify ontological research through a history of philosophy—but that would be negative: one would show the outcome of metaphysics in Hegel and the collapse of German idealism. But what after? Are Kierkegaard, Marx, and Nietzsche really after metaphysics? Or are we left with the nihilistic conclusion of its history? Markers for the future or for another expression of the same crisis of our philosophy?[5]

Ambiguous in any case; one reinterprets them from the present. So, let us transport ourselves into this present; let us characterize ontological research in terms of the philosophical void where we are, and which is linked to our entire history.

I do not postulate the identity philosophy-history, a punctual parallelism of philosophical and sociohistorical positions: the free yes and no are impossible—the free "answer"—but the question is given—It calls into question the philosophy given by our time. The reference to our time is necessary precisely because it is the time of nonphilosophy.

I. Our State of Nonphilosophy

There is a state of humanity, where we are, and that is (1) destruction of philosophy in the ordinary and classical sense;[1] (2) which calls us, however, to the highest point of philosophical consciousness—the "Phoenix," says Husserl.[2]

Hence, (1) the decadence of express, official philosophy; (2) the philosophical character of literature, art, etc.

My thesis: this decadence of philosophy is inessential [2]; it is a certain manner of philosophizing (according to substance, subject-object, causality). Philosophy will find help in poetry, art, etc., in a much closer relationship with them; it will revive itself and reinterpret its own metaphysical past—which is not past.

But it remains the case that, for the moment, philosophy is in crisis. What can take shape is either stammering, or quasi-silence, or even what expressly presents itself as nonphilosophy. Features of this historical state of nonphilosophy: they have been emerging gradually for the past twenty-five years—some are recent. I will not distinguish the older ones: the sense is the same. [40]

1) Crisis of rationality in relations between human beings.
It is a question of knowing whether there even is de jure the compossibility of human beings—possibility of an organic society.

The question actually posed since Marx: see society (capitalism) torn apart by class antagonism.

No universalism [means] class thought, morality—But for Marx, there is [a] principle of rationality from below: the foundational class for a new civilization that is liberated in power from all contradictions, as we are within all the domains ruined by contradiction. As a matter of fact, seen closely, it is less simple: how is this new civilization to be fashioned by the leadership of the new class? How will it be able to express its profound historical sense? The unrepresentable future: civilizing action takes place under the guarantee that the universal class de-structures itself as a class. Marx remains classical: praxis prolongs a historical truth (while accomplishing it). Marx remains Hegelian: Hegel not ruined but realized.

It is only with 1917 that Marxism puts rationality into question, i.e., from the moment that it is a matter of forcing history and not giving birth to it alone. Task of the revolution: not the transfer of the apparatus but the creation of the apparatus. Bolshevik voluntarism and subjectivism. Control, rationality, universalism of the regressive enterprise. It is not our concern to know if the enterprise does not become something *other* than a classless society (class abolished as class)—what matters to us is that there is, within the enterprise, a legitimation of a certain irrationalism.

What matters to us is also this: this first fact has had backlash **[3]** all over the world (and it is not finished). A counterrevolution has developed that has given itself the task of suppressing the revolution, of taking up [*reprend*] its irrationalism against it. Even from the revolution, only this irrationalism is resumed [*reprend*]: not its philosophy of history, but its procedures, its political techniques and policies—fascism.

Fascism has not ended with the end of the Second World War. Because if the revolutionary movements in the West are weak, then a question is in order today that, in order to [41] differentiate itself from the question that Marx first asked (revolution in developed nations), nonetheless shows that the crisis of Western "rationality" is the fate of underdeveloped nations. For Marx, there was a suitable relation between the problem of underdeveloped nations and the problem of advanced countries—and for Marxists, from 1917 onward, [there was the] idea of unequal development and the idea of the direct passage from underdevelopment to revolution. But the model for the revolution among underdeveloped nations remained proletarian revolution. What actually happens is quite different: relative indifference of advanced proletariats, spontaneous movements of underdeveloped nations. Hence, a regressive attitude that re-creates fascist behaviors like it has for much of the West.

What is in question behind the visible facts [*faits voyants*]: the possibility, for Europe, of creating a global civilization. One realizes that what we thought was the law of things (all people promised to our future—ethnocentrism: back on the same road. Even for Marx: these problems are resolved through extending notions of the proletariat or universal class to the colony), is in reality contingent historical privilege. The contestation of this privilege shakes up Marx's consciousness of being within the order of things. The claim on behalf of development makes us feel as if the politics of understanding is not de jure but only de facto.

It is both: the negation of the classical social "philosophy," an urgent appeal to the reflection on history, to awareness [*prise de conscience*], but also, like all limited situations, the possibility of simple repression.

Disclosure of a "sedimentation"—disclosure of our ethnocentrism, our universalism as a naive belief, as the projection of our history that we thought to be a law of the world—realization of this sedimentation as historical *Stiftung*,[3] i.e., of both its value as well as what contests it. This realization can [lead to] decadence (by effacement or by the resistance [*lutte*] of pure force)—or may well be an occasion of rebirth. [42]

[4] 2) The crisis of rationality in our relationships with Nature; Logic of technological evolution; the bomb—atomic energy.[4]
Highlighting (1) energies that are not within the framework of the world but which condition it and could destroy it; (2) energies obtained through disintegration: true being is explosive; to be wise is to be present on the surface of this volcano.

Hence, (1) idea that our world could not be—the shock [*ébranlement*] of exterior annihilation by this absolute other; hence, the revitalization of all tasks—irrationalism; (2) But, there is another aspect: these energies have been brought forth by humanity. Thereby, this ultra-naturalism is also an ultra-artificialism—the highly technological character of modern physics: technology is not only the application of science but is the condition of science. The (artificialist) spirit of technology was already intentionally present from the beginning of physico-mathematical science—a universe of objects that are in principle transparent for the subject. But now, the visible envelopment of science within technology: hence a new Prometheanism. The universe is a universe of *constructa*, an entirely human and an entirely inhuman universe.

This mixture of naturalism and artificialism—See American thought: neo-Darwinism. A being is either contradictory and disappears or adapts itself. Hence the possibility of speaking the language of finality without finalism. Agreement of realist causal ontology (societies, like cells, are regulating things) with artificialist thought: these things are full of "*devices.*"[5] Ideology of competition: "success" of herbivorous feeding because carnivorous feeding would cause the animals to consume themselves. "*Feeding devices*"[6] of insects (the tongues of butterflies collecting nectar)—or even of plants: "The flower itself has developed nectar during the course of evolution (the flower is also an indicator of [where] the nectar is) for the specific purpose of attracting insects in order to [43] [facilitate] pollenization."[7] Gills and lungs attributed to the "need to develop a surface of exchange" that is always present and which "has been met in different ways by different animals in the course of evolution" is the same mixture of blind necessity and artificialism, artificialist indistinction of nature-finality, see cybernetics: idea of machines constructed by us that think better than us. Idea of a truth that [5] would be given to us by them: reduction of being true to being constructed, extreme artificialism—but which, at the same time and secretly, is human artifice's abdication of responsibility [*démission*]: human artifice has disclosed "natural" relations, thing-ists of communication, that are causes of the formation of human thought. Extreme repression of Nature by artificialism and "return of the repressed."

These manners of thinking are almost oneiric, a museum of horrors. They do not come forth from contradiction: we only have dealings with *constructa* inseparable from the human being, with objects transparent to him since he has made them, with human activity—and yet all of this is produced by Nature. Nature *naturwissenschaftlichen*[8] as in itself—and yet this Nature has been constructed in human history. This contradiction is a veritable complex of contemporary thought. This thought is twice false: in its affirmation of Nature as well as in its negation of Nature. The danger of this contradiction is already present at the beginning of modern science as (1) disclosure of a nature in itself; (2) a disclosure that is nonetheless conditioned by human history. Hence, the folly of wanting to understand the advent of science itself, current fact, as a fact of Nature (in itself) in the sense that science gives to this word. But this was masked for a long time by the mediation (between Nature [44] in itself and Nature constituted in human history) of divine Reason. Science today, on the contrary, cannot lay claim to such a foundation; it is manifestly human, and so the circle human being–nature is obvious.

But this, the crisis situation for our thought, could be the point of departure for a deepening: the energies that come forth from the framework of the constituted world disclose contingency. But this realization of a *Boden* [ground], a sedimentation, could be rediscovered from Nature (on the condition that one does not conceive Nature as that described by objectivist science and as universal cause in itself): the rediscovery of a Nature-for-us as *soil* [*sol*] of all our culture, and where it is particularly rooted in creative activity that, in this way, is not unconditioned, which must maintain culture in contact with brute being, in the confrontation with it. This is the logic of the world of technology that reduces being to the alternative and to the antinomy of the pure object in itself and the artifact.

[6] 3) [Modern science—world and truth.]

The cosmic Rocket and the way it calls our relationship with Nature, our relationship with truth, with the in-itself (by the intermediary of other possible thinking beings) into question. One constructs the means to dwell on [*habiter*] other planets through technology, and as above, with ambiguous consequences: skeptics, irrationalists, ultra-humanists, ultra-rationalists.[9]

(1) The Earth deposed of its privilege as "metaphysical center": it becomes practically, and not only theoretically, one celestial body among others—the point of view from Sirius, from Micromégas—skeptical relativization of human things—all the more so since the "celestial bodies," reciprocally, will perhaps be possibly inhabited lands [*terres*], possibly inhabited by thinkers put together otherwise than us in terms of body and mind.

(2) Reaction against this shock [*ébranlement*], this encounter with the other: violence and reaffirmation of the human—the peasant [45] who has shot at the "martians"[10,11]—Promethean accent of "humanity": socialism is the domination of humanity over Nature thanks to humanity's reconciliation with itself—Propaganda of *Sputnik* and the alteration of Marxism. The same theme could have already been used with respect to atomic energy: but (1) it was not possible because of America's advance—one could not say that it was socialism that has discovered atomic energy; (2) it was dangerous because it risked showing that the problems of the domination of Nature are (a) relatively independent of social structure, (b) perhaps much more important than them.

Thus, here again, we are playing on an extremely complex confusion: anxiety, as a mixture of desire and fear in the face of the other. But this experience can at the same time be an occasion for profound philosophical realization (See above: underdevelopment as a problem).[12]

Show that access to other planets does not relativize the Earth and does not make a *Körper* out of the others, but on the contrary, that such access extends to other planets the function of a pre-objective *Boden*. The other planets become annexes of the Earth or the Earth expands, but one is always someplace. For example, the encounter with other thinking beings: if we can recognize [7] them as such, this signifies that we can establish communication with them.[13] And learned communication (for example, if they have language based on another corporeity), finally, always stands in connection with our human universe, which can thus be extended, generalized, but not annihilated [*anéanti*].

Thus, neither terror before the absolute other nor anthropocentric revindication.[14] . . . But in order to think this, it is not necessary [46] to take the situation as unjustifiable contingency, pure fact without truth, and it is not necessary take the mind as non-situated mind, pure *theoria* without place. See Husserl in *Umsturz*[15]—the disclosure of a *Lebenswelt* that subsists beneath idealizations, nourishing them and nourishing our history and which belongs to a type of being without which the law [*droit relatif*] of "construction" is unfounded.

4) [Cultural symptoms and the possibility of philosophy.]
All of the preceding are the emotional "resonators" that amplify and are felt as an immense public backlash against the development of technology—calling into question, by its consequences, this "technological world" itself.

One would have to cite other less visible phenomena, less understood, that attest to the same crisis situation, i.e., both the peril and possibility of a renaissance of philosophy: for example, in our Western ideology: poetry, music, painting, and psychoanalysis. The phenomena perhaps illuminate themselves in the perspective of the previous ones. Everywhere the soil [*sol*] is recognized as contingent, not only as possible, and one responds to this contingency either by irrationalism or by artificialism, opposite symptoms of the same difficulty.

a) Literature

"Poetry" in the modern sense—(Mallarmé and Rimbaud) contestation of language's "soil."

Mallarmé: language that indicates perceptible things (objective Nature), that directly returns to perception according to established correlations: [the] sign [is] an index. It is *selbstverständlich* [self-evident] language: Mallarmé understands it as result, [47] sedimentation of a founding language. This language, without a pre-given code, must signify by itself. The child, but us as well, when we speak of the new. The given language **[8]** functions by posing an enigma in tracing the contours of lacunae—thus language with a lateral, immanent signification, i.e., inseparable from signification, induced by it. It is only through signification that there can be the usual language of available significations.

Mallarmé: replace things, feelings, *selbstverständlich* [self-evident] anecdotes with their hollow mold—with what they are not, the absence that they cause to cease (the rose "absent from any bouquet").

More guarded language, language prevented from speaking too fast, given back to a kind of mutism, subtracted from the positivity of the world—with the risk that it becomes a too literal language, a writer's language, preciosity—speaking of "something else" (Giraudoux), visible danger in Mallarmé's prose where the prosaic is avoided not by the great means of poetry, but by the singing phrase colored by the "fin de siècle."[16]

Rimbaud: overcomes the correlation of sign-signification not by turning away from the positivity of the world, but, on the contrary, by entering without reserve into its pre-logical unity, by awakening its connections and its wild resonances (methodical disruption of sense, test of their sensical unity by an exercise of limits), and by placing language in this school, by letting it live as a thing of the world—clusters of words as there are clusters of colors and of qualities in things.

> Long after the seasons and days, the living and land . . .[17]
> Surviving old heroic fanfares still assaulting hearts and heads, far from
>   earlier assassins . . .
> Infernos hailing frosty gusts—such sweetness! Fires in a rain of
>   diamond wind,
>   Tossed [48] [9] by an earthly heart, endlessly burned to black, for
>   us.
>   —O world!—
> O sweetness; O world; O music! And look: shapes; hair and eyes,
>   floating. And white tears, boiling. O sweetness! And a feminine
>   voice at volcanic depths, in arctic caves. . . .
>   (*Les Illuminations*, XXIX, "Barbarian")[18]

In this way, Mallarmé and Rimbaud break the parallelism of the signifying-signified, either by the overlapping [*empiétement*] of the first on the second (reduction of things to their sense or to their purity), or by training the first in the life of the world—the two attempts, by the way, not being absolutely discernible because there is overlapping and because they may occasionally coincide.

Resumption of this enterprise in Surrealism:[19] destruction of "literature" (antithesis of Mallarmé: the world is to lead to the "book")—but a destruction that is also the sacralization of literature: first automatic writing, opposed to concrete literature, gives voice to the undivided life, to the unconscious's "clots of significations," abandonment to anything whatsoever (notebooks), objective chance as nonsense—"Holocaust of words," "the words make love"[20]—Then, very quickly in Breton, this destruction is understood as the reconquest of profound speech [*parole profonde*]: "Words without wrinkles"[21]—the "mouth of shadow."[22]

This recovery is, in reality, attempted by all the literature of the century, even nonpoetic, even in the "objective" forms of art such as the novel. Even the classical novel is sometimes "objective" (a character seen from the outside by an ordinary spectator = X); sometimes the narrative is accomplished by one of them from their point of view, sometimes a certain "voice" is accomplished by a narrator or with the [49] intervention of an author. It is not by subjective-objective categories that one can define its transformation.

It is in the relation of the signifier to the signified—subjective or objective, the classical novel wants to be thetic or thematic: a description of a framework, an analysis of feelings, that is to say, statements [*énoncés*][23] (it signifies beyond but unbeknownst to it).

After Proust, Joyce, the Americans, the mode of signification is indirect: self-other-the world deliberately mixed, one implicated in the other, the one expressing the other in a lateral relationship—Proust: the call to write is launched by things (the steeples of Martinville, three trees): **[10]** evidence of there being mute things demanding speech, speech whose purpose is to restore their silence—paradoxically, essence in appearance—transcendence as this paradox—one finds it everywhere: in myself, I am intermittent, a micro-description showing discontinuity (death of the grandmother discovered several months later), and yet I recover myself in this discontinuity—the Other is only myself: I make a stranger of him, infidelity in my mistrust (Albertine, inaccessible except in her sleep—as soon as she wakes [*vit*] she is under suspicion, and this suspicion creates distance and infidelity)[24]—it is never reached. And yet, this jealousy, at its limit, is pure love for the other (to suspect him at this point is truly getting out of the self and living in him, selflessness, love of the truth). This missing love will have been love: we will see it as soon as the tension of presence will have ceased: I loved him, said the Narrator, she loved me; there is no more reason to be wary of this appearance than the experience of *La Prisonniere*.

The relation of self-the world, self-self, self-other, is the slipping [*glissant*] relationship of transcendence—See time, which is also absence, dispossession, and to that extent, also possession: each person seated on a pyramid of time that is their own. As a result, Proust's expression is not thetic: each aspect is expressed in the classical, thetic manner, but what is to be expressed is enveloped by these opposites, and [50] this is not said positively; it is *between* the descriptions (Proust is deceiving himself when he speaks of philosophy and believes he is expressing his thought in a relativist-skeptical philosophy). The true thought of Proust: not everything is a lie, but truth in the lie, the impossibility of binding together the false and the true in the same story.

Joyce: the mist of interior monologue pierced by the irruption of the others. *The Americans*: the novel in the third person, from behavior, speeches of the characters without commentary, making anxiety appear in the highest degree (Hemingway) and thus close to free oneirism without contradiction (Faulkner).

Hence, neither subjective nor objective, but the implication and lateral relation of characters, one within the other and within the world, and all within the author, and this through indirect signification.[25] Here, as above, there is surface destruction, dissociation—and search for a more fundamental link, for a solidity.

[11] b) Painting

"Soil" of painting: the trompe-l'oeil, i.e., the picture, a collection of poorer signs arousing an equivalent of objective perception within the eye—in search of the appropriate technique: the representation of velvet, of "tactile values" (Berenson[26]) through visual givens. More generally, the picture as making present [a] feeling or [a] situation, arousing illusory "representation": a substitute for the real world (for pain, for love, for Watteau's anxiety), representational painting, founded on natural perception's system of correspondence and ingeniously putting it into play with respect to an artifact.

Painting and science (necessary natural relations)—model of the art of painting: perspective—natural signs [51] of relief or of depth—Nature's soil conceived in a realist manner → causal → finalist (Descartes: institution of Nature)—Art [is] technology, [is] science—ontology of the identity of compossibles—the truth [is] ideal, [is] *theoria*—the world killed, overcome.

The relativist soil: not Nature in itself but the sedimented product of culture—in fact, painting before the Renaissance is not that—the child, other cultures—Perceptions. But these facts are valued only by praxis: one realizes the expression of spatiality otherwise: Cézanne, deformations—Not the keyboard of preestablished signs: in establishing one—once established, [it] appears to be nature and soil: this is culture, sedimentation, *Sinn ent leerung* [emptying of sense]. But in the *Etablierung* [establishing], [there is the] foundation of a system (opposite, relative, diacritical) of signs that signify to each other relatively, are significant of themselves, signs that require invention. The amorphous perceived world is not by default but by excess.

More generally, da Vinci: find faces for things, a certain line, a certain "snaking" [*serpentement*], its generative principle.[27] In what "principle," in what "generation"? It is a line, nothing more—and a line that is not of the world, that is not in appearance—In relation to what does it signify? A norm or a level. It is necessary that a line, as a trace of movement, must be a rhythm, a law—a law not only of a real displacement in space but also of a field of possibilities beyond the probable. [52] This spatiality is meta-spatial.[28] The sign speaks to a field of existential possibilities within us, like a certain gap [*écart*] in relation to it.[29] Klee: "genius is the inconsistencies within the system."[30] It is a systematic error, "coherent deformation"—thus each painting is the creation of a dimensionality—thus (1) the painting is a world for itself, not a copy of the world; (2) it expresses indirectly and not **[12]** by returning to the object. A "world for itself" remains to be specified—it does not mean "constructivism," or another fabricated object, assembled colors, "decoration."

The autonomy of the painting in a certain relationship with the pre-pictorial world: Renoir in Cassis: look at the water . . . and cover the canvas with everything else—Painting not the pure absence but the gap [*écart*]. It is evident that one paints with one's hand upon the visible and that the hand is suspended on a look . . . [53]

Specify the reference to the world: it is not only *resemblance*: Masson's bright red cloud in the wheatfield at noon.[31] The picture as a whole is not objectively or immediately identifiable as a wheatfield at noon. Evidence: it needs a title. Klee invented 9,000 titles. The frequency of titles in non-figural painters. Bazaine: *Le Ruisseau*—without the title one would see the colors but not a picture; the red of Masson's cloud does not function as "threat" and "heat"[32] but as the red of the flag. But the role of the title [is not] substituted for a failed painting in order to ensure the univocal designation of the object. The role of the title is to allow pictorial signs to function as pictorial signs. To exonerate the picture of the function of resemblance is to permit it to exercise the function of expression, i.e., of presenting an alogical essence of the world that, like the line of which da Vinci speaks, is not in the world empirically and yet which brings it back to its pure accent of being, putting in relief its manner of *Welten*, of being world. Bazaine's picture, with its title, [is not] water and pebbles but aqueous and mineral essence.

See the lines of a critique concerning a young painter of the Paris School (Gianni Bertini):

> . . . panoramic weft . . . that unites the different biological and historic *reigns*. One thinks of a show in which a single non-Euclidean continuum would juxtapose, without a break, the moment when the Iron Crown sinks into the rock and the one when the *Titanic* sinks into the sea. An invincible Armada of steel and quartz cruises within sight of coral reefs . . . [it][33] couples, in short-circuits generating durable storms,

the most disparate realities in time and structure. In him we witness
the analogical symbiosis of barbaric splendors of long ago, of hypo-
thetical fauna and of themes tuned to the most vertiginous immediate: [54] atomic disintegration, supersonic speed, etc. . . . search for a
fertile collision between several principles or substances that are very
different . . .[34]

The Paris School: taking hold of certain symbolic matrices, certain
hinges of the World which are at work in various empirical objects—unity
beyond space, time, reigns, beyond distinctions such as nature-history,
beyond the distinction of waking and dreaming (little of reality), distinctions of real-possible: [it is] the original unity of indistinction.[35]

Likewise, with respect to Wilfred Moser:

A great book of pictures, in which are reflected towns and landscapes,
one does not know whether the painter has seen them or dreamed them,
or if he has heard their melancholy history. Sometimes we perceive the
night space through porous and crumbled walls, transparent despite
numerous superimposed layers. [13] Sometimes we catch an odd tang of
virgin forest, we find ourselves in an anguishing jungle from which only
those who can cut their way through emerge alive. But the darkness may
brighten at any moment, with the light hiding in all the cracks ready to
burst forth.[36]

Thus, relationship to the world in painting. It is precisely this relationship
(given, for example, by the title) that permits the picture to function as
picture, i.e., not to copy [but] to give the essence.

Question of non-figuratives: wouldn't the picture be even freer to give the
essence if all links were cut? Painting of being?

In reality, it can happen that it then falls back into itself precisely
as a thing: again it resembles things, bacteria, awkward biological forms.
One is limited to rendering (moving besides) more general physical structures: a torn-down wall where only the colored thing or even matter in
general neither vibrates nor dreams.

It is not necessary to impose any limit on the freedom of the painter:
[55] he is free to move away from exterior resemblance as much as he
can—but in order to obtain the *Welten*—"I am not romantic. The im-
mensity, the torrent of the world in a small point of matter, do you believe
it is impossible? What I am trying to translate is more mysterious, en-
tangled in the very roots of being, at the impalpable source of sensations"

(J. Gasquet, *Cézanne*). Lapoujade's[37] rendering of the hell-like mine lacks any "resemblance."

The solution to this search is in a study by Klee:[38] Klee is concrete: identification with the color, with Tunis—*Stiftung* of the painter through the nature that exactly fulfills the spirit of painting[39] (Klee text 1);[40] what one calls "abstract" is the concrete in memory (Klee text 2).[41] [56] The abstract is still the world: it is simply the world as terrifying, the search for its transcendence (Klee text 3).[42] But "the artist is man, nature himself and a piece of nature in nature's space."[43]

Painting is a movement,[44] a movement that sprouts within the appearance, which is dictated by it, by no means a movement inspired by the intellect (the left hand rather than the right hand). Subjects: an apple tree, a sleeper (4)[45] as *totum simul*. So why is painting so different from appearances? Precisely because it is Nature, not of appearances, not the "skin of things;" because it is *natura naturans* [*nature naturante*]:[46] its "hand nothing but the instrument of a distant will," because it provides what nature wants to say but has not said: the "generative principle" that makes things and the world be (5),[47] [57] "first Cause," "brain or heart of creation," "absolute knowledge," is the principle older than God himself (Schelling), raw being [*être brut*]—the indelible-indestructible (Michaux)—And its intelligibility to itself: a center "far from centers"— The center of the circle: technical center and center of understanding. The center of a circular organism is distinct from this center—The center of perspective and the focus of a modern picture.

Transcendence (the artist among those who are not yet born or among the dead) (6)[48] (before or after the world, not correlated with the world).

The "prototype," that is to say the *selbstverstandlich* [self-evident] world placed in a halo of possibilities of which it is only an "example" (7, 8, 9).[49] One deforms precisely [58] in order to seize upon the form in its birth (10).[50]

Thus painting is a kind of philosophy: seizing upon the genesis (11)[51] of philosophy in action. ("The painter knows a great deal, but he only knows it afterwards").[52] The painting is not "abstract," Klee said, but "absolute"[53] (i.e., radical), i.e., finding a position of being that is incomprehensible for science and for the everyday, i.e., the being already there that is presupposed in any "explication." Appearances are grasped as a "parable" of this being. Art giving symbols of appearances (i.e., their generalization, their derivation from part of a vaster possibility). It is a non-express philosophy ("without willingly expressing it"). The symbol is not even the thing, "an image focused in the mirror of the mind and yet identical with the object"[54] (Goethe). It reveals only by concealing [*Il ne dévoile qu'en voilant*]—(and philosophy?).

Hence the irony of art so that "ethical gravity rules, along with hobgoblin laughter at the learned ones"[55] (Klee). (This "irony" could also be philosophy.) (Does philosophy *possess*[56] being?) Irony is detachment, consciousness of contingency, of a kind of equivalence between possibilities, of the contemporaneity of all things.[57] "Were I [59] a God . . . I should also do a lot of historical theater; the times would be liberated from their age" (Klee).[58]

Another (inevitable) way to render contingency: mythical, epic, childlike expression—Michaux: This trace, that which "children have and then subsequently forget, the one they put into all their drawings at that age: locating things, leave here, go there, the distance, the directions, the path leading to the house as necessary as the house itself . . . that was his problem, too"[59]—original drawing, the world as seen from an unaccustomed eye, which has not yet accomplished the separation between the serious and the ludicrous, the "objective" from "subjectivities" (where one confines magic).

In principle[60] this mode of vision should lead [60] to the adult universe itself, the universe of "immanence" not confined to childhood. If it is "childish," it is only for the sake of rendering the adult universe as it is; the painter "would have required 'such a bewildering confusion of lines that there could be no question of a purely basic representation; it would be so opaque as to be almost unrecognizable'"[61] (Klee).[62]

From there, from the trace, titles (in the sense defined above: not in order to identify the object that the drawing leaves equivocal, to return to the everyday object, but to metamorphosize it, that is to say: a pine tree that in reality, in its essence, is what it is,[63] a folding of individual fibers, one within the other, with their burgeoning apex: it is "*In sich*,"[64] *in itself* [*en soi*], envelopment before the deployment of the for itself [*pour soi*], the possible)[65] animals, possible plants[66] obtained through variations of the real (*Giant Aphid*)[67] (duplication of a clown) (*Bird Drama*:[68] variations and contestations of our universe through that of birds that are figured through superimposed forms of anger, beings who are all claws, beaks, intertwined looks)[69] *The Tear*[70]—diagram with double contour shifted by a skull, lips in lateral relief, active, attracting attention, calm shoulders as in a plaster bust, the eyes and mouth are three perfectly sharp black holes, and also the tear like a perfectly clear annex [61] from the left eye, this production from within, which unbalances everything and changes the entire meaning of the whole: acute feeling from within the body[71]—*Family Matters (Among Fruit)*:[72] fruits of several plants or branches from the same plant, one connecting to the other—*Group with the Fleeing Scold*[73] (the unanimous plurality of little girls), *Brotherhood*[74] (a frieze of men with an emphasis on calves and jackets), "angels" (*Forgetful Angel*,[75] *Angelus Militans*,[76] *Poor Angel*[77]).

Why this insistence on Klee? Sign of our shifting "soil": the everyday world is always shaken by the painting—but [it] believes itself to be communicating by means of (1) the senses and of their system of "natural" equivalence, (2) of linguistic significations, of the "subject" in the pictorial sense—in short, the *logos* in principle reduced to logic.

The contemporary painting's search: not destruction of this world of signification and of being—but replaced in a more general communication and in a pre-objective being.

c) [Music]

One could (and we will do it later) make the same analysis with music. Generalization (and "purification") of music as with painting: there were privileged forms of tonality—with definitions of the gaps [*écarts*], intervals, simultaneous combinations and "valid" successions on this "soil," assuring musical communication—this being *selbstverstandlich* [self-evident]. None of this is physically suppressed but is reintegrated into a wider musical possibility [62] where the privileged structures are only some variants of the twelve-tone scale.

The "soil" turns out to be a historical formation or cultural contingency: music reenters into itself. This neither covers nor justifies all "generalized" music: there remains the mysterious problem of knowing what it truly is to be a musician in this freedom (like truly being a painter or being Mondrian)—i.e., not inventorying abstract possibilities (the other as "new," the nondescript other, the combinatory, blind combination—Boulez—the engineer "trying" anything, but his goal is fixed by a certain work to be realized—The musician has no aim, like the painter, except that *he wants* to attain interior "necessity"), but to bring possibilities into reality, i.e., existential possibilities—to do "otherwise" than what the musician has found to be required in preceding music—under this reservation: music itself may only be found by not taking aim—i.e., the painter—in this respect, a sign that generalized music finds it difficult to balance: at the same time as looking away from the habitual, titles or even very "impure" procedures (recitation on a musical background,[78] incorporation of waltzes or "profane" music, Alban Berg) perhaps attesting to external means for "passing off" a symbolism that is not sufficient—Romanticism and rationalism—it is necessary that titles or references to the lived are, as in painting, ways to transform it and not plated pieces of lived experience.

Under these reservations: there is truth in the will to liberate music, to render it as itself—this, which in the very sense of music, which is not speech, says everything.

Michaux: "There is what one calls music."[79] These tiny waves relieve the weight of things, the gravity of things, the hardness and sharpness of things, their lengths and heights, the dirtiness of things, as well as their defenders [*tenants*] (what defenders!) their entanglements [*intrications*], the [63] implications and consequences of things.

They know how to make night come upon the object, and upon beings when these have become like objects. They can disembody the flesh, abstract the concrete, de-problematize the situation. One breathes, one lives again, everything else is forgotten, the good flood having returned to recover the earth from geometry, from walls, ugliness, the innumerable, undesirable encumbrances that had filled it and had become necessary . . . three wars and as many revolutions to be eliminated and nothing as effective as this simple and prodigious covering.

Music, marvel that surely preceded the fire. We definitely needed it. . . . Inner life passes: astonishing inner life that proceeds both through flows and snaps.

Its gropings, its hesitations, its brusqueness, accentuations, drafts, resumptions [*reprises*], its backsliding [*retours en arriere*] are exposed here, what the other arts keep carefully hidden. . . . Music returns [*remplace*] what beings (mother, woman, child, friends) have of the marvelous, such that one would want, without suspecting it (through a marvelous subtraction of what is uncomfortable), to keep only what expresses them, to render them as inoffensive as those waves of delight that lift the heart. Music, profound center [*axe*], archaic center that holds multiple centers. Center before ambivalence, as one would say.

Art that sings the divine without having to believe in God, neither to be part of a religion nor to refrain from dogmas, without even knowing if what it composes is really a hymn or simply a way of wanting to happen "divinely."

Music, art of perpetual engagements—Art that sings love without knowing whether it is for a woman, without an engagement [*contrat*], without her being aware, without having to be at all and without even having to exist more personally than a ray of sunlight, a pink cloud in the high mountains or the fever of a returning springtime. Art where impossible love and its royal road are viable. . . .

It is spoken thought above all that creates ambivalence, even more than the life that is lived. The thought that defines and makes a definitive declaration, that makes prison bars it will later need to break to pieces in order to advance toward [64] a new state that it will define once again, that is to say, it will put itself behind bars that it will have to break anew with brilliance or with betrayal and lies.[80] . . .

Music, performance art [*art de comportement*], although without references to the physical, exterior world. Routes and passages, nothing better to express an attitude. A means not to be but to live, to feel alive [*de se sentir vivre*]—what is more communicable? Eight minutes of folk music says more about an unknown people than a hundred pages of notes and surveys. . . .

Impossible to project as such on an exterior screen in material markings visible on the outside; music: when one listens to it you are obliged to follow it through *routes internal to it.*

So it brings you naturally to an identification and to the illusion of a decanting [*transvasement*] from being to being . . .[81]

Beings and being enveloped in the "night" of music, and yet indicated, expressed, put in communication with us through it, in what they have of wonder, of what is not embarrassing, of the accessible beyond contradiction, without resistance and without "taking a stance."

Danger: narcissistic musical signification, oneiric (possible illusion: does folk music make its true sense legible in eight minutes?) ("illusion of a decanting from being to being").

Truth: there is access to the exterior through the interior, a relation there to being and to beings that is absolute, beneath ambivalence and the *thesis*—Taken at its source, the gesticulation of the man who is thinking and living through being and beings: the origin of music.[82] [65]

d) [Psychoanalysis]

A final "cultural" symptom as well (not from the world of technology), but more general than literature, music, painting: phenomenon of chain disintegration, of the liberation of energy, but only at the level of knowledge and at the level of human relationships: psychoanalysis.[83] [66]

[II. Philosophy in the Face of This Nonphilosophy][1]

[26] [A.] Husserl: Philosophy as a Problem

Ambition, from the beginning, to remake a philosophy after the psychologism, the historicism, the positivism that followed the collapse of Hegel[2]—academic forms of nihilism. [Husserl] himself rediscovers all philosophy through "his" naivete.

I. The period of the *Logical Investigations*[3]

This new philosophy first appears in the form of a domain of themes about which the sciences and history do not speak: essences beyond induction—blindness of induction—it presupposes essences, structures, invariants to be highlighted by eidetic variation—already physical induction—for example, history or linguistics presuppose that their universe has a characteristic [*typique*] (universal grammar).

This *Was heißen* [what is meant] beyond *Wortbedeutungen* [word meanings]—regulates the usage of words—But then where do we go? *Zu den Sachen selbst* [to the things themselves]: return to a core of concrete signification.

This domain of essences will be general logic and regional ontology: "prolegomena to pure logic" after *The Philosophy of Arithmetic*, "Philosophy as Rigorous [67] Science"[4]—it would be necessary to generalize the mode of knowledge for which the mathematical sciences have set the example—A priori, not only for nature but for everything else as well. Objective orientation: this a priori gives what descriptively makes sense of being; project of a generalized ontology: ontology of the *etwas überhaupt* [anything whatsoever]—regional ontologies. But Husserl is not a "realist": these essences are already realities with respect to an intentionality (*Über intentionalen Erlebnisse* [with respect to intentional experiences] in the second volume of the *Logical Investigations*). But intentionality, consciousness of . . . , conceived as spiritual relation to sense or essence.

Nevertheless, from this first expression of the philosophical will, we see that it is not a matter of "Platonism" in the current sense of the word. *Motives* [*motifs*] for *Umbildung* [transformation] are already present in this essentialist, objectivist philosophy.

The search for the *Wesen*[5] (*es gehört zum Wesen* . . . [it belongs to *Wesen*]) is the explication of an experience. It is a matter of a "phenomenology," i.e., the expression of being as it is actually encountered. For example, the world, the thing, defined through their mode of appearance, i.e., (1) the essence expresses facticity; (2) it expresses a relationship to a concrete subject. Already in the *Logical Investigations*, the universal is not essentialist: angels.[6] The universal value of our logic founded on the fact of communication.

II. From the *Ideas*[7] to the *Cartesian Meditations*[8]

[**27**] It is these two themes that will become deepened with the "period of the *Ideas*." Surprise of the first "phenomenologists": [68] the objectivist and essentialist orientation is revealed to be a philosophy of subjectivity, and of a subjectivity that is not only the "essence of subjectivity" but experience.

Rediscovery of transcendental idealism: all being is being-constituted. All being is to be converted into a noema by reflection or reduction to sense. A transcendental reduction *is added* to the eidetic reduction.

And in what does the transcendental reduction consist? It is disclosure of intentionality—but of an intentionality that is no longer immediate participation in an essence (First period) or (unlike Kant) operation of active and purely spiritual connection—intentionality (through the analysis of the perceived world): an objective multiplicity that refers itself to a *noema* of which it is the *Erscheinung Weise* [means of appearance]. Constitution: *Auffassung als* . . . [apprehension as . . .] *Auffassungsinhalt-Auffassung*—[apprehension content-apprehension], *Hyle* [matter], and *morphé* [form]—instability of this result: (1) *Auffassung* is *Sinngebung* [sense-giving], [imposition?][9] of sense and essence—but consciousness is not only this activity: problem of the status of *Hyle* evoked by the *Lectures on Internal Time Consciousness*,[10] where there is a seizing upon of the *Urerlebnis* [primordial experince] that is not *Auffassungsinhalt-Auffasung*, not objectification, [but] an encounter with the non-thetic at the heart of consciousness. Of that which is before acts: act intentionality and operative or latent intentionality—Problems of passive syntheses—Originary and secondary passivity at the heart of ourselves. Cumbersome intentionality, "fluent essences"; (2) Correlatively, the sense of the world's being is not being-posited by these acts—priority of the perceived, impressional world, over the world of *Gebilde* [accomplishment]; (3) Repercussion for the conception of reflection—reflection or transcendental reduction that discloses tiered layers of intentionalities, intentionalities that cannot be adequation with a **[28]** universal constituting Mind, that cannot consist in placing ourselves within it, that do not get carried away as coincidence with it. It knows itself second. It discloses an unreflected which is in principle not outside of its grasp but which it also does not [69] reabsorb. All reduction is eidetic: it does not put us in possession of our existence. A conscious reflection on itself knows this: it knows itself as indefinite iteration—surmounted by knowledge of its law: it would "always be the same." The subject escapes itself in seizing itself or seizes itself in its escape. Consequently, how does one rigorously maintain distinctions between the immanence of consciousness and the transcendence of the world or of the thing? Both take all or nothing. Resistance to intentionality as the *Sinngebung* of spiritual immanence, both within us and outside of us.

The same dialectic of the natural and transcendental attitude—the natural attitude overcome and preserved—the *Weltthesis* [world thesis] as *Urdoxa* [original opinion], *Urglaube* [original belief]. A contact with being that is before *theoria*—philosophy is this *theoria* that discloses the pretheoretical. A contact with the being that is *Verborgenheit* [concealment] as well as ἀλήθεια.

Appearance of a paradox of constitution: interrogating the thesis of the world, developing its intentional implications, is no longer revealing a reference to essences or to noema as immanent signification: it is often (*Ideen II*) within the "deepest" layers that one discovers an inherence in the world (in the body, to others),[11] layers upon which any thought of the in-itself, the *bloße Sachen*, is founded: will we go on to say that my body or the sensible, as *urpräsentierbar* [originally present], are themselves constituted by the system of *Auffassungen*, by the game of these "attitudes" and correlations, by a multiplicity of *Erlebnisse*—intentional object? It is nevertheless what Husserl maintains: *Leiblichkeit* [corporeality] itself is described in the natural attitude. It remains beyond a final constitution, accomplished in the immanence of a complete reduction, where there is only the "subjective," consciousness and its acts—But the question [70] **[29]** becomes pressing: is constitution centrifugal? If it is not immediation to a Spinozistic thought, if the analytic of consciousness always comes too late, after; if the world is always pre-constituted, *vorgegeben* [pre-given], *selbstverständlich* [self-evident], what do we call that which makes it emerge? Non-publication of *Ideen II*.[12]

All of these paradoxes and problems are made more acute around 1929 (*Cartesian Meditations*). Deepening of the theme of reflection and the reduction—the reduction increasingly appears as progressive: many stages. There is a phenomenology of the first degree (body and corporeity, *Einfühlung* [empathy]), then of the second degree: reduction to the immanence of the mind. But to say that it is progressive, that it is a construction, means that the *unbeteiligte Zuschauer* [disinterested spectator] knows himself (1) [with] universal authority, (2) but also that precisely in order to be absolute consciousness, he must provide for his act of origination, since he was born into a life beforehand. Philosophy *is* called into question by its own authority as philosophy.

In particular, Husserl perceives a residual "naïveté" within the conceptualization of the reduction. We speak of *the* consciousness, of *the* intentionality in general. It was implied that what the philosopher said was understood by the reader and immediately concerned him. But, the reduction remained an act of infidelity to the rule of *absolute Voraussetzungslosigkeit* [absolute unconditionality]: if we follow suit, it is necessary that the philosopher introduce into his philosophy the possibility of communicating it as a theme. Do not take this as something that goes without saying.

Hence a "reduction within the reduction," a reflection within reflection: [if] I must be a philosopher, I must explain how my reflection can be reflection for all, **[30]** that I see that it is first of all only a reflection for me. Reduction to the sphere of belonging or to [the] egological. Show how the other is possible for me (and me for him) as an *alter ego* within this sphere, an *alter ego* of which I can say a priori what [71] I say of myself. The theme of *Einfühlung*, which, in *Ideen II*, existed only at the first level of reflection, reappears at the higher level. How can I constitute the other as constituting (and as constituting me)?

This calls into question all the above distinctions:[13] because if the other is constituting, then the other, obviously, is the person and not only the mind. I must, therefore, say that it is the person who is constituting. And, moreover, if I am ultimately constituted myself (as is necessary for others to be constituting), [then] I am, as the final subject, not an *unbeteiligte Zuschauer* but a person within the world—identity of transcendental subjectivity and the person within the world—is a complete reduction impossible, is philosophy impossible?

This is where Husserl is in 1929 in the *Cartesian Meditations*—through the immanent development of his research, or rather as a result of its reflexive approach to itself (each step changes the landscape, discloses a *remainder* to be integrated, opens a new field whose exploration modifies the approach to the opening), the immediate will to remake a philosophy (i.e., a *strenge Wissenschaft*, i.e., a generalization of mathematical evidence, i.e., a universal right of *Vernunft* [reason]) has resulted, not in failure (these "difficulties" are philosophy itself), but characterizes the universal as problematic (*Vernunftproblem* [problem of reason]), since the philosopher is brought back to the world through it. There would be a failure if we were brought back to the naive attitude. But there is no question of this. We are not brought back to naïveté. We find another sense. There is nonphilosophy before and nonphilosophy after: that is philosophy. But at least philosophy is no longer a direct march toward apodicticity: it is this march [but] hampered by *Situationwahrheiten* [situational truths] or rather: it consists **[31]** in discovering our attachments and situations.

It is, therefore, the most coherent movement of *Selbstbesinnung* [self-reflection] that brings us back to the world. At the same time, [72] we are in the prewar years of fascism. Husserl feels that fascism puts rationality, the philosophy of understanding, and *Aufklärung* [enlightenment] all to the test.[14] He wants to show (1) that this crisis is motivated—that the rationalism of understanding has been emptied of its sense—that the existential crisis should not be judged from above by philosophy, as if there were no responsibility—that it is a crisis of philosophy—that the history of philosophy communicates with general history: we have the manner in which human beings go about constituting the world, the relations they develop with it. Philosophy is in the World. (2) But this crisis, which is total, which calls philosophy into question with good reason, only condemns it to rebirth on a new basis and does not signify the end of all philosophy. It is the end of a philosophy that has believed in founding rationality outside of the existential too easily. Philosophy, in the traditional sense, is to be reexamined, to be given the life it rightly lost—the Phoenix—the Greek and Renaissance idea of knowledge, both the center and perspective for our entire history, even for our existential history (it is the history of its decline). And the telos of the new philosophy is still [to be] brought back to its first vigor, with some *Welträtseln* [riddles about the world] and some *Vernunftprobleme* [problems of reason] of which it is ignorant.

The meditation on the relation of essence-facticity intersects with facts that implicate the essence of **[32]** philosophy.[15] From this meeting must result: a deepening of philosophy in the sense of facticity, and comprehension of these facts—but also reestablishment of philosophy, precisely because it includes the shock of reason, reestablishment of philosophy [73] precisely as the fullest consciousness of nonphilosophy.[16]

III. The last period **[33]**

European science and philosophy represent [a] valid telos but [a] telos that can only be attained through a radical reform. [Husserl] insists, especially at first, on the validity of the telos ("Vienna Conference"),[17] and then afterward insists on the radical modification that gives philosophy its dignity—and which is a true upheaval [*bouleversement*].

The valid telos: philosophy (and the sciences that are its branches) [is] an idea founded (*Gestiftet*) by the Greeks as a horizon of infinite research, a truth to be attained by the deployment of a process of indefinite approximation. This is radically original: the South, China are anthropological examples—Greece is the founding event of humanity—[the] historical-practical scope of planning of the world, but most importantly, the creation of a human universe of truth, of universality, knowledge—thus of responsibility, of communication,[18] etc.—Being faithful to *oneself*, being *through oneself* [*Être fidèle à soi, être par soi*]—Rationality, consciousness.

The "Vienna Conference,"[19] protestation against irrationalism (*Weltanschauung*)—the philosopher [as] "functionary of humanity"—philosophy *is* rationalism—philosophy [is the] "brain of history"—philosophy is theoretical attitude (*RMM*, 1950, 241),[20] *Idealisierung* [idealization], logification (*Krisis*, 335/288). The mind exists only in itself and for itself (*RMM*, 255)[21]—the philosopher [as] *unbeteiligte Zuschauer*. [74]

But, in the *Krisis* (I and II published in Belgrade,[22] III in preparation and recently published by Louvain),[23] [Husserl] insists on this: philosophy can only fulfill its task through [a] total transformation—made necessary by the philosophical error[24] contained in the evolution of science and philosophy since the Renaissance. The Renaissance—Descartes, creation of a *Wissenschaftlichkeit* [scientific discipline][25] and of a philosophy of the highest degree of dignity—but one that was naive, that was not conscious of itself—it is necessary to return to the founding act and to see there both its justification and its *Einseitigkeit* [one-sidedness], which was preparing for *Entleerung* [emptying], (for *Aufklärung* [clarification]), in order to learn how to rebuild philosophy as full philosophy and on a basis other than empty rationalism.

[34] Science and philosophy since Descartes—

The highest ideal of knowledge:
Science: to determine the world in itself as a mathematical multiplicity—Nature mathematized by Galileo—conception of the *bloße Sachen* [mere things], non-qualitative variables, geometrically or at least numerically defined—indirect mathematization of the qualitatively "full"—*Vorbild* [exemplar]: the universe of spatial forms. Idea that the world "in itself" [*en soi*] is (1) submitted to this systematic a priori in all

of its domains; (2) to conquer through the indefinite progress of inductivity with a possible deductive return; (3) to construct only according to this ideal existence; (4) such as it is in itself or before an infinite subjectivity.[26]

[75] Philosophy: continuity of mathematical knowledge with total philosophical knowledge (Descartes—the Cartesians)—same "substructure," but generalized: Being in itself, God as being without restriction, Object—of objects, Ideality: not only the world, but also "mathematized" God and humanity.

This mathematization and idealization involves: (1) the postulate that all qualitative change is assignable in qualitative terms; (2) the postulate that the world is made entirely of *bloße Sachen*. The spiritual-human universe is only made into a world through this infrastructure. The rest is not an object of science, is not an object of ontology—the domain of *Geist* [spirit] (of the objective spirit, of the world where there are human beings or organisms) has no *Weltlichkeit* [worldhood]: it is lacunary; it is necessary to place it back within the only really continuous whole, the whole of the *bloße Sachen*.

Hence, the *abstraction* of the *bloße Sachen*, and *ergänzend abstraktion* [complementary abstraction] (or *Gegen-abstraktion* [counter-abstraction]) of the spiritual-human as "psychological," "to conceive [it] as second nature or appearance," in itself "*fragmentarisch* [fragmentary]."[27]

Universal mathematics

This transformation of the given is legitimated by [these] results: fecundity-discoveries, establishing law [*droit relatif*]. But it postulates precisely an absolute right [*droit absolu*]. It forgets that it results from a creation of human *Gebilde*, from a *Tat* [deed] (the *Tat* of Galileo), and it gives itself as self-evident; at this moment, it loses the truth that it had placed within its framework: it becomes a false ontology—empowerment of the method (*Methodierung* [methodology]). It at the same time forgets that it discloses theoretical praxis. It at the same time forgets that it discloses "pure thought"—not forgetting pure thought as such would be to know that it arises from *Erfahrung* [experience].

Entdeckung [discovery] and *Verdeckung*.[28]

[76] **[35]** Double forgetting: Forgetting of Nature before idealization, before mathematization—forgetting of the pre-scientific, pre-theoretical, pre-objective world. The analysis of perception itself is idealizing: one believes that it is a question of giving an account of its own *identification*, whereas it is [actually] about its *Einigung* [unification]: identity is logical, the *Einigung* is pre-logical (enrichment). Analysis in

Empfindungen [sensations], or in properties, or in perspectives is idealizing. The carnal unity of the thing—the world has its "habits"—non-exact causality. Style and characteristic are "reduced." Characteristic reappears in modern physics (types or styles in groupings of quanta), but within the framework of the same substructure of idealities. Now this ignorance of the lived world sterilizes science itself by long imprisoning it in rigid representations of matter. It forgets the operation of *Stiftung* [institution][29] masked by its own results. It comes from the *Lebenswelt* [lifeworld] that differentiates these operations. But precisely for this reason it ignores itself as a creation of human *Gebilde* [accomplishment]. There is *Stiftung* and then *Sinnentleerung* [meaninglessness], forgetting of origins, traditionality, sedimentation. It is like pliers and drills: one believes that they are seen as such. Likewise, the sense of a *Gebilde* seems self-evident; it is nature but also culture.

Hence the *Technisierung* [technization][30] of thought—which becomes art (in the sense of fine art but also in the sense of technologies), i.e., treatment or maintenance without consciousness of its origins, consciousness of the source of its sense. Hence, [there is] a crisis of rationality so understood when there is theoretical or practical inadequacy in relation to being and in relation to the universe of *Geist* that [77] has not been penetrated (no *Geistenwissenschaften* [sciences of spirit, the humanities] for founding a scientific politics).

These forgettings are not a coincidence:[31] (apparent) solidity can be purchased at this price through *Verkörperung* [embodiment];[32] progress can be purchased at this price, one no longer reactivates—*Tatsachenwissenschaft* [fact-minded sciences] and *Tatsachenmensch* [fact-minded people].[33] All of this is false only as autonomous, only as nothingness.

It is necessary to return, through *Selbstbesinnung* [self-reflection], to the *Urstiftung* [original institution], i.e., (1) to the *Lebenswelt* as Nature (the ensemble of *Selbstverstandlichkeiten-Boden*-Thesis of the world);[34] (2) to the *Lebenswelt* as history. It "receives" all cultural acquisitions from the time in which they were sedimented. It contains science, "objective" or positive philosophy. The *communis opinio* of science and the pretension to completely logicize—[36] necessity of history, even for science.

The return to the *Lebenswelt* as characteristic of phenomenology— the *Lebenswelt* is a "universal" problem[35]—contains "everything." It is necessary to return to the dimension before objectivation. A world that will not be theoretical: *theoria* is a type of praxis for the human attitude— Return to a savage world before—[a] world where the distinction between the subjective (psychic) and the objective (in itself) will not yet be made. Philosophy should not be an "attitude"; it circles in on itself as *theoria*, paradox of a science of the pre-scientific and of science. Being motivated by the crisis, Husserl finds his problem: the dialectic of the transcendental and non-transcendental.

The beginning of all this is in the above: the thesis of the world *vor aller Thesis* [before any thesis]—The paradox of the world or *Welträtsel*; the *Selbigkeit* [self-identity] of the world and the *Selbigkeit* of the mind.[36] [78] The world conserved by phenomenological reflection—transcendence conserved in immanence—the reduction is not doubt. Doubt leaves the *mens sive anima* [mind or soul] untouched. The true philosophical attitude is not the hypothesis of the *Nichtigkeit* [annihilation] of the world but astonishment before the world. Philosophy is not *natürlich* but *natural* (*Ideen II*). The reduction is the intelligibility of what precedes it if it wants to be intelligibility of itself.

Only previously Husserl said: the reduction results in transcendental idealism, in the immanence of the consciousness of its acts and their objects—solely apodictic—i.e., in constitution—for example, in a descriptive phenomenology of the body, of *Einfühlung*, the sensible must cede its place, in a second degree of constitution, to an analytic that shows how noematic unities are constituted through the *Erscheinungsweisen* [modes of appearance] that give the ideas.

He says it still: he sometimes speaks of the reduction to the *Lebenswelt* as a preliminary phase in the natural attitude. History knows the *Lebenswelt*—yet he increasingly identifies transcendental philosophy with passage to the *Lebenswelt*, the universality of this "layer"—which contains all the problems of being and of reason. One comes to wonder whether the transcendental, as a system of *Auffassungen* and attitudes, is not rightly abandoned; does such a system shed light on the body when, reduced in these terms, the body ceases to have its evidence?—and so, reduced in these terms, the other is no longer graspable as other: they are "immanent." Others and bodies are themselves only as transcendents, *ek-stases*. The pre-theoretical *Leistungen* [achievements] would be such transcendences.

The "paradoxes" of the transcendental: its thought without "soil" [*sol*] is alogical. The paradoxes must be "illuminated." But can "illumination" be returned to immanence? For example: the problem of intersubjectivity—identity of the empirical self with the reduced self—for the most part, the other can only be [37] the empirical other,[37] exterior, not immanent. Hence the question: if it is truly transcendental, it is because the complete transcendental reduction (to self) is not possible. [79] "Solution": there is the community of transcendental subjects[38] (transcendental intersubjectivity), and this does not preclude the *Einsamkeit* [solitude] of the indeclinable Ego. Any affirmation of the indeclinable

Ego reverberates in the others. The negation of everything that is not it spreads out from it. *Ineinander* [interleaving] of the Ego, which precisely makes up each of the others, is posited with the same impossible *Einsamkeit*. They are incompossibles and yet simultaneities: *Urpräsens* [originary presence] . . . of the absent as absent. All of this presupposes, all the same, that constitution is not reduction to immanence and to the positivity of my intentional system. The bond of Egos is this absolute opposition common to them, and which presupposes their *belonging together* [*appartenance*], (absence) to the same world, the *Vergemeinschaftung* [co-belonging] of their lives and not only their parallel functioning.[39] The *Lebenswelt* is the index for the *Vergemeinschaftung* of constituent multiplicities. It is in the *Lebenswelt* that the constituents have the generality of *Ichlichkeit* [egoism].[40]

If this is the case, what is philosophy? To define it as reconquering the *Lebenswelt* by a *Wissenschaftlichkeit* of a new type[41]—knowing what not knowing is.

His characterization of "science" after the Beilage on philosophy *als strenge Wissenschaft* is philosophically "subjective" and "negative." It must be neither "positive" nor "objective" to make the pre-ideal foundation of ideality, the pre-subjective of subjectivity, intelligible. Philosophy is doubt regarding philosophy as human *Gebilde*. [80] It is a circle; it closes in on itself. It is construction of that which is *von Selbst*.

It is anticipated in biology (Beilage on biology);[42] one cannot conceive that philosophy is realized immediately.[43] The new notion of "constituent life," the notion of "teleology."

The transcendental: Kant's borrows from the *Lebenswelt*—Kant does not question the possibility of the world—Hume's *Welträtsel*[44]—the paradox of the transcendental—Descartes: there is a *Fundamentalbetrachtung*[45] [fundamental investigation] in him that is lacking in Kant and that is: [the] paradox of the world—but Descartes lacks it because the Ego is a piece of the world (*anima*)—the true transcendental, immanent to me in the psychological sense—therefore being itself speaks in us.

There is a philosophical "id," an instinct or a transcendental life— that only becomes will, philosophy, by my effort of *Selbstdenker* [thinking self],[46] and that is, in the sedimented past, only an anonymous "*es*"[47] (*Krisis*, 74/73), bond of philosophical intersubjectivty behind its back, *Ineinander* only seizable for each in their solitude—The *lebendige Gegenwart* [living present] as totality of time (*Krisis*, 73/71–72)—The hidden *lebendige Geistigkeit* [living spirit] (*Krisis*, 121/118)—none of this can be understood in terms of parallel consciousnesses [**38**] with their private acts. *Tiefensphäre* [sphere of depth] (*Krisis*, 121/119), third dimension (*Krisis*, 126/123), patent *Flächenleben* [life of the plane] and latent *Tiefenleben* [life of depth] (*Krisis*, 122/120)—Depth is characterized by paradox, by *Widersinn* [absurdity] (*Krisis*, 123/120). But I have taken this path and it is *begehbar* [able to be taken again] (*Krisis*, 123/120).

[81] Goethean metaphors of the "mothers of knowledge" (*Krisis* 156/153)—The reduction is access to their domain. The disclosure of this domain, without *Boden*, is a *Tat* [deed] (*Krisis*, 158/156)—exclusive task: "to comprehend precisely this style, precisely this whole merely subjective and apparently incomprehensible 'Heraclitean flux.'"[48] Reference to the *vorsokratischen Philosophie* [pre-Socratic philosophy] and to the sophistry of philosophical trial and error before the correlation *welt-Subjektivität Gegebenheitsweisen* [subjective manners of givenness] (*Krisis*, 168/165).

> In truth, this is a whole world—and if we could equate this subjectivity with the ψυχή of Heraclitus, his saying would doubtless be true of it: "You will never find the boundaries of the soul, even if you follow every road, so deep is its ground." Indeed, every "ground" [*Grund*] that is reached points to farther grounds, every horizon opened up awakens new horizons, and yet the endless whole, in its infinity of flowing movement, is oriented toward the unity of one meaning.[49]

Circularity of philosophy:[50] *Gebilde* [accomplishment] that wants to grasp [82] what is *von Selbst—überschauen* [in itself—surveyal], which *einströmt* [flows in on itself]—Reflection on the a priori of history that makes use of it (*Krisis*, 362/349, Beilage II, "Objectivity and the World of Experience"). Philosophy is the same in all, but from a *Selbigkeit* that is the *Selbigkeit* of the world (*Krisis*, 394, Beilage V).[51]

The *Epochè* itself makes use of a *Seinsgeltung* [validity]—the *Epochè* is not *Epochè*—the very will to recover in immanence is *Bodenständigkeit* [bound to the earth] (*Krisis*, 431, Beilage X).[52]

Philosophy beyond any *Absicht* [aim], any "goal"—as the *Lebenswelt* that is "*von Selbst*" (*Krisis*, 431, Beilage X), (*Krisis*, Beilage XVI, 462; see *Krisis*, 466, Beilage XIX).[53]

"Objective" philosophy as total interrogation and total response becomes problematic (*Krisis*, 467, Beilage XIX). Philosophy is a problem for itself (*Krisis*, 508/389, Beilage XXVIII, "Denial of Scientific Philosophy. Necessity of Reflection. The Reflection [Must Be] Historical. How Is History Required?").

Problems of our "kinship" with animals, biological problems, are a way to access *Sinnes Quellen* [sources of sense] by way of "technological" knowledge (*Krisis*, 482, Beilage XXIII; and *Krisis*, 491, Beilage XXV).[54]

[36ⁱ] Rediscovery of the *Lebenswelt* as *allenspannende Seinsweise* [all-encompassing manner of being], i.e., of the world before idealization, the in-itself, the object; of the spirit, history, before the ideal analysis that renders it into a "fragmentary" domain without proper *Weltlichkeit* [worldhood].

Descartes as Galilean: *Entdeckung* [discovery] and *Verdeckung* [covering]— *Entdeckung* of the psycho-mathematical; *Verdeckung* of the prior world on which it is founded, and of its proper *Fundamentalbetrachtung*; The *Fundamentalbetrachtung*: the *Cogito*, as *Eingangstor* [entrance] to the proper *Welträtsel*—this requires [83] a purified *Cogito* and not a *mens sive anima* [mind or soul], a piece of the world from which one reconstructs everything, but a truly transcendental *Cogito* radically distinguishes itself from the world and sees the world and the *anima* as paradoxes.

The union of the soul and body recognized as original order—but the soul and body still thought as substances.

Created eternal truths: not priority of the ideal; *verborgene Vernunft* [hidden reason] or teleology that goes back to the "covered" truth, as in Descartes. But this *Fundamentalbetrachtung* is covered over by the dogmatism of science. The dimension of the transcendental is identified with consciousness of the *Lebenswelt*. Husserl says again a few times: the *Lebenswelt* is not the transcendental attitude: the historian understands it in the natural attitude.

But in any case, the transcendental is no longer immanent consciousness of constituting *Auffassungen*. This would be what he calls in the "Vienna Conference" "*einseitige Rationalität*" [unilateral rationality]—there is also, for example, the history that functions within us, not as processes, chains of visible events, but intentional or "vertical" history with *Stiftungen* [institutions], the forgetting that tradition is, resumptions [*reprises*], interiority in exteriority—*Ineinander* of the present within the past. As long as we have not recovered this transcendental, rationality is in crisis.

In this way, Husserl recovers the paradoxes that guided the *Cartesian Meditations*, the paradox of intersubjectivity (past-present) with transcendental-[**37**[i]] empirical, constituted-constituting identification. This paradox is overcome because there is no longer transparent constitution: *Sinngebung* [sense-giving] as *Urstiftung* [originary institution] always entails *Sinnverschiebungen* [shifts in sense], intentional transgressions— there is no absolute spirit: the philosopher is not absolute spirit.

Apply this to the problem of simultaneous intersubjectivity: (1) *Einsamkeit* [solitude] of the indeclinable subject, solipsism: it is through me that any thought "other" lives again: *noch vollzug* [still completed]; [84] (2) Plurality of transcendental subjects, transcendental intersubjectivity.

No contradiction because they are truly the others that live again in me. I alone can rethink [*re-pense*] as *cogito*. Our bond is precisely our rivalry as subjects, this gap [*écart*] that we maintain between us, our absence in presence, our noncoincidence with others—*Ineinander* of the ego—The reduction, in this way, is recuperated in principle within everything, the egological reduction takes place through many iterations; it is neither in one alone nor gradually in several; it is simultaneous. There is no *auseinander* [outside-the-other]; there is *Vergemeinschaftung* [co-belonging], objective Spirit, *Ichlichkeit* [I-ness] and "spiritual generativity" (*Krisis*).

What is philosophy? To understand this, we must think the mind even before its idealization: philosophy is not *theoria* or human attitude (*theoria* has presuppositions, includes idealization, sedimentation)—it is thought, and thought of *theoria*, of the pre-theoretical, of their communal tissue—philosophy circles in upon itself—as human *Gebilde* [accomplishment]: it returns to the *Lebenswelt* and to history and sediments it, whereas philosophy should be total reactivation, thought of sedimentation, contact with total Being before the separation of pre-theoretical life from human *Gebilde*, the *lebendige Gegenwart* [living present] expanded to contain everything within the present, *Selbigkeit* [self-identity] of the same order as that of the world: it is experience, still silent, which must speak, i.e., without presupposing anything that presupposes language.

"Transcendental life" before any particular "*Absicht*" [aim]—Patent *Flächenleben* [life of the plane] and latent *Tiefenleben* [life of depth]. The "Heraclitean flux" (*Krisis*, 159/156).

> In truth, this is a whole world—and if we could equate this subjectivity with the ψυχή of Heraclitus, his saying would doubtless be true of it: "You will never find the boundaries of the soul, even if you follow every road, so deep is its ground (*so* [**38ⁱ**] *tiefen Grund hat sie*)." Indeed, every "ground" [*Grund*] that is reached points to farther grounds, every horizon opened up awakens new horizons, and yet the endless whole, in its infinity of flowing movement, is oriented toward the unity of one meaning.[55]

[85] Reference to pre-Socratic philosophy and to the Sophists. Other formulations, p. **37ff**.

Beilage XXVIII,[56] *Philosophie als strenge Wissenschaft*.

[57] Hence a revision of the relations philosophy–non-transcendental thought. Psychology is philosophy. Biology is philosophy. Philosophy is

already there in a recognition of lateral participation of life and psyche [*psychisme*] for me, of "ὅμον ην παντα" in the *intentionales Ineinander* within everything. It is this philosophy of everything's interconnection that we attempt to create.

* * *

Husserl end. [38ª]

Meditations on Philosophy (Summer 1935),[58] (Beilage XXVIII) *ernstliche, strenge, ja apodiktisch strenge Wissenschaft* [seriousness, rigor, apodictically rigorous science].[59]

Is this [an] "imaginary goal"? Can one hope to bring forth a philosophy that has never been? If one hopes to do so, it is through tradition, and this tradition is only comprehensible by the elucidation of the past. The philosophical universal is made of culture, by history—but perhaps history, showing that this telos is privileged, is synonymous with humanity?

But how could I claim to reach the truth of history? My history of philosophy is *Dichtung* [poetic invention][60] and always to be remade. The philosopher finds nothing stable, neither within himself nor outside. "Is the work lost that he, unconcerned about scientific historical study, has done under the guidance of, through the use of, his 'unhistorical,' untrue Plato? [*seines 'unhistorischen,' unwahren Plato?*]"[61]

The failure of objectivity—but there is "still a success in this failure [*eines Gelingens in deisen Versagen*]."[62] The work done with inexact instruments [86] is not lost. Because this is not deduction from premises. Plato was such deduction. Spinoza was, and there is such a relation of hierarchy between them that philosophy is such deduction, truth is such deduction . . . not horizontal history.

It is rather: my imaginary Plato is this, my imaginary Spinoza is that, and both are situated in relation to my philosophical view in such a way (a view that interrogates them and that is interrogated by them). The "past" is *my* past (my "*Dichtung der Philosophiegeschichte*" [poetic invention of the history of philosophy])[63] and reciprocally, what I think, as a philosopher, is the work of this past in myself. My "*philosophierendes Leben* [philosophizing life]"[64] is this back and forth, this zigzag.[65] And similarly, my work against and with others *in kritischer Freundschaft und Fiendschaft* [in critical friendship and enmity][66]—and similarly, my work against and with my past—"*connex*"[67] and not deduction.

Philosophy is not outside of time nor outside of itself; philosophy lies within a *lebendige Gegenwart* [living present], i.e., Being is vertical: it is everything within my *Präsenz-Feld* [field of presence] in the shape of "*dunkles Wissen*" [obscure knowledge][68] and not a result of definition or *Wortbedeutung*—"transcendental Life"—open in principle. Error of believing that philosophy is ideas; this is a field with an interrogation[69] that does not itself know what it asks (philosophy is a problem for the philosopher himself).

[38[b]]Therefore: "subjective" work is not lost, "and yet every 'intention' serves him and can serve him in understanding himself and his aim (*sein Absehen*), and his own aim in relation to that of others and their 'inventions,' their aims, and finally what it is that is common to all (*Das Allgemeinsame*), which makes up philosophy 'as such' as a unitary *telos* and makes the systems attempts at its fulfillment for us all."[70]

Philosophy becomes philosophy of philosophy, [87] thinking itself as *Gebilde* and ceases to be a simple *Gebilde* when it is taken nascently in a "philosophical life": in my living present there is an overcoming of the "wandering" [*baladeuse*] philosophy that will fall back into historical relativity and into the *Lebenswelt*. And that which overcomes historical relativity and is the seat of philosophy is myself as well as other philosophers taken as living minds (and not within some intemporal minds); it is the mind not as objective mind (historical process), nor as subjective mind (what I know of philosophy, my definitions, my "consciousness"), but the mind as the *Ineinander* of philosophies, one inside the other, their common root: pure interrogation.

"'[T]he point of it' ultimately was, in the hidden unity of intentional inwardness [*intentionaler Innerlichkeit*] which alone constitutes the unity of history."[71]

The key word: *intentionaler Innerlichkeit*; not the immediate interiority of the constituting ego, but indirect interiority, several, referred by each step of the Ego that gives itself as the feasible principle for everything—this is not thinkable through reflection but is feasible by *Praxis*: see Paulhan: "In this light at least, I have been you" (*Fleurs de Tarbes*).[72]

The mind, Reason, the Universal as "hidden," i.e., not objects for solving problems through the determination of an unknown (a knowable being and simply veiled). *Verborgene Vernunft in der Geschichte* [hidden reason in history], this is not a reason in the sense that philosophers have called everything else reason, simply transcendent (in a cloud, but reason in itself and for itself). The latent, the possible is as latent, is as possible. No explicative hypothesis: [88] visible as invisible in the field of presence, provided [38[c]] that one considers the world of the *lebendige Gegenwart* [living present].[73]

This new sense of philosophy: not philosophy that projects itself over [*surplombe*] the *Strom,* the flux, the plurality, and proceeds by way of the substructure of an ideal unity—but philosophy that enters the *Tiefenleben* [life of depth] where the flux premeditates itself [*sa prémédité*] ("*es*" [id], "*hinauswollte*" [meant to be]), philosophy of lateral unity, of *Ineinander*— unity at the edge, at the jointure of human beings, of philosophies, of cultures.

This philosophy is itself the end toward which all knowledge [*connaissance*] of *Geist* moves: psychological reflection leads to philosophical reflection. There is a complete psychology: it is philosophy, that is to say, the *Psyche* confined to the auto-revelation of Being (hence, reference to the *Psyche* of Heraclitus). If philosophy is true psychology, psychology is an incipient philosophy. But this is not only true of *Psyche*; the body as bearer of *Psyche* returns to Being where all things are together. We say: they are only human bodies—but no: animals are bearers of *Psyche* in their manner. Whatever we may *think*, we practice *Einfühlung* [empathy] towards them. They enter into intersubjectivity at least as variants, like the mad are "not quite" transcendental, similarly to plants, even to things, generalized *Einfühlung*, i.e., lateral relation and not frontal, *Ineinander*. It is true that for things, there is a reduction to Cartesian *bloße Sachen*. Reduction that reunites but that is not reabsorption—hence, a new ontology of nature in modern physics.

Even more so for the organism: its being cannot be defined as *Sache*. Every living body is more or less vaguely thought as "*anima*." It is only in the human, by "kinship" with us humans, that organisms can be thought.

Why? Not because everything returns to the constituting consciousness of which the human is the bearer, but because the human being, life, organisms understand [89] themselves: "Such is the guiding thread for all biology, and for all the variant forms of *Einfühlung* [empathy], only through which the animal can have sense [*sens*]."[74] The transcendental is no longer consciousness constituting everything: everything comes to consciousness in the human; the human as microcosm, see Bergson.

See Heidegger: "biology as a 'science [38ᵈ] of life' is founded upon the ontology of Dasein, even if not entirely. Life, in its own right, is a kind of Being; but essentially it is accessible only in Dasein. The ontology of life is accomplished by way of a privative Interpretation; it determines what must be the case if there can by anything like mere-aliveness. Life is not a mere Being-present-at-hand, nor is it Dasein."[75]

Thus biology, to the extent that it speaks of life, speaks necessarily of the incarnation of consciousness, of this first *Einfühlung* through which our body becomes *Leib*, waiting for other bodies to become "other bodies" for us and, for example, for animals to become animals. The *Ineinander* of intersubjectivity is extended to our relationship with our body, with animals, plants—a universal ontology, no longer as [the] determination of essences or significations that we constitute, but as our kinship, our coexistence with an "unknown ontology" of Others, whence the concept of "teleology" (i.e., *verborgene Vernunft*) marks the decline of idealism. It is not the return to a finality (animals "for humanity," or human "totality" of which they are abstract moments: they are an unknown for us), no longer [90] a transcendent finality; what binds them to Us is what we can only reach of them through our existence—i.e., others. It is necessary that they enter in order for us to have knowledge of them, necessary that they lend themselves. See teleology of history: "instinct" of history, return of the repressed. The hidden is not another manifestation (see Heidegger, *Verborgenheit* and *Unverborgenheit*).

Biology is, moreover, a technical science, i.e., treating the living as an artifact, as physico-chemically composed. But all of this is suspended by an image of the organism that is not *bloße Sachen*, the organism of *Einfühlung*—Resistance of the perceived organism, of *Einfühlung*, to these determinations. It is not a residue of pre-science within science, as Cartesian [38ᵉ] ontology believes; it is the proximity of the "sources" (i.e., of the total image of the world in *Ineinander*), proximity of the *Tiefe* [depth] that always leads biology to transcendental questions, leads it to always burst onto the terrain of the *Lebenswelt*.

Biology, thus, has an ontological scope; [it] does not tell us about a local sector of being (entirely terrestrial—and limited, on the same earth, limited to a canton). It has the same *Welt-allegemeinheit* [world-generality] as physics. It has its descriptive *Weltlichkeit* [worldliness], that of *geistiges Sein* [spiritual being]. Because (1) what could be recognized by us as "life" on Venus could only be on the condition of it entering into our *Lebenswelt* (this is the argument for the universality of the existence of consciousness and for the laws of fact extended from our thought to our being. Whence the uniqueness [*unicité*] of the world, not only through the uniqueness of consciousness, but from there, extended to the uniqueness of life—See Husserl saying: the *Selbigkeit* [self-identity] of philosophy is of the same kind as the *Selbigkeit* of the *world*); (2) More profoundly, it is not a matter only of repeating the idealist argument (what is, is for us, according to the synthetic unity of apperception), not just extending it from the constitutive to the regulating (for Kant already, there is a universal without concept); it is a matter of seeing that intentional implication reveals a reference to the *Umwelt* [environment] in life and to the *Welt* [world] that cannot be reconstituted from the *bloße* [91] *Sachen*: it is the universe of physics that is *enveloped* in that of life and not the reverse. And as that [universe] of life is enveloped in that of humanity, mindful biology tends toward philosophy.[76]

[B.] Heidegger: Philosophy as a Problem[1] **[39]**

Not to expound upon the old and new Heidegger, but to reveal within the new what is related to our question: [the] possibility of philosophy.

[92] In truth, his relative silence is not a pure and simple failure—or Heidegger's "turn" [*changement*][2]—but is significant, as the shorter writings indicate. For reasons of principle that make the task assigned by the "Introduction" to *Being and Time* impossible: more radical resumption [*reprise*] of the metaphysical interrogation of Being; it is our language, perhaps, the very nature of "truth" (always assuming non-radicalism), the very nature of "philosophy" (deeply linked to the accidental destiny of Being, and thus a revolt against a larger explication of Being) that would make this task impossible. Philosophy is to be replaced by *Denken*.

Thus, it is quite the same Heidegger—but, seeing the reasons in principle for the failure. He has "turned" [*change*] only in relation to popular interpretation, i.e.: (1) negativism: final phenomena—totality as death, anxiety as source of the negative, freedom as resolution in the face of death and thus authenticity; (2) anthropology: transcendence, i.e., the overcoming of *Seiende* [beings] in favor of *Sein* [Being] as an attribute of humanity—Being [*L'être*] understood through time and as human being (*Being and Time*); (3) all of this leaving the metaphysical question open (positive—superhuman) that Heidegger appeared to resume at the end of *What Is Metaphysics?*[3] in the Leibnizian form: Why is there something rather than nothing?

This was the position of *Being and Time*: The "Introduction" presents the analytic of *Dasein* as access to the question [93] of *Sein*—*Dasein* is considered only insofar as it is the interrogation of Being [*l'Être*], that this being [*étant*] has a privileged relationship to Being [*L'être*],[4] *being* [*étant*] itself the *Fragen* [question], being the being [*étant l'être*] who is in question in its being [*être*].[5]

[This] development is not a reversal of anthropology into the mysticism of Being [*l'Être*]: the beginning was not anthropology and the end is not mysticism. There is a turn [*changement*] **[40]** but one that is not reversal—but a deepening of the same research, with a displacement of the accents, and the experience of its impossibility—Turn, but within the same formulations:[6]

Freedom: "In grounding, freedom *gives* and *takes* ground";[7] "As this ground . . . freedom is the *abyss of ground*."[8] It was already not freedom that created the ground, since it receives it [thought?],[9] but [freedom] that gave ground [*donnait fondement*]. Now, it is *Sein* that is *Grund* (*The Principle of Reason*),[10] and freedom is the abyss; however, *On the Essence of Truth*: "freedom . . . receives its own essence from the more originary essence of uniquely essential truth."[11]

The human being: "a lieutenant of the Nothing" [*Platzhalter des Nichts*] (*What Is Metaphysics?*),[12] "Shepherd of Being" (*Letter on Humanism*).[13] The second formulation does not destroy the first, as we will see—but rather places the accent differently.

Truth: "*Because the kind of Being that is essential to truth is of the character of Dasein*, [94] *all truth is relative to Dasein's Being.*"[14] He would certainly explain that this does not place truth in the arbitrariness of our *Dasein*— and he still thinks that there is a kind of synonymy between the human being and transcendence toward being, i.e., truth. However, he no longer feels the need to speak the language of *Dasein* in *On the Essence of Truth*— but rather that of *Offenheit* [openness].

What happened? The deepening of the being internal to *Dasein* reveals that, negative in relation to the *Innerweltlich*, to the ontic, it is an opening onto a positive different from that of the ontic, [a positive] which is *Sein*. Its negativity is only an external view, **[41]** preliminary. Henceforth Heidegger concentrates on the expression of this new domain. There is no longer: the positive, the *Seiend*, the ontic, opposed to *Dasein*, the abyss, which is, as abyss, *its* possibilities, which is *je meinig*. This *Dasein* itself opens onto a domain for which it is essential that it remain hidden, to present itself only as withdrawal—a domain that encompasses both the *Welt* and *Dasein* and *Zeitigung* [temporalization].[15] Insofar as it is hidden, it does not offer positive aspects; the *Dasein* transcending toward it seems to transcend toward nothing. And yet it is not nothing; it is Being. The *nichtiges Nichts* [nothing nothings] is eliminated: *Sein* is only *nicht-Seiend* [not-beings]. But [as] *nicht-Seiend*, it is always! There was a direct philosophy in *Being and Time*: one describes *Dasein*; it was said that it was, i.e., abyss, in opposition to beings [*étant*]. Then one sees that this direct description is not radical because of its dogmatic use of *Wesen*; it says what *Dasein* is, namely, non-being. By interrogating the medium of *Wesen*, one comes to think that the question of the *Wesen der Wahrheit* assumes that the question of the *Wahrheit des Wesens* is resolved. It is not sufficient to have the truth, to say the essence; it must be taken into account that it is already the truth reduced to [95] its *was* [what]. The full essence is not that: it is the *verbal Wesen*, undivided from existence. This meditation on the truth of essence (which was to follow *On the Essence of Truth*) marks a turn toward an analysis that is not more direct—the non-distinction essence-existence [was] already expressed in *Being and Time*: the essence of *Dasein* is its existence—But, this was *stated* [*énoncé*] as the truth of essence[16] and limited to *Dasein*, i.e., "humanity's Being."[17] As for the rest, Heidegger used the notion of essence or of idea unscrupulously. For example, [the] description of the *Weltlichkeit überhaupt* [worldhood of the world in general][18] in the idea of *Weltlichkeit überhaupt*. The bias of looking for the *Wesen* is the renunciation of the alternative. Everything that is, is, either in the sense of *existieren* (*Dasein*) or in the sense of "world"—There is a universal Being that envelops the two correlatives of *Dasein* and world.

So, there is a turn, but one that is [a] passage from the analytic of *Dasein* to *Fundamentalontologie*, expected from the beginning, resulting in the elimination of **[42]** negativism (revision of the concept of nothing-ness [*néant*]), elimination of anthropological equivocation (one studies, for themselves, the relations to *Sein* that function at the interiority of the human being), elimination of the metaphysical problem: *Being and Time* already said that this resumption [*reprise*] is "phenomenological destruction"—It was, Heidegger says again today, the first book where the question of Being was posed as a question. But, one could have the impression that the question was a question in the old sense (see the end of *What Is Metaphysics?*: the Leibnizean question resumed)—Now, the "problem of metaphysics" disappears as a "problem," i.e., as having an "answer." Precisely because we have passed from *Dasein* to *Sein*, one sees more clearly that *Sein* is not the occasion for the "problem" but that it is the secret or mystery. [96]

We see (1) the passage to *Sein*; (2) Consequences touching on "humanism": Being and humanity, Being and language; (3) Consequences touching on history: the idea of the *Seinsgeschichte* [the history of Being]; (4) Conclusion: {end of metaphysics and nihilism, philosophy and nonphilosophy}.

I. From the analytic of *Dasein* to the *Seinsfrage*.[19]

[45] 1) From *Dasein* to *Seyn*

Motivated passage, which is nevertheless reversed. *Da-Sein* [is] being-there—more clearly (to distinguish it from intra-worldly objects, to underline the active sense of being), being-the-there, being-the-world.

Refusal to say "I," "subject," "consciousness"—even purified of all *Verdinglichung* [reification]—"*Aktzentrum* [center of its actions] and *Erlebnisse* [experiences]" (*Being and Time*), because if one does this, Being becomes "non-I," "object," bound—ipseity becomes first in the relation to Being such that ipseity is indirect, grasps itself only from the world as the "place" X from where the world is seen. It is not false to say that the *Dasein* of which I speak is me, or that *"Ich es bin,"* but it is the formal index upon which the analysis reveals its contrary: *Weltlichkeit* (*SZ* 116). That *Dasein* be mine, *je meines*, does not mean that it is first and foremost *es selbst*,[20] on the contrary:

> We do not represent distant things merely in our mind—as the textbooks have it—so that only mental representations of distant things run through our mind and heads as substitutes for the things. If all of us now think, from where we are right here, of the old bridge in Heidelberg, this thinking toward that location is not a mere experience inside the persons present here; rather, it belongs to the nature of our thinking *of* that bridge that *in itself* thinking gets through, persists through, the distance to that location. From this [97] spot right here, we are there at the bridge—we are by no means at some representational content in our consciousness.[21]

Will it not be said: this is a magical relationship—and I see quite well, in looking at the others, that they are here, not on the bridge at Heidelberg, that they are dealing only with their representations . . . ? Heidegger does not believe that we are going to walk among the things-objects coming out of our eyes.

What he wants to say is: if one replaces our presence to the thing itself with *Vorstellung* [representation], one will never find it. It is therefore necessary to retain this experience of *Inhalt gegeben* [given content] as true—and try to understand it from the resistant "facts," for example, the fact that others appear to me to be cut off from the thing itself, exterior to it—(For example, I would say: between the others and the bridge of Heidelberg, there is exteriority only if one places oneself in a world in itself, without *Dasein*. When they speak about it, I see quite well that they are there—what remains to be explained is the difference between this experience of the absent thing (theirs or mine) and the experience of a present thing. But it is the difference, interior to a Being with respect to which I am, in any case, always present.)

Da-sein, first, is being to [*être à*] . . . the thing itself, the world itself, the being itself. It is this that, from the start, Heidegger wanted to save from all analysis.

But the unity *Dasein-Welt* was expressed somewhat "subjectively": *Weltlichkeit* considered as "a characteristic of Dasein itself."[22] Similarly: *"Because the kind of Being that is essential to truth is of the character of Dasein, all truth is relative to Dasein's Being."*[23] Now, the same relation is no longer expressed in terms of *Ek-stase* or transcendence (i.e., with respect to *Dasein*); *"'Dasein'* names that which is first of all to be experienced, and subsequently thought accordingly, as a place—namely, as the locality of the truth of [98] Being."[24] It is the same idea, but followed better. We can no longer even speak of *Dasein* as an independent moment. It is *Dasein* only from its opening toward Being, in an ontological functioning of which it is only the "place," and which passes to the foreground. Describe this ontological functioning.[25]

[42] 2) Truth, *Offenheit* [Openness], *Verborgenheit* [Concealment], and *Unverborgenheit* [Unconcealment]

First step: insistence on the theme of truth rather than the thesis of freedom: *On the Essence of Truth.*

Truth as *Richtigkeit* [correctness], *Sichrichten nach* [correspondence to], both in the conception of *Satzwahrheit* [sentential truth] (correspondence of the *intellectus* to the thing) and that of *Sachwahrheit* [factual truth] (conformity of the thing to the intellect: of real gold) (which is [a] Kantian and Christian idea).

One cannot, without presupposing truth accomplished *elsewhere*, confine oneself to *Richtigkeit*. On what is *Richtigkeit* itself based?

Experience of *Richtigkeit*: application of a measure of which one is sure that it is measuring what is before us, i.e., that it has a homogeneity with the thing, that it is capable of the thing, i.e., that it has a domain of reference, that it is applied to the interior of an *offenen* [open]— Prepossession (*Vorhabe*) of a measure in the function of measuring. In other words, **[43]** pre-openness to the being that conditions all *vor-stellen* [re-presentation]. This "openness" to . . . , this "liberation for . . . ," conditions all truth—(see Husserl, experience of *Deckung* [coincidence])— A freedom [99] that is by no means arbitrary but rather consists in the *Seinlassen von Seiendem* [letting be of beings],[26] that is not lost in the *Seiend* but that confines itself to distance in order to reveal the *Seiend*. "Light" of Dasein that is this distance accomplished by *Offenheit*. The *Da* [is] "the openness of the open."[27]

Consequently: "The human being does not 'possess' freedom as a property. At best, the converse holds: freedom, ek-sistent, disclosive Dasein, possesses the human being. . . ."[28] *Dasein* becomes a movement of being that traverses man, that "possesses him."

This is not to be understood as *passivity*: Sartre (*The Flies*)[29] also says "freedom has fallen upon me like an eagle"—i.e., it is not myself as a being [*étant*] who is free; it is myself as existing, as a power for "no" who decides to "yes," otherwise unable to register, to do—similarly, openness to . . . is not receptivity with respect to an exterior term; it is a prior relationship to all *Vorstellen*, to a domain, to a "*Bezirk* [region]," the "prior givenness" of a measure. This means that (1) the relation is transcendence, transcending to . . . *Uberstieg* [transcendence],[30] the *Da* is horizon; (2) even after the reduction in *Vorstellen*, the relationship remains such in everything it has of living.

In other words, truth is not an exterior relation, receptivity—but is put in relation with a beyond, and thus is no longer immanence. In order to express this intrinsic and non-immanent relation, we cannot say that truth is given but that it is *not hidden*: ἀλήθεια, *Unverborgene* [the unconcealed]. This non-dissimulation is not evidence (*Sichtbarkeit*)—it maintains its distance—it implies a beyond of what we see, a Being, i.e., a *Verborgenheit* [concealment] in the unconcealment. That's why *On the Essence of Truth* refuses to [100] subtract the *Un-wahrheit* from the *Wahrheit*: *Un-entborgenheit* [un-concealment] "is older than every openedness of this or that being [*étant*]."[31]

Geheimnis [mystery]: any revealing of beings [*étant*] *is* the forgetting of what **[44]** is not revealed, the *Verborgung* [covering] that is *das erstlich Verborgene* [at first concealed].[32] In this, *Unwahrheit* [untruth] is not human negligence (no more than *Wahrheit* is human production, the result of an act, of a representation): "untruth must derive from the essence of truth."[33] It is necessary "to comprehend the non-essence in the essence of truth."[34] Truth cannot be defined in terms of essentiality.

Hence it is necessary to say that the "givenness" of Being [*L'être*] is also "withdrawal": "In this emerging-on-its-own, in φύσις, there reigns after all a self-withdrawal, and this so decisively that without the latter the former could not reign"[35]—Heraclitus: φύσις κρύπτεσθαι φιλεῖ.

This withdrawal of being, manifested by "truth," is ignored both by objective metaphysics, which reduces being to *ens realissimum*, to an immense *Seiende*, and by the subjectivist version of this metaphysics: Hegel, "Where the last trace of the concealing of being vanishes, namely in the absolute self-knowledge of absolute spirit in the metaphysics of German idealism, the revealing of beings respective of their being, that is, metaphysics, is complete and philosophy at an end."[36] [101]

Throughout his thought on Being [*L'être*], Heidegger wants to recover, against metaphysics, the experience of Being [*L'être*] that it has expressed and disfigured in its *Vorstellungen*: "to reattain the originary experiences of being belonging to metaphysics by deconstructing representations that have become commonplace and empty."[37] It is neither a matter of (1) breaking it into pieces, (2) nor surreptitiously conserving metaphysics. It is a question of converting it into its truth. Hence, the absurdity of Heidegger's reception: he is accused of destroying, while expressing, the truth of . . . metaphysics—and we want to use this expression of being for reconstituting a metaphysics, for "restoring" it, which also goes against his views: it is picking up fallen apples: "my attempts at thinking to be a demolishing of metaphysics and at the same time, with the aid of those attempts, [to] keep to paths of thought and ideas that have been taken from—I do not say, are thanks to—that alleged demolition."[38]

What is this *Wesen-Unwesen* of Being [*L'être*], which is the **[45]** truth of metaphysics—and which definitively discredits metaphysics, perhaps "Philosophy" (see above)?

II. *Seyn* or ~~*Sein*~~

This turn [*change*], which has just been described, can be expressed by saying: in *What Is Metaphysics?* the Analytic appeared to be presented in opposition to positive, actual (as defined by the sciences) Being, and **[47]** from a horizon of nothingness that it presupposes; there is, **[102]** say the sciences, only this and that—"and nothing else"; the position of being determined by them implies the negation of the rest: the rest is nothingness (see Cartesianism: nothingness has no properties). Heidegger shows that the being of science envelops this thought pushed back from nothingness, that this thought produces a margin outside the being of science—a margin produced by the phenomenon of anxiety, for example, as revealing the possibility of nothingness, and that metaphysics was an explicit positing of the question: why being and not nothing? The scientific negation of nothingness does not prevail over itself.

In this way, Heidegger (1) seemed to leave open the metaphysical problem as such (discovering a positive Being that arises of itself); (2) seemed to conceive of thought as an alternative: nothingness or an entirely positive being.

Today (*New Preface*): it is certainly necessary to criticize the entirely positive, entirely actual, entirely objective being of the sciences—but the idea of an absolute nothingness (*nichtiges Nichts*), its inevitable counterpart (science), is no longer valid, and philosophical interrogation does not depart from it. They are placed on the same plane (see Hegel), indiscernibles—or at least combined [*solidaires*].

The *nichtiges Nichts*, because there is something, would at once attest to an objective being, determined, in itself, exactly like that of science—one that would simply efface itself, would be a nihilism returned: God as unlimited or infinite being.

It is necessary, of course, to find something other than the *Seiende* of science, something that will thus be *Nicht-Seiende*, non-being, no thing [*aucune chose*], but that does not posit the *nichtiges Nichts*: what he calls *Seyn* or ~~*Sein*~~ is what *is not nothing*; it is the "*es gibt*," the "*il y a*," the open "*etwas*" [something] onto which we have "openness," in whose truth we are. One no longer calls it *Welt*, but *Sein*, as we no longer speak about *Dasein*, because it includes *Welt* and *Dasein* together, being their pure difference with respect to *nothing*, what is not nothing in them. It is a question of describing this being that is the common source or milieu of positive-scientific-objective being and of nothingness insofar as it is spoken about, that one [103] thinks there, and that thus is not nothing: "Everything that is not [48] simply nothing, *is*—and for us, even Nothing 'belongs' to 'Being.'"[39]

Henceforth in agreement with the Bergsonian critique of the idea of nothingness, but sees not only, like Bergson, [a] motif of "positivism," an affirmation without a "vestige" of being, understands that it is necessary to incorporate nothingness into being, that being is not *that which is*, while Bergson (necessarily) proves actualism to be right and also pulverizes the possible. Thus, an agreement with Bergson, against negativism. Moreover, there is the idea of being as that which is itself in Bergson, opposed to Spinozist eternity, linked to the idea of nothingness.

In agreement with Sartre with a law of negation (not the simple absence of positive fact)—but not with the definition of being that "is what it is." For Heidegger, Being is "that which is not nothing," what stands out against the background of the "rather than nothing," what poses a resistance to the slope of "nothing," weak and invincible at the same time, what is always circumscribed by nothingness and is, at its center, only *nicht Nichts*, the "*Etwas*";[40] whereas Being for Sartre is entirely actual and entirely before nothingness and not menaced by it (Leibniz: "because nothingness is easier than being"), what moves up the slope of what is easy and is not self-evident and is not so much "evident" as "not hidden." For Sartre, it *closes* nothingness. For Heidegger, it is what *opens* nothingness. For Sartre, being and nothingness contradict, are inseparable *as such*. For Heidegger, presence presumably presupposes a reversal of nihilation, but also nihilation is "concealed presence": "the nothing, which as absence interrupts ('nullifies') presence, without ever annihilating it. Rather, insofar as the nothing 'nullifies,' it confirms itself as a distinctive presence, veiling itself [104] as such presence."[41] (See Husserl: others given [49] in *Urpraesenz* [originary presence] as *Nicht-urpraesentierbar* [not originarily presentable]—*Ideen II*.) Heideggerian "Being" (*Sein*) is not difficult to conceive based on the ideas of *Wahrheit* and *Offenheit*: not based on Sartre's *Offenheit* (not from transcendence in the Heideggerian sense), but from the moment of the opening, between non-being and being. There is a pseudo-transcendence (or *Ek-stase*) that implies the "interiority" of nothingness and the "exteriority" of being and basically the correlative facts, basically Cartesian, pre-phenomenological notions. Heideggerian being is difficult only from this point of view, i.e., as before me through a distance that is not nothing ("sleeve of nothingness"), as separated from me by . . . *nothing*. Heidegger's enterprise has always been to describe *Dasein* as an *Uberstieg* [transcendence] that truly overcomes me and not as an "immediate presence to the world" (Sartre), being thus a two-tier structure (*Dasein* is characterized by *Weltlichkeit* and the world is "*subjektiv*," *Being and Time* claimed; *Dasein* is part of the definition of Being, and Being is part of the definition of *Dasein*) and not as being that is what it is. Hence, for Sartre, the possible is "for consciousness," Being is entirely actual—not a distinction between being and nothingness—as it happens in Heidegger, there is a possibility for Being that is not simply *das möglicherweise Seiende* [the possibly existing],[42] that is possibly actual, that belongs to the Being of the *nichtiges Nichts* itself.

[1] The Heideggerian Notion of Being]

Based on the notions of *Offenheit* and *Wahrheit*, the Heideggerian notion of Being [*L'être*] is not difficult:

a) L'être, l'étant, l'essence: *Sein, Seiende, Wesen*[43]

The piece of chalk as being [*l'étant*], *Seiende*—this whitish-grey mass of a determined form, light, brittle, etc., properties that respond to the question *Was* [what], *Washeiten* [what-is] = τὰ ὄντα = at the same time *die Dinge selbst* [the thing itself] and οὐσία. [105]

But, there is "that which, as it were, 'makes' this be *ein Seiendes* instead of non-being,"[44] which makes its *Sein*, τό εἶναι, "beingness, to be in being, Being."[45]

Das Sein is between extension (all the pieces of chalk) and comprehension (the chalk substance)—existence in the sense of spatial-temporal individuation and essence. It is what founds both, because the essence is only **[50]** in these pieces of chalk, and these pieces of chalk are only deployed from this essence.[46]

Another example, the high school—the high school insofar as it is a high school, that is, mainly for the pupils—it is for them that it is, and in its proper *wie* [how], or for us as we remember it: "One can, as it were, smell (*riechen*) the Being of such buildings, and often after decades one still has the scent in one's nose. The scent provides the Being of this being much more directly and truly than it could be communicated by any description or inspection."[47]

Moreover, of course, "the subsistence [the *Bestand* opposed to the *Gegenstand*][48] of the building does not depend on this scent [*Richstoff*] which is hovering around somewhere."[49]

See Proust: it is not a matter of designating new ("affective," "olfactory") "contents" of ontological memory. As before, the piece of chalk, the ontological memory, reveals an anterior unity in the manner of the distinction essence-existence, οὐσία-*die Dinge*-τα ὄντα, the high school in its evidence that is, like the angels, an individual-species and also none of that: a spatial radiation of sense, a historical "region."

For example, silk, velvet (in their relations, their difference), what distinguishes them is their different manners [106] of *Sein*. "The one is in being distinctly from the other":[50] the differences of essence proceed from different manners of modulating the same being that becomes being-silk or being-velvet—So, *Sein* is the origin of the essence as well as of the things it incarnates. For example, a mountain range ("the Alps," for example, opposed to the "Pyrenees")—For example, a State: in what does it consist, *where* is the being of the State?[51] There are neither countable properties nor **[51]** localizable things but that in which both participate. Where is the Being of the State? In the police operation in progress, in the typewriter of the secretary, in the communication of the head of state with the ambassador? "The state *is*.[52] But where is Being to be found? Is it located anywhere at all?"[53] See Fabrice: where is the battle of Waterloo?[54] It is in everything we see and beyond—one may well say where the State is not any longer (i.e., beyond the border), but not *where* it is. Its locality is of a special type (like soul-body). However, this can be extended to all sensible things: the thing is always *between* its qualities, and this is why it is neither the spatial-temporal individual, nor the οὐσία or ensemble of characteristics.

Where is Van Gogh's picture? On the canvas? Outside of the canvas as signification? But no, it is not in my head; it cannot be said that I am left alone with it. (See *Einführung*.)[55] Sartre, *The Imaginary*: where is the Charles VI who "looks at" me? (but Sartre concludes: he is in the imaginary, forgetting the *analogon*, forgetting that he "appears" as a phantom. On the contrary, Heidegger takes this being of the work of art as a model for the same natural being), which is not in the sense of spatiotemporal individuation, but as "apparition," indivisibly in its *was* [what] and in its *daß* [that]. [107]

This *Sein* (which is not infinite extension and zero comprehension, which is on the contrary comprehension growing with extension, because it is what makes a thing what it is and what makes it other to its other) is the active or verbal *Wesen*, what makes the world *weltet* [world, in the verbal sense], and makes the thing *dingt* [thing, in the verbal sense], i.e., the being before being-thought (in extension . . . , in comprehension),[56] active being which *west*, which "*este*," opposed to beings [*être-été*].

b) Being and *Grund*

Thus, *Sein* that includes *So-Sein* [Being-thus] or *anders-Sein* [Being-another], which are different manners of (verbal) *Wesen*. Whatever the problem of generality may be (why there are many pebbles, many organisms, many people, etc.), what makes a pebble be a pebble in each case, it amounts to nothing to say that it is its essence: because the essence must be participated in by existence. The *Wesen* as it *west* reigns as essence: *Sein* is here (the possible as a pretense to existence). It is necessary to say that this being is not susceptible to explication, that it cannot be given a reason, that every *Grund* is interior to it. This is even evident from the explication of **[52]** *Sein* as φύσις: a presence that (1) manifests itself "*von selbst*" in Husserl's sense; (2) precisely for this reason is not *selbstverstandlich*; example: the rose, the Rose-*sein*: *Angelus Silesius*.

> The rose is without why; it blooms because it blooms,
> It neither concerns itself, asks nothing, nor desires to be seen.[57]

The rose as emergence [*poussée*] of being (φύω)—what Sartre wanted to say in speaking of the being that is and does not exist. Only (1) its *is* was passive: it was [*est-été*]—and in this way presupposed positiving activity. According to Heidegger, its being is its own possibility [*propre possible*], i.e., there is a continuous self-creation of the rose and this is [108] the Rose-*sein*—the perseverance, the redeployment of the rose, as opposed to a quarter moon, which is "complete"; (2) consequently, the question did not arise of extending this being to man. [For] Heidegger apparently, we are not like the rose: "we humans cannot come to be who we are without attending to the world that determines us."[58] The rose does not occupy itself with knowing whether someone sees it (profound sense of Being, which is not the *percipi, Sichtbarkeit* [visibility]; it becomes my *Vorstellung* through degradation and forgetting)—the human being pays attention (1) to the world, (2) thus to themselves, (3) thus to themselves being-seen.

However, when one has discovered the *ohne warum* [without why] (which is founded on what the rose neither knows, does not know, nor knows of others, which is thus not linked to another being as means or effect— it would only give conditions of appearance, not what appears and shines forth).

We see in this way that the manner of human being, though they are *for* the world or the world is *for* them, is not explained by this *warum* [why]; it is its own *warum*. "What is unsaid **[53]** in the fragment—and everything depends on this—instead says that humans, in the concealed grounds of their essential being, first truly are when in their own way they are like the rose—without why."[59] "Without why" is not "inexplicable" (i.e., there is a *Grund* but one that is not accessible to us, or is not known by us), neither "lack of a cause," nor "cause of itself" (supreme *Seiende*, extrapolation of *Seiende innerweltlich* [inner-worldly beings]); it is a being, an *ester* (G. Kahn) that is "a-causal."[60]

In this sense, φύσις includes, for the Greeks, human beings, [109] human history, the gods. On this point Heidegger says that *On the Essence of Ground* was unsatisfactory; [it] only spoke of the *Grund* in the sense of *Seiende* [and] did not show Being as that pure, a-causal principle.

In developing *The Principle of Reason*, he says: There is no *Grund der Sein*, it is *Sein* itself that is the *Grund* of everything else, that actively founds each reflective account [*rendre-compte*], each *Be-grundung*. This is given with the very idea of *Sein* as that which is for itself, like the rose that "blooms because it blooms."

> Being "is" in essence [*Wesen*]: *Grund*. Therefore being can never first have a *Grund* which would supposedly ground it. Accordingly, *Grund* is missing from being. *Grund* remains at a remove from being. Being "is" the abyss . . . We say: being and *Grund* "are" the same. Being "is" the abyss.[61]
>
> Insofar as being essentially comes to be as *Grund*, it has no *Grund*. However, this is not because it founds itself, but because every foundation—even and especially self-founded ones—remain inappropriate to being as *Grund*. . . . Insofar as being "is" what grounds, and only insofar as it is so, it has no *Grund*.[62]

Any idea of a *Begründbarkeit* [ground-ability] of Being would make it into a *Seiend*.

Being as "abyss," "abyssal ground"—perhaps, however, this is still *Sein* seen from the point of view of *Seiende*, as *Nicht-Seiend*. Perhaps he would rather say: *Sein* is not a *Grund* in the intra-worldly sense, given as an appearance, "perhaps necessary," *der* [110] *Gründung* [establishment], *Sein* is *Ungrund* (*Introduction to Metaphysics*, beginning), three responses to the question of metaphysics: *Grund* is *Urgrund* [originary ground], *Ab-grund* [abyss] (refuses any foundation), *Ungrund* [non-ground]. Heidegger's seems to be the third.

Hence Being is not God; God is (Leibniz) [the] *Ens reale*, **[54]** *Ens necessarium*, who gives the *ratio*, himself identical to the Nature of things, why things exist rather than not existing—he is the *Seiende Grund alles dinge* [reason for everything], the "security" of Being. The question of God is second: what comes first is the question of the divine. The philosophical divine is an absurdity for faith. It is true that what is faith [now] could become non-faith. In this sense, the desire is common to all philosophers and to those of faith.

c) [What can one say about *Sein?*]

If *Sein* is therefore repugnant to ordinary determinations—Essence, existence, *Grund,* it should not come as a surprise that one cannot make "propositions" about it; propositions have taken place in beings [*être-été*] and not in the Being that *is* [*este*].

About the latter, one can only have *thought on the way to* [*pensée en chemin*],[63] make *Sätze* [statements] that "are no longer 'propositions': Being and *Grund*: the same."[64]

> When we say something [*vom etwas*] "is" [*es ist*] and "is such and so," then that something is, in such an utterance, represented as a being [*être-été*] [*als Seiendes vorgestellt*]. Only a being "is"; the "is" itself—*Sein*—"is" not. This wall in front of you and behind me *is*. It immediately shows itself to us as something present [*etwas Anwesendes*]. But where is its "is"? Where should we seek the presencing of the wall [*das Anwesen der Wand*]? Probably these questions already run awry. Nevertheless the wall "is."[65] [111]

One cannot say that the "is" itself *is* [*soit*] (for example, is as "representations" in the same way that the wall is as thing). One can say where the wall is (for you, there where you see it, for me, there where I co-see it on the horizon—example taken in order to detach *Sein* from objective place; there is a pre-spatial being that grounds appearance in space, the being of the horizon). One cannot say that its *being* is its objective place, that its presence is in the place in itself. The analysis of all perceived things claims that being is pre-objective.

Neither in itself nor representation, being is thus not a referent of statements [*terme de référence d'énoncés*]. Being refers to the term that designates it quite differently than beings [*êtres-étés*] [do] to the words that designate them—Ordinarily one has a verbal signification form (that which *vorstellt* [represents] that)—the thing (*Sache*), for example, the clock. For the word *Sein*, there is no corresponding thing. It is not something in the building, like the roof or the cellar. But this is not to say that Being is only 1 word + 1 representation, which would miss the thing (Nietzsche: a vapor). Being itself is referred to directly by words but neither as a thing nor as a representation. "Being itself relies on the word in a totally different and more essential sense **[55]** than any being does."[66]

The "is" wells up for us in the saying.[67] Language is "Being become word" or poetry[68]—The *Sache* [matter] could not be *shown* [*exposée*] by the word because it is not enveloped by it but envelops it, in his view.

The "floating signification," the "polysemy" of the verb "to be" (attested to by the frequent encounter with several radicals in the verb "to be") does not mean that it is a vapor or only says nothing; it means, on the contrary, that we "understand" it as everything that is not *Nichtsein*,[69] as embracing categories. If "being" verbs contain several radicals, it is not because that complete verb has been "lost"—(why?) [112] it is because each of the integral verbs calls the others, that Being in its unity "unifies and blends . . . what is originally different"[70]—it is richness. For this reason *Sein* becomes *Seyn* or ~~*Sein*~~, p. **47**.[71]

We return to the relationship of being to language, which means, not that being is verbal but that language is the house of being, a product of being.

d) But is it necessary to positively say what it is?

Now, it is always easy to show that particular beings [*Seiende*], for example, the earth, the sea, the mountains, the flora and fauna at all times lie overtly over against us. . . . But contrary to this, that wherethrough all this [*das wohindurch*], that is, all that which comes to presence on its own [*Von-sich-her-Anwesende*]—emerges and comes to presence never lies over against us as do particular beings that are present here and there. . . . It is not as though being keeps itself completely concealed. . . . Were being not to shine, then there would be no province [*Gegend*] within which an "over against" [*ein Gegenuber*] can settle.[72]

Being is that through which being has come to us; it is the *Eröffnung* [opening, inauguration], the horizon, not as distant, but as the "milieu" of things. Or element: "language is the language of being, as clouds are the clouds of the sky"[73]—or again "dimension": "the measure accorded to us [*die zugemessene Durchmessung*] and that by which an in-between [*entre-deux*] of Sky and Earth is open, the dimension"[74]—**[56]** measure in the sense of capacity to measure, i.e., standard of measure + space of possible measures, etc. to . . . Being, [113] to dwell in Being.

What is essential is not the human being but being [*Sein*]—as the dimension of the ecstasis of ek-sistence. However, the dimension is not something spatial in the familiar sense. Rather, everything spatial and all time-space *is* [*este*] [*west*] essentially in the dimensionality that being itself is.[75]

This altogether eliminates any substantialist or essentialist idea of being; it is that in relation to which there is, in the broad sense, more or less, much or little. It is the level of the world, by taking the word in the sense in which one speaks of a spatial level in psychology—horizontal and vertical—phenomenal in relation to that through which every object appears straight or bent: "We are on a plane shared only by men."[76] Heidegger says: from the point of view of *Being and Time,* it should say:

"We are precisely in a situation [*plan*] where principally there is being." But where does *le plan* come from and what is it? *L'être et le plan* are the same. In *Being and Time* (*SZ,* 212) we purposely and cautiously say, *il y a L'être: "es gibt" das Sein. Il y a* translates *"es gibt"* imprecisely. For the "it" that here "gives" is being itself.[77]

In reality, the French *il y a* renders *es gibt* well (1) because it is not centrifugal, (2) because *es gibt* does not mean [114] "to give" [*donner*].[78] To cite Apollinaire: *il y a.*[79] This is exactly what Heidegger wants to say, especially when he cites Goethe:
"Over all the peaks / is peace," i.e., ???[80]
An *is* that wants to say "reign" and "*il y a.*"

e) "Activity" of being that "*is*" [*este*], "mysticism" of being

Truth, the "memory of the world," opposed to consciousness and to the prevailing time; "inscription" (the register of Bergson); the impossibility of doing a philosophy with "human" "acts" and their "objects"; "human actions and passions"; Being is entirely non-artifact.

Necessity for making the language of human passivity, inadequate language, understood: the human is no more passive than it is the creator in the intra-worldly sense of these words.[81]

[2] About the Passage from *Dasein* to ~~*Sein*~~]

[57] Thus, the passage from *Dasein* to ~~*Sein*~~ expresses what is brief, meager in the philosophy of the subject and its objects—or in the philosophy of "man" "creator"—as if he had accomplished everything in poetry, science, art, philosophy from scratch. It was not anyone else who made them, but through the human being relationships, institutions that are a world or being play—"site" and not "situation:" *Stätte* [site], whose *Sein* must be revealed for the sake of *Eröffnung* [opening].[82]

Truth: the openness to truth [?], to ontological, philosophical truth—it is a *Seinlassen* [letting be], as a shepherd does not "command" his sheep through prior agreement. The "decision" is not creative; it is always restrictive: Parmenides before the three paths of Being, one of nothingness and one of *Schein* [appearance]: "Accordingly, decision here does not mean the judgment and choice of human beings, but rather a separation [*Scheidung*] in the aforementioned belonging-together [115] of Being, unconcealment, seeming, and not-Being."[83] Being was surrounded, encircled by becoming, appearance, thought, *Sollen* [having to]: it must be understood that it is rather [Being] that encircles them.[84]

Because there is this *Gegend* [province] before us, there is also something other than the nothingness of the past + memories that have remained present behind us. There is the *Gewesen* that is not *Vergangen* [past] and that is not a represented past but often *Vergessen* [forgottenness], active forgetfulness, forgetfulness as work of the past. To the extent that the *Stätte*[85] of truth is not created by the decision, it is also not destroyed by its slipping into the past: memory of the world—Bergson's open register, where time is inscribed (the organism does not know—but one can only know the present state of this organism by its becoming; to describe it is to describe a history)—the "historical inscription" of Péguy[86] (this inscription, which embraces everything and wants a point of time that has been *gestiftet* [given] once and for all, cannot not have been [*ne peut pas ne pas avoir été*]: Being that which is not nothing) (and these privileged inscriptions of truth that not only were the truth of time but have been recognized as such—or are only passed off as truth without meriting historical inscription, which, however, presuppose that they were not simple non-truth—scissions [*Entscheidungen*] become true as scissions—a sort of historical "selection" of the logic of things). Being is this register.

It is the excess of our experience regarding "subject," "object," "humanity"—everything beyond these terms obtained by scission, [58] a beyond that is not nothing.

To speak about, to open this field, one must speak the language of human passivity. But this language is inadequate: the human being is no more passive than a creator in the intra-worldly sense, no more an effect than a cause. [116]

    a) "Passive" language and "mysticism" (Heidegger himself rejects the word)[87]

Thinking accomplishes [*vollbringt*] the relation of being to the essence [*Wesen*] of the human being. It does not make or cause the relation. Thinking brings this relation to being solely as something handed over to thought itself from being. Such offering consists in the fact that in thinking being comes to language.[88]

A kind of circuit: it is thanks to Being [*l'Être*] that thinking sustains the relation to being [*l'être*]. Its proper act is to "present" itself—In other words, Humanity presenting its own Creation to God, *Offenbarung* [revelation] by the human being, reconstitution of God as God where, nevertheless, humanity only uses forces taken from God.

But this difference: for Christianity the world is fabricated, division of Being into created (finite) and uncreated (infinite). For Heidegger, there is no such division: the *Seiend* is not created and *Sein* is not an infinite object or Nature; *Sein* is finite (at least in the *Vorlesung*, "What Is Metaphysics?").[89] No *Seiende* without *Sein* and no *Sein* without *Seiende*.

We will see, farther on, in what sense it is Being that speaks within the human being (idea of *Sage*) (idea of *Denken* as thinking speech). But the relation of Being–human being in speech is not a cause-effect relation.

"Before he speaks, the human being must first let himself be claimed again by being"[90]—such a claim is the right that being has over us, which is the right of truth, *Offenheit*.

Being "makes use of" (*branchte*) the essence of the human being—but this also means: to have need (*Zur Seinsfrage*, 10). "Flavor" of Being—*Gunst des Seins* (*What Is Metaphysics?* [117] "Postscript"),[91] thus *Denken* is *Widerhall* [echo]—the *Ruf* [call] of being and the *Gehör* [hearkening] of humanity. *Denken "heißt"* [thinking "means"] that we "breathe" being—i.e., the silent voice [*lautlose Stimme*] of anxiety in *Was ist Metaphysik?* ("Nachwort")[92] that we **[59]** *stimmt* [feel] if it is not excluded by "anxiety about anxiety," i.e., there is an anxiety of repression—and an anxiety of being.[93] My *Dasein* is only *zugeworfen* [thrown] (opposed? to *Geworfenheit* [thrownness] as existential) by Being: "Dasein is thrown to me so that my self may be *Dasein*."[94] The *Jemeinigkeit* [mine-ness] of *Dasein* is nothing other than its flight out of itself: "the wavering of the beings that sustain us and unbind us, half in being, half not in being, which is also why we cannot wholly belong to any thing, not even to ourselves."[95] Philosophy produced in being: "For philosophy . . . it is not just that its object does not lie at hand, but philosophy has no object at all. Philosophy is a happening that must at all times work out Being for itself anew (that is, Being in its openness that belongs to it). Only in this happening does philosophical truth open up."[96]

b) Are all these thoughts *mystical?*

Heidegger rejects the word mystical as well as passivity: Being is not "*etwas für sich*" [something for itself] that would from time to time apply to humanity (*Sich dem Menschen zuwendet*). "Presumably [118] the turning itself, albeit in a way that is as yet veiled, is That which, in a quite perplexed and indeterminate manner, we name 'being.'"[97] Being is not distinct from its *Zuwendung* [granting] to us.

See *Zur Seinsfrage*:

> A thoughtful look ahead into this realm can write *Sein* only in the following way: ~~*Sein*~~. The crossing-out of this word initially has only a preventative role, namely, that of preventing the almost ineradicable habit of representing "*Sein*" as something standing somewhere on its own that then on occasion first comes face-to-face with human beings.[98]

How are we to make the texts where the human being appears passive agree with those that reject the exteriority of Being? They will not agree through compromise. It is Heidegger's essential thought: the thought of being as ἀλήθεια, as emergence from latency, thus as never *Unverborgen* [unconcealed], and in this sense as "mystery"—this thought is by no means an evocation of being in itself. It is precisely the contrary. **[60]** In opening *Dasein* onto Being, by making it *Da-sein*, a *Da* that is itself thrown by Being, Heidegger is much farther away from a Being in itself than when he described *Dasein* as dereliction,[99] *Geworfenheit*, thrown by X. Negativism always includes an afterthought of pure positivism. Heidegger's evolution also frees him from this positivism. In introducing the "divine" (a question that for him organizes that of God, given the philosophical sense of God), he is farther from God in himself than when he made *Dasein* the place of nothingness.

That is why he insists on the dialectic of *verborgenheit* and *unverborgenheit*. Being hidden (in the sense of hidden God), which both remains and at the same time "withdraws" from us (what it gives us is precisely its withdrawal); this is not mystical passivity; it is the idea that hidden being is not, in itself, a second property (it would then be manifest "in itself" or "for itself"), [119] that there is no reverse side of things, that everything true is also *Unwahrheit*: precisely not the illusion of a total unconcealment. "The talk of withdrawal remained obscure and to many ears had the ring of a mystical assertion nowhere anchored in the matter at hand."[100] In reality withdrawal means: being hides itself as being by taking place as beings [*l'être se cache comme être en se faisant étant*]: "Rather, inasmuch as it conceals its essence, being allows something else to come to the fore, namely *Grund* in the shape of ἀρχή, αἰτία, of *rationes*, of *causae*, of Principles, *Ursachen* [causes] and rational grounds. In withdrawing, being leaves behind these shapes of *Grund* whose provenance goes unrecognized."[101]

To say that Being is hidden is to say that what comes *zum Vorschein* [to the fore] is in principle of the order of beings [*l'Étant*] and inadequate to *Sein*. Non-theological "mysticism" is farther from theology than the philosophy of nothingness. The philosophy of the non-positive is farther from theology than the philosophy of nothingness or than nihilism, which is the inevitable counterpart to theology. Recuperating the experience of being, which is at the origin of Metaphysics, Heidegger is farther from metaphysics than those who make a "vapor" (Nietzsche) of Being. This nihilism is "a concealment that conceals itself."[102] Heidegger's recognition of being consists in the *Verborgenheit* [concealment] that is not **[61]** dissimulated to itself. In this sense, Heidegger is farther from theological positivism than the nihilists.

The expressions "secret" (*Geheimnis*), "mysticisms," are nothing *other* than phenomenological expressions: "Being *is* [*west*] appearing"[103]— "Being means appearing. Appearing does not mean something derivative [*Nachträgliches*] [120] which would from time to time meet up with Being"[104]—"not an addendum to Being";[105] because from the beginning, phenomenology has been understood as ontology, the manifestation of something that being has done that goes farther than our *representations*.

Being and Time: *Sein* is *verborgen* [concealed] as opposed to that which shows itself in itself, "but at the same time it is something that belongs to what thus shows itself."[106] "And just because the phenomena are proximally and for the most part *not* given, there is need for phenomenology. Covered-up-ness [*Verdecktheit*] is the counter-concept to 'phenomena.'"[107]
    The idea is always mine: Being is *selbstgegeben* [self-given] precisely as inexhaustible; the thing *dingt*.[108] The world in fact *weltet*, and yet still beyond what we thetically or objectively have. Being is eminently *Sichtbarkeit* [visibility], although it is not simply a possibility of perception.
    [But then to what extent is it an ontology, since Being is hidden?—in fact, neither theology nor ontology (see *Identity and Difference*)[109]—*Sense*, the *als*, is the moving relationship Being-beings [*Être-étant*], a relation which cannot be fixed, that is encompassing with respect to sense → thus *Denken* and not philosophy.][110]

Consequently, one understands how Heidegger can maintain expressions that recall the negativism of *Being and Time* once the relationship to *Sein* is introduced: this being [121] is as distant from us as nothingness. No time before human being—not that human being is eternal, but because time is not an indefinite duration [*durée*], eternity that is only through human being (which does not mean created by humanity).[111] "We are a sign, meaningless"[112] (Hölderlin), (see Giraudoux "caryatids of the void . . .");[113] Human being as "breach": Historical humanity's *Da-sein* means: Being posited as the breach into which the excessive violence of Being breaks in its appearing so that this breach itself shatters against Being.[114] **[62]** "Dasein is the constant urgency of defeat and of the renewed resurgence of the act of violence against Being, in such a way that the almighty sway of Being violates Dasein (in the literal sense), makes Dasein into the site of its appearing, envelops and pervades Dasein in its sway, and thereby holds it within Being."[115]

The being of *Dasein* is this tearing-apart from the beginning [*L'être du Dasein étant de ce déchirement*]; there is no victory except to no longer be: "Not-being-here [*Nicht-dasein*] is the ultimate victory over Being."[116] We are "condemned to being."

This is not pessimism; it is beyond pessimism and optimism, which account for life as if it were a business. "'Life is a business that does not cover its costs.' The proposition is untrue not because 'life' does cover [122] its costs in the end but because life (as Being-here) is not a business at all."[117]

In reality, these humanist-Sartrean expressions are not in discord with the thinking of *Sein*, which is by no means the restoration of metaphysics or even of ontology in the ancient sense—which rigorously establishes a reciprocal implication between *Sein* and *Mensch*:[118] each of them encloses the relation to the other—when one speaks of the one, one speaks of the other. Simply, Heidegger, having begun by going from human being to *Sein* (from time to being), now shows that it is also necessary to go from being to human being (from being to time).[119]

[63] III. Being and speech[120]

1) Problem of language and speech, cardinal problem of philosophy

Because (see above) the impossibility of determining and saying being as a *Sache* indicates the special relation [123] between being and speech: it is on the side of speech and not on the side *of what* one speaks about— *Between* created speech [*parole créée*] and received speech [*parole recue*], nothingness and exterior being.

The problem of language is not regional for philosophy. Even if it were, one could depart from it in order to arrive at Being (like departing from *Leben → Dasein → Sein*). But besides this banal ontological signification, λόγος has a more direct link. It is in this link that one will truly see the relation of *Sein-Seiende*. The essence of being is "intertwined" with the essence of speech: "[its] inherent involvement with the essence of language").[121]

Speech experiences a decline as the seizing-upon of being, an analysis that makes its ontological signification disappear, that expresses it in terms of *Seiende* cut off from being, from *Gegenstand*, [124] from *Objekt*. Privileged example: applying itself to rendering being is how speech is degraded in terms of *Seinde*.

Heidegger: "Thinking builds upon the house of being."[122] One believes that this is an image: being as dwelling [*habitant*] in a house that is language.

Heidegger: it is not an image that should be applied to being here (an *alagon*—an unclarified concept in Sartre, *The Imaginary*, and in Husserl, when it says that life, the organism are thought as an "*analogon*" of *Ichlichkeit* [I-ness] (*Krisis*, Beilage on Biology)—The *analogon*, the image, the symbol, are conceptualized in terms of *Seinde*, which only postpones the problem: because where does the image-object, which is inhabited by the signification that it is responsible for symbolizing, come from? With Sartre, one unloads what is positive in the image onto the *analogon* in order to be free to define the imaginary negatively (as with Husserl: in order to be **[64]** free to define *Ichlichkeit* as pure consciousness).

Heidegger: there is no "image," "*analogon*"; one doesn't think being through the house;[123] it is only when one has thought being that one can comprehend what a house is. One thinks beings through being [*l'étant par l'être*] or through the difference between beings and being [*étant-être*] (See Klee, it is through the "*an sich*" that one understands such an image arrangement). And beings [*étant*] already return to Being [*L'être*], already contain Being [*L'être*].

Thus (1) a trap in everything that we say about Being: speech hides Being from us because it is presupposed by everything said; (2) speech also reveals Being to us: *Besinnung* [mindfulness] about speech is the unconcealment of being [*L'être*].

"Symbol," "image," "*analogon*," these notions, employed in the analysis of language, are borrowed from a being that was reflexively reduced beforehand: See the bridge in the essay "Building, Dwelling, Thinking":

> To be sure, people think of the bridge as primarily [125] and really *merely* a bridge [*bloss eine Brucke*]; after that, and occasionally, it might possibly express much else besides; and as such an expression [*Ausdruck*] it would then become a symbol, for instance a symbol of those things we mentioned before [symbol of union, of established communication, etc.].
> But the bridge, if it is a true bridge, is never first of all a mere bridge and then afterward a symbol. And just as little is the bridge in the first place exclusively a symbol, in the sense that it expresses something that strictly

speaking does not belong to it. If we take the bridge strictly as such, it never appears as an expression [*Ausdruck*]. The bridge is a thing [*ein Ding*] and *only that.* Only? As this thing it gathers the fourfold [*das Geviert*: the sky-earth-divine-mortals].

Our thinking has of course long been accustomed to *understate* the nature of the thing [*Wesen des Dinges*]. The consequence, in the course of Western thought, has been that the thing is represented as an unknown X to which perceptible properties are attached. From this point of view, everything *that already belongs to the gathering* [*versammelnde*] *nature* [*Wesen*] *of this thing* does, of course appear as something that is afterward read into it.

The bridge . . . gathers the Fourfold in *such* a way that it allows for a *site* [*eine* Stätte] for it.[124]

This is to say that each thing is the manner in which the fourfold takes place.

The bridge is a trace, a modulation in the field polarized by sky-earth-divine-human. This field is the field **[65]** of Being. "Weak" Being, *Sein* marked ~~Sein~~, is the negation of the negation, a pre-object, because it is [a] node of the *Geviert*, the place where the "dimensions" cross. The four points of the cross indicate one of the poles. The "imaginary" and the "real" are forms by prevailing upon the "mythic," where "proper sense" and "figurative sense" are reversed, or rather stand in a reversible relationship. The "proper sense," [a] notion related to that of the *Objekt* or to the *Gegenstand*.[125] **[126]**

In reality, like the thing, the word is not an "object" (defined by "properties," recognized by "properties") and endowed with a linguistic sense; it is like the bridge, a node in the phonetic order that is a node in the semantic order.

Now, this examination of the "symbol" leads to consequences for all relations of "sign-signification"—one presupposed a relation of exterior correspondence between words and sense as between "comparative" things. There is the sense (idealized, or thing *that was* [*ou chose étée*]) and there is the word—and as one rightly understands that there is no comparative thing (the house and its inhabitant, language and Being), but that one is the other, that they stand in the relationship of beings [*L'être-été*] to being [*à L'être-étant*], so similarly one must see speech as signification, opening of Being.

Naming does not come afterward, providing a being [*l'étant*] that is already otherwise manifest with a designation and a token called a word, but on the contrary: from the height of its originary act of violence

[*Gewalt-tat*] as the opening up of being [*Eroffnung des Seins*], the word sinks down to become a mere sign, and this sign thrusts itself in front of beings [*l'étant*].[126]

2) It is necessary to recover operative speech as the pre-imaginary myth

a) Fallen language is phonetic or linguistic material. One tries to explain how it works by way of reanimation. There is (1) the signification (idealized or taken in beings); (2) the linguistic material. In order to understand the reference of one to the other, one founds speech on a *Sinnverbildungsakte* [act of meaning], acts of thought that infuse a sense: (a) the phonetic sense; (b) the semantic sense.

Particular case of the problem of *Sinngebung*: one only finds in things what one puts there—but if one puts it there, there is no acquisition, no communication, no efficacy proper to speech. But, if there is [such efficacy], is this not speech's own finality substituted for our activity?

[66] It is necessary: (1) that sense is never foreign, purely received, that it is understood from what we have; (2) that it is not [127] put into words by acts, otherwise there would be no gain.[127] Latency, i.e., the implicit, operative presence, is not a solution if it is only that development folded into its beginning.

It is necessary that *Sinngebung* is initially not the possession of significations and of a code, but the possession of the "differences between significations" and of "diacritical" signs—yet something else can be pre-traced within this field of significations and within this diacritical field—but then the "signifier" and "signified" are no longer exterior, being homologous relations. Hence, reservations to be made about the notion of convention: it assumes that they are exterior and bound by decree. But the decree presupposes language—convention in the sense of non-natural, yes, but not in the sense of artifact. Language is not nature but also not convention: it is history, i.e., the variation of always *vorgegeben* [pre-given] "conventions." Language is presupposed; i.e., when [Heidegger] wants to think its origin, he can only think of it as a *Gewalt-tat* [act of violence], institutive action of unlimited fecundity, myth[128] (mythical time is the past-present)—but if it is this at the origin, it is so at each instant—crisscrossing [*enjambement*] or overlapping [*empiètement*].

Consequently, the problem of *Sinngebung*: describe the sense of the field that is the phonetic field and the semantic field. The history of these fields, i.e., the production of the next from the previous, is not *Sinnverleibend* [meaningfully abiding] acts, but intentional synthesis (Husserl, *Krisis*), production of a whole new meaning from elements that are retained there, that no longer need to be considered separately—sedimentation.

To understand history not as acts but as institution that is produced and reproduced, to conceive it in the sense of φύσις (this φύσις, as the Greeks thought, which includes men, the gods, and not only animals and plants). [128]

b) "Wild" historicity

Sense "lines" words—vegetation of words—[the countenance?] of their sense through usage—i.e., the spontaneity of speech—the life of language.

c) The true signification of the etymological method: **[67]** Establishing

> old and often obsolete meanings of terms, the snatching up of these meanings with the aim of using them in some new way, leads to nothing if not to arbitrariness. What counts, rather, is for us, in reliance on the early meaning of a word and its changes, to catch sight of the realm [*Sach-bereich*] pertaining to the matter in question into which the word speaks [*in den das Wort hineinspricht*]. What counts is to ponder [*bedenken*] that essential realm [*Wesensbereich*] as the one in which the matter [*Sache*] named through the word moves. Only in this way does the word speak, and speak in the complex [*Zusammenhang*] of meanings into which the matter [*Sache*] that is named by it unfolds throughout the history of poetry [*Dichten*] and thought [*Denkens*].[129]

Heidegger, "The Question Concerning Technology":[130] It is not a question of transforming philosophy into an etymological dictionary. Our *Denken* does not live on etymology; it only serves to *bedenken* (to give thought) to the relations of being (*Wesens verhalte*) and what the words name in an undivided manner (*unentfaltet*)—Support (*Wink*) for Thinking, and not the reception of a thought possessed by words.

See *What Is Called Thinking?*:[131] The historical signification of the word (the history of its "vegetation"): the "'realm' [*Spielraum*] of speech from which the words 'thought' and 'thinking' speak."[132] It is a matter of knowing what the words *Sagen* [say] and not the sum of semantic changes. To say that the speaking power of words is reducible to these changes would amount to saying that $2 \times 2 = 4$ is justified by the [129] observable fact that people always say that $2 \times 2 = 4$. With etymology, it is a matter of retrieving a destiny that is *Geschick* [destining] and that is not History. Philosophy is *uberhistorische Erkenntnis* [supra-historical knowledge].[133]

See *The Principle of Reason*: "our languages speak historically"[134]— Heidegger (in agreement with phonologists against Saussure himself) thinks that the phonetic is not an "employee" of the semantic and the semantic the employer. There is a "labor market," and it this market that has occupied structuralism—i.e., in the function of institutions and not of individual acts.

To grasp language is to grasp this *Geschichte* [history], this crisscrossing, this deployment of the *Stiftung*, which is well beyond "lived states." The operation that Heidegger calls *Besinnung* [mindfulness], i.e., "just the opposite"[135] of the return to *Erlebnisse* [lived experience].

d) For example, the blindness of the philosophy of *Erlebnisse* or of *Sinnverleihende* [meaning-giving] acts for all interrogative thought. Platonic dilemma: either one knows what one is looking for and then does not look for it or one does not know, in which case how would one know to find it? The search, the interrogation, the *Fragen* is only understood in the vegetation of language and in its history, the wild state, **[68]** where there is no longer the dilemma of immanent-transcendent. And this dilemma does not exist because we have a permanent interrogation there: the significations are only divergences [*écarts*] between significations. It is rather our illusion to try to understand something that produces [*fait*] the mystery. Interrogation is to be understood, then, as a manner of existing (and not as an operation of thought or an operation of speech). It is speech itself that interrogates. The question is not a statement about *Erlebnisse*, about an *Erlebnis* interrogative in itself—nor again is it a simple form of expression to which it would answer, in *Erlebnisse* as lacunae. The question becomes thinking with speech. It **[130]** is not situated within the *cogito*, as one of my thoughts, thus the verbal question would be the "*statement*"[136] (the questioner is not a variant of the I think that . . . not knowing is not knowing that . . . not [*ne pas savoir n'est pas savoir que . . . ne pas*])—it is not situated in the simple verbal formula[137] (point of interrogation, inversion of the *statement*)—(thesis that is brought back to the first inasmuch as in both cases "thought" in the Cartesian sense is taken as possession of itself, *es selbst*)—The *Fragen* is made from speech, i.e., from open thought, i.e., from thought related to diacritical systems always in divergence, eccentric, and not *es selbst*—is therefore a question for itself, is never more than relatively a *statement* (an *innerweltlich* question, as such susceptible to *answer*—but that already carries the power of the *Fragen* within it: it is *Sein* that makes it so that *Seiende* are not nothing, and thus every question about *Seiende* involves *Sein*).

e) Language in its (verbal) *wesen* is not *statement* (*Richtigkeit* [correctness]).[138] It is interrogation—interrogation and not "question"—"proposition." There are no statements, no representations of being; this does not mean: being is unspeakable in the sense of a transcendent (which in itself would be adequation)—it means: the statement, the representation are in principle outside of the saying of Being, being productions of Being, particularizations of Being. Being dwells, *bewohnen*, in language; it is the motor, and it is why Being is not attained by language as object, *gewohnlich* [common] language (*Was heisst Denken?*).[139]

The being that *is* [*este*] is not an object of a statement. But it *is* [*este*] in speech. There is a speech of Being—speech that does not say it in the sense one says of a *Seiende* that it *is* [*est*]; *Sein* is not [*n'est pas*]—the speech that gives it (*es gibt*).

What will this speech be? It will not be *statement*. In a poem (*What Is Called Thinking?*),[140] the phrase "the moon [131] is risen" is not a statement. It is a matter of introducing, of installing an "element" (in the sense of water, sky, etc.). Being is such an element, the element of elements— For example, the child says "the moon" "instead of" "I see the moon"— criticize this idea of the "implied," which presupposes *Aussage* [assertion] as canonical language. "Parataxic" language and not the "syntactic" language of Parmenides. An inexact term anyway: the intervals of words speak (*Was heisst Denken?*).[141] This antepredicative speech is thus **[69]** not *Aussage* about a delocution, the expression of a lived state of the speaker; it consists (opposed to "conversation," "*Konversation*"—the interlocutor of the "*Gespräch*") in introducing the other "in *that* realm and abode about which they are speaking."[142] It does not express *Erlebnisse* but a *site*, a *place*, a durable institution, a *Geschick*, that is not familiar to the thinker himself: "No thinker—and no poet—understands himself."[143]

3) What does the *sense* of this *Sage* consist of?

Sense that is not reference to beings [*étants*], reference to essences in the sense of *Washeiten* [whatness]; reference to *Sach-verhalt* [entity]?

What are the *interior* and speech made of? Logic says: sense is "idea" or "*Begriff* [concept]."

Since the 1934 Conference, "Logic," Heidegger means by this "'the transformation of logic into the question of the essential nature of language'—a question that is something else again other than the philosophy of language."[144] "Logic" as variant of speech and not the reverse. Transformation, by Greek philosophy, of φύσις into ἰδέα (visibility), of λόγος as "gathering" (necessarily identical to the *Dinge* of the thing) into λόγος as [132] "*Rede*," "narrative," "statement"—consequently the reduction of the truth of opening to the truth of *Richtigkeit* [correctness]—the categories as modes of *Gesagtsein* [being-said]—The possible defined by the pure formal property of non-ἀντίφασις.[145]

The forgotten *Seinsmöglich* [possibility of being]: there is only the possibility of beings [*l'étant*]—the rehabilitation of ἀντίφασις with Hegel, the fact that he called metaphysics "logic," that is to say, his "Physics" does not prove that he found the order of [**70**] φύσις beneath λόγος, prove that he arrived at the point of crisis where the object destroys itself without revealing what it was taken from, the true *Sein*.[146]

Thus, it is not logic that one must ask for the sense of *Sage*. It is necessary to ask our experience of Being.

Sense, said *Being and Time*,[147] is the *als* [as] (like Husserl), but the *Auffassung als . . .* [apprehended as] is the *als* brought back to the *act*. *Being and Time*, already, no longer defines *Sinn* by act but by *Entwurf* [projection]. "*Meaning is the 'upon-which' of a projection in terms of which something becomes intelligible as something; it gets its structure from a fore-having, a fore-sight, and a fore-conception.*"[148] The new preface to *What Is Metaphysics?*[149] further discourages the "subjective" elements of the definition: "The realm [*Bereich*] that opens up for us in projection, in order that something (Being in this case) may prove itself as something (in this case, Being as itself in its unconcealedness), is called meaning [*Sinn*]."[150] *Sinn* has an element of "spatiality" (*Bereich*) not as a condition without which there would be no object (Kant), i.e., restrictive condition imposed onto being de jure—but as a synonym of Being: see *supra*, Being is "*Gegend* [province]," is "that to which there is an openness," that in which the intentionality of acts is deployed. Being's relation to itself, i.e., the relation of Being as *Seiend*, derivative, to being as *Sein*, is-ing [*estant*]—becomes the definition of *Sinn*. This [133] is no longer an attribute of subjectivity; it is the relation *Sein*, *Seiende* or the ontological difference.

This definition of *Sinn*—animation of the *Seiende* by a *Sein*, animation of *Sein* by itself, its relation to itself *als es selbst* [as it itself][151]—clarifies the identity of sense and speech, because the essence of speech (*supra*) is the power that it has to crystallize a simple "divergence" [*écart*] in being, to make it be "*als es selbst*"—and the identity of seizing upon Being and Speech: if we do not understand Being, there can be no speech, i.e., it could not happen "that in words beings as beings as such are opened up."[152] And inversely, if our "essence did not stand within the power of language, then all beings would remain closed off to us—the beings that we ourselves are, no less than the beings that we are not."[153] And this, even if we had a thousand hands and a thousand ears.

4) Hence the relation of language to being and to human being: [**71**]

a) It is not the human being who speaks, or who has language: it is language that speaks in them. This is to be understood not in the sense of causality and of the *Grund* internal to the world and to the *Seiend*; the operation of the λόγος is not accomplished on its own. We need our power to realize it, but in the sense of an *Eröffnung* [establishment] of a field, a field of *Sein*, the sense of which is not contained in humanity as being [*étant*]. "Language speaks, not humans. Humans only speak inasmuch as they respond to language on the basis of the *Geschick*."[154] Language is "the master of man" . . . "Man first speaks when, and only when, he responds to language by listening to its appeal."[155] [134]

b) We have an extraordinary impression, not of the "decision" (equivocal: it does not represent our authentic, formative, fecund moment), but of decisive actions or speech, that this speech is drawn from us by things or by others. And yet they are at most ourselves. This is already true in the word of the spirit that is the spirit of words: it is not we who play, it is "the *Wesen* of language" that "plays with us."[156] Its play takes place "behind our backs," those superficial significations of the word that lead us to say something that has more sense than we could know, in order to consider these associated significations "fortuitously" in the same word. The life of language gives us depth. "It is as though man had to make an effort to live [*bewohnen*] properly with language."[157] Hence, the appearance of passivity, of a language [*langue*] that knows more than we do, and yet this "unconscious" that plays there is we ourselves at the highest point: another would not have made that word—these essential traits of Being are guarded here by language under the cover [*à la faveur*] of our life.

The play of words expresses that *there is play* in language, and there must be; it can signify only in this way because sense is openness and not closure. Hence: the equivocity of language is absolutely necessary: it is life; it does not come from us, it comes from being. "The multiplicity of meanings is the element in which all thought must move in order to be strict thought."[158] The "*Gedachte*" [thought] is "*Ungedachte*" [unthought]: "The more original the thinking, the richer will be what is unthought in it."[159] [72] "The polysemy of a word does not primarily stem from the fact that when we humans talk and write we at times mean different things with one word. Polysemy is always a historical polysemy. It springs from the fact that in the [135] speaking of language we ourselves are at times, according to the *Geschick* of being, struck, that means addressed, differently by the being of beings."[160]

The equivocity of language is the pluralism of being, not the confused thought of the subject. It is delivered to us by being through language. It is thus through language that we who are arrested [*interpellés*] by Being, claimed by it, can only *Seinlassen* language [let language be].

"Instead, what is to be named now, language, understanding, mood, passion, and building, are no less a part of the overwhelming violence [of any permanent violence][161] than sea and earth and animal."[162] The difference is only, Heidegger adds, that "what is to be named now pervades them in its sway as that which they have to take over [*übernehmen*] expressly as the beings [*l'étant*] that they themselves are."[163] The origin of language and the origin of human being are the same thing, and both are violence, myth, secret. "The character of mystery belongs to the essence of the origin of language. But this implies that language can have begun only from the overwhelming and the uncanny, of the breakaway of humanity into Being. In this breakaway, language, the happening in which being becomes word, was poetry."[164] As Hölderlin said, *Ein Zeichen sind wir, deutungslos.*[165] [136]

[73] IV. *Being and Time*: The *Seinsgeschichte*

1) *Zeit*: *Vorname* for *Sein*

a) In *Sein und Zeit,* being is approached through time in order to avoid an objectivist conception of *Sein* as supreme *Seiende.* But this gives rise to "humanist" equivocations: one believes that *Zeit* (and Being) are attached to *Dasein* like "cosmic time" at the "time of consciousness" [*innere ZeitBewußtseins*].

This was doubtless never Heidegger's thought. Openness, the temporal *ek-stasis*, is not an "act" of consciousness, but any equivocation is diverted [*écartée*] by the passage to *Sein.* Just as *Dasein* is no longer *zugeworfen* [thrown] by *Sein*, at the same time it ceases to be the product of an *Entwurf* [projection], of an "intentionality."

Before an intentionality can take place, it is necessary to have an openness, a *Spielraum* ["realm," clearing], a *Gegend* [province] where it can be deployed. Time is this *Gegend*. This margin, where the *ek-stase* can take place, is *not nothing.*

So time will not only be simple succession in the sense of non-simultaneous "presents" (*Nacheinander der Jetztpunkte* [successive now-points]), minimal being—time will be the swelling or the "budding" of being. But then it would be better to say "history," which evokes an operation of being, rather than time, which evokes a "form." And to avoid confusing it with the correlative notion of time-contents ("history" in the sense of a series of human acts and passions—History), it will be necessary to say *Geschichte* [history] or better *Seinsgeschichte* [history of being]: i.e., what happens, not as *innerzeitig* [within time], intra-temporal, spatio-temporally individuated, but as an element of a budding process of being, as an advent, as given as a share to *Dasein* and to *Mit-Dasein*, as Μοῖρα [fate] or *Geschick* [destining].

b) But this is something that is not nothing and which *zuwirft* [throws] me this and that to live, something that overcomes the anthropology of *Dasein*—it is also known that this "Being" is not [137] a supreme Being, which is neither "creative evolution," nor *causa sui*, nor continuous creation—it will be remembered that this Being "is" only as a withdrawal, the last withdrawal, inexplicable by any unveiled presence—the *Seinsgeschichte* will be the manners in which Being conceals itself or turns away: the presentation of beings [*l'étant*] is in principle the *Verborgenheit* [concealment] of Being [*l'Être*]. These "withdrawals" are not constructive explication through an In-Itself. They are recognized in **[74]** our experience of Being [*l'Être*] and even in the Beings [*l'Étant*] that we are; Heidegger: we only know what we are after we have lost it; each is for themselves the most distant; i.e., presence to self is imperception, perception is what we are no longer, our *were* [*étions*]; the being [*l'être*] that *is* [*este*] within us does so only by remaining within our perception; all perception is imperception. Such is true nothingness: that which is not *nichtiges Nichts* but *Sein*.

The *Seinsgeschichte*, a new occasion to see the metaphysical operation of Being, its fecund withdrawal, these gifts that it gives without diminishing it, gifts that would increase it instead—an operation that is the truth of metaphysical "representations" of the infinite.

In the same way, applied to space, the quasi-intuition of Being gives: the space of *Umfasste* [inclusion], not the condition imposed on our grasp of what is "not nothing," and not "restriction" (in the Kantian sense), but is the manner in which it *zuwirft* [throws] us something that we have to be—in the same way, "applied to time," it gives: not the subjection of a Being in itself, forced to be only in *Nacheinander* [succession], but a time of *Seinsgeschichte*, the manner in which the Being that *is* [*este*] comes to have been, passage to beings [*l'être-été*].

2) Hence the *Seinsgeschichte* is a point of view on the philosophy of history; it is history as the product of Being and the history of philosophy = the experience of being and expression themselves include a certain indirect course, inevitably have a history—which, from what we have just said, is not the variation of "conceptualizations" of being but [is] itself a product of being. Being as the common life of history and philosophy. [138]

Thus the question: what is this Heideggerian absolute knowledge, and how are history and philosophy to be understood? Is what we have ordinarily called "philosophy" still itself?

Before arriving at this conclusive question, we must clearly see that, from the perspective of the *Seinsfrage*, we have (1) the profound unity of history and philosophy in the *Seinsgeschichte*; (2) the profound unity, in each, of sense and non-sense, which belong to the unity of being and non-being in (verbal) *wesen*.

[First] history and the philosophy of history

[75] a) History has a sense, is legible in the light of the ontological difference between Being-beings [*Être-étant*]. It is a perpetual commentary on this relationship—sense is a domain where what is projected out of itself . . . as *es selbst* or as difference from itself . . . (see *supra*, definition from *Being and Time*)—such a field exists in the successive as it does in the simultaneous. There is a *Stätte* for each city where it gradually comes out of itself little by little . . . and a *das Selbe* for all cities that makes them comparable, that makes them a single enterprise.

b) But at each time, this sense, this single "project," is not the realization of a certain type of state or human being that would be more true: the true State, the true human being. *Das Selbe* [the same thing] is not *das Gleiche* [sameness]. The "put in perspective" does not thus entail any conceptualization of history as marching toward a privileged being [*étant*]. These variations are due to the relationship Being-being, which cannot be hierarchized, objectively classified—Neither "progress" nor "decadence."

No progress, no march of history without end—one does not "overcome" history. One only finds rest at the center of the vortex ("enchanted circle" of Nothingness) and not by leaving the vortex. No decadence—this is less clear: Heidegger's descriptions and evaluations that appear to evoke decadence—the *Forgetting* of Being in our civilization—i.e., forgetting what is *von selbst* and *presents itself*—privilege given to being made, fabricated, created (Christianity)—that is, to the being that is an object for a subject, "made" by humanity, correlate of our vision [139] (ἰδέα), for our technical, criteriological *Aussage* [assertions]. The essence of technology (which was to reveal itself according to History only later) is already present in *science*. Security of being ("anxiety before anxiety," infecund anxiety)—Difficulty of "dwelling" within the world (prior to the "housing crisis")—an uninhabitable world whose technology is both the symptom and aggravation—Planeterization (relationship of humanity with itself) realized by purely technological, i.e., abstract action (to become the master of being, religion of what humanity accomplishes). And that consequently leads to the impossibility of peace, to the indistinctness of war-peace (a war that is false war, a peace that is false peace). All of this is founded on the fact that abstract action no longer has a *site*, a *Stätte*.

> The world wars are the antecedent form [*Vorform*] of the removal of the difference between war and peace. This removal is necessary [*nötig*] since the "world" has become an unworld [*Unwelt*] as a consequence of the abandonment of beings by Being's truth.[166]

> But since the emptiness of Being can never be filled up by the fullness of beings [science, technology, ignorant of their (verbal) *Wesen*, the world's quaking is hidden from them **[76]**—in order for there to be a consciousness of it, there would have to be a *Welt*, a relationship to being],[167] especially when this emptiness can never be experienced as such, the only way to escape it is incessantly to arrange beings in the constant possibility of being ordered as the form of guaranteeing aimless activity. . . . Technology is the organization of a lack [*die Organisation des Mangels*].[168]

All of this is put in perspective by a pre-technological, pre-planetary, pagan-rural past.

Yet is this an idea of decadence, of a golden age? Heidegger is against any idea of restoration (concerning Metaphysics): restoration is picking up fallen apples—but could this be filled with pessimism: *irreversible* decadence?

There is more: Heidegger does not think that technology—(or science)—is [140] ever without truth—nor [is it] an evil: "What is dangerous is not technology. There is no demonry of technology [*es gibt keine Damonie der Technik*], but rather there is the mystery of its essence [*das Geheimnis ihres Wesens*]. The essence of technology, as a destining [*Geschick*] of revealing, is the danger."[169] A danger that carries its remedy within it; because if technology is a certain manner of unconcealment, [then that means] it is a certain use we make of the power of truth. "The essence of technology is in a lofty sense ambiguous [*zweideutig*]. Such ambiguity points to the mystery [*Geheimnis*] of all revealing, i.e., of truth."[170] It does not suffice to say: technology remains under human control; technology has a *being* [*L'être*] that changes humanity—but technology brought back from beings [*être-été*] to the Being that *is* [*este*] does not pose any "danger."

Link this problem with that of "Culture": "culture" as technology;

art, the "artistic," becomes a vector for "culture" instead of being linked to *Da-sein*—Now what does Heidegger say about "culture"?

> The age of intellectual cultivation [*Bildung*] is coming to an end, not because the uncultured are gaining the ascendancy, but because the signs are appearing of a world-age in which that which is worthy of questioning [*das Fragwurdige*] will someday again open the door that leads to what is essential [*Wesenhaften*] in all things and in all destinings.[171] **[77]**

In truth, Heidegger puts the past in perspective to the extent that the past alone is accessible to us: it is in the past alone that *Sein* has been, becoming legible and manifest. But it is the past as *gewesen* and not as *vergangen*. There is a pessimism that is inevitable, but it is not absolute. Heidegger is neither an optimist nor a pessimist absolutely; as he says,[172] Schopenhauer is wrong to say: life, a business that does not cover its fees—not that it doesn't pay its fees but because it is not a [141] "business," because there is no sense in writing up a balance of *Dasein* and *Nicht-dasein*.

3) Secondly, the history of philosophy and philosophy

Thus, there is a sense of history that is never its "propositional" sense. This sense is the modalization of the relationship of being-beings [*être-étant*]. This sense is ontological, and if one wishes, "philosophical."

Philosophies are going to have a deep relationship with history; as history, they are modalizations of the relationship of being-beings [*être-étant*]. The relationship between them and history is also as close, in the sense of the *Seinsgeschichte*, as it could be in a dialectical materialism. In reality, dialectical materialism is, for Heidegger, an inadequate expression of the *Weltlichkeit* [worldhood] of which it has the sense. Because the historical *Wesen* of materialism is not material. Brought back to its *Wesen*, it is true because it (badly) expresses the unity of the *Welt* in simultaneity and succession, the undivided thrust of *Welten*.

The history of philosophy (without any intra-worldly or intra-historical parallelism, at the level of acts, of *Erlebnisse*, of "processes") is parallel to history. Heidegger thus places the history of philosophy in the perspective of the same conditions, with the same idea of sense (of *Selbstkeit*, which is not *Sichkeit*)—and of non-sense (impossibility of assigning a philosophy as *the truth*)—with the same refusal to take sides in the ideology of "progress" and "decadence." Apparently, the history of philosophy is the description of decadence: the forgetting of Being immediately after the pre-Socratics—the passage from φύσις to a philosophy of the ἰδέα, from λόγος as gathering **[78]** (definition of the "*thing*") to λόγος as that which is said, *Aussage* [assertion], as reason indebted to that which speaks (*principium reddendae rationis*); from there: *rationalism*, being is thought, self-consciousness, the achievement of this philosophy in Hegel—after Hegel: anti-philosophy, being is a "vapor" (Nietzsche), the unconditioned is weak, willingness to will, God is dead. Irrationalism or nihilism deeply related to previous [142] Metaphysics; it is the counterpart, the disappointment, but it does not bring us back to the pre-metaphysical innocence of indistinctness. It seems that the description is pessimistic and backward-looking. A flattening of the world has taken place since Hegel, a flattening that is the *cause* of the "collapse of German idealism," i.e., the world without relief, like a mirror that no longer reflects anything, a single surface of "facts," of the measurable and of the indifferent, of the *masslose Und-so-weiter* [measureless so on and so forth], of the *Immergleiche* [ever identical]. All that is "*welthaft Geistige*" [world-spiritual] is destroyed, considered to be a lie (see Heidegger, *Einführung*, 35: more than the *Weltlichkeit der Geist* [worldhood of spirit]), humanity no longer acts at the interior of a *Stiftung.* . . .[173]

There is *a* decadence—but it is not conceptualizing the history of philosophy *as* decadence: Plato is not simple "decadence" in relation to the pre-Socratics. Plato: "the fulfillment of the inception."[174] Being as ἰδέα is the consequence of defining Being as "emergent shining."[175] The consequence (*Vernehmung, Gerichtetheit* [interrogation, directionality]) is simply taken as essence. Thus: (1) the beginning *requires* this end, the end that "completes" it—Plato is the "typical" end, end-inception, "inceptive end of the great inception."[176] Plato and Aristotle (ibid., 137)—Plato is not a *Klassizist* [classicist], he is *der Klassiker* [the classic of classicism].[177] Socrates as thinker of the [143] "flow of air," the highest of thinkers;[178] (2) This very end, to unconceal its sense in its entirety, must be historically resumed [*reprise*]: what derives from Plato is not "the negative."

The inception, as incipient, must, in a certain way, leave itself behind. (It thus necessarily conceals itself, but this self-concealing is not nothing).[179] The inception that initiates can never directly preserve [*bewahren*] its initiating; it can never preserve it in the only way that it can be preserved, namely, by re-trieving [*wieder-holt wird*] it more originally in its [79] originality. Therefore, we can address the inception and the collapse of truth solely in a thoughtful re-trieval. The urgency of Being [*Not des Seins*] and the greatness of its inception are not merely an object for historians to observe, explain, and evaluate [*historischen Feststellung*]. This does not preclude but instead demands the possibility that this collapse be displayed as far as possible in its historical course [*geschichtlichen Verlauf*].[180]

Thus, even after Plato, one does not have vain repetitions; one has the solemn resumption [*reprise*] of the "exemplary end." And up until Hegel, who achieves the *Auslegung des Seins als Idee* [the interpretation of Being as Idea]. "The final closure of the first phase of Western thinking"; "the actuality of the actual, Being in the absolute sense, as 'idea' and explicitly calls it this."[181] This was neither useless nor the end of all *Denken*—it was only the end of what the West has called Philosophy.

Thus, philosophy, like all history founded on technology and science, derives from an interpretation of being [144] provoked by being itself. It is because being is at first φύσις, a power that appears and is unconcealed (*aufgehend-entbergendes Walten*) that it then is represented as εἶδος and ἰδέα. "This exposition is never based exclusively or even primarily on its being interpreted by philosophy."[182] Philosophy is "a happening [*Geschehnis*] that must at all times work out [*sich erwirken muß*] Being for itself anew (that is, Being in its openness that belongs to it)."[183] In this sense, philosophy expresses the history of being and not the history of conceptualizations of being—See Husserl: the reduction transforms the world; it is not the history of ideas, but changing the world itself. Philosophy is entirely "effect" and entirely "cause" because one has left the "causal" (dialectical materialist or Hegelian) thought where the problem of the subjectivity-world relation is insoluble. In this sense, philosophy is entirely truth, but simply of a truth that is not the last.

4) Relations of philosophy and history—but Heidegger can only maintain these relationships between philosophy and history (profound identity, without rivalry) and between philosophy and its history (which is entirely true in what it affirms, false **[80]** only in what it denies)[184] because he has a sort of absolute knowledge inside of which all the rest (the entire past of philosophy—the entire past of human history) is true or false, reconciled. If this "absolute knowledge" is no longer philosophy in the classical sense, or history in the sense of *historische Feststellung* [historical finding], then what is it exactly?

Conclusion

The determinateness [*Bestimmtheit*] of Being . . . is *the* power [*die Macht*] that today still sustains and prevails over *all our* relations to being as a whole, to [145] becoming, to seeming, to thinking, to *Sollen* [the ought]. . . . Everywhere we are underway amid beings, and yet we no longer know how it stands with Being. We do not even know that we no longer know it.[185]

Thus, restituting an experience of Being that is the truth of all metaphysics, but which is not itself a metaphysics, and which makes possible a *Zwiesprache* [conversation] between the West and civilizations without philosophy, that is to say, the Orient: "Being must be experienced again anew [*neu erfahren warden*], from the bottom up, and in the full breadth of its possible *ester* [*seines moglichen Wesens*]."[186]

This experience of being is not *Forschung* [research] (i.e., inventory of a domain); it does not lead to "results" like in the sciences; it does not privilege [*favorise*]; on the contrary, it makes "culture" more difficult and more cumbersome; it can only be true on the condition that it is not "precise" ("precision" is a technological criterion); it responds to a *Fragen* that does not know what it asks, that does not ask in all cases for an "answer," that does not lead to "propositions" or *Aussagen* [assertions]—is what philosophy seeks not at bottom the impossible since all our speech is "metaphysics"? Is it not the case that the forgetting of Being is "the only possibility for mortals to arrive at the truth"?[187] Heidegger, citing *Oedipus at Colonus* Μὴ φῦναι τὸν ἄπαντα νικᾷ λόγον.[188] *Dasein is* the possibility of *Nichtdasein*; it is by abandoning its essence[189] that *Dasein* is accomplished, i.e., by shattering itself on being. The return to being is "to exist in that which is without name" [*im Namenlosen zu existieren*]. "The human being must first let himself be claimed again by being, taking the risk that under this claim he will seldom have much to say."[190] Is this "philosophy" not nihilism? Silence? "Anyone today who is acquainted with the standards of such a thinking discourse [like that of Parmenides][191] must lose all desire to write books."[192] Knowledge would be non-knowledge—[81] nihilism. [146]

However, Heidegger explained his views on "nihilism," irrationalism: it is a false liberation from rationalism; it is the "regression" of rationalism. "God is dead" is no more his philosophy than metaphysics. Nihilism as conclusion is metaphysics. Nihilism has its truth, like metaphysics (it is unsurpassable, like metaphysics), but this truth is not nihilism. One says "surpass nihilism"—"and if," answers Heidegger, "What if the language of metaphysics and metaphysics itself, whether it is that of the living god or of the dead god, in fact constituted, as metaphysics, that limit which prevents a transition over the line, i.e., the overcoming of nihilism?"[193] The question is one of knowing whether one can ever have an experience of Being that is not metaphysical and thus nihilistic—but this nihilism is really not in every case one that formulates itself in negative propositions, one that treats *Sein* as a *Nichts* in the name of beings [*l'étant*]. True nihilism is a sublimated nihilism which understands that *Sein* is *also* nothingness, "which in a certain way it even 'is,' insofar as it essentially unfolds [*west*]."[194]—Incorporating nothingness into Being.[195]

Heidegger's conclusion is not negative. There is a thought that is not reflection (= thematization, objectivation, light coming from the one who thinks, and not from the thinking), but precisely from the very fact of *Denken* (= from this "leap," this call of Being (*Heißen* [being called], *Geheiß* [behest]), from this putting into correspondence with *Bedenklich* [what can be questioned], with what "gives to thinking," from this light which illuminates itself)—This *Denken*, which does everything, is also called *Besinnung* [mindfulness]: "To follow the direction that is the way that something has, of itself, already taken."[196] Because *Denken* as leap is put in relation with the "topology of Being" (*Zur seinsfrage*). *Denken*, thus, which is "*unterwegs*" [on the way to], for which one is no closer to the goal when one is there than when one is on the way (dialectical thought: Heidegger does not reproach the dialectic for being [147] in the order of φάσις, even if it was anti-φάσις, and thus "maneuver," of artifice). And this is certainly no longer constructive, "positive," "objective" philosophy (Husserl), but as Beaufret has put it, this is also not "a-philosophy": "Heidegger's thought, if it is no longer philosophy, is also not therefore extra-philosophical" ("Preface" to *Essais et conférences*).[197]

Moreover, one can not only ask whether this path of truth **[82]** is possible or healthy, but whether it should even be disclosed:

> Now it always remains possible, of course, and very often actually is the case, that we dislike a way of this sort from the start, because we consider it hopeless or superfluous, or because we consider it foolishness. If that is our attitude, we should refrain from looking at the way even from outside. But perhaps it is not fitting anyhow to let the way be seen in public [*ihn öffentlich sichtbar zu machen*]. With this hint, we shall break off our general remarks on the ways of *Denken*.[198]

But this may simply be *alt sein* [being old].

> To be old means: to stop in time at
> that place where the unique
> thought of a thought train has
> swung into its joint.[199]

As to the essential malaise of this thought (not the one due to years), there has always been a malaise in Heidegger's thought: (1) His gifts are "philosophical," and he has more to express than "philosophy"; (2) His language, put under way only slowly, rarely leads [148] to *Sage* (see *What Is Philosophy?*);[200] (3) Similarly (1): he looks for a direct expression of being whereas he also shows that it is not susceptible to direct expression. It would be necessary to attempt an indirect expression, i.e., show Being through the *Winke* of life, of science, etc. So philosophy is perhaps possible as *"das rechte Schweigen"* [the proper silence][201] of which the *Letter on Humanism* speaks. For example, he says, one can already "think" about "the being of a stone or even life as the being of plants and animals."[202]

Denken the living is the quasi-ontological problem of its relationship to us: it is our closest relative and yet separated from us by an abyss: "our scarcely conceivable, abysmal bodily kinship with the beast."[203]

A kinship with us that is stranger than the distance of man to God, so immense is it—distant proximity—the living and its *Umgebung* [surroundings], which is not *Welt* [world], which is not *Being*. Language that is neither *Äußerung* [utterance] of the organism, nor the *Ausdruck* [expression] of life, nor even a sign, nor even a *Bedeutung* [meaning], but the advent of being . . . (60). (See Husserl, *Ineinander* and *Einfühlung*.) This is what we are proposing, and the philosophical sense of the course on nature.

[Supplements]

[d] Psychoanalysis[1]

Double sense of psychoanalysis as a cultural **[20]** fact:

(1) Disintegration, contingency, psychologism, and the significant brought back to the insignificant or to the less significant, destruction of truth; (2) a more profound reintegration, new solidity that is not repression.

It is (1) if it is understood as a positivist explication by way of the sexual or the opposite by way of the ego.

It is (2) if one understands that the "sexual" which everything is based on is not the genital—that everything is based on it because human desire is an entirely different thing from an automatic function. It becomes autonomous precisely in the pathological case. And the ego is nothing *other* than sex, nor does it go "beyond."

(a) unconscious "id"[2] and the ego

The unconscious as thing, second consciousness. The psychoanalysis of the ego and its defense mechanisms as the counteroffensive of consciousness. These two theses = causal thought and its repression—two forms of disintegration.

Superficial conceptualizations, positivist deformations of a great truth: there is the id as perception that is [150] imperception, nonconventional thought (and not hidden adequate thought); there is the ego, the perception-consciousness apparatus, like a system of attitudes which avoid, bypass the id—(without going so far as to be consciousness of the unconscious).

The inner censure of instinct[3] and the flight instinct is its own causal censorship or externally summative and dialectical conceptualization.

In this way, our entire life is supported on a sexual soil, but (1) myth of an integrated sexuality: "pure" sexuality does not exist. "Left to itself," it has its contradictions; (2) there is an efficacy of superstructures like a vaulted ceiling—and even certain superstructural values can be linked to the fissuring of the infrastructure.

(b) Ego and others

Pansexualism: Reply = correlatively to the accentuation of the ego, one accentuates the struggle of the ego against the ego, competitions frustration-aggression, aggressive relation superimposed on sexual relation.[4]

More profound conceptualization: there is no sexuality + aggression, nor ego + ego—aggression has [its] roots in sexuality and the other ego [has] roots in my ego [*l'autre raciness en moi*]—aggression is explicated through the archaeology of the id[5] and not through the visible relations of the ego. And aggression before being in relation to others is a relation to my own ego. Sadomasochism and the *füreinander* (badly expressed as projection or introjection). It is impossible to think in terms of the ego or of consciousness, i.e., tissue of decisions and empirical acts—It requires monumental grounding, and that is what Freud wants to say in speaking of the libido.

Thus, no social adjustment preceding total reworking.

(c) Integration; (d) the cure—See p. **23**.

[21] The true (+ understood) formulation is not entirely sexual, but: there is *nothing* that is *not* sexual, nothing is *asexual*, overcoming the genital is not a distinction or [151] absolute break → ontological character of sexuality, i.e., it is a major contribution to our relationship with being (i.e.: with the world, others, and ourselves).

Psychoanalysis tends toward pure thought if it makes use of an objectivist-technical ontology in the description of the human being, of structures [*instances*]—on the contrary, it does not destroy; it acquires (and it sketches a philosophy), if it allows itself to be guided by the relationship to being as it is revealed in humanity—(the case of Freud—passage from causal thought to dialectical thought).

We confront these two on the following points (structures): (a) The ego and the unconscious; (b) Others and aggressivity; (c) Overcoming and sublimation; (d) The cure.

a) "Structures": The unconscious and "perception-consciousness apparatus" or ego.

Philosophy of consciousness prevalent at the beginning of the century—Everything that is not the deliberate positing of a sense, of an aim, necessarily appears as unconscious—Everything that is not first-person as third-person—i.e., as another first person, consciousness behind consciousness, the "id" (*Es*).

Difficulties: relation of the two—psychic existence = existence as consciousness → the unconscious = what one does not want to assume → suppression or even active repression → the unconscious results from putting "defense mechanisms" in place → highlighting the *ego*—Center of psychoanalysis shifted to the ego.

Is this a solution?—It is palliative: the insufficiency of the "unconscious" is not corrected but masked by accentuating the ego—passage to its antithesis—It would be necessary to resume everything.

To posit the unconscious not as a first consciousness to be masked, i.e., forgotten adequation (postulate of priority for conventional thought, of priority for the thinking subject), but as indirect consciousness or without exactitude or thinking for itself, close to the self, according to a system of signs weakly articulated, equivalences "approached," if it is not spiritual adequation but signifying or speaking subject.

As a result, the ego and its "defense mechanisms" are [152] also to be conceived in these terms: their avoidance of the repressed **[22]** is not knowledge of the unconscious but indirect consciousness as well; that which is to be avoided is not denied (which would be to say known) but bypassed—the ego as official, thetic, recognized domain, and the id are instances of ipseity.

Through this reform, one will no longer have causality of the id or causality of the ego—one will have [a] relationship that is not face to face—[a] relationship of infrastructure to superstructure, i.e., [the] sexual = the Soil [*Sol*] that supports life: (1) it is not necessary for there to be sexual perfection for there to be vital perfection: what is required is that there will be no destructive conflict; (2) it is not necessary to attribute all efficacity to the infrastructure; there is an efficacity of superstructures like vaulted ceilings ("defense mechanisms" and the equilibrium that they achieve: it is only necessary that this equilibrium not be pathological = anxiety, fleeing from situations, total impasse); (3) it can happen that a crack in the infrastructure is translated into the value of the superstructure—the "good" and the "bad" are mixed. In brief: structures are only structures = this in front of that [*ce devant quoi*] . . . compared to [a] life that is one.

   b) Ego and others

In the conceptualization of the ego as pure consciousness, absolute spontaneity, the other is the exterior—conflict or competition of consciousnesses—frustration-aggression—highlighting this relationship, which is numerically different from the relation to the id or to the ego—"sexual-aggressive."

As above, with respect to the introduction of the ego and its defense mechanisms, it is a bad, external correction.

The solution in a conceptualization of this kind can only be compromise: adjustment—the manipulation of the human being to obtain the adjustment, i.e., unity through integration of an abstract type.

Through [this] conceptualization + depth: relations between others and myself [*moi*] are intertwined and simultaneous—aggression ≠ a response to an objective frustration (and thus the remedy is not an objective gratification). Aggression is also masochism: it is myself that I pursue in others; it is others that I pursue in myself. Freud: sadomasochism. I am not at all simple: others are in me; I destroy myself for them; there is an exchange—not being for itself [*L'être pour soi*] + being [153] for others [*L'être pour autrui*] but the *Füreinander,* i.e., sadomasochism—what I am "for myself" I am also "for others"; what he is "for himself," he is also "for me"—This **[23]** is impossible to think for "consciousness": it can feel itself annulled only by the absolute other, absolutely guilty, absolutely unjustifiable, responsible, condemned—but if I am an existence, i.e., always bound to inertia, to others different from myself, this generativity absolves me: I know I will not be a consciousness by negating it

c) Integration

Suppression, censure, complexes considered impurities of life as long as one remains within first person–third person philosophy. The interior and exterior correlate without intrusion. Dreams of the total person "without complexes"—dreams of access to a pure objectal [*l'objectal pur*] without narcissistic inherence. Passage from the captive to the oblative[6]—good and bad, one next to the other—psychoanalytic wisdom through the total overcoming of contradictions—energetic metaphor of sublimation (and of transference): the same energy taken from the symptoms is transported from beyond life to the ends of the superego [*sur-moi*].

In conceptualizations of the relation between the concrete and the subtle ego-id, censure is not exterior, suppression is not conflict with another; there is no return to the immediacy of ascertainment (the false freedom of Americans talking about sex: there is no freedom through shamelessness that is a counter-modesty); there is no one without complexes, neither eliminations of the captive, nor pure objectal [*l'objectal pur*], nor transference without rest: pathological character, ritualism of certain sublimations. The complex as formative = Oedipus: humanity learns its role as humanity through Oedipus; it is initiated into love by Oedipus; there is no other way. Overcoming is also conservation and not quietism. [The] "sweetness of the superego" is humor. No energetic metaphor of sublimation: architectonic metaphor: the unconscious is the "indestructible." [154]

d) The cure—the psychoanalysis
In the external conceptualization of ego-id-other, with its overemphasis on the ego and on adjustment to others, one has (1) an underestimation of history and of its weight. Technical [24] interventionism: call upon medical technique in order to obtain the medical key through a concise idea (as if the problem were not to reestablish communication between self and self, as if it were to find a key and give it to the patient in the shape of an interpretation)[7]—or in any case, intervention of the analyst who still has the character of a technical action: questions, discussions, counsels, reports of submissions (or, if not, failure)—transference becomes conditioning by the analyst. What is necessary is for the analyst to be blunt [*cru*], that the past is effaced by a stronger present—technicism results in irrationalism.[8] The cure becomes suggestion. Although ineffective in truly pathological cases—but, in clinical practice, psychoanalysis is applied to everything so that there is no longer a crucial experience. The institution of psychoanalysis prepares subjects that it can (apparently) "cure." But they are not cured because they are not sick: they are the normal for this historical milieu. Alternation of immodesty and seriousness. Transference in order to manifest [?], i.e., of everyday reality and passage beyond. . . .

On the contrary, in the Freudian spirit: psychoanalysis as therapeutic and not institution—it remains in the observable—it does not provide objective proof of its truth: truth is here brought into relation to transference; one cannot affirm that it is imposed only through its clarity or explicative force. All action on humanity is action on someone who sees and thinks, and success can be due to in part to what they think. Nevertheless, a maximum of precautions are taken so that there is no simple shamanism: non-intervention, slow psychoanalysis, non-manipulation, one does not aim for the ego and its passing emotions; one tends toward the liberation of what is imprisoned, i.e., toward its reintegration into the entire life of the subject. One aims at the domain of our "archaeology" [155]—The analyst does not have the key. It is to be made for each case. He is not the one who knows in the face of the one who does not know. He is in the game (counter-transference). It is necessary that he continue to know himself in order to know the other. Socratic dialectic (almost silent Socrates)[9] = emergence of truth in the dialogue—transference, as Platonic love, is the condition, not the cause of the ascension toward truth. Psychoanalysis is not a technique for manipulation but for culture.[10] Importance of this "symptom," [i.e.,] psychoanalysis. Born from a **[25]** "crisis" (of which Freud would already speak, of a malaise), it can be [a] deepening, [an] enrichment of culture, or an aggravation of the crisis to the extent that it accentuates the objectivist and technicianist spirit[11] from which it proceeds (the neuroses submit to objective knowledge, become objects of science), or whether it is that spirit which recognizes its limits, rediscovering our archaeology as not being made by decisions of the ego or of consciousness's *Erlebnisse*—mythical time = time before time or before things and always present. Withdrawn into "subjectivity" through *Aufklärung* [clarification]. It is not a matter of becoming wild again: psychoanalysis is not a destiny, letting blood back into the choice. But the options are not decisions in the life of the instant = choice of sickness or of health. Always resumption, one cannot date it—Sartre himself: choice of the intelligible character = Kantian myth → one does not change, existential eternity. A dimension other than that of "consciousness": the relation to others, mythical-oneiric others, subject-object, overlapping [*empiètement*]—on the side of the self: indifference, one does what one wants and has no remorse, recognizing its pre-objective and mythical sources. Psychoanalysis: either the last conquest of scientific and technitionist ontology or the rediscovery of a remedy in another contact with being: being that is neither being for itself nor being object, but the contradictory being of human desire: ruin of "paternity" in the American world (and even in the European). [156] Oedipus is no longer able to shape—or to regain the strength of the Oedipal relation which seems to have conditioned Europe's creations (incest turned bad rather than prohibited, Nature in tension with culture and not assimilated by it)—Recovering the pre-objective that has made the civilization of consciousness and the object great.[12]

II. Philosophy in the Face of This Nonphilosophy

These symptoms are more and more "apparent" [*conscient*]: crisis of the notions of object and subject through their very development—either moving toward nihilism or else toward a new philosophy founded on a being other than subject-object being.

The philosophers—motivated by these experiences and *problemgeschichtlich* [conceptual historicity], motivated by the maturation of these problems (there is no need to decide: if philosophy is always reflection, the two motivations lead to the same point: [as a] reflection of our time, our philosophy can be deduced from precedents just as our time can be deduced from precedents. Even in a theory of reflection, the path of *problemgeschichtlich* is not closed)—how do they react? How do they understand the crisis and the solutions they propose? [157]

Husserl: fascism—is his first encounter with nihilism—*Die Krisis der Europäischen Wissenschaften.* Heidegger: his career coincides with the development of public nihilism. Sartre: already a child of the nihilistic period that begins with the war of 1914.

Brief examinations of Husserl and Heidegger—what the crisis means, according to them, for the future of philosophy.

1) Husserl and the idea of instituting philosophy anew.[13]

Course Notes from the
Collège de France, 1960–1961

Cartesian Ontology and Ontology Today[1]

[Course Outline]

[Our Questions Today]

I. The fundamental thought in art.
    [A.Vision and contemporary painting].
    [B.Vision:] Descartes.
        1) Treatment of light through *models.*
        2) Disjunction of resemblance as a component of Being.
        3) Vision is nothing made to be seen.
    [C.The philosophy of the visible and literature].
        [1) Vision and its signification].
        [2) The writer and the visible].
            I. The visible and the invisible: Proust.
            II. "Simultaneity": Claudel.
        [3) Claude Simon].
            1) Time.
            2) Space.
            3) The magma of humanity.
            4) The world as total existence.
            5) Art
            Claude Simon (Conclusion).

II. Descartes.
    Class of April 13, 1961.
        1) [a] The Cartesian "beginning"—vision of the eyes and vision
            of the mind.
    Class of April 13, 1961.
        1) [b] The Cartesian "beginning"—Positivism and vision of the
            mind.
        2) [a] The night of doubt: positivism and humanism.
    Class of April 20, 1961.
        2) [b] The night of doubt and the critique of the natural light.
        3) [a] *Cogito.*
    Class of April 27, 1961.
        3) [b] *Ego sum, ego existo.*

[Resumption of the April 27 class].

3) [c] The "I am"—change in the sense of the natural light.
Class of May 4, 1961 [Class not held].

4) God as light and abyss.

[Our Questions Today]

[163] **[1]**[2] This is not history of philosophy: the past for itself—but the past invoked for the sake of understanding what we think—within the horizon of being understood from the present. Aim: contemporary ontology, philosophy today.

Why this detour? Because we do not know what we think. Easier to say in what respect we are not Cartesians.

We do not know what we think: for 100 years, there is a fundamental thought that is not explicit "philosophy" in every case.[3] Everything art has searched for, that the "underground man" has searched for:[4] Dostoevsky, Nietzsche. Especially in France, the lateness [*retard*] of official philosophy with respect to these inquiries [*recherches*][5] (Bergson, Brunschvicq, even Alain, Blondel)—Russell even more—Croce less—Germany: Schopenhauer. [164]

> The difference between the person who inflicts suffering and the one who must bear it is only phenomenon, and has no bearing on the thing-in-itself, which is will living in both. Deceived by the knowledge bound to its service, the will fails to recognize itself here, and in promoting the well-being of *one* of its phenomena, produces great suffering in *another.* So in its passion it sinks its teeth into its own flesh, not knowing that it is injuring only itself.
>
> Thus, through the medium of individuation, the will reveals its own inherent self-conflict. The inflicter of suffering and the sufferer are one. The former errs in believing he does not share the suffering; the latter, in believing he does not share the guilt. If the eyes of both were opened, the inflicter of suffering would see that he lives in everything that in this wide world suffers pain, and which, if endowed with reasoning, wonders in vain why it was called into existence for such great suffering, through no fault of its own that it can discern. And the sufferer would see that all the wickedness which is, or ever was, committed in the world flows from that will which constitutes *his* own nature also, is manifest also in *him,* and that through this phenomenon and its affirmation he has taken upon himself all the sufferings arising from such a will, and justly endures them as long as he is this will.[6] **[2]**

Persecutor and persecuted are identical (Baudelaire)—One lives "at the bottom of the other" [*au fond de l'autre*]. There is only one fundamental will that is torn apart—abused by representation, intelligibility, apparent exteriority. Individuation: this tension, this inner fissure of the universal and particular will.

Schopenhauer, philosophy at the margins—but finally in consonance with the search of the "underground man"—anticipates: Freudian projection-introjection, sadomasochism, the death instinct—anticipates the Sartrean intersubjective: [the] world as representation [is] for others—[the] world as will [is] consistent for itself, [165] co-responsible, assuming everything, sacrificing itself so that the exterior is . . . Certainly, this is the myth of the will, but a search for an inner bond with others beneath representation.

Husserl ingeniously finds Schopenhauer again, whom German academic philosophers have neglected: sexuality, two intentionalities that have a similar *Erfühlung* [fulfillment] (*dasselbe*). Program for an explanation of *Sichtigkeit* [the visible], for the uniqueness of the visible world. Heidegger deepens *Nietzsche,* (Book forthcoming),[7] but is initially quite far from the "underground man."

In any case, in France today, philosophically, we do not know what we think—a whole part of the philosophy of tragedy takes place in Camus, Sartre—but appears as a "literary" novelty. There is a philosophy around psychoanalytic research, ethnological research, or even physics—but pure philosophy is going to be in crisis (Revel).[8] It lives mostly in the past as the history of philosophy.

Gueroult's severe critique of those who read Descartes without following the order of reasons as such, without looking for *Descartes's* problems and *Descartes's* arguments, which he turns toward his own problems. It is true that Gueroult admits that this objectivity is required only for Descartes. For others, "structures" are something other than "reasons": "These structures have the common character of being rational or irrational demonstratives, whatever path is chosen. This is always a process of validation. This demonstration combines logical means with architectonic means. [The architectonic] . . . of philosophical work looks to incline or to constrain the intelligibility of the subject to a judgment of ratification relative to the truth of doctrinal teaching."[9]

For example, for Malebranche:

Malebranche does not proceed through decomposition, dissociation, recomposition: he sees the immense being that supports his soul and on whose surface [166] [3], here or there, his capacity for thought condenses. . . . This system is not discovered through one, but through many, indeed, even through an infinity of ways: through as many ways as there are points of possible concentration for our attention on the surface of infinite being.[10]

. . . Analysis knocks down the façade of clear and distinct ideas in order to discover a vast intuition that is given or is wholly refused; that, far from being able to be demonstrated, is anterior to all evidence and absolves all reasonings, helpless in themselves, that is made less to prove than to procure a vision.[11]

But in this case, is Descartes himself even understood through the order of reasons? Gueroult shows that this has lacunae (for example, Gueroult says, it is missing a philosophy of the individual soul). The order of reasons is also the acceptance of these lacunae, tacit acceptance, mask, [a] view of being that turns away from these lacunae, intuition . . . So much the better because that is where there is still philosophy in the history of philosophy.

It remains the case that, for Gueroult, it is all the same a forfeiture [*déchéance*] of philosophy—Descartes remains the model: nondogmatic rationalism that recognizes but [also] measures the order of feeling [*sentiment*]—that admits other truths but not what is false according to the understanding.

Philosophy remains separated from the fundamental search that conveys, in a confused manner, much of philosophy.

Hence, the aim of this course is to look to philosophically formulate our ontology, which remains implicit, in the air, and to contrast it with Cartesian ontology (Descartes and his successors).

Order to follow: make contact with our questions through samples of fundamental thought (art, literature); to confront these questions with Cartesian thought (Descartes and his successors)—to see if they appear or are hidden there, or whether they are not at all and why; hence, return to the present, search for the formulation of our ontology, of philosophy today.

I. Fundamental Thought in Art [4]

[A. Vision and contemporary painting].

"What I'm trying to translate is more mysterious, tangled in the very roots of being, at the impalpable source of sensations" (J. Gasquet, *Cézanne*). Something that only offers itself through sensations but is beyond, at the root, at the source, hidden-revealed.

Space—"I believe Cézanne was seeking depth all his life";[1] Robert Delaunay, *Du cubism à l'art abstrait*[2] (P. Francastel, 1957): "Depth is the new inspiration."[3]

What is this "search" for depth that lasts "a lifetime" (and not "once in his life")? It is not the depth that is soared over [*profondeur survolee*], explained, changed into presence, or the depth implied by perspective drawing, the simple absence of certain parts.

It is *overlapping*[4]—the latency that is not possibility in the sense of another actuality of recognition, of another actuality simply coordinated with ours, which is possibility in the sense of pregnancy, envelopment of the inaccessible actuality in the accessible actuality. It is there right now. The [168] spectacle is there, outside of all vision; it is what is ready to be seen (light). It is because there is no exhaustion that the hidden thing is actual. It is because it is actual, as actual as the visible thing, that it hides itself from me, since it is there, behind. Depth is "between" the projection and the flight over [*survol*] and is not the coordination of the two.

No better commentary from Heidegger: *Identity and Difference* (I).[5]

Heidegger recalls the principle of identity in the *Sophist*: rest and change are each respectively αὐτο δ'έαυτω ταυτόν:[6] each itself is the same for itself with itself—mediated identity, fissure that closes on itself—"unity with itself."[7] Identity is [5] not a second and inert property of a Being in itself: it challenges us, the thing speaks to us, and it is how the thing can "appear in [its] Being."[8] Each "identical" place in depth is not a positive "where," but the reverse or the inverse of an alterity, other than the other. And it is because Being (here the where) and Thought (from the point of view of this where, the "who" is not here) belong to the same—it is because all of our efforts to think the spectacle in itself can only evoke it as visible. (Berkeley—only this does not mean: things are ideas, this means:

ideas are things, or rather: it is necessary to get rid of these two notions in order (Bergson) to conceive the thing as eminently Visible, [a] Visible whose empirical visions are only privations.)

This is depth:[9] in reality, the other "dimensions" are not different—Forms, planes, systems, height-width [169] are only crystallized by hiding the rest—are variants of depth—or reversal.

Abandon the notion of dimension as relation or point of view from where measurement is made. "Point of view" evokes projection. Precisely: there is no projection other than [the] free attendance of space. The dimensions are derived from a dimensionality, from a global locality, from a voluminosity where they are reversible, expressible, one through the other.

[The] search for depth or for form is a search for a unity through transcendence as well and not within the in-itself [*en soi*]—For example, "breaking the fruit bowl": it is remade from the pieces—it breaks, not for the sake of "cubes," "spheres," "cones," which would place space on one side and the contents on the other (Cézanne's second period), the colors modulating in *instability* in order to obtain spatialization to which the contents contribute.

Thus, the problem becomes generalized from space to color. Color: "place where our spirit and the universe meet"[10] (Cézanne)—Thus, color, not as second attribute of the "spectacle form," "simulacra of the colors of nature" (R. Delaunay),[11] but as dimension itself, genesis of identity, of difference, of texture, of something. . . .[12]

But is color the recipe of the visible? No: *Portrait of Vallier*, with its whites—the colors are there to **[6]** cut up [*découper*], to be richer than the being-colored. For example, space in the watercolors of the final years: there are no "places"; it radiates around planes that are in themselves non-localized, "floating movement of planes of color which overlap, which advance and recede" (G. Schmidt, *Les Aquarelles de Cézanne*).[13] Painting is the segregation of Being where we first are and not the construction of "traits of Being" that would give an illusion or analogy of it.

[170] A third dimension [is not] fictitiously added to the painting in addition to those of the canvas, organizing a perception without an object as similar as possible to perception with an object:[14] The backing board has two dimensions; the contemplated canvas has an infinity. And the perception of the world as well. The gaze [*regard*] interrogates the thing. It asks it how it makes itself a thing and how the world makes itself a world. It is necessary to see the *means* that we habitually traverse without seeing them, to broaden visibility (the hand of the captain in *The Night-watch*,[15] and its shadow over the body in profile—but many of the other

means of visibility are much more subtle: for example, the color and expression of a look). It is necessary to substitute the system of equivalences proper to the painter, who eminently contains it,[16] for the visibility of the "skin of things."[17] The painter "takes his body with him,"[18] i.e., his eye and his hand; he lets things live within his body and gives rise there to an internal double, a spectacle of something, only by being a "spectacle of nothing," "auto-figurative" (Bru).[19] Product, in the visible world, a second, larger visibility, makes everything become visible (against Berenson and tactile values).[20] Madness of vision: a partial world that wants total being. Vision is no longer looking upon an "outside," representation. It is the painter who is born into the things [171] as if through a concentration and coming-to-be of the visible.[21] Space especially comes to be from we don't know where, germinates upon the substrate [*le support*]—Henri Michaux: Klee's colors emanate as though through profound natural phenomena, "exhaled in the right spot,"[22] like a patina or moisture— "inarticulate scream . . . that seemed to be the voice of light" (Hermes Trismegistus). One no longer knows who sees and who is seen: "the role of the painter is to circumscribe and project what sees itself within him"[23] (M. Ernst). André Marchand: "In a forest, I have felt many times that it was not I who was looking at the forest. I felt, certain days, that it was the trees that looked at me, spoke to me . . . I was there, listening . . . I believe that the painter must be pierced by the universe and not want to pierce it . . . I am waiting to be [7] internally overwhelmed, buried. I may be painting to emerge."[24]

The line in painting—thus contact with polymorphous Being, giving rise to an expression, i.e., advent of created systems of equivalence. This sometimes implies new materials, new means of expression, but can also be accomplished by reinvesting in the old.

Creation, novelty, does not consist in privileging one of them, color over the line or signs over figuration, but in employing them like moments of a diacritical system, moments of an internal differentiation.

For example, the line is in no way excluded by color (Klee's lines, Matisse's lines)—What is contested:[25] the prosaic line, the line *of the* thing (the contour of the apple). Already da Vinci, "the sinuous" [*le serpentement*] and Bergson: the line "could be no one of the visible lines of the figure."[26] Even more so: there are no objective lines; they are always before or after the look. The line does not imitate the visible, it "makes visible" (Klee).

[172] Michaux: we have never "let a line dream";[27] we have never at this point used this manner of making a line go in the direction of being a line [*d'aller, ligne*].[28] The line can thus be reinvested, become an autonomous power. The difference between figuration and non-figuration is

then as small as we want—figuration: the line gives a prosaic signaling together with formula of activity and carnal passivity[29] (Matisse). Klee: the line only gives the "invisible" figure [*chiffre*], the title providing the prosaic reference—but Matisse's women were not women for the first visitors, and Klee's holly leaves are incredible for their "exactitude."[30]

Movement—does the picture give traces of movement like the comet on my retina?—But the unstable attitudes, blurred snapshots, freeze movement.

Rodin: it is necessary that the parts of the body are each in different phases of movement. Thus [producing a] position that the body in motion never had. These are incompossible moments that secrete the transition. Why? Because each of them, according to the logic of the body, gives me **[8]** another relationship to space, precisely because they are incompossibles and yet nonetheless of the same body, [because] the body explodes [*éclate*] in temporality: the human being, with two feet on the ground, the horses of the *Epsom Derby*, embracing the trail of their hooves, have a foot in each instant.[31] *Ineinander* of space-time—the photo keeps open the instant that time overcomes through overlapping [*empiétement*] and metamorphosis; the painting includes the body, "leave here, go there"[32]—movement is not first change of place but [an] internal formula of a doing, the explosion of a body through what it leaves and what it approaches.

[173] What is it to see? To see something . . . some part . . .

Depth: identity in depth, in latency, not alterity, not dissimulation rather than positive presence, unity in thickness *with itself*. . . ; Color: not *quale* but texture, dimension, world, (monochrome)—Line: trace; Movement (explicit or monumental) has an inside, a latency that is differentiation, a diacritical system of space-time.

One seeks a definition of the *quale*, of the thing, of the world, of Being, *what it is*. But to understand them precisely, it is necessary not to define them but to see them.

The red, the thing, the world, Being are what make these *Abschattungen* [adumbrations] eminently substitutable—not departing from *Abschattungen* but from the transition of one to the other, from segregation to the interior unity that is not a trait of Being, to which Being belongs.

To see is precisely not to have need of a definition, of thinking, of *vor-stellen* of being to . . . (my body, my house)—Presence of an absence if you will—(the hidden God).

This investment of the visible, in the narrow sense, by an invisible is given well with all vision—but extensible: there is nothing that cannot become visible (second visibility of the painting). To understand this pregnancy of the **[9]** invisible within the visible, this flesh of the imaginary (immanent visibility), it is necessary to elucidate our flesh, i.e., how our vision emerges from our body. It is related to movement, movement that cannot be blind, where it precedes itself. To see and to be moved are two faces of the same phenomenon: my body counts in the visible world and the world is included within the "scope" of my body. Identity in both cases and not difference, and identity of the two cases through non-difference. Forms are "scars" of forces and forces vibrate within forms. No question of synthesis or even of *Verflechtung* [entanglement].[33] This overlapping of vision-movement means that the moving body is a visible, tangible, and touched body, seen, is internally animated—reflexivity of the body, reversibility of seeing-visible, without any coinciding: complementarity.

Now, this padding [*capitonnage*] of a visible, or this outside from within, is extended from the body to all exterior things that the body sees, the whole spectacle related to one of its parts where it strangely resides. Relation to distance between the things and [174] what secretly doubles them in my body. If I am flesh, i.e., seer-visible, there is also a flesh of the world (Cézanne: Nature is in the inside).

This is how there can be beings that are not in-themselves and that are not nothing: pictures—icons. It is the internal double of things descending into them, vision reversed, that lines its descent into the visible. The imaginary, said properly (in what it has of freedom, beyond the seen *analogon*), is not sight of an absent in-itself (and of value as present through forgetting the entire in-itself, nothingness that is as valuable as being). It is the carnal double, internal equivalent, the secret figure of the real—macrocosm and microcosm and "parent forms" (Chastel, *Da Vinci*).[34]

Let us return to *seeing* (Leonardo): to see is not to have a *quale* but to have access to a principal figure of Being: the "absolute image" (Chastel), the *proporzionalita in instanti* [proportionality in instants];[35] simultaneity is openness to what we are not,[36] fission of being from what we are and not a property of seeing—"window of the soul."[37] Light is that through which one sees as well as what one sees, which in a sense "sees"—Vision is a thing entirely different from projection: it is not anamorphic, fixed point of view. It happens [*se fait*] everywhere as well. It is *ek-stase*; it is "natural vision"—(spherical, Leonardo).

But it is also a capacity for the imaginary; it is *l'occhio tenebroso*[38] [the dark eye], pictorial "science" of the visible through painting. **[10]** Created systems of equivalence that are applied to [175] natural forms whose "seal has not yet been broken" (Rilke).[39] In each visible, all of the visible: in marks and bells, all of the colors, sounds, and words. Overlapping, total part—no break between Nature and humanity.

Rectify Valéry's image of Leonardo, *Science and magic*.
  Valéry: "I felt that this master of means, this possessor of destiny, possessor of drawing, of images, of calculation, had found the central attitude thanks to which the enterprises of knowledge and operations of art are equally possible; the happy exchange between analysis and singularly probable acts. . . ."[40]
  It is a myth of the young Valéry. (Painting: *"cosa mentale"* [mental thing])[41] there is also, for Leonardo, a glorification of the visible, the idea of *componimento inculto* [uncultured composition] (oneirism, participation in the indivisible totality of the visible, marks).
  The growing predominance of *Sfumato*,[42] of the *non finito* [unfinished] (emergence of forms without contours) over "painting in relief . . . smooth and shiny forms" (Chastel). Science is integrated with a more general, non-central contact with being.

Such is this modern search (which discovers the Renaissance above Descartes). What does Descartes tell us about the same subjects? Next (Leonardo praises [*fait cet éloge*] painting *against* poetry, which would be incapable of "simultaneity"). Consider literature's search and see if its aim is different. If speaking sense is different from mute sense.[43] [176]

[11] [B: Vision:] Descartes[44]

1) Treatment of light through *models* [*modèles*]

Aim in the *Optics*: to fabricate "artificial organs"[45]—technology to manipulate light—and initially thanks to thought.
  Not experience (*Erfahrung*), interrogation of light, of vision. One does not dwell within light. One does not occupy the phenomenon: how light illuminates [*comment lumière eclaire*]. One begins from the light that enters the eye, that upon which we can act, from the light which acts.

> Now since my only reason for speaking of light here is to explain how its rays enter into the eye, and how they may be deflected by the various bodies they encounter, I need not attempt to say what its true nature is. It will, I think, suffice if I use two or three comparisons in order to facilitate that conception of light which seems most suitable for explaining all those of its properties that we cannot observe so easily. In this I

am imitating the astronomers, whose suppositions are almost all false or uncertain, but who nevertheless draw many very true and certain consequences from them because they are related to various observations they have made.[46]

Thought through *models*: not that our thought imposes any necessity on things but because we have no other—*Intuitus mentis* [mental vision]—Construction and operation[47] that must rejoin the consequences—natural light substituted [177] for light—(we will see further analysis of Cartesian "light").

Now, this *intuitus mentis* reduces the phenomenon of light; the results of light are taken as acquired: simultaneity, instantaneity, assimilation of light to solidity, identity, *lux-lumen*. *Lumen* is *lux* continued, assimilation of vision-touching with canes—the blind "see with their hands." The model of vision is contact—light stripped of its distance, of its transcendence—vision is a flight over, not openness to. . . .

2) Disjunction of resemblance as a component of Being

Reflections, specular images ("phantoms") are of *things*—For example, the bouncing of a ball—clear relation of projection—the resulting resemblance is extrinsic denomination.

The reflection, the specular images act on bodies like things and give a perception without object, illusion—notably, my reflection in the mirror (or vision of others) is a mannequin—I do not see *myself*, I do not see others—I think myself, I think the other—Visibility is no longer the structuration of Being (Schilder):[48] my phantom body, in the mirror, pulls out all of my tactile experience, invests it outside—other people are mirrors for me through their bodies—My body and theirs overlap—No intercorporeity.

3) Vision is not a thing to be seen—over there and **[12]** within us. The painting is not operant communication with the visible, but the employment of a code of signs or of given discriminations. Philosophers believe they notice small images of things within us and believe that vision is the entrance to the κοινός κόσμος [common universe] through the ἴδιος κόσμος [private universe]—but, for these εἴδωλα [images, phantoms],

their sole reason for positing such images was that they saw how easily [178] a picture can stimulate our mind to conceive the objects depicted in it, and so it seemed to them that the mind must be stimulated to conceive the objects that affect our senses in the same way—that is, by little pictures formed in our head. We should, however, recall that our mind can be stimulated by many things other than images—by signs and words, for example, which in no way resemble the things they signify. And if, in order to depart as little as possible from accepted views, we prefer to maintain that the objects which we perceive by our senses really send images of themselves to the inside of our brain, we must at least observe that in no case does an image have to resemble the object it represents in all respects, for otherwise there would be no distinction between the object and its image. It is enough that the image resembles its object in a few respects. Indeed, the perfection of an image often depends on its not resembling its object as much as it might. You can see this in the case of engravings: consisting simply of a little ink placed here and there on a piece of paper, they represent to us forests, towns, people, and even battles and storms; and although they make us think of countless different qualities in these objects, it is only in respect of shape that there is any real resemblance. And even this resemblance is very imperfect, since engravings represent to us bodies of varying relief and depth on a surface which is entirely flat. Moreover, in accordance with the rules of perspective they often represent circles by ovals better than by other circles, squares by rhombuses better than by other squares, and similarly for other shapes. Thus it often happens that in order to be more perfect as an image and to represent an object better, an engraving ought not to resemble it. Now we must think of the images formed in our brain in just the same way, and note that the problem is to know simply [13] how they can enable the soul to have sensory awareness of all the various qualities of the objects to which they correspond—not to know how they can resemble these objects. For instance, when our blind man [179] touches bodies with his stick, they certainly do not transmit anything to him except in so far as they cause his stick to move in different ways according to the different qualities in them, thus likewise setting in motion the nerves in his hand, and then the regions of his brain where these nerves originate. This is what occasions his soul to have sensory awareness of just as many different qualities in these bodies as there are differences in the movements caused by them in his brain.[49]

Descartes (1) is right to oppose the εἴδωλα in itself—there is no question of taking them up again—the problem is not with that, but to know precisely if Being is to be conceived as causally related to us In Itself; (2) is right to consider the resemblance of the retinal image to the thing as secondary: (a) it would still be necessary for there to be other eyes inside the brain in order to see—we have not advanced one step in the problem of vision by giving ourselves double objectives that are not an opening onto the thing; (b) resemblance to another is not realized in the picture. Figuration is a very peculiar case of the *Darstellung* [presentation] of being.

There, where it exists, it is not the picture that opens itself onto Being. But if there is no exterior resemblance picture-thing, there is also no longer a difference between round and oval, square and rhombus, that is to say, the picture is not something else, substituted thing, *signaling* the thing. The difference is much more profound.

Here is Descartes's weakness: (1) For him, the sign is the adequate occasion for thinking the signified. Perception and vision of the picture are "thought"—the sufficiently discriminating sign permits us "our representation" of things. For example, oval for circle, rhombus for square. There is the true in itself (circle) and the sign for us (oval), and thought reconstitutes the in-itself from the sign for us. But—as [180] he explains elsewhere—signs[50] are not given to us. One does not shift attention from the body's dimension to things in their extension, from perception of the hand to perception of the thing enclosed in it—perception of the body is perception of the world—the body's space is the matrix of all space—but this bodily space is not thought; the soul is not a pilot thinking its ship, but dwelling within the body and thus within the world.

The analysis in terms of thought is a two-part analysis; it is *as if* our bodies had been instituted through such a Thought—that what *is there* is causality—which produces a magical appearance of adaptation outside because the body has been so disposed by Thought of the All—disjointed vision in Thought and Causality.

Now, in the order of the visible, of the union, the body is the measuring of things and not an object—and the circle is not the thought cause of the oval—there is no oval or circle in itself; there is an equivalence for my body through the polymorphous being of these two "projections"—In the order of thinking, reconstitution of the divine thought that gave us this body.

[14ⁱ] What Descartes says about the picture is that the picture is before the thought of God, of Micromegas: three "true" dimensions figured by two dimensions.

[181] Projection deciphered: space in itself reconstituted from a leaf of space, *partes extra partes*, space of juxtaposition, from *overlapping*.[51]

"Thought" of Being that is what it is (circle, square), i.e., thought of a thinker who is everywhere—retrieved from sufficient discriminations.

The painting is artificially calling to this code, trompe-l'oeil, perception without object, which is possible because no perception opens onto its object directly: it only corresponds to it through divine regulation—God's guarantee that my thought is true—picture and prosaic thing are homogeneous: the perceived does not look like Being, nor does what is painted, but the perceived thing and the picture look alike: deciphered signs; use the same code, natural-divine, the equivalences are not to be created, not from "culture," not from "poetry," neither from latency nor from the teachings of the visible—painting is drawing, and drawing is understood as coding according to the institution of nature—the word of Pascal: vanity of the painting that makes one admire what the original would leave indifferent: the original, the world itself—Cartesian word: the painting signifies to us a preexistent In-itself, not as good as but not differently than perception does.

In brief: negation of openness to the visible (and to Being through the visible), like the negation of the consciousness of automata—openness to the visible is replaced by the thinking of engineers. Text of *Treatise on Man*, p. **14–15**.[52]

[14] *Treatise on Man*:

External objects, which by their mere presence stimulate its sense organs and thereby cause them to move in many different ways depending on how the parts of its brain are disposed, are like visitors who enter the grottos of these fountains and unwittingly cause the movements which take place before their [15] eyes. For they cannot enter without stepping on certain tiles which are so arranged that if, for example, they approach a Diana who is bathing they will cause her to hide in the reeds, and if they move forward to pursue her they will cause a Neptune to advance and threaten them with his trident; or if they go in another direction [182] they will cause a sea-monster to emerge and spew water onto their faces; or other such things according to the whim of the engineers who made the fountains.[53]

Problem of automata: responses within a meaningful relationship to a situation. But this relationship is not thought by them, operant—it was thought by the engineer—in the same way, things acting on my senses give rise to a vision in a meaningful relationship with them. But this relation is not operant. It was thought by God, and the body [was] instituted accordingly. Hence, the possibility of illusions is linked to natural inclination—Thus, it is not the world that one sees—true perception and illusion are homogeneous—the "natural magic" of Perspective is the Great Lie, solitude: I am confined to my nature and brought into accordance with the world through God alone. Perceptual magic is reduced to identity in God for understanding and will, body, "finalized" soul.

Cartesian ontology: truth defined through immanent certainty (thought), which opens onto Being only because the Being of God is connected to it. Descartes: anthropology-theology—diplopia—my thought—validated by God—which is there without me having to think it more than once in my life—which is there in order to confirm me—metaphysics that chases me out of metaphysics (not deepening the *Meditations*) that (1) limits, (2) grounds my lights. Ontology of painting: communication with Being through vision, opening to . . . , always incomplete, to be done.

"Natural light" and "scream of light."

* * *

[C. The Philosophy of the Visible and
Literature]

Now this disclosure of the "*voyance*"[54] in modern art, *voyance* that is not Cartesian thought—may have [183] an analogue in the arts of speech. Perhaps it is necessary, not to bring vision back to the legibility of signs through thought, but inversely, to find within speech a transcendence of the same type that there is in vision. Da Vinci demands *voyance against* poetry. The moderns make poetry into a *voyance* too—Max Ernst compares the painter projecting what *sees itself* within him to the poet. Since Rimbaud (*Lettre du voyant*), writing [happens] "under the dictation of that which is thought, that which is articulated in him." Look for what expands the philosophy of the visible within literature. Descartes: idea of a universal language where signs would have their meanings circumscribed exactly—this is equivalent to the theory of perspective.

Since we have arrived at Descartes, let us read the text on language ("Lettre à Mersenne"). Descartes to Mersenne, [16] November 20, 1629— speaking about a proposed project for a universal language:

> I believe, however, that it would be possible to devise a further system to
> enable one to make up the primitive words and their symbols in such a
> language so that it could be taught very quickly. Order is what is needed:

all the thoughts which can come into the human mind must be arranged in an order like the natural order of the numbers. In a single day one can learn to name every one of the infinite series of numbers, and thus to write infinitely many different words in an unknown language. The same could be done for all the other words necessary to express all the other things which fall within the purview of the human mind . . . But I do not think that your author has thought of this. There is nothing in all his propositions to suggest it, and in any case the discovery of such a language depends upon the true philosophy. For without that philosophy it is impossible to number and order all the thoughts of men or even to separate them out into clear and simple thoughts, which in my opinion is the great secret for acquiring sound knowledge. If someone were to explain correctly what are the simple ideas [184] in the human imagination out of which all human thoughts are compounded, and if his explanation were generally received, I would dare to hope for a universal language very easy to learn, to speak and to write. The greatest advantage of such a language would be the assistance it would give to men's judgment, representing matters so clearly that it would be almost impossible to go wrong. As it is, almost all our words have confused meanings, and men's minds are so accustomed to them that there is hardly anything which they can perfectly understand. I maintain that such a language is possible and that the knowledge on which it depends can be discovered, thus enabling peasants to be better judges of the truth of things than philosophers are now. But I do not hope ever to see such a language in use. For that, the order of nature would have to change so that the world turned into a terrestrial paradise; and that is too much to suggest outside of fairyland.[55]

Always the same mode of thought: one can find this science, order proceeding from the simple to the complex—thought's *point d'honneur*—in fact its disorder.

Pure understanding—"possible"—which is not to say realizable in language and used in imagination—For example, thought of the corporeal.

The order of all possible thoughts—symbol and writing are composed following this order, reflecting it—For example, numbers: systematic writing—the principle, once acquired, indefinitely forms "different words" corresponding to always different thoughts and always the same.

True philosophy: "enumerating all the thoughts of man"—putting them in order in terms of clarity and simplicity. The universal language formed through this analysis "would distinctly represent all things," "would be an aid to judgment," would render error almost impossible—would be transparent—would no longer include "confused significations," a simple, customary connection between thoughts such that nothing is understood perfectly—a real language of truth [185] that would make every human being more of a philosopher than philosophers at present.

What there is to say are "thoughts,"—and these are countable and susceptible to being ordered from the simple to the complex (linearly).

Language as an algorithm[56] resembles these thoughts, being embraced by them, composed by thought. To speak is to provide an adequate analogue of this composition—New thoughts are always composed of the same elements, and new language is always composed of the same elements. *Intuitus mentis* that envelops speech like vision.

Not all of Descartes's thought is there—or rather: [17[i]] it is his thought in principle (order) in a kind of heaven on earth; [is it the case that] this pure understanding is in fact only "possible" in a fairyland, that nothing invincibly opposes it except in exercise? Even for the human being alone? Even for spiritual things, metaphysics, it may be necessary to speak about the imaginative (and further) (light).

Olympica:[57] Henri Gouhier: it is pre-Cartesian, these are student notes (24 years):

> The things which are perceivable by the senses are helpful in enabling us to conceive of Olympian matters. The wind signifies the spirit; movement with the passage of time signifies life; light signifies creation.[58]

> Just as the imagination employs figures in order to conceive of bodies, so, in order to frame ideas of spiritual things, the intellect makes use of certain bodies which are perceived through the senses, such as wind and light . . . It may seem surprising to find weighty judgments in the writings of the poets rather than the philosophers. The reason is that the poets were driven to write by enthusiasm and the force of imagination. We have within us the sparks of knowledge, [186] as in a flint: philosophers extract them through reason, but poets force them out through the sharp blows of the imagination, so that they shine more brightly.[59]

There is a question: we will see the difficulty of seizing upon the understanding through the understanding—(*Cogito*);[60] still, the light of the *intuitus mentis* is in principle the only light: the imagination participates; note the contrast [17[ii]] with the moderns. The moderns: language not as instrument whereby thought would be like the pilot in his ship—but, a kind of substantial union of thought and language—language not governed, [but] endowed with its own efficacity: Max Ernst, that which "thinks itself" and is articulated within the poet.

Rimbaud's *Lettre du voyant* (cited **16**). One often quotes "derange-ment of the senses [*dérèglement des sens*], "I am another"; it is necessary to cite the other words: (1) "one thinks me"; (2) "the wood that becomes a violin."[61]

(1) It is not about thinking anymore—the derangement of the senses is to break the partitions between them in order to regain their indivision—And through this, a thought not mine but theirs—A contact with the visible totality; (2) The wood that becomes violin—like my body (above) sees my resounding and singing words as visible, are (of the vis-ible, sensible) what becomes expression. Things speak through me.

[1] Vision and its signification]

Not only parallel problems: vision and its signification, speech and its signification—but a single problem: the visible and poetic signified are intertwined; poetry, speech of things (Valéry)—Text p. **18**; and even the philosopher (Husserl).

[187] Valéry: **[18]**

Honor of Mankind, Sacred LANGUAGE,
Ordered and prophetic speech,
Chains of beauty that enwind
The god bewildered in the flesh,
Illumination, and largess!   The pythia who speaks in classical
Here speaks a Wisdom   verse.
Now a Wisdom makes utterance,
And rings out in that sovereign voice
Which when it rings can only know
It is no longer anyone's
So much as the woods' and waters' voice![62]

Literature and the disclosure of the visible, speech of things—

Look in literature for the attestation of the writer writing "under the dictate of that which is thought, of what is articulated in him" and which retains the very essence of the visible. Do not take this as a diagnosis of all modern literature—or only of modern poetry after Rimbaud. There are many other diagnoses (Jacques Rivière,[63] see **18**).[64] Rimbaud [is a] brilliant stage in the development of literature that began before and continues after him. Perhaps a change in the relationship with being in the writer since Romanticism—It is often said: it is a world where "God is dead" (Lessing), predominance of subjectivity; even Jacques Rivière (*Nouvelles Études, Reconnaissance a Dada*—1920):

It is quite evident that in the eyes of any of the great writers of the classical age, the germ, the intelligible plasma that they felt upholstered their brains and in which they recognized the substance of their work, appeared only as things they simply had to hunt, to expel such things before them. Like an object, rather, which they had to explore, penetrate, conquer. . . . All the classics were implicitly positivist: they accepted the fact of both the [188] interior and exterior world and the obligation to learn about it.[65]

Hence, modern literature, "pure exteriorization and simple in themselves." See Malraux[66] in *Psychologie de l'art.*

A questionable perspective: if it is no longer the object, it is the subject—In reality, it is a new relationship to Being rather than a rupture favoring the subject.

Rivière himself, in the same article, with respect to Flaubert:

Nothing less than his eyes enter. He sees nothing and searches for nothing to see beyond what he needs. If he bends upon nature, winded, groaning, obstinate, like a miner on the vein that he cuts, it is that he must extract his goods; it is that he wants to extract the necessary materials for his edifice. From the stone, from the plank, from the slate or tiles: all that observation is charged to get him, the only utility he knows.

In the end, he wants nothing but to find a material for a kind of indefinable and precise, one would say poetic or even plastic, image [18ii] of an order that his brain incubates. Albert Thibaudet[67] was a thousand times right to make him [Flaubert] appear "as the most arresting type among us novelists who think by way of themes"—a thousand times right to emphasize the importance of his famous joke: "In *Salammbo,* I wanted to give the impression of the color yellow. In *Madame Bovary,* I wanted to make something that was the color of those moldy nooks where wood lice can be found. As for the rest, the plot, the characters, I do not care." Yes, if one looks at it closely, Flaubert, in sum, writes only to give a body to certain whims that haunt him: the formidable flock of concrete details that he sets in motion and that push him is simply in the hope that it will rid him of the demons who torment him.[68] [Note]:[69] He wrote the accidents of the world himself . . . as soon as they are perceived you appear as if transposed [189] for the employment of an illusion to be described, so that all things, including our existence, seem to have no other use.

This does not quite prove what J. Rivière wanted to prove:

Never, perhaps, has one demonstrated with so much weight, strength, and naiveté, a more complete disdain for the given, a more serene irreligion of reality, a more purely *poetic* conception of the novel, a more complete will to "fiction."[70]

—No, Flaubert: each thing is perceived as a symbol or as equivalent to an image that it will serve to render: event, anecdote, dialogue, but which would not be without these things, which needs them, which goes to them. Being is their encounter, neither "interior" nor "exterior," and "our own existence" is for it, at its service.

For example, the yellow, or the grey-moldiness: the grey wood louse is a region or texture of Being (i.e., geographical, climatic, cultural, historic, inter-human being, etc.)—Painter [18[iii]] and writer take up the same relation in two opposite directions: the painter gives the yellow or the grey in question and hence the flock of details, indirect figuration—The Novelist gives the details, inversely, but does not give the color directly. Both of them make use of equivalences that seem given to them within the perceived and which result in the intermixing [*mélange*] of themselves with the visible world and of the regions of the visible between them.

This is not to lose interest in the world; it is to find access through intermixing, through an imaginary within us that welcomes it and makes it at home. In a sense, it discovers it.

By virtue of the same *intermixing*, the speaking human being does not designate "significations"—this does not necessarily mean, as for Dadaism and the initial Surrealism, "nothing linguistic" (Rivière, 309)—In other words:

Language, for the Dadaists, is no longer a means: it is a being (298). As it is for Mallarmé, so it is in Rimbaud that words have begun to debauch themselves (one could even go back farther on this point: Flaubert is not without responsibility). And no doubt I am in need of a very brilliant and very important discovery: this secret virtue in them, distinct from what they have to signify, and which [190] permits them to absorb a little of the writer's sensibility and to lead him away to the state of a simple seed, to another world where it will flourish again. No one admires more than I the way, in Mallarmé, they slowly emerge from their individual sense, then from their logical solidarity, to simply end, having met elsewhere, hatching out, being born to many. But in the end, in this sense [*acception*], they cease to be signs; the value they receive is from a post-intellectual order. What determines their appearance is henceforth only their inner kinship with this or that aspect of the subject. They come only upon his [**18ⁱᵛ**] injunction, under pressure, and to compose a new, foreign figure . . . they become simple effects. It is necessary to see with what promptitude they follow, not to say the thought of, but, for example, the person of Rimbaud. Obedience is all that the poet demands of them. Lines are drawn in space; elusive paths are declared where they have only to precipitate; they gather a thousand directions in the moment; they are as precise and useless as lightning.[71]

(1) Why useless if they are included without having been "unsealed"—if they are precise—if they have a definite power of arousal? (2) And in any case, is it myself? Is it not the world—along with me? Is it not the case that any "objective" thought, when it is new and teaches, involves a passage through this transcendence to which it adds immanent motivations, which, moreover, do not compensate it? Immanence is transcendence that has cooled down—this does not mean that any discontinuity, irrationality, has the same virtues.

[2] The writer and the visible]
Thus, one should not speak of subjective literature but of a new node between the writer and the visible and what he has to say.

> It is with Romanticism alone that the literary act has begun to be conceived as a sort of attempt at the absolute and its result as a revelation; literature had gathered together the inheritance of religion at that time . . . ; all of these gestures only tended to bring into this host what the work was, its "real presence."[72]

—Yes, but the postwar period after 1918 was not to bring them about as J. Rivière believed, and the *NRF* liquidated this [191] literature for the sake of returning to classicism—simply put, the subjectivist equivocation should be dismissed [*écartée*] along with the equivocation of any speech, and the attempt at the absolute became the discovery of the visible world more resolutely; oversignification and not non-sense—the signifying elements not being *excluded*. We ask [**18ᵛ**] for some examples of this attestation: Proust, Claudel, and even recent Literature.

One could do it in two ways: (1) on one hand, the best way, would be to give an example of writers' speech practices, showing how they disclose oversignifications or "alogical" essences—notably that of the sensible—But this would require a study of what one (wrongly) calls their "technique"—and of the work as a whole; (2) on the other hand, the imperfect but shorter way: taking samples of this speech at the level of the sentence; gathering declarations (in a direct, signifying, reflexive style) of writers talking about their own relationship with the world and their own artistic intention—something in the course of the narrative (narrative often done through a narrator, e.g., Proust)—Claude Simon, who reflects on what he is in the process of narrating, not only to show his world but thought as well).

(See text of Proust, **p. 19**, above).[73]

I. The visible and the invisible: Proust **[19]**

But ever since, more than a year before, discovering to him many of the riches of his own soul, the love of music had, for a time at least, been born in him, Swann had regarded musical motifs as actual *ideas*, of another world, of another order, ideas *veiled in shadow, unknown,* impenetrable to the intelligence, but nonetheless perfectly *distinct from one another, unequal among themselves in value and significance.* . . . He knew that the very memory of the piano falsified still further the plane in which he saw the things of the music, that the field open to the musician [192] is not a miserable keyboard of seven notes, but an immeasurable keyboard (still almost entirely unknown) on which, here and there only, separated by the thick darkness of its unexplored tracts, some few among *the millions of keys of tenderness, of passion, of courage, of serenity,* which compose it, each one differing from all the rest as one universe differs from another, have been *discovered* by a few great artists who do us the service, when they awaken in us the emotion corresponding to the theme they have discovered, of showing us what *richness, what variety lies hidden, the unknown to us, in that vast, unfathomed and forbidding night of our soul which we take to be an impenetrable void or nothingness.* Vinteuil had been one of those musicians. In his little phrase, although it might present a clouded surface to reason, one sensed a content so solid, so consistent, so explicit, to which it gave so new, so original a force, that those who had once heard it preserved the memory of it on an equal footing with the ideas of the intellect. Swann referred back to it as to a conception of love and happiness whose distinctive character he recognized at once as he would that of the *Princess of Clèves,* or of *René,* should either of those titles present themselves to his memory. Even when he was not thinking of the little phrase, it existed *latent* in his mind on the same footing as certain other *notions without equivalent,* such as our notions *of light, of sound, of relief,* of physical pleasure, the rich possessions that *diversify and adorn our inner domain.* Perhaps we shall lose them, perhaps they will be obliterated, if we return to nothingness. But so long as we are alive, *we can do more about having known them* than we can about some real object, than we can, for example, *doubt the light of a lamp that we lit before the metamorphosized objects of our room, from which even the memory of the darkness escaped.* In that way, Vinteuil's phrase, like some theme, say, in *Tristan*, which represents to us also a certain emotional acquisition, had *wedded our mortal condition,* had taken something of humanity that was peculiarly touching. Its destiny was linked to the future, to the reality of the human soul, of which it was one of the most special and distinctive ornaments. Perhaps it is nothingness that is true, and all [193] our dream is inexistent; but, if so, we feel that these [20] musical phrases, these conceptions which exist in relation to our dream, *must also be nothing* [*ne soient rien non plus*]. We shall perish, but we have as hostages these divine captives who will follow and share our fate. And death in their company is somehow less bitter, less inglorious, perhaps even less probable.[74]

Musical ideas opposed first to intellectual ideas: veiled in shadow, opaque to the intellect (to the light). They have an "obscure surface," yet they are resistant in their own manner: distinct; unequal value and signification— less identical to themselves than non-different, *Dasselbe* [selfsame] and not *das Gleiche* [sameness]; consistent, "differentiated," explicit; (elsewhere: they descend into the piano and violin that are hurrying to join them); "entities" (p. 189) founding their intellectual equivalents ("small diver- gence [*écart*] between the five notes which compose the little phrase"); "keys"[75] of tenderness, passion, courage, serenity; "themes"—preexisting in us (where the themes awaken them); latent within ourselves when we do not think about it.

Is it not a general conceptualization of ideas? Because the *"Princess de Clèves,"* *"René"* are compared to them—they are "conceptions of love and happiness" locked up in these essences as well as in the words—Is the writer not also in search of these essences?

In any case, this conceptualization of the idea applies *to notions of the sensible*: like music, the sensible gives "notions without equivalent":[76] light, sound, relief, sensuousness. Question: what are these essences?

Light is not a *quale*; it is the impossibility of *obscurity*, the entrance into a *world*, i.e., a henceforth *inalienable* dimension, irreversible initiation; luminosity is the structure of being: Eternity of light as it is. [194]

Thus, there is (1) *intuitus mentis*, intellectual ideas and (2) ideas at [this] "obscure surface" related to notions of the [21] sensible, notably light. What relationship [is there] between the ideas of the visible and musical ideas?

The "inner domain" borrows in order to adorn itself—"ornament"—and to differentiate itself from the visible (light, non-relief, sensuousness) (everything that we say about the soul, which is *night*, makes use of the visible) and there is a richness *awakened* by art in its apparent night or emptiness, richness that art "reveals," which through it, becomes almost visible but signifies beyond. Riches related to those of the visible in that (1) once known "*we can do more about having known them*": facts and dimensions— singular and general like the sensible, indestructible for life—like the past (Claudel) (which precisely is kept by the body); (2) it is sometimes about (intellectual) "notions without equivalent," not possessed in the manner in which one can say *what it is*, but which has "wedded our mortal condition," i.e., can be grasped precisely only in the oneirism (dream) of the sensible, the figures or linings of our experience.

We have said Platonism, but these ideas exist without intelligible sunlight and are related to visible light: a frame [*membrure*] of the visible. Secret, unveiled and veiled, "alogical" (Scheler) essences, some addressing the aesthesiological body, others the libidinal body.

In relation to them, the language of the writer would be what music means in relation to the little phrase itself—symbolic matrices.

Proust: literature built upon the writer's landscape, where he reads everything he writes—art is the operation of the "acquisition" of these "entities."

What is fundamental: under any intellectual idea, penetrable, graspable by the *intuitus mentis*, there is one of those entities that is not [a matter of] positives but differences, "differentiated" and collectively hidden from the night or from the void of the soul—i.e., their consistency, the possibility of identifying each one, is primarily due to their non-difference with themselves because they are poles of carnal life = invisible frame [195] or structure of the visible—vision participates in these *cogitatio caeca* [blind thoughts], entails a secret, more than empirical visibility.

Thus, a nocturnal reality of the soul, of the incorporeal—which is not nothing—but which needs to "adorn" itself with the visible—which is like the opposite of the visible—The visible opens onto an invisible that is its relief or its structure and where identity is rather non-difference.

Here we can study time and space in Proust—their mode of cohesion: cohesion of scales (the butterfly and the boat)—the two paths are not identical[77] (perspective), but one is deferred [*reportés*] to the other in their absolute difference—

Time: the past is lost—reality is only formed in memory (by language)—world at a distance—and yet is itself (through the body).

I. Proust[78] **[24]**[79]

Musical ideas: (1) musical ideas [are not] intellectual ideas, veiled by darkness; opaque to the intellect; "obscure surface"; (2) nevertheless resistant; distinct; unequal in value and signification—they "descend" into the piano and violin which are hurrying to join them; "differentiated"; explicit; less identical to themselves than not different—*Dasselbe* and not *das Gleiche*; (3) "keyboard," preexisting "keys" [*touches*] in us that they come to touch [*viennent toucher*]; latent within ourselves when we do not think about it, exactly like the significance of the Pythagorean theorem; (4) "entities" that found their "intellectual equivalents," for the "little phrase": "small divergence between the five notes that compose it"; "themes."

The notions of the visible: "notions without equivalent" (whose intellectual equivalents are reported) light, sound, [196] relief, sensuousness—Light: is not merely a *quale*, it is the impossibility of obscurity, initiation to a *world*, to a little eternity, to a henceforth inalienable dimension—Universality by singularity (i.e., the past) (which is precisely guarded by the body).

Relationship of the two: The notions of the visible resemble musical ideas in this: they are less *positive* than not absent, "we cannot be sure that we did not know them"—presence by radiance; they are inscribed by experience, they have "wedded our mortal condition," they are the eternal of the ephemeral, figures of the singular.

Here like there, in light as in the musical idea, we have an idea that is not *what* we see but behind it: night or void of the soul that "adorns itself," "differentiates itself" or "decorates itself" by borrowing from the visible, the "other side" of the visible; this "other side" is revealed to be rich through art but would not be without it; only through a borrowing from what art accomplishes within the visible and speech do a universe and plurality of universes and millions of themes come out of their night.

Thus this is not Platonism: these ideas have no intelligible sun and are related to the frame of the visible.

The ideas of art: it is not only music; "*The Princess of Cleves*," "*René*"; the writer's language is to the work's signification as the five notes are to Vinteuil's little phrase, as light is to luminosity, as the visible is to visibility.

[25] Confirmation: *Time Regained*. All of this expresses as light makes both itself and things visible. This is not an *analogy*: Theme of the visible, sensible, and theme of the speech of the world; *Time Regained* II,

21–24. The sensible world is hieroglyphics[80] and the writer's speech is the conquest of these things-words [*choses-paroles*], what they want to say.

The visible (with all the invisible that it drags behind it) is the Being common to us, and the language of the artist (as indirect and unconscious) is our way of achieving participation in this Being: [197]

> means awareness of our own life, means also awareness of the lives of others—because style for the writer, no less than for the painter, is a question not of technique but of vision. It is the revelation, which by direct and conscious methods would be impossible, of the qualitative difference that there is in the way the world appears to us, a difference which, if there were not art, would remain the eternal secret of each. Through art alone are we able to emerge from ourselves, to know what another person sees of a universe which is not the same as our own and whose landscapes would remain as unknown to us as those that may exist on the moon.[81]

Explosion of the visible world that offers itself to me as the world of all (despite the reflection that tells me that this may be only a private world). Explosion of the language or of the speech that comes to reanimate and recommence this wonder by touching what I believed most hidden within me and that reveals itself to be participable and to this extent an "idea."

Among the most celebrated accomplishments of Proust: the cohesion of time and space as we live it: Time is always lost.

Time: it always seems to us that the *true* hawthorns are those of the past—or because in effect the faith that creates exists only at the beginning—which is to say that reality is formed only in memory: i.e., at a distance, by evocation and especially by the re-creation of language. The past is lost—but strange resurrection by means of speech. Absence that rejoins (which can even alone *create*) presence—the sensible is no longer called to speech (last years of *Proust*)—whether by the body and memory or by speech, time becomes something other than succession: pyramid of "simultaneity." **[26]**

Space, we are speaking less about Proust's space; yet something of an analogue: the butterfly and the boat, the two paths that are perspectivally identical, are not at all so in my life; they have an entirely different ontological amplitude: the boat that silently goes from one branch of the rosebush to the other, that rumor, that crossing of space it envelops . . . Opposed to perspectivism: projection [198] onto a plane, immediate access to the depth of time or space—"promiscuity"—Identity and difference to be understood in terms of *Dasselbe* and not *das Gleiche*.

This = contributions to the presentation of the visible world's miracle and of its simultaneity, "notions without equivalent"—Now, on this point, Claudel, among more recent writers, resumes the same enterprise in a more violent manner.[82]

[27] More likely to seek this out in another.

II. "Simultaneity": Claudel[83] (See Wahl,[84] *Cahiers P. Claudel*)

With respect to this: description, neither a connection nor a composition (synthesis)—of a cohesion of being (against linear, serialized thought), which does not happen so much above [199] us (in a superior Being)[85] as it does below;[86] cohesion of space; cohesion of time; cohesion of space and time; cohesion of the human being with their space-time or of human being with human being, replacing all things for them; but cohesion that is not indistinction, that is of incompossibles, that is overlapping [*empiéte-ment*], absence or *Ek-stase*.

To be represented not by two lines: the line of successions and the line of simultaneities and myself at their crossing: the past is no more, the elsewhere is not here, so one ends up restituting the past and the elsewhere as *Vorstellung*, thus sacrificing their distance in order to maintain them in Being.

Successions do not make a line: where would we line them up? This does not only mean (Bergson): the spatial symbolization of time transforms it, deforms it; it is the exterior substituted for the interior, division with respect to indivision, of the kind that should find contact with "fusion" and with "interpenetration": this would still be a simply immaterial series; the critique covers all series, spiritual as well as spatial. The cohesion of time is not that of a chain, which comes from *Matter and Memory*:[87] the past exists for me because I have seen, i.e., through its flesh and my flesh, and as it is, not melded with my present but exactly incompossible with it. Cohesion through incompossibility—"time has become Ek-stase."[88] And this return to time is not a polemic against space: it is precisely the spatiality of what I have seen, its rivalry with what I see in the same space, where its phantom remains (which has *its* past), which makes the past exist, is not "virtual."

Neither simultaneous: I cannot truly think the antipodes as existing in the sense of this room. They are much "farther" than it. Simultaneity through the overlapping [*recoupement*] [200] of finite visible fields, carnal coexistence, co-duration.

Time and space are horizons and not series of things. And horizons that overlap [*empiètent*], one over the other: I read time in space and read space in time (what would a time be which would not happen in a Space and in the same space?). A single great differentiation of a single Being.

And I myself am not at the crossroads of these lines because there are no lines but at the hollow of a vortex of ontogenesis that projects and distributes spaces and times.

Claudelian "simultaneity" is this co-presence of horizon in the midst of parts of space, parts of time and of time to space and space to time. "I see Waterloo; and, over there, in the Indian Ocean, I see, at the same time, a pearl-diver, with head suddenly cutting the water, close to his cata-maran."[89] I am over there (past), over there (spatial) and here, at each hour is all hours, each season all seasons. Not reference to essence or idea but through differentiation within the flesh of Being. As each side of the chair is the entire chair.

The human being and their space-time.

So what, for example, is a country? It is a precipitate of space-time, a manner of spatializing and of temporalizing across that which humanity learns to Be, i.e., not only a geography and a history,[90] but a formula of inside-outside relationships.

Dutch painting[91] is not the external imitation of this space-time but bears the figures of Holland as the "Boundary of two worlds,"[92] relation of inside and outside.[93] "Interiors" "invite us more effectively than a treatise on asceticism . . . to the consciousness of our inner being, the contact with our ontological secret" (cited by Wahl, 239). [The inside is seen in the outside—grasps it better than itself. "Simultaneity" of the interior and exterior]—[201] [Relation to the outside that is not "representation" but ecstasy: "the gradual mounting and descending of the light **[28]** along the wall that we present to it."[94] And reciprocally, the visible is the transactions, the chemistry, the music, the interrelationship and the "operation of interests" of *Anima*.][95]

Human being and human being: passion.

Passion is, between two temporalities, something like the cohesion of a temporality with its past: it is the transfer onto a being of our own indistinction with all being.

> We are both alone in this horrible desert.
> Two human souls in the nothingness, who are able to give themselves
> to each other.
> And in a single second, like the detonation of time that annihilates
> itself, to replace all things, one by the other!
> (*Le Pain dur*).[96]

But this adhesion to the other is like everything that can only be maintained in distance. Because what desire takes is only a being and no longer Being—a "poor woman" who carries everything.

All of these themes in the Double Shadow (end of the second day of *The Satin Slipper*).[97] Passion created a "new being" in an instant, but it comes to pass in the "land of shadows"—by the light of the moon. In the visible, Rodrigue and Prouhèze are separated.

What is, exactly, the land of shadows, the sun of the night? Reconciliation in death?[98] The Double Shadow metamorphosized into a palm branch?[99]

No, it is, on the contrary, the most real: the "indestructible archives," "the page of eternity." The no-longer is founded on "having-been"—anti-Platonism: certainly [202] the visible is not everything—but what is truer than it is its double or shadow, which "only exists."[100] Each is the impossibility of the other, and the adhesion of one to the other was only "a single second"; but this being behind the present, which could not remain, has been inaugurated and created in the present. See Proust: "reality is only formed in memory"—It was not a matter of an *illusion* of reality. No, it is as good as what was remembered. The present "develops" all of its sense through distance. The past is not pure (immaterial) memory, and not image memory (conserved or re-created in the present), but past-shadow, visibility inscribed forever, flesh become essence. The past is another invisibility of the visible (there is the invisibility of present latency: that which is, behind me—that which is between the visibles). The past is what has been seen as a variant of the same being with which one still has dealings. The one who saw was the same eye who still sees, or rather who "listens," beyond the visible of fact, the universal visible. Not spiritualism but philosophy of the flesh and of the incorporeal as the front and back of the same Being.

[29] Disclosure of the visible world; And: speech as "intelligible mouthful"[101] [is] [a] signification thrown away as impure by the body and consumed by it; Speech bearing "the common essence to the sensations of past and present outside of time" (Proust, *Time Regained*, II, 47), [bearing] more generally "the common essence" to space and to time, [bearing] "the common essence" to the supported characters, the one over the other, one confused with the other, the common essence with the real and the imaginary. In brief, bearing not a signification that is an "the idea of intellect," but a signification that is a *metaphor*, put in relation to everything that our habits and our regulations [*contrôles*] separate, while the intelligence "directly releases from reality" its truths—Speech signifies through context, as a tatter [*lambeau*].

In this way, literary creation is clarified: How is it creation if what the writer says must be understood? On the other hand, how can one pretend that what he says preexists?

[203] Solution: the world that he says is a visible, sensible, mute World onto which we are all open. What he says comes to join the "keyboard," "keys" of our life preexisting in a sense. But there is precisely no preexistence as thing said. The light is for all what Proust's phrase says above—but this phrase is creation because signification only existed as the mute frame of the visible, hieroglyph, and these are the words that make it exist for itself.

Descartes, saying that not everyone is equal in their application but is equal in their capacity for understanding.[102] Inequality results, for him, from a methodical, deliberate use of a light that is the same for everyone. He underestimates speech and the exercise of speech here, which is something different from the use of the method. As for the natural light, there is one, but it is first of all the light of the visible.

Writers don't have the impression that they are creating or inventing because they are, in effect, in the process of deciphering the hieroglyphics of their landscape. But they create because (1) nobody would make these mute truths, taken from their landscape, speak for them; (2) once converted into things said, they take their place, if not as a picture within the visible, then at least within the World that is, like the visible, a call to speech—by reading them, others learn to say *something else* [*d'autres*].

This is not created ex nihilo, and one doesn't know exactly *what* is created (metamorphosis), but what is certain is that [204] one cannot prevent this from having been said; neither things nor the world are the same—the history of literature and of philosophy is not only the history of thought but the history of Being. Simply put, the writer himself does not always know where or how he changes the world—nor do his contemporaries.

Claude Simon:[103] I have invented nothing . . . of course, he says only his contact with things. But because it comes from, and is addressed to, this region beneath ideas, literature has an irreplaceable function. Because the solid, the durable, Being is there—Irreplaceable for philosophy itself:

Why? The "Preface" to *The Nigger of the "Narcissus"*[104] has immense value for Claude Simon: because of its "ideas," its "credulity," "persuasion," changing wisdom, and what is visible is the durable: that which traverses time, that which is outside of time. Conrad, "Preface" to *The Nigger of the "Narcissus,"* v–vi, viii, ix.

* * *

[3) Claude Simon].

Claude Simon: Time as "magma" and its deposit in space—monumental space and the "flesh of the world"—the promiscuity of the human being within the world—the event and history.

[30] Sartre on Lapoujade:[105]

There is a painting that cannot express pain and death without it being such or naked horror without beauty, clear style, that is to say old style become convention or the betrayal of pain and death by beauty (Titian);

Dilemma that exists each time one paints the figure;

It no longer exists if the painting, instead of presenting a figure from the outside, "invests" us with "created presences that are an integral part of each composition and yet transcend them [205] all."[106] "His presences could not be communicated through figurative art. The human figure, in particular, disguised men's suffering [*peine*]."[107] There is torture appearing as transparent fire with its hearth of pain [*douleur*]—or love appearing as nudes, couples who are not given through imitated contours, volumes, mass, perspective, but through being "put in the presence" of the flesh, of its radiation—or a crowd or gathering, painted not from the outside but in accordance with the link between activity and passivity that makes them a crowd: "How was the artist to paint the crowd seen by itself, as it experienced itself and makes itself, here and everywhere? How was he to curve space to inscribe in it the infinite circle whose center is everywhere entwined with its circumference?"[108]

Through the disintegration of the figurative, one finds a Beauty sought after by an internal requirement of the painting, which no longer hides pain and death while being the deep chord. Even the call of time accomplishes this consciousness of pain and death and this deepening of the painting—it also places the painter somewhere that is no longer in front of and outside of what he paints, but the painter paints himself by painting [*peignant*].

Generally valid: Claude Simon: his profound newness, no longer rendering what is outside space, time, human beings, according to their figure as "figures," external contours in transparency, but as "a thing that exists totally" (interview with Madeleine)[109] from which each experience we have is taken, the totality always showing through as a sort of encompassing of the magma.

Claude Simon: speaking about *The Flanders Road*: "everything **[30]** jumped up to my mind, all together, a kind of violent gust" (Madeleine's interview). "It was only a matter of writing the . . . [206] perception or the . . . I would not say thought, I do not believe that I think . . ." (Madeleine interview). He thinks like Cézanne "thought in painting";[110] he speaks with his voice and shows the world, lets it see with a certain gesture—but this type of disclosure of the world, without separated thought, is precisely modern ontology.

Demonstrating this not through the total study of his art, his language, his mode of presenting the world (indication at the end), but through some passages where he himself formulates, resumes his world.

[32] 1) Time[111]

There is another experience of time (1) of its very structure, (2) of its relationships with the rest; time that is a "presence" and not a "figure," and where the one who speaks is grasped.

[112] Second-degree silence of hooves in the night—these "thousands" of hooves: these noises are no longer something in time, figure, but background, gradient of time—something "majestic," "monumental," absolutely great, ultra-thing. "The progress of time itself," "invisible immaterial with neither beginning nor end nor point of reference." This is not a container; it is time itself as presence. Nor is it something in space (on account of their resemblance, the sounds of the hooves do everything) and not even a collective, great mobile thing, the regiment moving in space: the cavalry is "slouching," "advance without progression."[113]

This sound is like the rain, like the night is "encompassing." Time is an "element," the "nibbling sound . . . thousands of insects would make gnawing away at the world."[114] Time becomes that which [207] digs into and weakly shifts the world. Amplification toward the past and toward nature, insects, crustaceans within (under) an icy mass. Is it present, is it past? *Element* time.

[115] This is an oneiric structure of time. There are others—but in every case, opposed to a "threadlike" time,[116] for "thick" time (arrested in space)—i.e., space of the present made into part of time—Which thus believes in the multiple—and consequently: the past-present relation of a space-time to a space-time, and not of an object that was and is no longer to another that is. The past-present relation is a relation of a time-space to another that tears it apart;[117] this is not to conceive it as the degradation of continuous, ideal time but as time itself. Time lacks Italian perspective[118]—this means, says Claude Simon, that our memories are not stored chronologically in order [33] of decreasing clarity. But this would only affect our "consciousness" of time: time in itself would remain

in place, subject to perspectival representation, with the exception of the possibility of more violent memories—This means something more: that, as the path traveled includes trees hidden in the perspective of the point of arrival, presents linked in time are not reconcilable within a single view, such that when you open one you find behind it another present that clarifies the first—trundled present [*présent-gigogne*], but moreover the past that it includes decenters it, is another world. The simultaneity of time is this: the coexistence of incompossible presents within it.

Time[119] must not be thought separately from space, without which there would be no present. It is a property of [208] this space and not only of "consciousness"—Monumental time of the clock, time of the rail-like night, of cars, time of the world that is its immense clock, a clock that is not only a landmark of time but at the limit of time itself.[120] Space can be a symbol for time only because it first participates in time's genesis.

Hence the wall is not a symbol of time alone—a support that we would hang onto in order to think the pure relationships of filiform succession that would need no space. The years pile up on top of each other; time is this very wall—or a face[121]—built by lifting up the preceding years.[122]

[123] Because time is this: sedimentation and tearing apart—sedimentation means that each new situation effaces everything, that being is always complete—and yet we know quite well that there has been something else. . . .[124]

There is something else: the present torn apart by *sensation*.[125]

[34] In total, there is no serial Time—not only spatialized—but also no series where the existence of an end annuls and replaces the existence of the precedents such that only one term would exist at a time.

What is there is not a series but a nesting [*emboîtement*]: the present (always sensible and always spatial) holds other presents within its depths (that which has passed in this same visible before this same seer). Ordinarily one does not open it; it seems to be enough, complete, and the other presents have reality only in general (the catch-all of memory). Sometimes tearing apart, abyss, true memory occurs through the sensible itself, but it is still a dimension of the sensible: it is only in this odor in the landscape that the individual past palpitates. Past and present do not rise in a series. Besides, the present itself, when looked at carefully, is neither a point nor a segment of time: the unity of time is always a cycle (for example: the day, or the course [209] of 6¼ hours) in the sense that we take the word in nature (the nitrogen cycle)—For example, afternoon is the day that "has happened" (Sartre). The day is like the opening of a bud.

And the structure of a cycle is general like those of buds or clustered flowers. The generality of time, the concept of time (which is not only irreversibility but also eternal return: it is different only because it is the same), which is lived even in the present, derives from this nesting [*emboîtement*] inside the present that is "under way." One cannot set presents up in a series where they form a series of another degree and where each present, moreover, carries, alters, and maintains all of the preceding ones.

Thus, there is no line or series of time but a trans-temporal core—Visible or World—a kind of eternity of the visible, like a container that secretly "leaks" [*perd*], and thus is always ahead of and late to the present, never on time.

(2) Space **[35]**

As nesting [*emboîtement*] time, nesting space, vegetative space, like the one over which the bud has power, space of proliferation, akin to our flesh.

The alternative: it understands us—I understand it—it is transformed—it is no longer thinking nature-reed, it is two modes of our being-flesh: either we are statues or we are flesh in the "flesh of the world."[126]

Space is the relationship of our flesh to the flesh of the world. Hence, [such an] extraordinary description[127] of the space of the body. It is a space of ubiquity where bodies are overprinted, one upon the other (mirrors [*les glaces*] are here only a limit case), where the places are nested [*s'emboîtent*], one within the other, each sensible given (the sound of the stopper against the bottle) opening the trundled [*en gigogne*] latencies (the latency of the neighboring bathroom for Louise, of the [210] room beyond this bathroom for Sabine). Louise sees herself in the mirror while Sabine speaks to her, i.e., she is within Sabine and outside of herself. It is no longer even she who looks: it is her image in the mirror who is looking at her and insulting her because it is true and miserable; one can say this, and it is stupid that one can say it, because she is this ridiculous idea of herself that she gives off that she sees . . .

For example, the death of Reixach—"thoughtful and futile" Reixach—thinking about a revulsion—"the murderer" in front of Reixach, the narrator behind, "that is, between us—I following him and the other man watching him advance—we possessed the totality of the enigma (the murderer knowing what was going to happen to him and I knowing what had happened to him, that is, after and before, that is, like the two parts of a shared orange cut in half and that fit together perfectly) in the center of which he rode ignoring or wanting to ignore what had happened as well as what would happen, in that kind of nothingness (as it is said that in the center, the eye of a hurricane there exists a perfectly calm zone) [36] of knowledge, that zero-point. . . ."[128] Space, the surrounding world, morally as well as physically close through me because they are full of hidden others who know many things that I don't think about, who are, one says, myself, and who fit exactly, one over the other—and me in the middle thinking nothing, at least not all of that, zero-point, impalpable space, invisible fault of space. "Some good eyes that we have, that we can't see both sides of an orange at once" (Stendhal—Blin, *Problemes du roman*).[129] And yet they are both, and we see "an orange," and we are installed in the middle of a visible that we do not know . . . [211]

(3) The magma of humanity

The "flesh of the world" is not a metaphor for our body in the world. One could say inversely: it is just as much our body that is made of the same sensible fabric as the world—Neither naturalism nor anthropology: human beings and time, space, are made of the same magma.

For example, as time is nesting time, there is a sort of overlapping [*empiétement*] of bodies, one on the other, and what happens to one, its life and its death, metamorphoses the duration, the age of the other.

—The flesh of Rose: flesh of woman, that is, mother, that is, containing the human-witness, that is, protecting him from time, and now by death bringing him into the world in a "void," and is thus older than him since she has touched the common goal before him and since he has only just been born. . . .[130]

Coming to the age given to him by Rose's death—Promiscuity of birth, of love, and of death.

This mixture and overlapping [*empiétement*] already exists because we see, that is to say, we see the others see with an extraordinary subtlety; we see with the eyes of others as soon as we have eyes. See *The Grass*: "something that emanated from the raised hand (although it didn't move) from the eyes (although they didn't move either) fixed on her. . . . , this constant physical pressure of the eyes, of the hand."[131] It seems like a sixth sense because we believe that one can only see visible things or qualities: but I see bodies stretched over [37] the world and over the same world that I see, their infinite gestures, I wed them, I see them from within.

Human beings are also trundled-human beings—if we could open one, we would find all the others, as in Russian dolls, or rather less well-ordered, in a state of indivision.

The meeting of human beings is rumor, argument.[132] For example, Maurice, in *The Wind* [212] seeking consolation from Montès because he has been prevented from serving time for blackmailing a letter he stole from Montès.[133]

Human beings speak in order to discharge what they have to say; what they have to say is neither thought nor understood as signification; they are like projectiles they throw at each other, "something stronger than blows, harder than matter itself: words."[134] So strong and so hard that when one removes it from the spectacle, it is transformed: (breakdown of sound film) "like under the influence of narcotics or corrosions"—language [is] incrusted within the visible and holds its place.

This magma is not only disorder, change, unreason. It is also the excess of sense. A kind of surplus of sense that comes upon human speech and action as if they couldn't help it; a human being is the carrier of ideas (passions, qualities, intelligence, idiocy) who has infinitely more sense than "what we think is us and makes us talk act hate love"[135]—come and dwell within us—draw a picture. Again, a face is an enormous emblem full of sense: Iglesia falling asleep is like an Aztec or Incan death mask, "set motionless, impenetrable and empty on the surface of time, that is to say that kind of glue, of greyness without dimensions in which they were sleeping, waking, moving, falling asleep and waking again without, from one day to the next, any variation whatever to make them think it was the next day and not the day before or even the [38] same day."[136] Masked man or marionette posed on the magma of time, precise form that covers the formless and which makes it so that there is nonetheless something to say about it, a history to recount . . . For example, the old woman in *The Grass*: her face, her makeup, reminiscent of a "primitive and barbaric cult."[137] Any face, perhaps, any passion, any action takes on this monumental aspect when one compares them to the shapeless time upon which they are placed: for example, Helene, in *The Wind*, watching her father and Maurice through a window, "immobilized in time's [213] density," "seeing her then (Helene) stopping in mid-stride in the shadowy vestibule . . ."[138] and so forth.

Human and inter-human magma draw these monumental figures, lacking common measure with our "thoughts." Of the kind where the formula of the world is not the absurd: "I think that non-sense is still an invention of poets and philosophers. A replacement value of some kind. The absurd destroys itself. To say that this world is absurd is to admit that one still persists in believing in reason. It took me a long time to discover that this is how it was and to convince myself of it. To discover that there was nothing to correct, only to take—everything to take—and that everything which has been, was, and would be was sufficient in itself, was sufficient and well beyond satisfying the more urgent desires, that one would never arrive at satisfaction with the sumptuous magnificence of this world as long as one manages to be a conscious being."[139]

(4) The world as total existence

Mixture is chaos but is also the proliferation of sense. Mixture of the past, present and future, of the imaginary and the real, one communicating with the other (daydreams about a portrait of an ancestor that has a bloodstain on his forehead, the stories about him—crystallizing on Reixach and his death—and all this, through what Iglesia the jockey says, crystallizes on Corinne, whom the narrator will love after the war)—(the three themes preceding each other, tying one to the other, constituting not a chaos but a sort of circular growth where each is determining and determined). Especially in terms of the imaginary, discovery of a new imaginary: that of the stories of others, of people about whom others speak, and who are unobservable but constitute a real associate (past or future): Sartre had only thought of the "ego" in order to go beyond the [39] observable . . .—mixture of others and myself—

In all this, what is a "decision"? A kind [214] of failure, like the cracking of a falling tree[140]—decision is not ex nihilo, is not of the now, always anticipated, because we are everything, everything has accomplices in us. One does not decide to do but to allow to happen.

And what is the event, the composition of beings and things? The same event occurring from outside (the death of Rose) does not come from outside, is anticipated in Montès and also matures in him, like everything.[141] It is less something that happens than something that cannot not have been—"last sentence of a slow and inexorable genesis." For example, the scream: "As if the one who moaned was only a passage taken by the scream," ". . . the woman screaming in terror at this mysterious thing that used her body, mistreated it, tearing it apart in order to accomplish what must be accomplished"[142]—like birth and like death—prepared, planned, desired—feared, done, and undergone and out of all proportion with the planned. "I hadn't thought of that" and "I always knew it" (oneiric consciousness).

For example, the war: the pre-human within humanity, disgust, fear, and joy of the "all is permitted." "This alleviation, this illusion of freedom that comes with the taste and feeling of being irresponsible, joyous and frightened at the sight of this flouted universe without facades, stripped of everything except nudity and sacrifice and where, despite the codes of what you were taught about your own character and that of others, something is happening: blood, fire, shards beyond all human measure, escaping all human will, something grand, a mystery, like music or birth, leaving you wondering, dizzy, and confused."[143]

When it doesn't pretend to do something, history still contains this knot of forces and of means dispersed in what happens [*ce qui advient*], carries a name, will henceforth be, can no longer not have been. . . .

Thus history is not "the united and reassuring process of an adventure" (i.e., of a project, of an enterprise), but [215] something that "is done" without a direction fixed in advance, without apparent order, without respite (commentary on *The Grass*). All objects, all the visible, all characters, one "transparent" to the others, one dwelling within the other, one implicated or nested within the other, all start to breathe "with an imperceptible and total respiration like that of vegetation"; "no one makes history, it is not visible, just as it is impossible to see grass grow."[144]

(5) Art

We understand "technique" through what it means to show (and if one doesn't understand it, it's through a lack of curiosity, because one does not sense what it is to show and what immediately insinuates it); the deleted punctuation (not always, not when it chants [*scande*] the narrator's emotion), deleted when it "cuts off," when it breaks the "violent gust" of the world. The relative or total substitution of the interlocutors [40]—not only in order to show that one has misunderstood—or that the others are indistinct—but to show that we do not live with consciousnesses, each of which would be an inalienable, unsubstitutable I, but with people gifted with a verbal body and who change this verbal body. Each one can be, according to the moment, I or You or They, or (which is something else) element of a We, You or They and that in its own eyes. Insofar as we live in language, we are not only I; we haunt all grammatical persons, as we are at their intersection, at their crossroads, at their tuft. The usage of pronouns and grammatical persons in the novel (Michel Butor)[145] expresses a certain relation, among all of these, of the author to the characters and the reader. In Claude Simon there is no employment of pronouns but the employment of undivided sentences within the magma.

The narrator's recitation (not in the same sense as Proust—In Proust it is the writer living and passing from there to the work, the story of this passage constituting the same work). [216] Here it is rather a story told by someone who hasn't seen everything, and who relates to what is told to him, a story thus opening onto nested stories—like the world abounds in associated aspects—of stories with an archaic structure.

The figures [*personnages*] are (more than "characters" [*caractères*] defined through the interior point of view or personal project) the bearers of ideas that descend into them without their knowledge, like the figures of an altarpiece.

"It is no longer a question of translating time through time, but [of a] simultaneity, "a thing which exists totally" . . . (Madeleine interview).

[41] Claude Simon is referring to the "Preface" of *The Nigger of the "Narcissus."* Conrad: "the visible universe"—he finds the "fundamental," the "durable" and "essential," "the very truth" of his existence.[146]

Thinkers: they go "beneath the visible world," they are addressed to "credulity," intelligence [and] inquietude or desire for peace, they serve our *profound interests*.

"The artist" returns to this region "of effort and intimate struggle"; he discovers a "message" that is not addressed to our combative nature, a more reticent message, "less precise," "more profound," and which addresses itself not to "wisdom," not to "acquired" qualities, but to the most "durable" in all men; addresses itself in accordance with and to our capacity for "joy," "admiration," for "mystery," or solidarity with creation and with all solitudes (for example, the obscure existence of people who are "simple, naive and without voice"), who give value to all the places of the earth, "places of splendor" or "dark corners"; it is "temperament" speaking to "temperament," thus through impression of "the senses," "because temperament is individual or collective," is not subject to persuasion" (viii); for example, the arts; this sensoriality obtained through works of the style . . . ; "shows," "with the sole power of written words" (ix); which does not satisfy "wisdom," does not persuade, does not edify, [217] amuse, or ameliorate. But in *vision* everything is given in addition and then some: the "vision of truth" (ix).

To show a "fragment of life," to keep it against time, to show its "vibration," its "color," its "form" and hence the "substance . . . of its truth . . . ," "the evocative secret, the force and passion . . . at the heart of each persuasive instant" (x).

Solidarity "in the mysterious origin" and for the uncertain destiny that unites human beings with themselves and with the visible world.[147]

Art stops human beings from working at their lives for a moment, and in that instant the entire truth of life is found: "a moment of vision, a sigh, a smile, and the return to an eternal repose" (xii).

Claude Simon (Conclusion) [42]

What is literature? How is literature possible? More precisely: how is the literary work (1) created, i.e., absolutely new, i.e., definitively modifying the universe of culture, (2) yet understood, which presupposes pre-existing "keys" in the reader? In any case, the capacity to apprehend this language—thus immanence of the new—this amounts to asking (a) what does *true* literature consist in? (b) What is the nature of "literary ideas"?

The literary work is created and yet understood because (a) it is created *as a thing said* but not ex nihilo: from what the writer sees. The writer: I have invented nothing. I say of things what I have seen. Claude Simon and the mirrors of the two bathrooms. Butor: "the novelist is the one for whom nothing is lost"—Claude Simon: the visible is infinite and literature is infinite—one can always find things to say at a higher magnification. One has always lived enough to write. Does he mean: copy of what is? Duplication of what is? For the writer: what he says is what he has seen—but the thing seen is [218] polymorphous or amorphous. To see is not to think.[148] To write *what one has seen* is in reality to shape it. Like drawing is something other than connecting the dotted lines of vision. Like a picture is something other than a copy. Everyone has seen mirrors, had the experience of adjoining rooms where one can hear what is said in the other room, etc. But when what is not ignored is said (emphatically, in preference to something else) and read, then that thing, through isolation as well as passage into the imaginary (the reader does not see, does not make use of his visible world and his constituted language as a *means without which* there is no literature, but which is in no way a *means by which* there is literature: neither "images" nor even evocation of the *sense of words* when one reads) becomes, not a thing seen, but *dimension,* "coherent deformation" (Malraux). Another, who "had" all that in his field, would not have "thought" to say it. In what sense can one say that he *had* that in his field? In the sense only that, when one speaks to him he finds it there. Like the amateur seeing the painting, [one] finds a means to "see it" without being able to make it. *Coherent* deformation: what is important is *coherent.* Because everyone can deform and does. But that the deformation is *coherent,* i.e., overlaps from one landscape to another, from the landscape to human beings and their discourse: from the discourse of one to the discourse of the other. What does this overlapping consist in? In diverse visibles (or: the present and the past: Proust) or insofar as visibles and human beings include differentiations, reliefs of the same order, or are mounted on the same axes, participate in the same essences, or are *metaphors* for each other, even attest to "divergence" [*écart*]. The universe is defined not by *what one sees, what one says,* but precisely by what one does not see, precisely what one does not say: by the difference between one and the other. From this *difference,* the author is author, as she is in her own manner of dealing with the visible through the gestures of her body: *someone,* that's it, these invariant symbolic matrices. Vision is style. In hearkening to [*entendant*] a divergence through vision, a manner of not being everything. Thus, there is creation, although nothing is done from scratch. [219]

(b) And there is comprehension, although what the writer brings forth does not preexist absolutely—whoever is not a writer always has the impression that there is nothing to say—and yet when something is said, they "comprehend" it—See Descartes: not everyone is equal in their application but is equal in their capacity for understanding. He explains this through a difference of *art*. But exactly: in what does art consist? Is it a method? But it is spontaneous method first. Does it always remain so? The rules of the method presuppose what is in question (Leibniz's: see what there is to see, etc.). Intellectual "vision" is not equal in everyone. Would it be through labor? But not everyone knows how to labor. Claude Simon says the same thing. *Labor* is speech and vision, i.e., decentering, relief, dimensionality, a manner of relating to *Sein* through such-and-such *Seiende*. Thus, there is no equal capacity for labor. There is a common capacity for comprehension because (it is the fact of vision in the nonartistic but common sense) the given is polymorphous, amorphous, not fixed. Descartes has defined vision badly, which is not the seizure of a *simple* element that cannot be given in half but first of all the constitution of a field, of a background, and of a kind of relief on this background—as such not intellectual vision—style is vision. The capacity to comprehend is not the same in all: there are those who simply understand that the things said rejoin and transform their experience. And there are those who comprehend or recognize [*recomprennent*] in the sense that it makes them want to write in turn *something else* . . . Fecundity of art. One speech arouses another speech. Why? By virtue of the power of continuous metaphor. All literature is grafting, surgery [*surgeon*]. "Ideas" (even those "of the intelligence") always grow sideways, laterally (even in philosophy). By definition (dialectically), an idea is never *what it is.*

All of this [is]: (1) conceptualization of visibility not as possession of a system of qualities but as possession of a grid, of a typical relief, of gradients (dimensions); (2) conceptualization of speech not as invention but as dictated by this structure of vision, this texture not only in black and white, but still in [220] color. Speech is structuring—indirect speech and not modeled on significations.

Hence, the literary work is not the addition of a positive surplus to what exists (progress). But rather means that nothing can be as before. The path of the future is not traced, but certain paths are blocked or downgraded. [221]

II. Descartes

Why this beginning? Useless if it were to say what **[1]** Descartes has said, in the order he said it, in response to *his* problems. Is it for him to pose our problems? Illegitimate if they didn't exist—absurd even—but neither "our problems" nor "his problems." In other words, determination of unknown terms in relation to known ones—Descartes in the *Regulae* has defined the questions he poses in this way—but these are questions that do not cover over his philosophy: the questions are arranged in a series according to dependence—to know according to order—but does the order of his reasons account for (1) what was before (sensual man)? Is his philosophy simply implicit, inseminant, in nonphilosophy? A few hours a year—in the *Meditations*, he does not advise anyone to undertake this endeavor like the author. It distracts one from the world. Thus philosophy concludes the world, validates the world, but in very diverted, contrary ways.[1] Baillet[2] describing [Descartes's] rupture of 1619—Rendering the mind *naked*. The science within humanity, of which there are vestiges, is well hidden. The method is natural but that means: recurrence of the method implicated in its own presentation, which presupposes itself, which is constructed, hence finally questions its own value. This question uproots—transforms—it opens the field of Cartesian reasons. But this field is not everything: it is instituted through reversal. (2) Especially as these reasons end up validating not only the natural light, of which they [222] are a part, but also natural inclination, feeling, the union. And this is necessary for there to be truth in the natural light: "If everything is true, nothing is false" and "if nothing is false, nothing is true."[3]

Truth of understanding and truth of feeling is troubled by the understanding and the inverse, in relation to [feeling] the understanding is negative (Gueroult I, 323).

Hence relationship philosophy–nonphilosophy: one leads to the other but leads there through reversal—the first reversal is passage to the *Cogito*, the second reversal, return to the existing world, to the union.[4]

If Descartes conceives of *his* philosophy in this way, it is not a series of positive truths in linear order, or a simple explication of given seeds. It is movement, a path [*chemin*] and truth that is only here in the ensemble;

the precept of observing the order means precisely that any proposition should be resumed in totality—"Night" of doubt, hypothesis that *nihil esse*, immediately discovering the *natural light*, that which *is*: it is the first moment of his philosophy; then the second moment: the natural light leads to the light of God, but this turns out to be incomprehensible, like an abyss of power ex nihilo, in particular, able to bind together two substances whose essences negate each other: the soul is corporeal.

If this is Descartes's philosophy, the establishment of an intelligible light against the sensual human being and the visible world, then it relatively justifies feeling; it must contain (if its second moment is not simply a denial of the first) an ambiguous relation of light and feeling, of the invisible and the visible, of the positive and negative. It is this relationship or mixture that we should seek.

It will not be found following Descartes's order (truth through knowledge, order of his thoughts): of course [223], it should not be preferred to the order of matters (nature, man, God) that would break the chain of reasons and would be acceptable only if there were separate reasons. We seek, on the contrary, not to separate them, but to find a central relationship operative throughout (in all matters), a certain manner of identifying and differentiating that is the principle of cohesion, the fiber of Cartesian being. That is different from the order of reasons insofar as this order is always made of a series of statements, of proofs. For example, the "Sixth Meditation" includes the more than moral certainty that feeling indicates the existing world. Not that this feeling communicates with this world, but because it is also validated by veracity. It is thus reasonable to feel [*de sentir*] with all the included inclinations. The framework for Cartesianism to seek would be, not this armature of statements about knowledge, but the experience, the relationship with being that it expresses (for example, the description of the objective reality of the sensible in the "Sixth Meditation," which is the "differential of Being and Nothingness," Gueroult). Perhaps, [one will] indeed find a fiber of Being, a nexus in experience, in contact with Being—not of reasons or thoughts. Wahl,[5] for example: the idea of the instant and the idea of light (physics—action of thought— auto-creation of God), the idea of the instant [2] or of light that includes inner movement (what Descartes has alternately said about the instant as a very small time, as the negation of time and that as fiction), these diverse significations being not one-to-one relations to a certain moment of the order of reasons, but connected together within a texture of Cartesian Being.

This is why we have said "Cartesian ontology." To take Descartes, precisely as he goes "from knowledge to being," not as someone to whom our idea of an experience of Being does not apply. But as someone who has had a certain experience of Being, expressed precisely in this official priority of knowledge.

We do not take Descartes at his word on this matter. Especially, [224] we do not follow his advice to stick to his conclusions, nor do we imitate him. But it is necessary to imitate him to understand him. And we don't pose a *problem* to him that he would ignore (we assume the problem of history). In truth, we don't pose any problem to him. We instead attempt to explicate a *mystery* (his mystery), to know his relationship to being indirectly attested to by certain recurrences from one end of his work to the other, recurrences of words, examples, notions (light, being and nothingness, *videre* [vision], *simul ac* [simultaneity]). [Recurrences] not exempt from restoring the order of reasons, but from which the order of reasons is not exempt (unless Descartes was perfectly successful and we only have to know his conclusions), because it is the Cartesian examination of Being.

By opposing his approach to ours, we do not impose on Descartes questions that he did not ask himself: if his philosophy were simply one of knowledge, it would be a special case of ontology, since it would be necessary to think the being of knowledge.

[6] So, under the order of reasons, before and after it (Descartes arranging his thought in a rigorous series), there is the natural functioning of the human being with their truths, especially in ambiguity, and the false questions of their "philosophy"—Then, the Cartesian *"search" "for truth" "through the natural light* which, entirely pure, and without help from Religion or philosophy, determines the opinions that an honest man must have on all the things that can occupy his thought."[7] But this natural light, which displaces so many problems (movement) (the *ubi* [when]) by bringing back the *per se nota* [that which is self-evident], presupposes itself. The rule of division being applied to the presentation of the method itself, the whole is justified by the development of knowledge. Is there not a residue that knowledge, according to our nature, does not exhaust? Yes— philosophy, which one doesn't do without. There is something deeper than the evidence of fact. Search no longer for a [225] "useful" method (*Regulae*), for a wise use of human vision, but for a veracity at the heart of things, for a veracity of Being.

Now this veracity, once discovered, guarantees the natural light put in suspense, but only partially: not as measure of what is. It does not close our universe. Especially if, in front of it, the *corpus esse animatum* [body to be animated] is a contingent proposition (*Regulae*); the experience of my body forces us to speak of an essential union, and of a body (the human body) that has a sort of indivisibility, that it is the body of a soul. Broadening [3] the natural light, which is going to recognize a "purity" of feeling that would be disturbed by the understanding. There is a truth of the false and a falsity of truth. This means that the "sensual man," justified in the "Sixth Meditation," [who] challenges the purification of the first two, would need to begin again. Blindness is relatively well-founded, and it is founded on the light itself. It contests the natural light and its name. Thus there is something after the series of reasons.

This circularity and dialectic—opposed to the linear—opposed to Descartes's manifest attitude: philosophy and nonphilosophy with neither overlap nor conflict, philosophy giving us reasons to stop doing philosophy.

But in saying dialectic, I want to say: thought that does not efface its traces, that does not forget its path [*chemin*], where the path co-defines truth, where the "conclusion" is not more true than the development [*cheminement*], where the end is also the beginning, and inversely. Therefore, recognized dissonance and movement that exist in Descartes (point of view of the naturing, point of view of the natured, to which the different views on the instant correspond, for example, instantaneous action, time, reconciled in the total view of continuous creation, even at the interior of the instant—and the continuous creation of God through himself), that make the order of reasons a pluralistic principle that Descartes disguises as a linear order leading to conclusions. I do not want to say: dialectic in the sense that moves around oppositions and differences. That is why I have not said dialectic but rather ontology, i.e., seeking [226] in Descartes the constant principle that assures differentiation and integration and that remains through the successive stages.

[1] APRIL 13, 1961

> For earlier and later in any duration are known to me by the earlier and later of the successive duration which I detect in my own thought, with which the other things coexist.[8]

1st Part: Being according to light and distinction.
2nd Part: Being according to feeling and its "coexistence."
Conclusion: Intellectual intuition and being.

1st Part: Being according to light and "distinction."

Ontology in the modern sense: these are all the problems (and first of all "knowledge") interior to a first circumscription of Being—To go "from knowledge to being" is to imply a certain ontology, a certain carving-out [*découpage*] of being.

Now, Descartes does speak of being, but as the contrary to the interior of knowledge—hence we ask him a question he does not pose to himself, to which he does not respond—But if the question is posed, is dominant, he must implicitly respond to it—the meanderings of the order of reasons must attest to the impact of the initial carving-out [*découpage*]—"return" of Being (as Freud said "return" of the repressed).

Therefore we follow this order of reasons; we do not ignore it—but we do not take his word for it—we confront everything with experience. Besides, is there not an indication of a Cartesian ontology in the modern sense in Descartes himself? Not at the *interior* of the demonstration, of the [227] argumentation, but through a problematic conceptualization.

Of Descartes, as of Malebranche, should we not say that "the analysis collapses the façade of clear and distinct ideas in order to discover a vast intuition given or refused as a whole; which, far from the power of being demonstrated, is anterior to all proofs" (Gueroult, *Malebranche* I, 25–26)? This implied intuition would be attested to especially by favorite examples, recurring metaphors (light, eye, *intuitus mentis*),[9] favorite words (pure, naked, specific), or even prepositions (*simul ac . . .*), "evident" principles often invoked ("nothingness has no properties").

It is not a matter of a psychological *explication* of Descartes,[10] and still less reading Descartes like a thinking machine might—the explication makes the order of reasons into a simple *appearance*—now Descartes is not the debris of an entire life; he is that which has made those givens into language, a universe of thought.

It is a matter of detecting the piles that undergird the order of reasons itself—Gueroult himself makes great use **[2]** of the concept of light (See Laporte:[11] seeing—to know is to see—even in God there is *vision*, *videre* and *velle*)—And J. Wahl, at first, as well as the notion of the instant and of simultaneity—it is not a matter of saying "visual" philosophy, or of considering this metaphor as a sort of false philosophy. Descartes himself teaches us that there is a symbolization of spiritual things by visible things (wind → mind → light → instantaneous [228] action), that perhaps the imagination extracts the sparks of truth from reason better—overall, he teaches us that there is a spatial "*integumentum*"[12] of the mind, that presentation through the sensible is useful for "man only [as] man," that what makes the character of metaphysics exceptional and must limit it to "once in a lifetime" and to "a few hours per year" is that it must do without the imagination, that in the end maybe we should say that for human beings, composed of soul and body, and whose whole soul must be united to a body, there is no absolutely pure intellection . . . Hence, in marking the constitutive role of "light" or "simultaneity" in it, we indicate not a psychological explication but the figures of his ontology.

Therefore, taking into account the order of reasons, let us attempt to identify the ontology that it expresses and hides. And first, opposite to the opening onto the world we have spoken about (relationship to Being accomplished from the inside—carnal—the seer-visible, relationship that is the interrogation of ourselves by the world as much as of the world by us), we place the Cartesian "beginning": his vision of the visible and the analysis through which he metamorphosizes it into vision of the mind.

1) [a] The Cartesian "beginning"—vision of the eyes and vision of the mind

Model of vision through the eyes: Descartes is aware that speaking about the vision of the mind is something new: "In case anyone should be troubled by my new use of the word intuition. . . ."[13]

Deliberately, expressly, he constructs the *intuitus mentis* upon vision of the eyes:[14] it is necessary, like artisans, to direct the gaze onto [a] *singula puncta*.[15] [229] Likewise, the *Principles*,[16] defining *perceptio clara et distincta*, gives the comparison: "I call a perception 'clear' when [3] it is present and accessible to the attentive mind—just as we say that we see something clearly when it is present to the eye's gaze and stimulates it with a sufficient degree of strength and accessibility."[17]

The initial relation with the visible is given as a model for the visible, the figure, the details, the irreducible elements—will say more later with respect to God, in the "Objections and Replies,"[18] to see the sea from afar and at once is entirely the same as seeing "the sea." But here he takes the figure in a field or against a background as a model and not the field or the background—i.e., what he calls the object of the gaze and what consequently is "present." This presence of the figure is all that is retained of vision. The rest of the field is composed of such figures not present. This eliminates the relationship to the background, which is of another kind (relationship of envelopment by the visual background, which includes a zero degree of vision, is not nothingness: the night that surrounds me and surrounds my body-figure). Openness to the *Umfang* [expanse], i.e., the figure being "over" a background, the *singula puncta* are integrated into a field of visibility that is not the sum of *singula puncta*, of visibles, that is the establishment of a *Sichtigkeit* [visibility],[19] openness to the visible *vor aller Thesis* [before any thesis]—Reduction by Descartes of being visible to consciousness of the visible: "from knowledge to being, the reasoning is sound."

Now, it is this reduction of visible being that orders the definition of the vision of the mind. After the comparison between clear perception and the fixation of the eye, "'distinct' if, as well as being clear, it is so sharply separated [230] from all other perceptions that it contains within itself only what is clear."[20] The distinct is that which not only is present, like the *singula puncta*, but contains *only* what is clear. No hidden lacunae—but how can we ever know, since Descartes denies that we ever have adequate ideas: "a fully adequate conception of things (and no one has this sort of conception either of the infinite or of anything else, however small it may be)"?[21]

We know that the clear contains only what is clear because we distinguish it from everything else—See the letter to Hyperaspertes.[22] The *positive*, truly productive faculty being able to conceive two things as completely separated from one another: and it is vision's loss to see two things as one. To see is to see not so much that one [4] thing is itself but that it is not the others: "In the same way, eyesight is more perfect when it distinguishes accurately between the different parts of an object than when it perceives them all together as a single thing."[23]

Thus the distinction, which makes the difference for the *intuitus mentis*, insists that it involves an exclusion of the other that the vision of the eyes never involves except only relatively.

Why? There is a *mentis acies* turned toward the things,[24] a gaze of the mind, which, like the gaze, will be a carving-out [*découpant*], isolating light and which will doubtless arrive, not at elements which would be adequately known, but at "things," [elements] about which we are sure that if they are known so little, [known] so completely, that they are *not* complex—one says that they are "self-evident"; one doesn't learn to see them; one sees them or one does not see them: the job is only [231] to "separate" them and "intuit each one separately with steadfast mental gaze."[25]

The operation of seeing, as far as they are concerned, is always the same—and moreover also the same with respect to more complex truths, if knowledge is knowledge—the light operating here is the same for all natures, like that of the sun, the same for all objects.

Thanks to the analysis of the vision of the eyes as vision of figures, a vision of the mind and an all-or-nothing intellection are thus defined—in the name of which most of the *problems* of philosophers are revoked in doubt.

Descartes rejects the problem of movement,[26] problems of the *ubi* [when],[27] in the name of this clarity that all other effort would obscure. Descartes even renounces, in the *Regulae*, treating the *extensio* through the *intellectus purus*—the imaginative conception that one has suffices. The *intellectus purus* would be philosophy.[28] [29]

Descartes defines legitimate questions in the name of the natural light. These are the ones where the unknown is designated through conditions that determine us, [conditions which] "point us decidedly in one direction of inquiry rather than another,"[30] i.e., where sought and given quantities are engaged in relations such that one can extract the *equality* of what is sought to certain givens[31]—i.e., not conceiving of a *new* being when one tackles a new phenomenon, seeking to think it separately from that for which one has evidence (the magnet)—in a sense, [232] is this not the contrary of philosophy? And doesn't Descartes say this himself, since what is most difficult, as he says, is to truly know what we *see*. . . . The heading "*The search for truth through the natural light, which, entirely pure and without borrowing from religion or from philosophy, determines the opinions that honest men must have on all things which come to occupy their thought.*"[32]

[5] Thus there is no sensible-intelligible break (there may be a distinction between sensible things). In *The Search for Truth*, the light of the intelligible is compared to that of a white color that one cannot conceive without having seen it. Simply put, it is prescribed to focus on the distinct that is necessarily clear.

One says: but is this not proven? *Regulae*, AT X, 417:[33] it is necessary only to proceed like the Astronomers—by constructing a model of the mind's function—the rest is nothing for us—a kind of humanist positivism—the vision of intellectual vision is itself presupposed; the method is born from natural *semina*; the rules of the method will be to construct the method. This is not the dialectic of phenomenology-absolute knowledge; this is only a constructive-humanist process, thought that no longer seeks to dwell in being—the intelligible is our vision.

But this is not all: Descartes was to enter philosophy upon the wind of doubt.[34]

APRIL 13, 1961[35]

1st Part: Our opening onto the world, relationship to being from the inside, carnal, the seer being visible—interrogative relationship. [233]

 1) [b] The Cartesian "beginning"—Positivism of the mind's vision.

Descartes is opposed to (1) interpretation of the relationship vision-thing—it is conceived as a relation to what is in itself: *extra nos, in re* (*Regulae*—the *details* that the artisan sees)—it is a relationship to figures and not to backgrounds.[36] This presupposes a thing in itself given to philosophy, the problem being only to know how the gaze carves out [*découpe*] the figures. No awareness or analysis of the [*Umfange?*], of the first opening through which there is the visible, the thesis of the world—it is a *consciousness*—reduction to sensible being.[37] (2) It is for this reason that, by simple explication, one discovers that seeing is an operation of the mind, inspection of the mind. Having removed the envelopes of vision, *naked* or *pure* vision can appear only in an emaciated [*décharnée*] way, pure reference to something,[38] position of a being in all or nothing, which is or is not for me, without medium [*milieu*], a grain of being, simple Nature. The distinction is the truth: clarity is not sufficient and adequation is impossible.[39]

 Hence, also the construction of the *intuitus mentis* according to the model [234] of this "reduced" sensible being: attention and the gaze—like this reduced being, the *intuitus mentis* is circumscription, abstraction, concentrated rather than diffuse light, the ensemble of ideas being assumed to be virtually given and only needing actualization—this is not learned—these presuppositions do not have to be justified—they are the spontaneous fruits of my nature—the method is implied in the construction of the method (division implied in the rules of division)—but: I touch my intellectual nature here at the same time that I exercise it—take it or leave it: that or nothing—the rest is like nothing for a human being—being is brittle.

 2) [a] The night of doubt: positivism and humanism

Yet is being, having been thus *reduced*, still being? In fact, I cannot doubt it—but my nature is presupposed, my involuntary and not posited being—they call into question the *intuitus mentis*—is it really a vision of the mind, or is it still my nature that speaks?

 In this very *question* Cartesian thought and ontology are attested:

Descartes will transform the question into a negative statement: deem everything false that can be called into doubt—doubt is voluntary, free; it consists in thinking that everything that is not absolutely is nothing. For Descartes, this is philosophy (his response to Gassendi: a philosopher would not have said that). For Descartes, a philosopher is the one who poses an alternative between Being and Nothingness—doubt takes place as if everything *nihil esse*—similarly, Descartes's refusal to consider Gassendi's objection that the dream's illusion is not proof against perception—Descartes: as soon as there is ambiguity, the possibility of error, it condemns the perceived in its entirety—Descartes does not wonder if this voluntary, thetic doubt itself presupposes a perceptual relationship to truth.

The question being posed in this way, the return of reduced or repressed being is accomplished under the form of a hypothesis of nothingness; this very manner of interrogation (this negativism) will go back [235] to the positivism that has been shaken: there will be a purification, a new reduction of being, but what remains will be absolutely pure and positive: the being of thought. Purification, stripped of the wax and of the *inspectio mentis*.

[40] The *cogito* as reflection that is contemplation—grasped in myself as an intellectual nature—inner knowledge that always precedes acquisition—the refusal of an indefinite reflexive regression—I grasp an idea of the mind in myself—I grasp myself as illuminating-illuminated light—Spinozist reflexivity—the *facultas cogitendi* contains in it the possibility of all ideas, the treasury of my mind, which are not separated from it. It is *virtus nativa*. And in this sense, it is spontaneity, although the understanding is passive and open to being through representation or to objective "reality." To know is to see, but here what one sees and what sees are one; it is the light disclosing itself at the same time as its objects—parallel with Malebranche, who never doubted being, for whom we are only darkness to ourselves and for whom the light is not mine. But is it really mine for Descartes?[41] [236]

[1] APRIL 20, 1961

[42] Descartes's initial reference to a clarity that overcomes interrogation: one would obscure it by interrogating it; *The Search for Truth*: against those who "cannot distinguish between what is clear and what is obscure, nor tell the difference between something which needs and merits a definition

if it is to be known and something which is best known just on its own."[43] "Thus it would be pointless trying to define, for someone totally blind, what it is to be white: in order to know what that is, all that is needed is to have one's eyes open and to see white. In the same way, in order to know what doubt and thought are, all one needs to do is to doubt or to think. That tells us all it is possible to know about them, and explains more about them than even the most precise definitions."[44]

This clarity-distinction is only clarified in reference to the senses, themselves understood in relation to *figures*, to non-complex forms rather than simple ones (without consideration of backgrounds, of inner and outer horizons).

Justification of this reference: distinction between simple and compound natures cannot be true, but it is *useful*. One will make certain assumptions: "certain assumptions must be made in this context which perhaps not everyone will accept. But even if they are thought to be no more real than the imaginary circles which astronomers use to describe the phenomena they study, this matters little, provided they help us to pick out the kind of apprehension of any given thing [237] that may be true and to distinguish it from the kind that may be false."[45]—It is "useful" to conceive sensing [*le sens*], even light, as corresponding to an action coming from the outside and imprinting a "figure" onto the body—this is useful because the figure "touches and sees itself [*se touche et se voit*]"—it is sufficient that "the consequences of this supposition are no more false than those of any other"[46]—thus, disregard everything in color except that it is figured and an expression of qualities by figures.

One distinguishes the true from the false in knowledge by means of concepts that are not necessarily true—See the *Optics*, thought through constructed models and not through submission to the phenomena; for example, light is defined by contact—it is the true and the false that matter for us—if I pose a question about instantaneous physical action, don't look at the magnet, or even at the light, but at a transmission of movement since "*Nihil magis sensibile* [Nothing is more sensitive]": the stone moves in time, but it transmits its motile power in the instant only if it is "*nuda* [naked]." For example, the solidarity of the two extremities of a stick—or again contrary effects of the same cause affirmed in accordance with a scale model—or again: instantaneousness of nervous actions without the material transport, by analogy to the movements of the top and bottom of a pen: what is transmitted does not necessarily resemble the image printed through the senses—the distinction itself[47] can only be acquired by these sensible models—principle of all of this: knowledge of a new being is not **[2]** access to a new type of being, or else I would need a sixth sense or a divine revelation to have knowledge of the magnet. All that will be knowable in it for the human being [238] must be composed of unknown simple natures—the rest would be nothing for us, and it is also sufficient to show that it is beyond our reach to know some proposition. The not-known—or at least the not knowable—is nothingness.

The same positivism for extension: everything that has length, width, and depth, without distinguishing *verum corpus* [true body] and *spatium* [space].[48] Descartes is not occupied with *extensio* without a subject or with "philosophical entities of this sort that are not genuinely imaginable"[49]— certainly, for the *intellectus purus* this *en abstractum* has a consistency, but these too-sharp distinctions dissipate the "natural light" (AT X, Rule XIV, 442ff.). [Descartes] no more wants to define place by the surfaces of bodies than to distinguish place as "intrinsic place,"[50] spatiality without subject: because it is a matter there of "the simple and self-evident nature by virtue of which something is said to be here or there. This nature consists entirely in a certain relation between the thing said to be at the place and the parts of extended space."[51]

[Yes, but does this exteriority not give rise to any questioning? What would Descartes have said if he had heard Hegel wonder about [*s'interroger*] the sense of Nature as absolute exteriority, to find precisely in this something to question, the answer being speculation, i.e., the fissure of the absolute subject . . . But he himself [Descartes] will not encounter questions of this kind, the problem of its composition in timeless instants or *minima* of time, if not for space then at least for movement, finally resolved by divine action as continuous creation.][52]

However: simple propositions of simple sight which cannot be sought and do not include the true and [239] the false can give rise to questions: there is a question of *dubitatione Socratis* as soon as Socrates turned toward his doubt; he wondered about doubting everything and affirmed that he did.[53] In this doubt about doubt, there is something that is not *per se notam* [self-evident].

Descartes could apply [these questions] to the *Regulae* and ask them if they didn't envelop a question of this kind: Laporte, the rule of division applied in order to arrive at formulating the rule of division—the method precedes itself—the *spontaneae fruges* [spontaneous fruits];[54] the *prima cogitationem utilium*[55] *semina* [first seeds of useful ways of thinking], *mentis lumine* [light of the mind].[56] The *vertigo* of the method among the ancients. He accepts this circularity because it is the condition of all human knowledge—but this requires that we do not do philosophy and that certainty remains pragmatic. If one wants to found it as certainty, one must show that this nature (*a natura in nobis insita*) is not chance; to wonder about it to show that the circle which makes the method assume the method (spontaneous) is not vicious, that one is justified by the other, that being is this very circle and does not remain on the outside. That human experience (Hegel) is [the] presentation of the absolute and that the absolute [is] *bei uns* [with us] in our experience.

It is this kind of *question* that engenders the *Meditations*, and which occupies a disproportionate place—Descartes always tries to repress it or resolve it through the natural light—but the kind of interrogation which introduces it with the first two "Meditations" represents a calling into question of its positivism, of its initial restriction of Being to the Being of figures.

2) [b] The night of doubt and the critique of the natural light

The natural light in the *Regulae* [is] valid because it is myself, human light. It is precisely this [240] same reason that makes it subject to doubt. The vision of the mind is in fact irrefutable and so forth; as to mathematical ideas, [they are] clear and distinct—but ("Fifth Meditation") is it not precisely "the Nature of my mind" which is such that "I cannot but help consider them true as long as I conceive them clearly and distinctly" (AT IX, 52)?[57]—Idea of facticity as opaque—perhaps there is something behind the "figures"—what do this hyperbolic interrogation (deem false what is doubtful) and this metaphysics (assume a malicious demon) signify when placed back into this zigzag?

"As if suddenly I had fallen into very deep water, I am so surprised that I can neither secure my feet on the ground nor swim to support myself above" ("Second Meditation," AT IX, 18)—new depth or dimension. How will we get out? By finding a ground, a *Grund* to walk on? Return to the positive—will the positive be what it was before?

Descartes tries (afterwards) to maintain the line of the *Regulae*: the construction of the malicious demon like that of the astronomers—twist a stick in the opposite direction [*sens*] to straighten it ("Responses to the Objections")—elimination of the negative, like auxiliary lines in demonstrations. It is through freedom that he has posited [3] doubt as false, that he "pretends" to doubt. This doubt will turn around and will be forgotten in what is negative: it will reveal a new positivity; that of thought about thought . . .

No, doubt is free and feigned, as well as hyperbolic and metaphysical (founded on contingent conceptions)—it cannot be otherwise: one naturally believes the evidence—but it is not reduced to these excessive negations: they are there to balance the custom of believing—it is the stick that one twists in reverse—but Descartes's attitude is not entirely defined by this "process": "it is necessary that I now stop and suspend my judgment on these thoughts" (AT IX, 17). "First Meditation": I cut the body, exterior things, off from myself, and if that doesn't give me the truth, at least "it is in my power to suspend my judgment" (AT IX, 17)—"Suspension." [241]

For example, the voluntarist *Cogito* of the *Principles*: even if I am deceived, I can suspend my judgment. Metaphysical doubt thus does not disclose a positive thought but a thought in suspense—thereby shedding light on other, more central formulations of the *cogito*: the thought that makes indubitable is thought in suspense, and doubt itself is not negatively rather than positively stated; it is thought in suspense which has this title, since being *what I seem* to see and see with evidence, is as such incontestable and alone right.

The Evil Demon, metaphysical doubt (i.e., even the obvious) is not [a] final scruple or an objection that would disappear without leaving a trace, leaving the same naive natural light as before. The Evil Demon is eliminated from the result, becoming a good Demon when one thinks about it better—but Cartesian reflection is not simply the elimination of the shadow [and] making way for the light, forgetting its own path. There is an overcoming of the Evil Demon, but it is an *Aufhebung* that conserves.

In grasping the notion of the Evil Demon as a hypothesis, opinion (but Descartes indicates that any dependence, especially toward a less powerful being, is more likely to lead me astray), one finds it inconsistent.

Power is being and if this power produced error, it would produce nothingness within me. Nothing in common with the Power of God, creator of eternal truths, whose principle is, on the contrary, that being can only come from being. In effect, upon reflection, one will see that the Demon is not a malevolent Demon but is God. But the Evil Demon at least resembles God in that, like him, he overflows the being of figures. He is contested by the *ground* but God will also be *ground*, abyss; he is [an] Under Being [*Sous Être*], upon reflection, but prefigures the Over Being [*Sur Être*] who takes his place—defect and excess: in the two cases, the simple being of the visible for the mind is contested.

That being so, does one find a *ground* upon which one can walk? Or else does one get used to living in the *Abgrund*? [242]

3) [a] *Cogito*

Two elements: (1) of fact: I think when I doubt—I am sure when I am not sure, sure of being not sure—the negation is a positing; it is not nothingness; (2) intelligible: "to think it is necessary to be"—in seeing this necessity (my thought is *not nothing*), there is certainty of certainty a fortiori because there is certainty of uncertainty. The first-person formula (God can't make me nothing) is stylized—it is uncreated necessity that is seized upon. Thought is to being as *Lumen* is to *lux*—pure understanding for pure understanding.

Cogito "simple, absolute nature," "My thinking in general," not certain general ideas of thought but an inalienable kernel obtained by cutting everything else off—"pure ego"—subordination of texts where Descartes speaks of a thought of several thoughts at once, subordination of texts where Descartes speaks about the thought of seeing and feeling.

Alternative: either psychological consciousness: notation, observation, or mathematically rational intelligence: grasping the rational necessities immanent to my essence, [4] clear and distinct idea of my soul in fact legible—but the *Cogito* is in this.

[The] *Cogito* [is] truth of a provisional type: not still truth "in itself" of the Self—this will be the *reines Für* [pure For].

In fact, the Ego who *cogitat* is individual but is grasped only as intellectual nature in general.

Question: can one make these distinctions? Doesn't the *Cogito* deny them? Are the in-itself or the for-itself not called into question?

According to this, the natural light is more aware of its limits; it is no longer the unscrupulous play of the "nature of my mind"—one has detected obscurity in it—like in the flame: it comes from a home [*foyer*] it doesn't know.[58] My capacity for forming ideas (for opening me [243] to being through representation) rests on my pre-significant contact with this natural thought that I am and with this body of mine whose union with me is *per se natum*—certainly there is nothing to confuse the natural light who "*ostendit* [shows]" with "eyes of the mind," *monstration*, pure domain of appearance with no irresistible impulse (natural inclination): it is manifestation, and there is nothing outside of it that can correct it. But precisely because one has opened the universe of the *cogitatio* as *universum*, one knows that it will have to think what it rejects. It poses itself as inside an obscure Being and is not satisfied with its "separated" essence (Gueroult), with its distinction or difference. Where, exactly, is the difference between the *cogito* and irresistible mathematical evidence? For Gueroult, it is only that it is simple, absolute nature, while they are relatively complex, decomposable. If this were true, the *Cogito* should immediately go outside of time and lead to the essence of thought and to the certainty that the soul always thinks. However, this is not the case.[59] Even after the *Cogito*, as soon as I turn my attention [away from it], it becomes obscure and the power of God within me makes me doubt. What has been gained? The instantaneous self is hardly more distinct than 2 + 2 = 4, i.e., there remains the relatively opaque presence of my nature to my nature—and without God, I would never know anything else— however, there is this difference (without which the passage through the *Cogito* would not change the philosophy of the *Regulae*): the *cogito* tends to get the upper hand; if I am at present, nothing will make it that I have not been—on the side of what is affirmed here (my *cogitatio*), there is nature (in reality supported by memory and the movement of my mind), there is the requirement of what has been and cannot cease having been, not as essence, but as past—presence of the past—the immutable, conservation becoming an ontological problem instead of being simple psychology, as in the *Regulae*. Gueroult: philosophy of the *Regulae* and of the *Meditations*: the second is clarity of the same [244] type as the *natures*, the *Meditations* adding to [the certainty of the *Regulae*] the certainty of certainty; going from *lumen* to *lux*, but it is only the disclosure of conditions of possibility—the *cogito* is one of intelligible necessity, *it + perfection* [*la + parfait*], *absolute* simple nature.

For myself: the *Meditations* show that the natural light of simple natures is borrowed from the flame of the *Cogito*, that it comes back to them as *cogitata*, and certainly we have nothing else to think other than the passage to appearance: the *cogitatio* as universal order of thought (as well as thought of seeing and of feeling). Gueroult is obliged to subordinate this text—also to subordinate the text where the *cogito* is founded on vision of many things at the same time—and to assume that Descartes goes from instantaneous and atemporal experience to atemporal nature—and to maintain the priority [of] simple natures over existential positions (philosophy of the *Regulae*).

For me, on the contrary, [a] strong sense of the order of the *cogitatio*'s inauguration; it is to the extent of saying: I am knowing, and the knowledge that I have cannot depend on something that I do not have—my thesis, on the contrary: there is the operative *cogito* or I am and the reflective *cogito* or statement, vertical *cogito* that *founds* the horizontal and which is not the simplicity of a pure nature (all the rest is no less "inseparable" from me).

[1] APRIL 27, 1961[60]

   3) [b] *Ego sum, ego existo*[61]

The *cogitatio* as universal milieu—change in the sense of the natural light.

Evidence of present mathematical ideas—the natural "yes"—what comes from the nature of my mind [is] evident for me. [245]

But at the same time, uncertain for me as soon as I don't see it: it is *only* evident for me—I can distance myself, and the nature of my mind becomes opaque before me—non-freedom.

It is a matter of remaining in suspense between custom, adherence to my nature—and denial, neutralizing custom through [the] "fiction" of metaphysical doubt working to deceive me, twisting the stick in the other direction.

The straightened stick, thought in "suspense": third domain between what is visible to the eyes of the mind and the *nihil esse*, [that is to say, between] object-being and nothingness: the domain of the *not nothing*, of the *something, aliquid esse* [something that]—not even a third domain: universe where the other two enter.

It is the universe of "my being"—*Ego sum, ego existo*—do not take this as *ego* (as well as *sum*) in the empirical and vague sense. These words are questions, indices. There is myself and there is *se esse*, and it is a matter of establishing these notions anew. What is found: whether to see or nullify, the two being part of a primordial function, equal in denial and evidence of fact: the "it appears to *me* that. . . ." There is the appearance of something to me (which implies: I appear to myself, I hide myself to myself, being a self is this dissimulation)—one can no longer say dissimulation: because *ego existo, ego sum*, I don't know what I am—I know only that the *reines Für* (Fichte) is not nothing and not simply a visible object-being.

The *ego existo, ego sum* is a shimmer of doubt and certainty, not a purely positive observation, the reestablishment of an object-being: one cannot think this: "The fact that I exist so long as I am thinking, or that what is done cannot be undone . . ."[62] without believing them to be true. More precisely, the process is this: "For we cannot doubt them unless we think of them; but we cannot think of them without at the same time believing that they are true. . . . Hence we cannot doubt them without at the same time believing they are true; that is, we can never [246] doubt them."[63] Doubt and belief are *simultaneous*—at the limit: doubt is here the manner of belief and belief is the good manner of doubt—for a moment one is beyond doubt and belief—See *The Search for Truth*:

> As soon as you showed me what little certainty we can have in the existence of things which we can know only by means of the senses, I began

to doubt them. This was enough to bring my doubt home to me and to make me certain of it. [2] Thus I can state that as soon as I began to doubt, I began to have knowledge which was certain. But my doubt and my certainty did not relate to the same objects: my doubt related to myself and my doubting. So Eudoxus was right when he said that there are things we cannot know about unless we see them.[64]

Vision has changed direction [*changé de sens*]: it is now vision of the invisible (my doubt), certainty of uncertainty. Hence my existence, my being, is not a piece of common existence or object-being conserved in universal destruction; it is presence to "self" of all vision as mine alone, of all negation as a mode of being or of appearing again, as not nothing, negation of the negation, but also not, like in algebra, a positive result. [247]

Let us specify this new type of being: The *Ego* before the idea of myself—the *Ego* that I am—that I find in the *Ego existo, ego sum.*[65]

> I would never have believed that there has ever existed anyone so dull that he had to be told what existence is before being able to conclude and assert that he exists. The same applies to doubt and thought. Furthermore, the only way we can learn such things is by ourselves: what convinces us of them is simply our own experience. . . . I can say for sure that I have never doubted what doubt is, though I only began to recognize it, or rather to give my attention to it, when Episton tried to cast doubt on it.[66]

Doubt about doubt creates the formulated doubt as an object of thought but does not create knowledge of doubt, which is prior in terms of inner testimony or pre-reflexive consciousness because it consists in having an experience of being oneself, because it is what we know from the mere fact that we are—there is a non-doubt of doubt, a non-dissimulation of doubt with respect to itself, and of thought, and of existence, and what one calls the *Ego* is this non-dissimulation. Knowledge of doubt and of the *cogitatio* is something else: it is the formulation of the idea of doubt. This idea rests on the layer of primary doubt that gives sense before [248] the significations of words. You must not imagine this primordial *Ego* as containing the answers to reflexive questions in advance: it is *ignorance* of these questions; as Claudel says, that is the best way to solve them.

> It is true that no one can be certain that he is thinking or that he exists unless[67] he knows what[68] thought is and what existence is. But this does not require reflective knowledge, or the kind of knowledge that is acquired by means of demonstrations; still less does it require knowledge

of reflective knowledge,[69] i.e., knowing that we know, and knowing that [3] we know that we know, and on *ad infinitum*. This kind of knowledge cannot possibly be obtained about anything. It is quite sufficient that we should know it by that internal awareness which always precedes reflective knowledge.[70] This inner awareness of one's thought and existence is so innate[71] in all men that, although we may pretend that we do not have it if we are overwhelmed by preconceived opinions and pay more attention to words than to their meanings,[72] we cannot in fact fail to have it.[73] [249]

"Innate" pre-reflexive knowledge, i.e., what we have through the sole fact that we are—so what defines us is not the express, reflexive *cogitatio* and *still* less the thought of this thought, both of which are "acquired" and do not have their answer in a constitution of thought by itself and for itself. These are idealization[s]—ideas [as] "the work of my mind" (*Meditations*)—ideas give me the "objective being" or the "by representation" of thought—the "objective being" or the "by representation" of myself. And the *I am, I exist* gives me its formal, actual, effective being, an existing thought. The idea of myself, like everything, is first within me only as a disposition; it is only in "the treasury of my mind" as long as I have the *vis nativa* to form it as part of myself. But the "true signification" of the *cogitatio*, the "innate" knowledge that I have within me, is not thanks to an idea but because "I alone am to be myself." One shouldn't say *cogito ergo sum* so much as *sum*, i.e., *cogito*. The *cogitatio* is what, within myself, understands and is not false: that which is derived from this observation or experience that I inalienably am for myself— The *Regulae* was saying: all that one knows are the simple natures and their composition—I can conceive of a triangle without *cogitare* that it contains the knowledge of angles, lines, the number 3, of the figure, of extension—and even more easily than these simple natures. These are nevertheless components of the triangle and are [known] *notiores* [better] than it since "it is just these natures that we understand to be present in it"[74]—and again, *Conversation with Burman*: "I could not conceive of an imperfect triangle unless there were in me the idea of a perfect one, since the former is the negation of the latter. Thus, when I see a triangle, I have a conception of a perfect triangle, and it is by comparison with this that I subsequently realize that what I am seeing is imperfect"[75]—and again: the circle seen has always been the naked, thought, reflexive circle—the sensible is only the negation of the idea, i.e., God could have created exact sensible triangles—[250] no idea of the being of the sensible as inexact in principle—but when it comes to myself, existence cannot be simple negation of essence, I exist before knowing myself expressly. Do

I know myself implicitly? Yes—but, this **[4]** means: there is a *semina* of the idea of myself within myself, operative *cogitatio* that has the *vis nativa* conceiving itself, realizing a reflection that is contemplation (by eidetic reduction, examining what is inseparable from myself and cannot be eliminated from me through imaginative variation) and not a return to a constituting self—there is sense before signification (*intellectus, mens, ratio, voces adhunc mihi significationiis iquotae—Meditations*), I exist before knowing that I am. And what am I then? I am a *natura cogitans*: "a thinking nature, which I think constitutes the essence of the human mind, is very different from any particular act of thinking, but not that it is a thinking thing; just as it depends on a flame, as an efficient cause, whether it turns to this side or that, but not that it is an extended thing."[76]—*Cogitatio* or *natura cogitans* is my essence but an active essence,[77] an essence that destines, disposes me to think, doubtless not this or that, but in every case to think, to have thoughts, which means that whatever happens, as long as I am, it is always thoughts that come to me, that even in doubt, even in the suspension of judgment, there are thoughts—experience in my present existence;[78] *Ego sum, ego existo,* is, from the inside, by coincidence, the observation of the identity between my being and my thought that I reflexively translate outside the order of ideas, in saying that the idea of myself or of intellectual nature is within me virtually as soon as I am, that it is innate to me as a disposition, [251] as capacity for thought. The *ego sum* is founding in relation to these "propositions"—("Meditation II," AT IX, 19): "This proposition: *I am, I exist,* is necessarily true every time that I pronounce or conceive it in my mind."[79] The *truth* of this statement comes from the fact that pre-reflexive existence supports and carries all statement, all conceptualization.

I am—what am I? *Cogitatio*—that is to say a being open to . . . disposed for . . . an openness (*facultas cogitendi*)—openness that is not simple emptiness [*béance*], *nichtiges Nichts,* which is not freedom to remain emptiness, even if it is free to think this or that: for it, even nothingness is transformed into something: thought. *Res cogitans* is not a substantialist construction but a way of saying that this openness to . . . something is not a zero of being, that this appearance, this presentation of someone to me and hence from myself to myself, suffices to constitute an entirely **[5]** new type of being—not one in itself opaque but a "true thing," i.e., a true thing and a thing of truth—*Cogitatio, cogito* is a subsequent and developed signification of this operative signification, of this shimmer—I am, I exist, ultimately means: there is thought, understanding, reason—but (Laporte)[80] Descartes does not say: *cogitatur* [thought], he says *cogito*—intellectual nature or thinking nature, reflectively extricated, is being through [the] representation or objectification of my primordial being, of this existing thought that is only thought because it is myself and because I am it, because it is mine.

Gueroult—*Cogito* and understanding—it is not a lived experience—it is an experience, a fact deciphered by reading an intelligible necessity, which is its condition of possibility, certainty of certainty—experience of thought that is not nothing—reading of essence: "it must be in order to think"—empirical contact with the existing, concrete self is the [252] inverse of an implication of certain "rational necessities" in my "essence" that are "immanent" to it—my essence, [the] "simple, absolute nature" of the *cogitatio*, "my thinking in general," do not proceed without being: "it must be in order to think"—existence and reason are like *lux* and *lumen*, and it is this entirely intelligible light that is reflected in the empirical *ego sum, ego existo*. The second-person formulation is only a stylization. The statement "God cannot bring it about that I am nothing as long as I think that I am something" is pronounced as an uncreated truth that imposes itself on God. Intellectual intuition is the absolute indivisibility of the understanding [in its act of] understanding and what is understood.

Is it Cartesian to base certainty about certainty on certainty? Is reflection as a recourse to conditions of possibility Cartesian?

Does it conform to the order of the *Meditations* to take the characteristic of lived experience away from the *cogito*? And [the] priority of the "*That*" over the "*What*"?[81]

Can one, precisely in relation to the *Cogito*, distinguish what my thought is in his eyes, as lived, and what it is in itself: the ego in itself or the ego for the ego? Is the *Cogito* not precisely saying that the being of the Ego is being for itself, *reines Für*? Certainly, Descartes himself says it: that the soul is *cogitatio* is established only by the "Second Meditation," "according to the order of my thought" and not "according to the order of the truth of the thing" (*Meditations*, "Preface," AT VII, 7)[82]—but the question is one of knowing whether, with the *Cogito*, Descartes has not disclosed an order where this distinction no longer makes sense. At the moment where the meditating mind finds itself in the "Second Meditation," it has no right to deny or affirm the order of the "truth of the thing"—it doesn't care—I dispute this only—perhaps one can get [6] out of there, but it is necessary to take this passage seriously: this kind of madness of reason, which makes it believe itself capable of thinking everything, that it comes into possession of a limited sphere of truth as soon as it realizes that we can never have dealings with anything but thought, that we know virtually everything.[83] "And yet may it not perhaps be the case [253] that these very things which I am supposing to be nothing, because they are unknown to me, are in reality identical with the 'I' of which I am aware? I do not know, and for the moment I shall not argue the point, since I can make judgments only about things which are known to me. I know that I exist; the question is, what is this 'I' that I know? If the 'I' is understood strictly as we have been taking it, then it is quite certain that knowledge of it does not depend on things of whose existence I am as yet unaware; so it cannot depend on things of whose existence I am as yet unaware; so it cannot depend on any of the things which I invent."[84] The order of my thoughts includes everything for the moment—I am in the order of universal appearance.

The *cogito*, [the] "simple absolute nature," [the] elimination that gives intellectual nature in general—but is this *simple* identity? In other words, the *simple* action of God, i.e., where understanding and will are indivisible—the elimination, the distinction—but the question is one of knowing whether they are not called into question here, if from now on the distinction is not made rather for the sake of disclosing cohesions, reflection in order to disclose the unreflected—for example, the reflection on the I am gives the I think as the true center of the I am, the completely naked I am as entirely naked or pure life. But is this not a way of recognizing that in being [an] I think, I am everything, everything I think I see, imagine?—it is not necessary to imagine myself: it would be closing my eyes in order to see better—but it is necessary to understand that I am what thinks in order to imagine and to feel.

Gueroult's alternative: either psychological or mathematical ascertainment, observation, introspection, and "Spinozist" reflexivity: the light was already there. It is the alternative of the event and the idea, of the temporal and atemporal—of idealism and empiricism. There is a third position: the *cogitatio* as openness, a tearing-apart of time that does not overcome time—as continuous *cogitatio* [254]—in fact, I'm certain only insofar as I think, and if I stopped thinking I might also cease to be. It would not be the beginning of idealism but the beginning of a philosophy of experience.

Gueroult: the *Ego* who *cogitat* is *in fact* an individual, but it is only intended as "a thinking ego (identical in each)" (implied: if there are others) as "intellectual nature in general," "condition for representation in general"—but it is precisely my factual [7] existence that is given to me, and the[85] *Cogito* leaves nothing to lose.

The true question is not [so much] knowing whether the *Cogito* is *intellectus purus* or not as it is knowing whether, in the order where we have been placed by doubt and by the ἐποχή, the distinction between the pure and the impure still has sense. Horizontal and vertical *Cogito*—far from me and near me. For the vertical *Cogito*, i.e., my existing self, the intellect of which I manage to form the idea secondarily, is the representative being or objectivity of an operative intellect that I am, and this one, which owes nothing "to the senses," is, however, not to be understood as light without any shadow, light without a drop point [*point de chute*] or support.

Descartes, "Second Meditation," *res cogitans* first defined [as] "a mind, or intelligence, or intellect, or reason"[86]—next: "A thing that doubts, understands, affirms, denies, is willing, is unwilling, and also imagines and has sensory perceptions"[87]—Gueroult: the second definition is enumerative, nominal; what appears to me is inseparable from myself, is the *cogitatio*[88]—response: with the *Cogitatio*, all of this becomes as inseparable from myself as what appears:

> This is a considerable list, if everything on it belongs to me. But does it?
> Is it not one and the same "I" who is now doubting almost everything . . .
> imagines many things even involuntarily, and is aware of many things
> which apparently come from the senses? Are not all these things just
> as true as the fact that I exist, even if I am asleep all the time, and even
> [255] if he who created me is doing all he can to deceive me? Which of all
> these activities is distinct from my thinking? Which of them can be said
> to be separate from myself? . . . the "I" who imagines is the same "I" . . .
> the power of imagination is something that really exists and is part of my
> thinking. Lastly, it is also the same "I" who has sensory perceptions . . .
> But I am asleep, so all this is false. Yet I certainly *seem* to see, to hear,
> and to be warmed. This cannot be false; what is called "having a sensory
> perception" is strictly just this, and in this restricted sense of the term it
> is simply thinking.[89] . . . When I see, or think I see (I am not here distinguishing the two).[90]

Ambiguity in Descartes: the wax is there to show that I see through the gaze of the mind what I thought I saw with my eyes—but in reading it: the wax has always been what I reflexively find there—i.e., the gaze of the mind passes "*tan quam oculis* [as its eyes]"—everything is *Cogitatio* and the *Cogitatio* is everything—latent content to the maximum in Descartes precisely because he is sharp: as aware of union and mixture as of intellectual purity—another purity, says Gueroult, that of feeling—but one that does not rest on the distinction as a goal but on the distinction as simple means, not on the philosophy of the idea but on the philosophy of experience. Similarly, *Conversation with Burman* [256] **[8]**—it is necessary that reflection is thinking about two things at the same time, otherwise one would think that one thought, one would not think that one thinks, that a thought crosses time from within and does not soar over it . . .

Gueroult: impossible, it is necessary that the *cogito* is simple in order to be evident—but in the end the text is there—should one not think that there is a search for a third dimension beyond the simple and the complex, the one and the multiple, the pure and the impure, [which is] no longer thought on the single plane of the *Regulae*? Time: there is no longer, as there was in the *Regulae*, psychological means of combating the mobility of thought through the movement of the mind (enumeration, numbering, memory *almost* eliminated—memory as simple *conservation*), but the idea of a simultaneity through the infrastructure of time, through continuous *cogitatio*, which overcomes the alternative of [*breviorum?*] *tempus* and an outside of time or eternal. Similarly, pure or impure no longer have sense if the understanding, to the extent that it is conceived separately and so forth, is like that to which . . . appears and what appears. The thought of seeing and of feeling is a toothing stone [*pierre d'attente*][91] for the problem of knowing what objective reality is, for feeling the "differential of being and nothingness." On the side of the *cogitatio*—through which feeling is no more explicable than through extension, an equivalent to this problem—Descartes has not purely and simply reestablished positivity at the level of *pure* understanding—this not a pure and simple reversal—profound modification of the *natural light*.[92] [93]

It will be necessary, similarly, to discern, next to the ideal position of God (through objective reality and being through representation) a real position (it is conceived by the same faculty as myself—separately from my freedom). The first gives it as evident, the second as incomprehensible.[94]

For example, the soul [is] more easily known than the body and yet: [257] "although indeed it is a very strange thing that the things I find doubtful and distant are more clearly and easily understood by myself than those which are veritable and certain and which appear to my own nature," "this part of myself—I don't know what—that does not fall under imagination" (IX, 23)—darkness to ourselves—the central I is . . . nothing.

Change in the sense of the natural light.

[RESUMPTION OF THE PRECEDING COURSE,
APRIL 27, 1961]

3) [c] The I am—change in the sense of the natural light [1]

Irresistible evidence of present mathematical ideas. Doubt about metaphysical opinion as soon as one ceases to look at them, as soon as one is given the freedom prior to which the nature of my mind is opaque. Evidence and uncertainty are together attributes of my factual nature.

"Suspension" obtained through (1) custom, adherence to my nature; (2) rejection of this custom by "fiction," negative judgments, deeming false everything that is only given, compensating custom—one stands between the natural yes and the free no.

In this situation, one perceives that a third domain is open: between immediate being and negation, the domain of the *not nothing*, of the *something*—between "what one sees" and "what one denies" or rather containing them both: I am, I exist, not as an entirely positive being, in itself, nor as pure refusal or rejection or nihilation [*néantisation*], but as *aliquid* [something], different from nothingness, like that to which all this appears, being of appearance, of *Erscheinung*, to which it is manifest that . . . , or at least that is manifest to the self, that is *not hidden* to self. Because he doesn't yet know what he is or who he is—(the formula of the *Meditations* is not *cogito ergo sum*—but I am, I exist—what am I?)—the first [258] truth is only the other side of doubt (text from *The Search for Truth*); it is of a tenuous stuff, tissue of negation: I am presence to self of the same negation and indeclinable negation of negation, not as pure and simple reestablishment of a positivity: the positive is forever enveloped by doubt. But the no that excludes it appears as a new manner of being[95] that subtends all negative judgments and through them all the truths of simple sight. What is this manner of being: I am, but what is my being? It is the being of appearance, a being (1) appearing to itself; (2) of the appearing.

(1) I doubt (at the limit I deny), but in this very thing: I cannot doubt doubt. Doubt about doubt, if I attempt it, would only be the disclosure of the first doubt—See the *Regulae,* Socrates doubting his doubt—See the text from *The Search for Truth* where it says that doubt about doubt *creates* methodical doubt,[96] doubt as object of thought, but that in no way reveals an infrastructure constitutive of primary doubt—All objectivation presupposes calling into question—before doubt focuses on doubt, there is the "inner consciousness" of doubt that "always precedes its acquisition." I know that I doubt and what it is; I know what [2] existence is for me before asking myself; I know the one for whom there is . . .—I know it through

a knowledge that is not ideal. I form the idea, the "work of my mind," beforehand. It is "being through representation," and so it has formal reality outside of it. The idea of myself is derived; at first it is only within me as disposition (*Notae in programma*). It is not distinct from myself at first (text on the treasury of my mind)—the existing, actual, formal self is that *for whom.* . . , before whom . . . the "witness" (inner testimony), (1) one cannot [259] positively designate it,[97] because it is the being of non-being—and it must be non-being or pre-being in order to be the last witness, behind that which there is no other—it is what Descartes calls *cogitatio*: openness to . . . ; (2) one cannot define it through negativity, *nichtiges Nichts*, because this openness, this emptiness is freedom only with respect to such and such a thought; it is not freedom with respect to oneself: it is necessarily fulfilled, if only through consciousness of negation or doubt that is not nothing. See the text of the *Principia* saying that the *cogitatio* is not free to be or not to be *cogitatio*, that it is free only to have this or that modality. The "I am," *res cogitans*, the something that thinks, is not a substantialist construction but the only way of saying that surely this is not nothing, i.e., that all particular thought, in order to be this indisputable excursion out of error, this neutral presentation (I am a *true thing* is not an incontestable in itself but, on the contrary, something defined entirely through its true presence), must include a center that is not nothing, an I . . . , a lack of . . . thoughts. This center, the *cogitatio*, freedom for . . . , of which we are currently forming the idea, is the developed, express signification (but preknown) of the words "*mens*," "*intellectus*," "*ratio*"—(words that, therefore, previously had for me only [an] "unknown" signification" (*Meditations*) and whose developed signification, provided here, was founded on an operative signification). It is **[3]** thus certain that the "I exist" ultimately means: there is thought, understanding, reason—but (Laporte) it is not *cogitatur*, it is *cogito*—the "thinking nature" that I perceive and reflexively set free is only actively thinking because it is mine, because it is taken in the nascent state, because I am it or because it is me. It is not, according to Gueroult, a lived experience [*un vécu*]. It is an experience that makes way for the apperception of an intelligible necessity as its condition of possibility, certainty of certainty, experience of thought—being that makes way for the legibility of essence: "to think it must be"—the blind empirical contact with the thought that I am, or with my thought's being, [260] therefore being only the inverse of an entirely clear operation, the implication in my "essence" of certain "rational necessities" which are "immanent" to it.[98] It is implied by my essence, by this "simple absolute nature" which is thought, the "thinking self in general" (in effect, *thought* is not a "universal" concept applicable to all thoughts but a certain *nature* of which they are its modes and not its species), that all of this cannot go without being, that "in order to think it must be," and the examination of the I am, I exist, is only the empirical echo of this implication. The first-person formulation is only stylistic (and style means nothing?)—when Descartes says that God cannot make me be nothing as long as I think that I am something, the evidence here, pronounced in terms of *I*, is derived from an uncreated necessity imposed on God himself: that thought is to being as emanated light is to emanating light, *lumen* to *lux*, intellectual intuition. The examination of my existence is certainty; the seizure of this intelligible necessity is certainty about certainty, absolute indivisibility of the understanding that understands and of the understanding that has understood.[99] Objection: (1) it is not Cartesian to support certainty with certainty about certainty—it does not conform to the order of the *Meditations* to derive, as far as I'm concerned, the *That* from the *What*—it does conform to the very principle of the "I think" as the first truth to distinguish here what my thought is in its own eyes from what it is in itself, the Self in itself from the myself for myself, since the *Cogito* is in the process of saying that the irrevocable being of the Self is being for Itself. (2) Gueroult's alternative: either psychological or mathematical ascertainment, observation, and Spinozist reflexivity. It is the alternative of the event and the idea. **[4]** But there is a third conception: the *cogitatio* as openness always to be done again (*Einströmung*) and seizing upon my being as continuous *cogitatio*.

In the same way, it will be necessary to replace the ideal position of God (founded on the consideration of objective realities or of being through representation) with his real position (we do not conceive God otherwise than through a faculty [261] different from ourselves, i.e., the formal reality of God is incomprehensible being while the objective reality is the most comprehensible being—i.e., the soul is more easily known than the body—and yet *nascio quid*).

The disclosure, through the Cartesian ἐποχή, of the *cogitatio*'s universe is not idealism but the advent of a dimension of experience. Descartes considers this order to be partial: there is *veritas rationum* and *veritas rerum* (text cited in Gueroult) that commence only after God—but he has discovered more than he was looking for: the two orders cannot be juxtaposed or superimposed. They necessarily encroach upon the ἐποχή [hence] dialectic. "Vertical" *cogito* and "horizontal" *cogito*.

(2) If the I and its existence are understood in this way . . . , i.e., as formal reality of a thought and not as its objective reality, as *Ego sum, ego existo* first, from which we draw the idea of the *cogitatio*, "signification" "reason," "*intellectus*" "*animus*," "*mens*"—if the distinction thus made between what can and what cannot be separated from myself (eidetic reduction) gives

a point of view on myself as an operative understanding that I *am*—does it follow that the I of the *cogito* is "pure understanding"? If I am that to whom everything appears—was it the nothingness of all things or all things as doubt-belief[100]—is the *cogitatio* exclusive?

Two texts say that, as *cogitatio*, I am also the one who senses and imagines things "as coming from the body"—*videor videre*—*videre* precisely taken as thought of seeing—Gueroult: it is an enumerative, nominal definition—the true definition of the self is *ratio, intellectus*. Similarly: the idea of *Conversation with Burman* (of a permanence of thought prior to the following thought, of a continuous thought, making me think that I think and **[5]** not only think that I thought)—this idea would make the *Cogito* complex thought and hence less evident than mathematical thought; it is only an ad hominem argument. It is necessary to seize upon the singular nature or essence of my thought—these arguments take from the *Cogito* its sense: the question is [262] knowing if the *cogitatio* that I am is forced into the dilemma: either attribute or mode, either simple or complex, i.e., thought on the single plane of the *Regulae*—the discovery of the *cogitatio*, on the contrary, is that of an order where the criterion of distinction is no longer sufficient:[101] Descartes, feeling and imagining, as thoughts, are also inseparable from myself.[102] This opens up a task: if one keeps everything in the reduction to the *cogitatio*, it would be necessary to understand what effective vision can be in the time of thought, and that will be the problem of quality and its objective reality, thought of seeing the same things—the toothing stone of the *cogitatio* as thought of seeing and of feeling already corresponds to this differential order of Being and Nothingness. Dimension of the *Cogitatio* does not involve the cleavage of the one or multiple, either pure self or impure self, with reference of *reines Für* to the truth of the thing (the truth of the thing that thinks is being the thing that thinks): in the vertical, there is no sense in asking whether the understanding is pure or not: what is it other than the one for whom all "content" is available, for whom they are, to whom they appear? It is not that the understanding is not pure; it is that one does not see how there would be something not of the understanding. I am knowing and am only knowing, and for this order, what does not figure there is like nothing (the knowledge that I have cannot depend on something that I do not have)—this is provisory (I do not dispute it)[103] but nonetheless constitutes a universal milieu.

Modification of the natural light—it is no longer seen as separable, distinct, by virtue of an organization like that of my body—it is thought of seeing and non-dissimulation of this thought to itself (overcoming of doubt), its belonging to itself and to myself—this property has to be accessible to itself to be able to reiterate itself, **[6]** reflect on itself, contemplate itself, short of being thought. This functioning light [263] of the mind's eyes becomes obscure to myself, and the contemplation that is now truly clear is the reflective contemplation that envelops all the others or the inner consciousness that precedes it. This is not a simple, irresistible impulse: thought "shows," the natural light *shows*, i.e., it opens onto a being through representation—natural inclination not [objective reality],[104] i.e., it is evidence for itself, monstration to itself; it can be corrected in name only. It *west* like the flame, it is *virtus nativa, facultas cogitandi*, working and opening mind and no longer a visible grain—but no more spontaneity, i.e., auto-production—it thinks by being and because it is a thought and would rather cease to be than to [cease to] think.

The relationship of *cogito*-mathematical evidence is not the relatively decomposable relationship between simple and absolute nature; the luminosity of my existence, its *Gelichtetheit* [clearedness], is not indivisible. Even after the *Cogito*, as soon as I stop thinking about it, the evil demon returns. The self apperceived in the instant is hardly more transparent than $2 + 2 = 4$.

It is not necessary to put mathematical evidence-*cogito* in the same series, which would be that of increasingly simple natures. It is necessary, on the contrary, to put them together on the side of the opaque: without God I will never know anything. So what has the *cogito* accomplished for us? This: it has made known to us, not a simple nature (thought is one, but second in relation to my contact with myself, to my non-dissimulation to myself) on the side of which one was looking for the stable, the immutable,[105] but a being-everything, a being forever that must exist, that exists automatically because it has existed: if I am at present, it will be eternally true that I have been—thus not as essence but as temporality, presence of the past. Conservation, continuous thought becomes the essential characteristic of the natural light, which is no longer an entirely given nature but a nature that is produced and which reproduces,[106] *vis native*: what [264] I touch in my present, in my presence to myself, is this nature and this light, this causality *in esse*. The naked is only dressed, *cogitatio* only in operation.

Why Descartes is the most difficult of authors: because he is the most radically ambiguous, he who says the most indirectly by virtue of his aversion to Being and who is therefore always badly understood, always presumptively rectified without being convincing due to latent content.

MAY 4, 1961 [COURSE NOT DELIVERED][107]

[108] From the *Ego sum, existo* to my essence, the *cogitatio*—"intellectual nature in general"—the understanding that I am and the understanding that I understand—the effective *cogito* that assures me of my existence now and the soul of which I know that it "always thinks," like I know that the flame can take on this or that figure, but in any case is always extended—the *Ego*, the operative, vertical *cogitatio* and the *ego*, the *cogitatio* spread out on the horizontal plane of "objective realities"—certainly, it is not through simple irresistible inclination that I believe that I exist: it is through natural light that "shows" (*ostendit*):[109] the understanding illuminates itself, and it is itself that it illuminates—I am not darkness for myself—but this reflexivity is not that of the idea, is not "Spinozist" (Gueroult); it is before the idea; it is not of the acquired, thetic type of reflexivity, already accomplished in things ("the light being already there"); it is contact with Self.

So: for this existing understanding there is no alternative [265] between the pure and the impure,[110] between what can or cannot be "separated from myself"; nothing can be "separated from it"—the method of *distinction* no longer serves so much to discern what can separately exist (eidetic variation) as to detect, on the contrary, the natural, pre-reflexive connections that make it the case that it is myself who senses and sees—to discern the *mixture.*[111] And that is why the *cogito* is not removed from the Evil Demon[112] as soon as I stop thinking about it. If it were a simple, absolute nature, different from mathematical truths in that they are still decomposable, it [would close?] time, it would destroy the Evil Demon, and we wouldn't need God in order to be certain of anything. It remains intermittent and temporal because it is thick and not simple. It is my contact with an existing soul, its virtualities, its non-constituent, pre-reflexive light, entirely concentrated in one actual *cogitatio*; it is, touched from within, this mind-treasury for which all its ideas are innate, i.e., which natively has the virtue of projecting itself into being through representation but which, within the current examination, as in infancy or sleep, is all of that only provisionally. Certainly, I have a complete experience of it (from the center of pure intellection to the body "as that by which" I think I see), but it is the effective operation of thinking that opens my access to the thought of thinking and not the reverse. This actuality of pure intellection pretends to be atemporal:[113] if I have existed, it will always be true that I have existed, says Descartes, but a problem is posed, not resolved: to know how this inner liaison of my time before the idea is possible in thickness. This question is the subjective correlate of the question (left in suspense) of the innateness of qualities and of objective realities to the sensible.[114]

Texts from the "Second Meditation" on the *Cogito* that [266] does not suppress anything: "Is it not one and the same 'I' who . . . imagines many things even involuntarily, and is aware of many things which apparently come from the senses? Are not all these things just as true as the fact that I exist . . . Which of all these activities is distinct from my thinking?"[115]

Descartes's ambiguity: distinction and "mixture" are *per se nota* in the same way. The *cogito* is not separate from my feeling; thought is within feeling in its entirety. The wax has always been seen by the mind when it was seen by the eyes: this does not mean that the impure *ego* is founded on the pure *ego* (in the Kantian sense) as its condition of possibility. Descartes warned us that we should not found operative thought on thought about thought, that it is only necessary to think or to exist in order to know what of knowledge is not knowledge, which is *to be oneself,* to have an open field of thoughts. . . . Hence, the wax has always been before the mind's inspection, which also means: I have eyes; it *makes sense* to say that I see with my eyes. And, if the *Cogito* were intellectual nature for itself, it would make no sense. *Simplicity* of the *Cogito* as *simplicity* of God's action: not by *identity* but by indivision-understanding-will. The same indivision thinks and feels— the *cogito* is not only individual "in fact" (Gueroult) while being through its pre-individual aim: its facticity is part of its definition.

What has one gained from the *Cogito*? Change in the sense of the natural light. One has not overcome the certainty of the instant—one has not left time—and in this sense, *my nature.* However, it is certain in a way that is different from mathematical truths—it is not certainty of what is seen as *distinct,* i.e., separable, i.e., eidetic, i.e., invariant residue of fact—it is certainty of presentation, of appearance to . . . , of inner testimony, of non-thetic "inner consciousness" [267], of the *non-dissimulation* of myself to myself and of all things to myself, and this monstration, *because it* renounces being immediate truth (distinction), because it welcomes everything (sleep, dreams, feeling, imagination) without repressing anything in the name of distinction, is no longer only my nature as contingent fact but my nature as ultimate witness ("Meditation III," AT VII, 38–39), after which there is nothing left. One has gained: in this sense, the purification of the natural light is no longer only my psychic constitution as it is, psychological evidence—but one has only gained this at the price of the ἐποχή that renounces the immediate distinction between truth and falsity and which, as *cogitationes,* welcomes everything. Hence, the natural light is more pure, no longer being the simple impossibility of not believing, being the ostentation of truth by itself, of the "true thing" by itself; but being more pure, it at the same time illuminates the mixture of itself with obscurity. It is consciousness of mixture as much as it is intellectual purity. Another purity, says Gueroult: that of feeling, but then there is a double sense of "pure": of "pure" and attentive mind, which is that being pure is not being without mixture.

4) God as light and abyss

The Evil Demon again—a facticity that is now only that of time—I do not have reasons to think that this facticity is diabolical—falsehood disguised as truth, and all the less since I have not examined reasons for thinking that there is an All-Powerful. But in order to scrutinize this Power that takes away my certainties, it is necessary that I see whether there is a God and if he can be deceptive,[116] but this traditional question must be taken in the "order of the meditation," i.e., from the point where I am, from the *Ego cogito* with its limits.

Proof of God: objective reality, the being through representation of one of my thoughts that cannot come from me (or from nothing), must open onto a Being equivalent to the thing [268] itself. Ideal position of God. But this only touches the *Cogito* through one of its *cogitata*. The second proof envelops the *cogito* itself in a Being and a causality *in esse* that subtends it in its entirety—realist position of God.[117]

The third proof relies on the first two by showing that the God-essence and the God-existence are the same God. The plan followed (meanderings of the "Fifth Meditation") shows that there is latency. But this basically means: objective infinity ("immense light")[118] is dialectically incomprehensible—to see is not to see.

The Cartesian circle, the dialectic of the positive and negative in God, of positive and negative Theology, are, like the *Cogito*, Being's reaction to Descartes's initial positivism.

The "Fourth Meditation"[119] and the "Fifth" seek to explore what is *between* God and the *Cogito* (many other things to say about the Nature of his mind, beginning of the "Fifth"). This in-between which has been revealed through the second proof by God existing and acting.

Theory of the trans-temporal *Cogitatio*; theory of the sensible and of the union (the time of things and their "coexistence" with myself); theory of movement; world of light.

Conclusion: light and feeling—the two "purities"—dialectic in Descartes—ambiguity in Descartes—like the expression of a "call from Being," felt by the philosophy of "certainty" or "consciousness."

Philosophy and Nonphilosophy since Hegel[1]

Introduction[2]

Claude Lefort

Maurice Merleau-Ponty was a professor at the Collège de France from 1952 until 1961. His courses during this period were the subject of summaries he wrote himself and published in *L'Annuaire du Collège*. These were later reassembled in a small volume (*Résumés de cours*, Paris: Gallimard, 1968). Only the classes of 1960–61, interrupted by the philosopher's sudden death at the beginning of May 1961, left no trace of any summaries. The year was divided between two series of courses: "Cartesian Ontology and Ontology Today" and "Philosophy and Nonphilosophy since Hegel." However, the preparatory notes for these two courses have been preserved. In reading and rereading those that concern the second course, the development of which was particularly thorough and whose deciphering did not pose any major problems, I was convinced of the interest there would be in filling, at least partially, the gaps left by the *Résumès*.

The notes presented here were not intended for a future publication. The first reason is that the discontinuities in the writing, the elliptical turns, the condensing of entire arguments into a sentence, into a word, and the profusion of German terms borrowed from the vocabulary of Hegel and Heidegger, make rendering this text intelligible to a larger audience difficult. However, these considerations are perhaps not decisive. More important in our eyes is the status of the text, which is equivocal enough to distort the relationship that the reader takes up with the printed page.

These course notes are in effect different from the working notes that have accompanied the publication of *The Visible and the Invisible*. In the latter, the shuffled writing, though often abrupt or allusive, proved to serve a thought that in the space of a few minutes or hours—no matter—reached its expression. Merleau-Ponty doubtless did not imagine that one day these working notes would be published; but at least he had dated, classified, and titled them (most of the time). They make up a sort of philosophical journal. On the other hand, the course notes were only the support for an expression that was accomplished in another place, at another time, by speech, in front of the Collège's audience.

Here, the writing is not sufficient. Let us understand that thought does not test its limit by falling back onto itself, by detaching itself from itself [272] in order to be imprinted on the visible. And so the reader is in turn deprived of the detachment that assures him his reading. Here the ultimate risk of engendering is returned to speech, a speech that we lack and which, being made, was articulated and returned to itself by another circuit.

Also make no mistake: the best-arranged sentences in these notes might never have been spoken. Merleau-Ponty—as everyone who took his classes remembers—did not read and only glanced at his notes in order to *speak*. He wasn't saying a text; he did not have the qualities that are usually attributed to the lecturer and which make him an actor. His thought prevailed in speech as otherwise it did in writing. Speech was, for him, an event, which also made it an event to hear.

The course notes do not exactly constitute a piece of writing. Beneath speech, they are beneath writing. But if one is willing to welcome their indecision, if one refrains from asking of them what they cannot give, if one approaches them in memory of the work of Merleau-Ponty—if, in addition, one knows from experience a writing that is still not yet writing, the movement which hastily leads to a deferred expression, the blanks left on the page, from whence we hope that speech will spring, these little chasms to where one must return in order to catch their breath—then there is no doubt that the work of thought will be felt in the breakthroughs, the retreats, the lacunae, the clash of sentences, of words; there is no doubt that the questions agitated during this last class, beyond all expectation, regain their force of attraction.

So we can hope that, in a journal like *Textures*, these pages will be read as they should be.

The course is entitled "Philosophy and Nonphilosophy since Hegel." As will be seen, its aim is far from being achieved. In fact, it is reduced to lessons on Hegel and Marx. In the course's title Merleau-Ponty says: "Since Hegel." But for whoever wants to part with him, it is impossible to leave Hegel behind. So, the first part of the course is entirely dedicated to the last pages of a fragment from the *Phenomenology of Spirit*: a fragment that we know under the name of the "Introduction," but which at first was left without a title.

The ambiguity of this text by Hegel is indicated by the fact that it both should not and yet should form an introduction, that it should and should not manifest a separation between a knowledge that would open up onto phenomenology and phenomenology itself. The ambiguity of this text testifies to that of phenomenology as such, which, in a sense, is sufficient to itself and in a sense is circumscribed at a distance from true science, conceived as Logic, both rejecting and demanding the division of knowledge.

Remarkably, Heidegger had already given, under the title "Hegels Begriff der Erfahrung" ("Hegel's Concept of Experience"), a long commentary on the "Introduction," which was included in *Holzwege* (*Off the Beaten Track*, Cambridge: Cambridge University Press, 2002). More remarkably still, it was in this essay (at the time untranslated) that Merleau-Ponty read Hegel's "Introduction" text, where it was reproduced. But if he proceeds in this way, it is not in order to spare himself the pain of consulting the edition of the *Phenomenology of Spirit* itself.

Merleau-Ponty's reading goes from this same movement to Hegel as well as to the great philosopher who reads Hegel today, the philosopher [273] who "since Hegel" thinks "philosophy and nonphilosophy." So, although the course is de facto reduced to lessons on Hegel and Marx and does not offer us the dialogue with Heidegger that we expected, it tacitly engages and dispenses the signs of a proximity and distance that require interrogation.

Merleau-Ponty says "philosophy and nonphilosophy." He does not make use of an artifice in order to speak of "modern thought," of "thought after Hegel." He doesn't care to lay the groundwork for a history of ideas. The question of the accomplishment and of the negation of philosophy is, for him, the question in which philosophical thought arises, and never ceases to arise, tested by the impossibility of occupying and withdrawing from its place. This question, which opened up for Merleau-Ponty the path of his work, was increasingly recognized as *his* question while he freed himself from the "point of view of consciousness," which he still held in the *Phenomenology of Perception*. In this sense, the interpretation of Hegel is inscribed within a work of self-interpretation.

But it should not escape our notice that the process involves a return to Hegel, not to the Hegel of the *Phenomenology*, freed from the Hegel of the *Logic*, but to the breaking point of Hegelian thought—a breaking point whose erasure is accomplished under the sign of Experience as much as it is under that of Science.

"Philosophy and Nonphilosophy since Hegel": Hegel makes the phantasm of philosophy and nonphilosophy legible: the phantasm of philosophy within nonphilosophy and that of nonphilosophy within philosophy. But if he makes them legible to us, he also inaugurates an interrogation that we can only accomplish by returning to him again, an interrogation such that it permits the legibility not only of its phantasms but of those of its heirs, blinded in their turn when they saw his own.

The notes are presented as is. I have only modified or added punctuation marks when these seemed indispensable, and, from time to time, inserted a word in brackets in order to facilitate the intelligibility of the text. I have conserved the references to the edition of *Holzwege* (Frankfurt am Main: Klostermann, 1950) because Hegel's text is short enough that it is easy to find the cited passages in the *Phenomenology of Spirit*.

An illegible word is signaled by a question mark: [?]; a dubious word by the sign: [knowledge?].

We express our gratitude to Madame Merleau-Ponty, who has amicably consented to this publication, and thank the journal *Textures* for authorizing the reproduction of this text published in numbers 8–9 and 10–11 (1974 and 1975).

Claude Lefort

[I. Hegel]

It's not a matter of a fight between philosophy and its adversaries (positivism), but of a philosophy that wants to be philosophy by being nonphilosophy—of a "negative philosophy" (in the sense of "negative theology"), which opens access to the absolute, not as "beyond," second positive order, but as another order that requires what is beneath, the double, accessible only through it—true philosophy mocks philosophy, is a-philosophy.

Principle posed by Hegel: it is through a phenomenology (appearance of spirit) (spirit in the phenomena) that one gains access to the absolute. Not that the phenomenon of spirit is a means, a ladder along which one passes on to the absolute, but because the absolute would not be absolute if it did not appear in this way. Phenomenology is all truth according to a certain point of view.

"Introduction" to the *Phenomenology of Spirit.*

Marx: the realization of philosophy is its destruction as separate philosophy (Hegel implied).

Kierkegaard: goes further; sacrifice philosophy—it masks existence, the absolute relationship, because it wants to be an integral existence that "understands" other existences and overcomes them from the inside, i.e., transforms them into a [chapter]—The relationship to the absolute can only be realized in non-integral, narrow, and therefore deep existence.

But this anti-philosophy is above all anti-system—against the scholastic Hegel—not against the Hegel of 1807 and before. [276]

Nietzsche: Preface to the second edition of *The Gay Science* (1886).[3]

All philosophy is life and life of the body "that eventually still has to inscribe itself in cosmic letters on the heaven of concepts."[4] In particular, the philosophy of the beyond is the remedy for an illness to which one must oppose only the "freedom of the spirit."[5]

After such self-questioning [*interrogation de soi*], self-temptation, one acquires a subtler eye for all philosophizing to date; one can infer better than before the involuntary detours, side lanes, the resting places, and *sunny* places of thought to which suffering thinkers are led and misled on account of their suffering . . . what was at stake in all philosophizing hitherto was not at all "truth" but something else—let us say, health, future, growth, power, life. . . .[6]

A philosopher

cannot keep from transposing his states every time into the most spiritual form and distance: this art of transfiguration *is* philosophy. We philosophers are not free to divide body from soul as the people do; we are even less free to divide soul from spirit. We are not thinking frogs, nor objectifying and registering mechanisms with their innards removed: constantly, we have to give birth to our thoughts out of pain and, like mothers, endow them with all we have of blood, heart, fire, pleasure, passion, agony, conscience, fate, and catastrophe. Life—that means for us constantly transforming all that we are into light and flame.

. . . Only great pain is the ultimate liberator of the spirit, being the teacher of *the great suspicion* . . . [that] compels us philosophers to descend into our ultimate depths and to put aside all trust [277], everything good-natured, everything that would interpose a veil, that is mild, that is medium—things in which formerly we may have found our humanity. I doubt that such pain makes us "better"; but I know that it makes us more *profound* [*plus profonds*].

. . . Out of such long and dangerous exercises of self-mastery one emerges as a different person, with a few more question marks—above all with the *will* henceforth to question further, more deeply [*profondeur*], severely, harshly, evilly, and quietly than one had questioned heretofore. The trust in life is gone: life itself has become a *problem*. Yet one should not jump to the conclusion that this necessarily makes one gloomy. Even love of life is still possible, only one loves differently. It is the love for a woman that causes doubts in us.

The attraction of everything problematic, the delight in an *x*, however, is so great in such more spiritual, more spiritualized men that this delight flares up again and again like a bright blaze over all the distress of what is problematic, over all the danger of uncertainty, and even over the jealousy of the lover. We know a new happiness.

. . . From such abysses, from such severe sickness, also from the sickness of severe suspicion, one returns *newborn*, having shed one's skin, more ticklish and malicious, with a more delicate taste for joy, with a tenderer tongue for all good things, with merrier senses, with a second dangerous innocence in joy, more childlike and yet a hundred times subtler than one has ever been before . . .

. . . No, this bad taste, this will to truth, to "truth at any price," this youthful madness in the love of truth, have lost their charm for us: for that we are too experienced, too serious, too merry, too burned, too *profound*. We no longer believe that truth remains truth when the veils are withdrawn; we have lived too much to believe this. Today we consider it a matter of decency not to wish to see everything naked [278], or to be present at everything, or to understand and "know" everything.

. . . One should have more respect for the bashfulness with which nature has hidden behind riddles and iridescent uncertainties. Perhaps truth is a woman who has reasons for not letting us see her reasons? . . .

. . . Oh, those Greeks! They knew how to live. What is required for that is to stop courageously at the surface, the fold, the skin, to adore appearance, to believe in forms, tones, words, in the whole Olympus of appearance. Those Greeks were superficial—*out of profundity* [*profondeur*]![7]

Commentary:

Philosophy separated from life is the remedy, search for the "sunny places of thought"—philosophy is "transfiguration" of what we live, of pain, of suspicion, because life is a "problem"—at the end of this clairvoyance, there is, not misanthropy and hatred of life but *another* love, "new happiness"—"abyss" and "regeneration"—second innocence—truth is only veiled truth—not the search to "see everything naked," "to know" everything—being superficial through depth (Apollo and Dionysus).

Idea that there is a philosophy that does not interrogate enough, that flees interrogation for "sunny places"—all philosophy is transfiguration (see Marx), that true philosophy is beyond: great suspicion, abyss, a-philosophy through fidelity to what we live, that this ends not in "knowing everything" (new positivism) and not in despair but in the will to appearance—See Hegel: appearance and depth are not contraries—Nietzsche cares about the quality of the "philosopher": the absolute of appearance.

If we have time:

Heidegger: the conclusion that he thinks his *denken* will bring to this movement toward overcoming metaphysics, toward philosophy a-philosophy [*philosophie a-philosophie*].

Sartre: a text from the *Critique of Dialectical Reason* in order to see whether, like he says, Marx is *the* philosophy not overcome or a moment of the history of a-philosophy.

Problems related to those of the below and the beyond as well as their relationship: [279]

1. Problem of Christianity—philosophy as the negation of separate philosophy; religion as the death of God—Death of God: Hegel's word, theory of ideologies in Marx, non-Pharisee Christianity in Kierke-

gaard, Nietzsche's word—this does not mean (Heidegger): *es gibt keinnen Gott*[8]—it means: it is necessary to think the absolute as capable of dying, not in the sense of the death of only living beings, which are uprooted from existence by an exterior cause, but in the sense of human death, prefigured in the human being because they are a consciousness, *Er-innerung* [re-collection], negativity putting itself to the test—the absolute requires all of this in order not to be *einsam* [solitary] and *leblos* [lifeless] (Hegel).

Question about the final sense of Christianity.

2. The problem of humanism:

Humanism must also include a kind of anti-humanism. Is the Dostoevskyan and Nietzschean overman [*surhomme*] to be understood as replacing God with humanity (mysticism of the Overman)—or is it the co-belonging of Being and humanity, not being able to think their relationship apart from humanity? The relationship being the proper domain of philosophy beyond all anthropology.

1. Hegel: we will explain the last four pages of the "Introduction" to the *Phenomenology*,[9] and analyze it with citations.

[2.] Philosophy is not access to the absolute through knowledge [*connaissance*]—it is (indissolubly) the unconcealment of phenomena, presence of the absolute.

Philosophy proceeds *"an die Sache selbst"* [to the things themselves]—but if this passage is made through *Erkennen*, one conceives it either as an instrument or as a medium through which the very thing is visible to us—Hence, a question of the critique of [280] knowledge: can consciousness acquire *was an sich ist* through this instrument? The question posed in this way, the answer is necessarily that "between knowledge and the absolute there lies a boundary which completely cuts off the one from the other."[10]

Because: the instrument modifies the thing, the milieu alters its image; the means is contrary to the end; there should be no means; "the absurdity lies in making use of any means at all."[11]

Will one say that one removes from the result what is due to the action of the instrument? But then one finds oneself faced with the initial problem: how does one know the absolute? If the instrument is only a trap, like glue for a bird, bringing the absolute closer to us without bringing us in, then the instrument is ridiculous, the absolute defies all the agitation of *Erkennen*; it only serves to "bring about a relation that is merely immediate and so a waste of time to establish"[12] and which would be powerless "if it did not, and did not intend to be, in and for itself with us from the start."[13]

Will one say that one rectifies *Erkennen* through a medium, given the deviation of rays of light? But *Erkennen* is not a certain refraction of light; it is the light itself, "the ray itself by which the truth comes in contact with us," and if one deducted this light, the *Erkennen* indicates to us only an empty place or a pure direction. . . .[14]

A philosophy of *Erkennen* (instrument or medium), placing philosophy and the absolute in front of each other, destroys itself. It is necessary that the relation to the absolute is prior to *Erkennen* by other means, that the absolute is *schon bei uns* [already with us], that it is the light itself that unconceals.

The critical attitude of *Erkennen*: distrust of a knowledge that "without any scruples of that sort goes to work [281] and really does know"[15]—but this mistrust is assumed, is not truly radicalism; it assumes the *Vorstellungen* [representations] of *Erkennen* as medium and instrument and "a *distinction of ourselves from this knowledge*,"[16] as well as the disjunction of the *Erkennen* and the absolute and thus the immanence of the *Erkennen* to a truth at the time where one speaks from the absolute; all of this is not "fear of error" but "fear of the truth"[17]—true radicalism would not be this mistrust but also "mistrust of mistrust."

It is not necessary to assume *Unterschied* [distinction] of ourselves and of *Erkennen*;[18] seeking an *Erkennen* that is ourselves (our being). . . .

In reality, it is necessary to start from this: "that the absolute alone is true or that the true alone is absolute."[19]

This seems to be a dogmatic leap into the absolute. An unproven proposition.[20] It is that:

1. This is implied in our existence as mistrust of mistrust, knowledge that makes itself, in fact, *Weltthesis* [world thesis], identity of our being and knowing.

2. The proof will be given by all that follows, that is to say, through the presentation of our history, the unconcealment of a spirit-phenomenon, of a life that makes itself known and thus of a knowledge that makes itself life.

In a sense: circle—the beginning is the end—but a conscious circle.[21] [282]

". . . that 'absolute,' 'knowledge,' and so on, are words which presuppose a meaning that first has to be got at."[22]

It is a matter of taking the relationship of *Erkennen* to the absolute as given in our life (thus an absolute that will be *Erkennen* as well), in order to truly recast the concepts of the subjective and objective, the absolute and knowledge in contact with our life, to grasp science in its nascent state in us: "science, in the very fact that it comes on the scene, is itself a phenomenon."[23]

The fact of knowing, not as a simple fact (Descartes) to be put on the same footing as any false knowledge, as certain as simple thought, but enclosing an appearance of knowledge *wie sie an sich und für sich ist* [how it is in and for itself]. The recourse is to the "presentation of knowledge as a phenomenon,"[24] to the "experience of its own self."[25]

Phenomenology: this auto-presentation of the spirit, appearance that is not an effect of the absolute but the absolute itself—of which philosophy is the experience.

I. Philosophy: not *Erkennen*, but the redefinition of everything from our experience, our knowing life opened onto *die Sache selbst* [the thing itself].

[The] separation of knowledge-absolute (critical attitude) is a false radicalism, has assumptions: (1) knowledge-instrument or alters the absolute (and so how do we know about it), or, if it is only a trap like the glue, assumes a "relation that is merely immediate and so a waste of time to establish"[26] and that the absolute "did not, and did not intend to be, in and for itself with us from the start";[27] (2) [283] knowledge-medium: this "milieu" is the contact of truth with us, "the ray itself by which the truth comes in contact with us."[28]

Thus, against these *Vor-stellungen* [pre-presentations] (exterior representations of *Erkennen*) (critical examination of *Erkennen*), this "fear of error"—"is itself error."[29]—To put it differently, we are in the truth;—in other words, *Erkennen* is not distinct from us; we are not distinct from *Erkennen*, no "*distinction of ourselves from this knowledge.*"[30]

And this knowledge, which is us, is also knowledge of the absolute because, if one denies it (Descartes), it is necessary to affirm that knowledge is true the moment that one says that it is outside of the absolute and thus of truth.[31] And what does this "other truth" mean? Absolute, knowledge: "words which presuppose a meaning that first has to be got at."[32] There is knowledge, science, "which without any scruples of that sort goes to work and really does know."[33]

Thus: there is the fact of the knowledge that is us and that is contact with the absolute—

the absolute alone is true, *das Absolute allein wahr*, the truth alone is absolute, *das Wahre allein absolut*. Implication of the absolute within us as interior to the truth, of an absolute that is not something other than our truth, which is not separated from *Erkennen*.

This attitude is not dogmatic, but on the contrary, [is] the truly critical, radical attitude: because it is the decision to grasp the trouble of "giving" the concept of the absolute, of *Erkennen*, of the objective, of the subjective ("to give this concept"),[34] in place of presupposing them as known to all or to imply the concept that one has.

Starting from the true as absolute and from the absolute as true, and from a knowledge that is one with our being as knowing being, without relating to "the emerging science,"[35] at the nexus in it of knowledge and the absolute, of our Being and of Being—To seize this nexus fully and not in the void of *Vorstellungen*. [284]

II. How the unconcealment of the phenomenon is the presence of the absolute.

The phenomenon: the *auftretende Wissenschaft* [emerging science]: it is *Erscheinung* (manifestation)—science which *auftritt* [appears], "which is still not explained and developed in its truth";[36] it is still not liberated from "*Schein* [appearance]."[37] It cannot be liberated simply as *Versichern* [assurance],[38] certainty of thought (in the Cartesian sense), "dry" certainty of its *Sein*, strength of *Sein*—because another *Sein*, that of false knowledge, is worth exactly as much—nor no longer showing a reference to a presentiment of itself in false knowledge: this would still be self-reference to a *Sein* (presentiment) and self-relation to itself such that it is in false knowledge, to a "bad" mode of its *Sein*; to its manifestation (*Erscheinung*) and not to it, science "how it is for and in itself."[39]

It is necessary to show science manifesting itself as reference to *science in- and for-itself*—this is done through the presentation (*Darstellung*) of science in the process of appearing, i.e., science proving itself to be science, exposing itself as science
(that is to say, not only the *Cogito*, but a *Cogito* that understands itself as well as the false).

This *Darstellung* is not still science "in its free form," but the path (*Weg*) of *naturliche Bewußtsein* [natural consciousness] that strives for true knowledge—or the soul's route through the stations that it is prescribed by its nature toward explicit *Geist*—this path: complete experience (*Erfahrung*) of itself which fulfills the knowledge (*Kenntnis*) of "that which it is in itself."[40]

Science in the process of becoming manifest, i.e., proving itself to be [285] science by resuming what precedes it, conserving and overcoming, and maintaining its identity in this becoming because it is itself what it develops, and that this setting forth [*aller*] is returning to what it is in its pure state, as pure *Wissen*.

A life that is made into knowing—and realizes that it is a knowing made into life.

The junction of the two, the reversal of one into the other, is the manifestation of knowledge—Identity of the phenomenon and of the absolute: the phenomenon, the path is, precisely as such, the absolute (in and for itself) or its presence—and reciprocally, the absolute is the phenomenon since it is that which "is in and for itself."[41]

Presence of the absolute and the unconcealment of the phenomenon are synonymous because the absolute is the subject, self-consciousness, and the phenomenon is the figuration of this self-consciousness in becoming. The phenomenon and the absolute are related because any phenomenon figures the relationship to self and because the absolute is self, i.e., relationship to self.

Any phenomenon is *Darstellung des erscheienden Wissens* [representation of the *Wissen* that appears];[42] exposition of knowing in the process of its manifestation.—Exposition, i.e. here: exteriorization, revelation, and not second in relation to knowing; the characteristic of knowing is to manifest itself as knowing—

Hence:

1. The phenomenon is a "figure" (*Gestalt*) and not "free" knowing—is "figured" knowing—thus relationship to a *Gestalt*, knowing some thing—but this knowing some thing is knowing of self: what I see, in the phenomena, are figures of the relationship to self—consciousness of something is consciousness of self (once deciphered).

2. Inversely, knowledge of self or in equilibrium with itself, or the absolute, is truly rejoined only by leaving itself;—reaching the absolute is nothing other than completely deciphering the *Erscheinung*—an absolute knowledge turns out to be absolute only in its self-manifestation, by being born into the phenomena.

The relationship between phenomenology and absolute knowledge (metaphysics) is that of perception and the thing: partial perception is not simply reconciled with the [286] thing; it is necessary that it be partial in order for it to be total. That, at least if one considers the "vertical," present world—and an *Erkennen* not distinct from our being. Phenomenology discloses this order where being toward the thing and being toward the self are synonymous—where the sequence of "*Gestalten*" leads to the Self, is the same thing as the Self and not a pre-given critique of metaphysics, and where inversely, metaphysics is nothing other than taking possession of what appears.

Phenomenology, in total: the entire system under a certain relationship—what is restrictive in the *Erscheinung* (what is *only* manifestation) is in reality not an impediment but an accomplishment for an absolute that is entirely manifestation of self, subjectivity.

It remains to make this nexus more precise, the "chiasm" of the relationship to self/relationship to the exterior.

III. Structure of consciousness as fundamental law of the phenomenon and of auto-presentation:[43] passage from *erscheinenden Wissen* to *Wissen*.

"Natural consciousness" (*naturliche Bewußtsein*) is not real, effectual knowledge (e.g., living a society, a religion is not Knowledge in its truth)—and yet stands for real knowledge: it is a concept of knowledge, a non-realized concept only realized through the sacrifice of this deceptive positivity, "loss of itself,"[44] recognition of its non-truth.

There is a natural consciousness that is naturally unconsciousness (see Marx; see Freud), naturally mystified: it is consciousness of the exterior, *Bewußtsein* [consciousness]. The truth is called by it, but it can only occur through its tearing-down and negation—the immediate is deceptive.

Passage from there to truth—difference with Descartes—the path is doubt or even despair, but Cartesian doubt results in the restoration of truth in its initial sense (through God); instead of doubt, the entire history of consciousness is inscribed here (object and the work of consciousness are reflected exactly); there is intuition of the non-truth of the immediate and of the superior truth that follows, realization (*Ausfuhrung*) of knowledge, laboring on the self of consciousness (*Bildung*). The school of truth is not the doubt [287] that converts everything into *my thoughts*; it is skepticism that no more spares my opinion than that of others, does not give precedence to my principles over those of others, does not save my thoughts, but is attached neither to myself (thought of the understanding) nor to authority but to the content, to its "necessities" (*Notwendigkeit*) and to its cohesion (*Zusammenhang*).

This consciousness, which is formed or cultivated or is laboring, is a negation (since the immediate is recognized as not-true), but a negation that does not come to *nothing, Nichts*, which comes to "the nothing out of which it comes as a result," which is thus at bottom the "true result."[45] Determined nothingness that has a content, which thus is not *Abgrund*[46] but passage (*Ubergang*) to a new form (*neue Form*) that is the truth of the old, its true overcoming. Question: but then, can there ever be a completion of this movement? Is it not necessary that the negation be absolute, negation that gets carried away, negation of the negation, without content? Only then would there be an end to the necessity of "going beyond itself,"[47] only then would the *Wissen* find itself, would the concept correspond to the object, [the object] to the concept: Sartre's solution: sacrifice the for-Itself so that the in-Itself is, [so that] nothingness is nothing [*le néant n'est rien*]. Impossible solution here for Hegel because *Bewußtsein* (embedded in the apparently solid reality of the immediate, in its flesh), as we were saying, *is only* its concept, project of oneself, being at a distance, not the realization of oneself; it is also necessary to say that it is its concept that is intentional with all its might, that projects itself into that of which it is conscious and thus *uber sich selbst* [beyond itself]. It is in its beyond: e.g., spatial perception is *von Jenseits* [from beyond]: the space beyond the limited segment. *Bewußtsein* is violence against self, passion for itself, auto-destruction ("Consciousness, therefore, suffers this violence at its own hands; it destroys its own limited satisfaction").[48] Hegel condemns a nihilistic solution that would conclude, because of this, in the *vanity* of self and others; because this solution through vanity detaches itself from all content and "[finds] instead of all the content, merely the [288] barren ego,"[49] remains in the "*Fürsichsein* [being for itself]."[50] Understanding, skepticism, pure nothingness are always "I."

But then if *Bewußtsein* is by definition outside of itself, fissure (and doesn't even feel like finding rest in nothingness), how is it that all consciousness is not unhappy; how can there be access to the absolute?

IV. The problem of the measuring and the measured—the exchange between measuring and measured or *Erfahrung*.[51]

The *Darstellung* as science's entry into knowledge in the process of appearing, and subject to a critical examination (*Prüfung*), assumes a *Maßstab* [criterion] that one applies to it[52] and which is grasped as *Wesen* or *Ansich*. Now, since science is only an appearance, where would we grasp the *Wesen* (the essential opposed to the inessential)? (How can consciousness learn? Either it knows or it ignores.)

Bewußtsein: it distinguishes itself from something to which it is in relation—this *etwas* [something] is *etwas for it*—and this being of something for a consciousness (*für ein anderes* [for another]) is what one calls *Wissen*. But what is known is also posited as being outside of this relationship. And this is what one calls *Wahrheit* [truth] or *Ansichsein* [being in itself]. All of this is grasped as phenomenon, in the state of *erscheinende* [appearance]. Here, we philosophers interrogate *die Wahrheit des Wissens* [the truth of essence], thus what the *Wissen* is in itself; but in this search, this *Ansich* of the *Wahrheit* that we reach is *für uns* [for us] and its alleged *Ansich* [in-itself] is not the truth but our knowledge of this truth. So here we do not have measuring not brought along by us, and the emerging knowledge to which we apply it will perhaps refuse it.

However: it is consciousness that we study, and therefore the measuring is it, i.e., us—philosophy is already in life. "Consciousness furnishes its own criterion in it itself, and the inquiry will thereby be a comparison of itself with own self."[53] The distinction between measuring-measured is interior, being for the other is proper to itself, and this other is not only in it another [289] for it, but another in itself; it is knowledge, *Wissen*; it is truth. In that it declares itself *Ansich* or *Wahre* [true], we have the measuring that it itself brings to measure its knowledge.

One can call the *Wissen* [essence] *Begriff* [concept], the *Wahre* [true] or *Wissen* [essence] can be called the object—there is a critical examination (*Prüfung*) of the correspondence of the concept to the object in consciousness. One can, inversely, call the essence of the object or in-itself the concept (consciousness-object) and [call] examining, philosophical consciousness the object since it is what we examine and, by examining *naturliche Bewußtsein* [natural consciousness], we make it appear in front of *naturliche Bewußtsein* and seek its being for natural consciousness.

The two presentations are *dasselbe* [selfsame]—exchanging their roles, natural and philosophical consciousness are both object and subject—we philosophers do not bring our measurings, our *Gedanken* [thoughts] and our inventions. We seize the thing (*die Sache*) "as it actually is in and for itself,"[54] i.e., absolutely.

1. §13 knowledge is experience; the absolute is the reversal of roles between the measured and the measuring.
§ 14 experience, ambiguity, dialectic.
2. §15 and §16: yet philosophy is not *reine Zusehen* [pure vision].[55]

1. §13 and §14

(13) But not only in this respect, that concept and object, the criterion and what is to be critically examined, are ready to hand in consciousness itself, is any contribution of ours [addition: *Zutat*] superfluous, but we are spared the trouble of comparing these two and of making an *examination [Prüfung]* in the strict sense of the term; so that in this respect, too, since consciousness critically examines itself, all we are left with is pure vision [*reine Zusehen*],[56] to look on. For consciousness is, on the one hand, consciousness of the object, on the other, consciousness of itself; consciousness of what to it is true, and consciousness [290] of its knowledge of that truth. Since both are *for the same consciousness [für dasselbe]*, it is itself their comparison; it is for *the same consciousness [für dasselbe]* to decide and know whether its knowledge of the object corresponds with this object or not. The object, it is true, appears only to be in such wise for consciousness as consciousness knows it. Consciousness does not seem able to get, so to say, behind it as it is (to where it is), not *for consciousness* (that knows it), but *in itself*, and consequently seems also unable to test knowledge by it. But just because consciousness has, in general [*überhaupt*], knowledge of an object, there is already present the distinction that what the object is *in itself* [*ihm etwas das Ansich . . . ist*], is one thing *to consciousness*, while knowledge, or the being of the object *for* consciousness, is another moment. Upon this distinction, which is present as a fact, the examination [*Prüfung*] turns. Should both, when thus compared, not correspond, consciousness seems bound to alter its knowledge, in order to make it fit the object. But in the alteration of the knowledge,

the object itself also, in point of fact, is altered; for the knowledge which existed was essentially a knowledge of the object; with change in the knowledge, the object also becomes different, since it belonged essentially to this knowledge. Hence consciousness comes to find that what formerly to it was the *in-itself* is not in itself, or rather that it was *in itself* only *for consciousness* [*für es an sich war*]. Since, then, in the case of its object consciousness finds its knowledge not corresponding with this object, the object likewise fails to hold out; or more precisely, the criterion for examining is altered when the intended object of the criterion does not hold its ground in the course of the examination; and the examination is not only an examination of knowledge, but also of the criterion used in the process.[57]

(14) This *dialectical* movement which consciousness executes [*ausübt*] on itself—on its knowledge as well as on its object—*in the sense that* out of it *the new and true object arises*, is precisely what is termed *experience*. In this connection, there is a moment in the process just mentioned which should be brought into more decided prominence, and by which a new light is cast on the scientific aspect [*die wissenschaftliche Seite*] of the following presentation [*Darstellung*]. [291] Consciousness knows *something*; this something, the object, is the essence or the *in-itself*. This object, however, is also the in-itself *for consciousness*. Hence comes the ambiguity [*Zweideutigkeit*] of this truth. Consciousness, as we see, has now two objects: one is the first *in-itself* [*Ansich*], the second is the *being-for-consciousness* of this *in-itself*. The last object appears at first sight to be merely the reflection [*vorstellen*] of consciousness into itself, i.e., an idea not of an object, but solely of its knowledge of that first object. But, as was already indicated, by that very process the first object is altered; it ceases to be the in-itself, and becomes something (a term) which is *in itself* only *for consciousness*. Consequently, then, *this being-for-consciousness of the in-itself* [*das Für-es-sein dieses Ansich*] is the true—which, however, means that this true is the *essence*, or the *object* which consciousness has. This new object contains the nothingness [*Nichtigkeit*] of the first; the new object is the experience concerning that first object.[58]

Literal commentary on fragments §13 and §14

Bewußtsein's development in knowledge happens without addition from us (*Zutat von uns*). Not only because the measuring and measured are both present in consciousness ("Consciousness furnishes its own criterion in it itself; and the inquiry will thereby be a comparison of itself with its own self"),[59] but again because there is not even comparison, subject to the critical examination of the self by the self, but pure intuition (*reine Zusehen*), pure spectacle. And in effect, it is itself the comparison to be made insofar as it relates to the object, on the one hand, [and] to the knowledge it has of it on the other, and that these two terms are for it, for the same consciousness (*für dasselbe*), thus immediately understood as coinciding or not. One could say: but consciousness cannot pass behind itself (*dahinter kommen*) in order to rejoin the in-itself and confront it with the knowledge that it has. However, it has a double reference by the very fact that it is consciousness of an object: to what is in itself for it and to what is knowledge or the being of the object for consciousness for it (*das Sein des Gegenstandes für das Bewußtsein*)—it is because of these two references that there is *Prüfung*. Hence there is a duality in the indivision of the process (intentionality).

If there is no correspondence between the in-itself for it and knowledge of the in-itself for it, one would think that it is [292] knowledge that must be modeled on the object (problem: how consciousness learns something). But this change of *Wissen* (towards the true) also brings about a change in the object because the initial *Wissen* was essentially linked to the object; if it changes, the object changes; and the initial object that passed itself off for *Ansich* becomes *für-es-an-sich*. The object, the in-itself that was measuring, changes due to the fact that the measured does not remain stable. The critical examination thus has a double sense: from the measured through the measuring and vice versa (see Lévi-Strauss).

1. This exchange is dialectical (action of A on B is also the action of B on A)—and also: self-movement; consciousness as relation to its object is modification of itself for itself; 2. And this dialectic is *Erfahrung* (pure *Zusehen*, concrete, without discourse) because it itself creates, through its content, new truth, without any contribution from us. Experience, i.e., the effective assumption of a being, is alone capable of giving rise to a dialectic because it alone is the opening onto something that can be unconcealed, that has depths, a latency, which thus can give rise to the *ek-stase* from whence a *new* truth will come; 3. Consciousness that was under discussion in this exhibition, being experience, is *zweideutig*: reference to an *Ansich* and reference to a *Für-es dieses Ansich*.

The introduction of the second element (consciousness of itself) modifies the object itself, becoming the second object, proven object. And this second object, which annuls the first, *is* what experience has made of it (it remains nothing other than the first become its truth, which, by being it, is another)—(thus exchange between the In itself-in itself and the In itself-for us, [an] exchange that assumes that consciousness or *Erfahrung* is both relation to itself and relation to a transcendent; and it is these two alternatively, not simultaneously)—(i.e., latent intentionality involving reversals and not a unidirectional dependence on a noema in relation to noesis).

Thus it seems that the dialectic (if this defines it completely) is essentially phenomenological (in the Hegelian sense), i.e., relation to self through relation to a transcendent and vice versa—intertwining of subject-object because they are abstract moments of an *Erfahrung*—dialectical movement being movements of contents that are not "given" [293] by consciousness, but that only exist in the relation of content with someone who experiences it, who lives it. No dialectical movement without duplicity in relation to the thing, relation to the Self—putting the dialectic back on its feet would be to destroy it (one forgets that it is Hegel who has deliberately said that the dialectic was the world on its head). Philosophy, i.e., access to the absolute, seems to be essentially experience, i.e., entry into the phenomena, taking part in their maturation, in experience. It is this because it is only in the relation of the *experiri*, in existing things, that one can attend to the advent of knowledge.

Correlatively: overcoming, conceived especially as conservation: the true (the measuring) is already there from the beginning; the beginning is the end or result; the creation of the new, the *Bildung*, is the explication of what was already there. However, the movement described includes a metempirical aspect.

2. §15 and §16

(15) In this presentation of the course of experience, there is a moment by virtue of which it does not seem to be in agreement with what is ordinarily understood by experience. The transition from the first object and the knowledge of it to the other object, in regard to which we say we have had experience, was so stated that the knowledge of the first object (the *for*-consciousness of the first in-itself) is itself to become the second object. But it usually seems that we learn by experience the untruth of our first concept by appealing to *some other* object which we may happen to find casually and externally; so that, in general what we have (falls on our side) is merely the bare and simple *apprehension* of what is in and for itself. On the view above given, however, the new object is seen to have come about by a *reversal* (Hyppolite: conversion) *of consciousness itself.* This way of looking at the matter (*der Sache*) is our doing, what we contribute; by its means the series of experiences through which consciousness passes is lifted into a scientific route, but this does not exist for the consciousness we contemplate. We have here, [294] however, the same sort of circumstance, again, of which we spoke a short time ago when dealing with the relation of this presentation to skepticism, viz. that the

result which at any time comes about in the case of an untrue mode of knowledge cannot possibly collapse into an empty nothing (*leeres Nichts*), but must necessarily be taken as the negation *of that which it is a result*—a result which contains what truth the preceding mode of knowledge has in it. What we have here is presented to us in this form: since what at first appeared as object is reduced, when it passes into consciousness, to a knowledge of the object, and since the *in-itself* becomes a *being-for-consciousness* of the *in-itself*, then as a result this latter is the new object, whereupon there appears also a new shape or embodiment of consciousness, the essence of which is something other than that of the preceding shape. It is this circumstance which carries forward the whole succession of the shapes of consciousness in their necessity. It is only this necessity, or this *origination* of the new object (which offers itself (*darbietet*) to consciousness without consciousness knowing how it comes by it), that takes place for us, so to say, behind its back. In this way there enters into the movement of consciousness a moment of the *being in itself or being for us*, which does not specifically present (*darstellt*) itself to consciousness which is in the grip (*begriffen*) of experience itself. The *content*, however, of what we see arising exists *for consciousness*, and we lay hold of and comprehend merely its formal character (*das Formelle*), i.e., its bare origination; *for consciousness*, what has thus arisen has merely the character of object, while, *for us*, it appears at the same time as movement and becoming.

In virtue of that necessity this pathway to *science* is itself already *science*, and is, moreover, as regards its content, science of the *experience of consciousness*.[60]

(16) The experience which consciousness has concerning itself can, by its own concept, conceive [*begreifen*] within itself nothing less than the entire system of consciousness, the whole realm of the truth of spirit, and in such wise that the moments of truth present themselves in the specific and peculiar character they here possess—i.e., not as abstract pure moments, but as they are for consciousness, or as consciousness itself appears in its relation to them, and in virtue of which the moments of the whole are *shapes or configurations of consciousness*. In pressing forward to its true existence, consciousness will come to a point at which it lays aside its [295] semblance of being hampered with what is foreign to it, with what is only for it and exists as an other; it will reach a position where appearance becomes identified with essence, where, in consequence, its (exterior) presentation coincides with just this very point, this very state of the genuine science of spirit. And, finally, when it grasps this its own essence, it will indicate the nature of absolute knowledge itself.[61]

Literal commentary on §15 and §16

This "experience," which one comes to describe as the unconcealment of knowledge and philosophy, is not, however, experience in the ordinary sense. Experience in the ordinary sense discovers the non-truth of its point of departure through the truth of another object which replaces it.

Here, on the contrary, the experience described brings the new object forth out of the negation of the old, from labor accomplished on the old; the fact appears as result, and only overcomes the old by conserving it in its truth. This necessity, seen in the unfolding of experience, is the contribution of philosophy. The philosopher sees an *Umkehrung des Bewußtseins* [reversal of consciousness] there, where common experience sees an object appear without knowing how it happens. The philosopher goes behind the back of consciousness. His view of experience is not, like that of man simply living, a grasping upon successive objects by a consciousness (according to the noesis-noema correlation considered as irreversible), but a view where what was an object (in itself) can become consciousness (*an sich für es*), where what was consciousness can become an object and where there is an inversion of consciousness. Common consciousness is "grasped" in experience—thought through experience, *in der Erfahrung selbst begriffen* [grasped in experience itself]—the philosopher thinks experience—content and form are newly distinguished. The path, if it leads somewhere, if it has a direction, is already science, and the experience of consciousness is only the content of this science.

Hence: experience contains everything, the whole realm of spirit under a particular determination: that of *"Gestalten des Bewußtsein"*—precisely in this experience, a moment happens when *Bewußtsein* is grasped in its own truth, is reintegrated with everything essential and hence indicates [296] absolute knowledge, i.e., knowledge that is absolute and an absolute that is knowledge.

1. *The absolute and us*: its *Parousia*—*an und für sich bei uns* [in and of itself with us]—chiasm—

From the beginning: the absolute: *an und für sich schon bei uns ware* [was in and of itself with us].—From it to us, all intermediation is "the itself by which the truth comes in contact with us"[62] and not "*distinction of ourselves from this knowledge.*"[63] Next: the absolute alone is true, truth alone is absolute.—Signifying not dogmatism (exterior link *Wissen*-absolute) but, on the contrary, an internal and reversible relationship (without hierarchy) between truth and the absolute: the absolute is in the nature of knowledge and knowledge is in the nature of the absolute.—What is given is their link, from which it is necessary to clarify *Subjekt-Objekt*.

2. The absolute

The Absolute is in the nature of knowledge: the absolute is the subject; it is not the *Objekt*: this would mean *an sich*, i.e., *für uns*. It is "for itself." If it is *an sich*, it is *an und für sich*, i.e., its resting in itself is due to that which is for itself. The only true *an sich* is *für sich*; but this means noncoincidence; what it knows is nothing other than itself—*Sich selbst wissends, Geist* [self-knowing Spirit], but it is objectified.

The phenomenon

We are not told here what this absolute is; it would be contrary to the point of departure. Notion of phenomenon: in considering human history and the we, one sees a *Wissen erscheinen* [appear] there.—And the absolute will be this *Wissen* for itself. All that is produced is never more than "*Gestalt*" ("bound" form, not "free," which has not yet conquered itself, which still doesn't quite know yet), due to the unique fact of *Wissen*—(e.g., the Greek city-state, Christianity).

Why bound? Because it is bogged down, not transparent to itself, not revealed, but in the process of *erscheinen* [appearing], which is its very nature.

Nevertheless, all of this variety is only a variant of the relationship to Itself. But it is not a complete relationship to Itself. It *erscheint* [appears], i.e., in front of us. That which knows is not what it knows and [297] vice versa. One can *darstellen* [present] it, recount it like an exterior spectacle.

Yet, to the extent that it unfolds, its sequence allows one to say that what follows is the truth of what has preceded; thus it is culmination and explication, not blind process; thus it "returns to itself," becomes itself. Its *Erscheinung* [appearance] undoes its *Schein* [seeming], and at the same time [undoes] myself, who contemplates; I realize that I am nothing other than it. It becomes Self that knows itself and becomes me while I become it. There is appearance (that is to say exterior manifestation) of an absolute knowledge knowing, all of whose phases pass, one into the other (its beginning in its end, its end in its beginning) and which passes into me as I [pass] into it. At this decisive moment, when *auftretende* [emerging] knowledge is grasped (*begreift*) *wie sei an und für sich ist*, we are at the absolute.

The Hegelian notion of the phenomenon (phenomenal spirit) is this: the for-Itself seen from the outside, appearing, and to this extent, not fully being for Itself, and yet being already, without which it would never fully be, on the path toward itself and toward the other—Identity leaving itself (*erscheinen*) and returning into itself.[64]

The phenomenon is not object and not subject. Not object: it concerns me: in presenting it I understand myself. Not subject: it still has to become for itself. It is the hidden frame of "subject" and "object"—object returning itself, subject outside of itself.

It is the conquest of this order of the phenomenon, the presentation of its series that is the only justification for the absolute. Justification that is not demonstration but auto-monstration of the becoming-absolute of the phenomenon (becoming-phenomenon of the absolute) through its own movement.

3. Phenomenon and structure of consciousness—passage from the phenomenon to knowledge.

Point of departure: *naturliche Bewußtsein*—knowledge of the exterior—belief seizing upon exterior, and belief truly having it [298]— but how would it have it if it is exterior? Perhaps it is only a dream—total skepticism: I know my thoughts as little as things (Montaigne?). What there is, is *labor*, not according to my rules but according to the content, knowledge laboring according to its needs and its *Zusammenhang* [cohesion]; thus negation which is *wahrhafte Resultat* [true result], negativity that is not *reine Nichts* [pure nothing] and not *Abgrund* [abyss] but passage to the truth of . . . (see Husserl: all perception that is crossed out is replaced by a truth).

This passage, triggered by consciousness of the exterior as such.

It is its own concept, i.e., *über sich selbst* [about itself], it is beyond itself, *über sich selbst hinausgeht*.—Hegelian equivalent of intentionality—it is its *begreifen* [grasping] of itself *to accomplish*—in this sense self-destruction in order to realize itself: "Consciousness, therefore, suffers this violence at its own hands; it destroys its own limited satisfaction."[65]

But it is necessary to specify this again. Because one could make the objection: consciousness is impossible, impossible in principle, being fissure and unstable [*port à faux*]. One could make the objection that one is tempted to do as Husserl does: consciousness is consciousness of something, always noesis-noema correlation—but how can it have its noema if it is not in possession of itself as noesis? Now, if it is in possession of itself as noesis, that is when it can take itself for an object (reflection) and, to this extent, there is not always a unidirectional correlation of noesis-noema but possible reversibility. It is precisely this that Hegel will say: consciousness is this reversibility, this exchange. (In Husserl, intentionality also takes on this sense.)

Measured and measuring.

A knowledge that proves itself to be knowledge: it is subject to critical examination (*Prüfung*), i.e., that one applies to it a measuring that is essential or *an sich*. Where does one grasp it? Answer: one is already in it.

Bewußtsein: this relationship to *etwas* that is for it, this being of *etwas* for a consciousness (*für ein anderes*) [is] *wissen*. But that something is also thought as outside of this relationship to consciousness: *Wahrheit* or *Ansichsein*. [299] When the philosopher is asked [*s'interroge*] about the truth of *Wissen*, about the *Ansich* of *Wissen*, we are only going to get its *sein für uns*. The enterprise seems absurd. These are our measures that we apply to our *Wissen* and this one perhaps challenges them. But philosophy is possible because the object to which we apply ourselves here is consciousness, and because this object is identical to our measurements. The consciousness we have of *Wissen* and of its truth cannot deform it because it is here consciousness that knows consciousness. "Consciousness furnishes its own criterion in it itself; and the inquiry will thereby be a comparison of itself with its own self."[66] The measuring is not external to the measured; being for another of knowledge, which it grasps, is consciousness itself; and the fact that, reflecting on *Wissen*, it makes it be for another does not diminish its value, since it is this being for another that consciousness is.

Here, the dichotomy *Wissen-Ansich* is broken and the *Wissen* of the philosopher rejoins *Ansich* because it is the *Ansich* of *Wissen*. Reflection returns to the unreflected.

Hegel: if one calls the *Wissen* "*Begriff*" or [calls] *Wahre* or *Wesen* "the object," now the object is proof of the concept. Consciousness is not separated from its object by this structure, constrained to have only one view of it "for itself" that [the object] could contest; because it is its relationship to the object—and subjecting their correspondence to critical examination is part of the definition of consciousness. To put it differently, one can also reverse it and call the essence or the In-itself under consideration the "*Begriff*" (the *Wissen* that I'm trying to assess), [call] this *Wissen* [an] object as I consider it and [the concept] thereby becomes *für ein anderes*, now the concept is proof of the object.

> It is clear, of course, that both of the processes are the same. The essential fact, however, to be borne in mind throughout the whole inquiry is that both these moments, *concept* and *object*, "being for another" and "being in itself," themselves fall within that knowledge we are examining. Consequently we do not require to bring criteria with us, nor to apply *our* fancies and thoughts in the inquiry; and just by our leaving these aside we are enabled to consider [300] the matter as it actually is *in itself* and *for itself*.[67]

The exchange in reflection between measuring and measured means that it is as much the object that measures the subject as the subject that measures the object and that we are thus at the absolute.

The close relationship of phenomenology and philosophy is confirmed: it is the structure of consciousness itself that makes: 1. absolute knowledge accessible to us, since when it comes to knowledge there is zero relativity in its apprehension of itself; 2. moreover, this absolute knowledge in a sense precedes itself since the measured is also measuring.

Thus the notion of phenomenon as neither object nor subject—as spirit appearing, seen for itself by another and that is proven from the outside, and that it is necessary to grasp as it is *present*—itself the united [notion] of the true structure of consciousness—the reversibility of measured-measuring that makes consciousness's learning [*apprentissage*] and the appearance of knowledge possible—leads immediately to a relationship to the absolute.

4. Relativization of subject-object. They are both *für dasseble*—consciousness is *ek-stase*.

§13 and §14.

§13: One cannot even say that there is a comparison as distinct act and added to *Bewußtsein*: because it is consciousness of the object and of itself and of the divergence [*écart*] between them; itself and the object are *für dasselbe*. It contains reference to the "back" of the object, to the sides where the object escapes it. It is not even necessary to speak of it rectifying its *Wissen* on the object, and when the *Wissen* changes, the object becomes [301] another as well. As a matter of fact, consciousness is put to the test of the object (of the measuring) by knowledge (the measured), just as much as the measured through the measuring. Consciousness, the true progress of knowledge, consists not in exterior comparison of the two terms, but in the *Ineinander* of objects-knowledge, noesis-noema, which arouse one another (see Lévi-Strauss, double critique—and in general relationship between concepts and research). The idea, thus, of consciousness not as *Sinngebung* but as adequation to manifestation—philosophy [is] *reine Zusehen*.

§14: This movement (interior to consciousness) is "dialectical" in the sense of reciprocal action, of the passage of one into the other, of *Füreinanderessein*, and thus of a movement which revives itself. Dialectical link to the structure of consciousness—this dialectic is *Erfahrung*: in the sense of an experience that someone has, for example, in the course of which the object and knowledge are modified. The dialectic is a movement of content, its openness to . . . its truth, without addition from us. This is only possible when its seat is the phenomenon. Because it is *Erfahrung*: contact with something that can be unconcealed, [that] has a latency, thus can give rise to *ek-stase*.

Ambiguity of truth: the In-itself become In-itself-for-us, i.e., subject-object. The progress of *Wissen* is the emergence of a new object.

The ambiguity is essential to the dialectic and to *Erfahrung* because it is through it that the object passes into the subject and vice versa. There is no immanence, there is truly learning [*apprentissage*]—*Erfahrung* as solution to the dilemma: either one seizes upon or one does not know.

It seems that the dialectical movement is bound—certainly not to consciousness in the sense of immanence, at least [not] to consciousness as that very one *for which* the In-itself and the In-itself-for-us are simultaneous, certainly not to *Sinngebung*, but to consciousness as the identity of wild-consciousness and reflecting-consciousness. The movement comes from the content, but from the content insofar as there is *Erfahrung*. Putting the dialectic "on its feet" would be to destroy it. Philosophy seems to have entered the phenomena. But §15. [302]

FEBRUARY 20, 1961

Reread translation of §13. Commentary:
The development *Bewußtsein*-knowledge, *Erscheinende Wissen* or the *Wissen* that *auftritt* is made without contribution or addition from us (philosophers), not only because consciousness is the comparison of itself with itself (says *HW* 113: *Vergleichung seiner mit sich selbst* [comparison of itself with itself]), nor does it receive its measuring from the outside (*gibt einen Maßstab an ihm selbst* [gives measure to itself])—what could be: banal theme of immanence, we only ask the questions that we can settle; the question is the inverse of an affirmation in the process of being made; the battle is victory; underestimation of the search; dogmatism—but for a more profound reason: there is not even comparison, putting itself to the test by itself, but pure vision, *reine Zusehen*. It is truly self-presentation of the *Wissen*: and not *Sinngebung* by us.

Because it is not necessary to imagine consciousness either as a relation to a pure exterior or as a pure relationship to itself, or as the sum of both (consciousness of truth plus consciousness of knowledge of truth). It is the third and only one for which both the truth and knowledge of the truth are, from which they are abstracted. That is to say: there is not truth and knowledge of truth; there is only one and the same third term: openness to . . . proof of itself in the presence of . . . openness before which: therefore what was knowledge can become object, and what was true can be reduced to the rank of simple *Wissen*. It is not necessary to alternatively think consciousness as relationship to itself and relationship to another, but as the place of a unique explosion [*éclatement*] that makes ipseity and the consciousness of something happen. Neither as positive nor as negative, but as negativity at work—so really one cannot speak of it as an entity or as negativity.

If one arrives at this point, one gets out of the banality of immanence. The immanentist objection: the reference to the true in itself is illusory; consciousness can only aim for what *it is* in itself. It cannot go behind the object which is offered in order to [303] glimpse the object itself (it cannot seize the old jacket as it will be in my absence); it cannot go behind itself as appearance of the *Erscheinende*; [hence] there is not only knowledge, comparison of itself with itself; [hence] relativization of any object in knowledge, of all knowledge, moreover, in a future object. Hegel rejects this objection: if this were so, there would be no consciousness: the words *Ansich* or being in itself, *Wissen* or being for consciousness, would never have any sense for us. As soon as there is consciousness (*Gerade darin, dass es überhaupt von einem Gegenstand weiss* [precisely since it even knows about an object]) there is a sense to the in-itself or truth and to being for consciousness or knowledge. The truth is not that there is only knowledge or that there is only the in-itself or object, but that both are in a kind of precession or gravitation of exchange or reversibility.

One can ask if here we are not beyond *Bewußtsein* and *SelbstBewußtsein*, two abstractions to designate the two sides of *dasselbe*. The Self (and philosophy) being neither receptivity nor *Sinngebung* (*Zutat*) but the spontaneous articulation of a *reine Zusehen*.

End of §13: what is "put to the test" or called into question from itself by itself?

How does consciousness learn something? It seems to be either by receiving from the object (but then how does it seek it?) or through reminiscence and contribution from itself (but then how does it ignore it?). It seems that the solution is either to deny knowledge or to deny non-knowledge.

Relationship to an external transcendent or, on the contrary, immanence (dogmatism of philosophy) are in reality equivalent. It is not necessary to say: I learn by changing my knowledge to conform to the object—nor, incidentally, do I learn by explicating a knowledge which rectifies the object; the truth is: I form my knowledge according to the object, and I model the object according to knowledge because there is no purely knowing knowledge or purely objective object; neither subject nor object but the work of one against the other. At the moment, for example, when I "rectify" my knowledge according to the object, this also changes the object: a layer of disillusionment is deposited in it, even if it is the object that teaches me, suddenly, [that] it is no longer the same as it was earlier. For example, I learn the truth about someone by spending time with him—the change in my knowledge is also a [304] change in the object: it is no longer yesterday's friend who is the enemy of today. It would be false to say that yesterday's friend is today's enemy or that my friendship has yielded its place to hatred; what is closed off is not annulled, and not even in the object. There is no absolute error. Essence is not a substitute for appearance: the appearance becomes the essence and the true is that which is *gewesen* [been]. It is essential to the *Wissen* to be *erscheinende Wissen*.

So: the theme of phenomenology (*erscheinende Wissen*, birth [*éclosion*] of knowledge) seems to lead to the upheaval of philosophy: not absolute *Ansich*, not absolute *für uns*—and for the same reasons, i.e., their reciprocal relativization, their *Ineinander*. That is to say: it is the same dimension of the absolute that is conceived otherwise than philosophy has done so far; neither as "free" knowledge (i.e., without attachment, without outside, without adherence to the In-itself); but as the *Ineinander* of the two. The (subsequent) formula "the absolute is subject" does not mean that it is the only subject. The "free" is liberated from the free and from the bound; the absolute is the *dasseble* of the absolute of the relative. The true subject is the subjectivity of the subject and of the object. There is a *leblos* [lifeless] and *einsame* [solitary] absolute that is not absolute. The true philosophy does not go *dahinter*: behind the *Erscheinung* and behind that which is in the world. It can only conceive the absolute as the other side of the *Erscheinung* or from the phenomenon.

Hence §14

Translate §14—[which is] essential:

1. What one calls dialectic—its jurisdiction: movement that consciousness exercises on itself; reaction of the *Wissen* to the object and of the object to *Wissen*: metamorphosis of one into the other—thus self-movement (solidity of the structure of *ek-stase*). Its product: movement that gives "rise" to a new true object; gives rise, i.e., [to] discontinuity, *reine Zusehen* and not *unsere Zutat*, novelty created by overcoming but emergence that has seen what has preceded it, which thus has its cohesion and its "necessity," which is reason and knowledge.—It is the subject becoming object and vice versa, or their exchange. [305]

2. The dialectic thus understood is *Erfahrung*, i.e., pre-objective relationship to being, relationship to a being in which we are *begriffen* [grasped] (p. 116), i.e., taken, i.e., thought—to think the other is to be thought by it.

Why is it necessary that it is *Erfahrung*? Because it is not *unsere Zutat, Sinngebung, für uns* alone, because it is the self-movement of the pre-objective and pre-subjective content, because it is *reine Zusehen*, vision, *erscheinende Wissen* inside of an outside, "bound" inside, and it would be nothing at all if it were immanence—between immanence and a relation to a transcendent exterior: the horizon and the richness, the fecundity of a content that is not a *dry object.*

3. The dialectic thus understood is *Zweideutigkeit* [equivocity]; it is necessary to underline this in order to put the *"Wissenschaftliche Seite"* (the side of knowledge) in a new light for the *Darstellung* that follows (for the phenomenon)—a new idea of light: the true is for itself *zweideutig* [equivocal] because it must be *Wesen* or *Ansich* and can only be these by being *für das Bewußtsein des Ansich,* i.e., by not being (see Kierkegaard: Phariseeism; as soon as I say "I am Christian" I am no longer Christian). The *Vieldeutigkeit* [ambiguity] is not a shadow to be eliminated by the true light. The true cannot be defined by coincidence and outside of any divergence in relation to the true. Any relationship to an *Ansich* (first object) inevitably includes a relationship to a "for myself" of this *Ansich* that is the destruction of the first object. One will say: it is not a second object there. It is only the reflection of consciousness on itself that adds my knowledge of the object to the object. The limits of the subjective and objective stay sharp. But not: because this "reflection" becomes "the true," the truth of the first openness to the object, and as such the essence in opposition to the appearance, the object. In fashioning the being of my knowledge, of the object (from the motifs of my naive experience), I integrate these motifs into the domain of knowledge; I annul the first object as abstract, and I bring forth a new object. This one, says Hegel, is *die über ihn gemachte Erfahrung* [the experience of it]. An "experience" signifies this assumption of the object that, because it assumes it, labors upon it (*über ihn*—knowledge that is not distinct from our being), is generative of truth, of an object of the second power, [306] object of the object, truth of truth.[68]—Truth and knowledge inseparable from a reciprocal *Begriff* where the object *begreift* me no less than I grasp the object.—Philosophy inseparable from phenomenon. (See modern phenomenology and the discovery of latent or operative intentionality, involving a reversible relationship to self/relationship to the other, and not only relationship in the narrow sense of noesis-noema.)

It seems that: the dialectic is certainly not accomplished by consciousness, in the spiritual motor sense—because then it would be *unsere Zutat*—but no longer objective movement (and for the same reason). It is the *movement of content,* of experience, i.e., of this new ontological milieu which is *Erscheinung* and that does not happen without a relationship to someone who in fact experiences it; it is not a property of consciousness; it is rather consciousness that is a property of the dialectic; the dialectic has consciousness (and seems unthinkable without the consciousness through which the production of the new object takes place—but opaque consciousness, experience).[69] "Putting it back on its feet" would destroy [307] the *Darstellung*, the productivity of science. When Marx says this, did he thus misunderstand Hegel? No, Hegel had also said that the dialectic is the world on its head.

Literal commentary of §15 and §16

§15

The experience of which Hegel comes to speak is not experience in the current sense. The current sense finds a new object that devalues the old externally, fortuitously. Here, on the contrary, one has to say: it is knowledge of the old object that becomes the new object. For example, it is what I projected from this friendship that, finally projected before me as an object, becomes the truth of this friendship. Now, this presupposes the *Umkehrung* (reversibility, conversion) of consciousness; the object becomes subject and vice versa. There was mystification: there is demystification. I was walking on my head; I put myself back on to my feet. How is this possible? It is necessary that there was an addition from the philosopher (*unsere Zutat*) that guides experience toward its truth.

If there is philosophy, not skepticism, it is necessary that past experience does not fall into nothingness, that the present is its result and the truth of the past, that what was in itself and is coming into being for consciousness, that this even constitutes, is the new object, that there is genesis of the latter, necessity. Hence the disjunction between consciousness *begriffen* in experience and the philosophy that *begreift* the becoming—human experience is only the content—philosophy is only the *Formelle*.—But then, from the point of view of philosophy, the path toward science is already science, and the experience of consciousness is only the content of this science. Is it not a reversal of the for or against in relation to what has come before?—*Unsere Zutat*—Why go through phenomenology if it means arriving at a science that projects over experience, as *das Formelle* projects over the *Inhalt*? [Hence] Logic.—Heidegger: this genitive, *Wissenschaft der Erfahrung* is neither objective nor subjective: it is speculative, dialectic, i.e., the chiasm of the two movements.

Answer:[70] phenomenology contains all spirit, but [308] under a particular determination; the moments are not "pure" but such that they are for consciousness (*Bewußtsein*) or as terms of reference for consciousness, so that these are *gestaltent des Bewußtseins*; i.e., the consciousness that considers them feels bound to another, exterior; it is not quite *Wissen* that appears. There comes a point where the *Gestalt* is fully understood, where it is itself that is seized, where what appears finds its center, where the phenomenon thus passes into the absolute, showing what the absolute is.

This means: there is something other than *Bewußtsein* or consciousness of the exterior; but yet nothing is outside of *Bewußtsein*; this other thing is achieved when *Bewußtsein* is equal to its outside, coincides with knowledge itself, which is not its attribute, its property, that [consciousness] doesn't have it, but which has [consciousness], and yet which turns out to be part of it. For the same reason (necessity, continuity, conservation of the truth of the past), it is necessary that experience is *Begriff*, but it is necessary that the *Begriff* is experience.—Equilibrium of 1807.

General commentary: philosophy and nonphilosophy.

Phenomenology poses the problem of an experience that is understood.

Two sides: discontinuous experience, skepticism; the experience that is only there for the sake of the form, and where the measuring is never put to the test.

Philosophy is defined in 1807 as this double critique of experience by the concept and of the concept by experience—excluding impressionism and dogmatism.—But these dangers exist to the second power: there is recourse to experience that is dogmatism (judgment of history—the facts show that . . . it is not myself who says it, it is the things.—See process of 1937).

There is recourse to the concept that is skepticism (*I think* [309] *that* this experience is absolute—that I have achieved the essence there—1937 [is] the new history). But can no experience as such coincide with the essence? A consciousness that is truly for itself is empty—*Nichts*—Any full consciousness is bound consciousness.

Phenomenology and logic represent these two dangers—there is no solution as long as one remains at the antithesis: subject-object or consciousness of the exterior-consciousness of itself.—Hegel has overcome this antithesis in the analysis of the Third term. But he restores the *unsere Zutat* of philosophy, and thus his very recourse to the phenomena is a more violent dogmatism; the others don't even know what they think anymore; the philosopher understands them better than they understand themselves.

In this, he aggravates the situation. The successors protest against his dogmatism (Kierkegaard and Marx), his skepticism or his conciliation (Marx and Kierkegaard): he freezes *Entäußerung* [alienation] in necessity; he takes bourgeois being for Being; he takes established religion for the truth; it is necessary that praxis is absolute. But they also, in their opposition to Hegel, have oscillated between dogmatism and skepticism. The problem of a philosophy that *is* nonphilosophy remains entirely as long as one thinks *consciousness* or *Gegenstand*.

CLASS OF MARCH 6, 1961

We have shown: the truth alone is absolute.

Truth: what is proven, the work, becoming, experience is alone absolute; released, non-captive, self-sufficient. No exterior relationship to the absolute, [no] instrument to reach it. No introduction to the absolute: we are here.

A manifestation is all there is (*Erscheinung, Offenbarung*) of Freedom, of identity to self, of *Wissen*, of science in the Cartesian sense of certainty.—Manifestation, that is to say, exteriority to *erscheinende Wissen* and *Wissen*.—But this exteriority is not an accident for *Wissen*. The *Zweideutigkeit* is not to be understood "as a lack of clarity [310] but rather as the mark of its essential unity."[71] Consciousness is equivocal, not in the skeptical sense, but because it is reversal (*Umkehrung*) (deriving from its *Verkehrtheit* [perversity]); it is in this movement that the concept and the in-itself exchange their roles and that the truth is manifest, that consciousness becomes what it is: its concept, that free *sense* arises, delivered, the *als*, the being of beings [*l'être de l'étant*].[72] As long as consciousness is *Bewußtsein*, it "does not admit this 'as.'"[73] It involves a horizon or a *Hintergrund* [background] that it has not explored. In order for it to become itself, it is necessary that it is torn apart (*Zerrissenheit*): "A mended sock is better than a torn one, but not so for self-consciousness."[74]

But this tearing-apart is its accomplishment—

> The presentation of phenomenal knowledge is not a route which natural consciousness can take. Nor, however, is it a path that at each step gains distance from natural consciousness in order to meet up with absolute knowledge somewhere in its subsequent course. Nonetheless, the presentation is a path. Nonetheless, it moves back and forth constantly in the interstice that obtains between natural consciousness and science.[75]

> If here we may still speak at all of a path, then we may [311] do so only of the path along which the absolute itself goes because it *is* this path.[76]

It is essential to the absolute that it involve this self-presentation because it is that which is living truth, experience, which makes up the life of the absolute-subject. . . . "The representation of the object represents, though unthinkingly, the object as object."[77] Natural consciousness, being pre-ontological, aims beyond the *Gegenstand* (but Hegel will find the *Unterscheidende* [distinctiveness] of the *Unterscheidung* [distinction][78] only on the side of the "subject").—*Erfahrung* is "the word of being"[79]—"the name for the being of beings";[80]—*the new object is the "truth of the true, the being of the beings,*[81] the *Erscheinen* of the *Erscheinende*";[82] it is experience itself. Here Hegel's approach to the overcoming of subject-object; (the Third term, *für dasseble,* for whom are the *Ansich* and the *für uns* and thus beyond).— *Erfahrung* is thus the "*Dasein des Absoluten.*"[83] "Experience is the being of beings."[84] Phenomenology [?] in the realm of spirit; phenomenology and science are *dasselbe* [selfsame] (grasped in *Gleiche* [sameness]).[85] *Wissenschaft der Erfahrung des Bewußtseins:*[86] the genitives are as much subjects as they are objects; the reversal indicates the double relationship of the *Seiende* and of *Sein,* a double relationship which "opens"[87] being— dialectical-speculative genitives.—"Phenomenology is itself being, in the mode of which the absolute in and for itself is with us"[88] and needs it to be not alone and *leblos.*—"For men, there is no introduction to the being of beings because the essence of man in the company of being is this company itself."[89] Natural consciousness has not been introduced to the absolute: it is there. [312] It is necessary only that it recognize the constitutive *Verkehrtheit* [perversity][90] that "we ourselves are in the experience which our being also *is . . .*"[91]

All of this is in this text: true philosophy is nonphilosophy— entering into the depths of *Erfahrung.*

But it is also the case that the absolute is true: the absolute alone is true, nothing that is related is true, nothing outside of consciousness is true, no *Gestalt* is true.

Experience in the ordinary sense is the external encounter with a new object with forgetting of the preceding one, hence skepticism. And not interiorization of the first object, which is the second—"pure seizing upon" what is in and for itself. For example, mastery (and its impasse) disappear, hence the truth of slaves, stoicism, Christianity. —In order to pass from ordinary to metaphysical experience, a conversion is necessary, a reversal through which what has been "for myself" is objectivity, what has been "in itself" is subjectivity, and so consciousness is *gestaltet* [formed] otherwise.[92]

Now, this is not, in the eyes of consciousness, grasped in experience; disjunction of lived "contents" and its *"Formelle"* or *"reines Entstehen"* or becoming. The slaves don't know that they bring about the future and the overcoming of the master.

In brief, experience is necessary but not sufficient; it is necessary that it be understood, that it requires "conversion" or "reversal."—The ground of natural consciousness is in reality the "foreground of light."[93] To convert this ground to a figure, to truly know what *erscheint* [appears], the *Sicherscheinen* [self-appearance] of the *Erscheinen* [appearance] or the *Erscheinen* [appearance] of the *Erscheinende* [appearing], is the contribution of the philosophical gaze that transforms "for us" (philosophers) what is in itself for bound consciousness.

But then the dilemma seems to be: either experience is truly assumed and it is wandering, skepticism; or it is understood, transformed into its truth, but then it is overcome. And the pretension to gain access to this second order through experience [313] is the most complete dogmatism because it is a dogmatism disguised as the movement of things.[94]

Read the text of §16.

Hegel's solution:

But from where would philosophy take exterior measurements of experience? It does not contribute anything else; its contribution is precisely the renunciation of all contribution so that the *Erscheinen* of the *Erscheinende* shows itself.[95] We have said that no consciousness was cut off from the reverse side of things that it sees. What is "behind the back" of consciousness is only that the real characters of the drama are not the *Gestalten* among whom it is played, but moments of the unique Self. It is experience itself, phenomenology, which is suppressed, the *Darstellung* which is interrogated, that is metamorphosized into absolute knowledge simply because the point it reaches is defined by coincidence: it is revealed as being allowed [314] to understand itself and everything else as not being a local event in the midst of the whole, but as always having been in another mode of Being, and even as giving reason to becoming. The *Umkehrung* is in the nature of consciousness. The moments of the truth of Spirit are in experience, not in a *pure* (*reine*) state, but like in a mirror: "as they are for consciousness [in the eyes of this consciousness of the exterior, in the face of exterior *Darstellung*], or as consciousness itself appears in its relation to them."[96] What appears in phenomenology are these structures of consciousness of the exterior that create, within it, dialectical movement without it knowing exactly why—without consciousness having taken possession of its own reversal, of its own chiasm, of this movement of self-genesis that crosses it. But this movement (which is consciousness) *pushes* it toward its true Existence (i.e., toward its existence revealed to itself), i.e., so that up to a certain *point* it knows that it is not consciousness of an *exterior*, that what it is aware of is itself, that the *Darstellung* is presentation of self to self, that the *Erscheinung* is equal to the *Wesen*, to the thing itself, and then coincides with the very point of Spirit's own knowledge. So consciousness "designates" absolute knowledge. The absolute is thus not an object of contemplation before consciousness or before philosophy (when it was [such an object] it was still only spirit-phenomenon). And this consciousness realizes that it is spirit in and for itself. From the fact that the sense of experience and its truth are, at bottom, only the full identity of Self, that the secret of things is only this: Being is Self ("formal" secret, i.e., structural secret that all experience possesses in what it has of the ontological); one can say that it is not revealed through philosophy to men, that it is also latent in them, and that it only receives from philosophy its rigorous, naked, direct (*and usually retrospective*) formulation. So that one can just as well say that they are entirely in error except for it and that they are entirely in the same truth as it. Philosophical *Sinngebung* is not [315] drawn from a source different from the very form of experience, which emerges when consciousness casts off [*dépose*] its alleged intentionality in order to discover *itself* as what it seeks, and at the same time, as absolute.

The Hegelian absolute (what sees philosophy behind the back of consciousness taken in experience) is of such a nature (the pure core of Self which tears itself apart, which does not have *its* Concepts of its Ideas, but the Ideas, the Concepts that we also have, which, as soon as it is seen from the outside, as object, is the same one we have under our eyes, the *Gestalten* of spirit-phenomenon) that one cannot say that it is *behind the back* of consciousnesses occupied with their experience. It is at their core and in their relationships, "divine universal man" as "element" (Hyppolite), where self-consciousness of the absolute is possible, this last not being exterior consciousness of "divine universal man."

This Hegelian absolute, which is full nothingness, would be *leblos* and *einsam* without the rest. Thus it is not to be thought apart.—"it is the mode of Hegelian thought itself . . . *the circularity of the thought or the finality of the self.*"[97]—"The truth is the becoming of itself, the circle which presupposes and has, at its beginning, its own end as its aim and which is real only with its developed actualization and with its end."[98] To think the absolute is not only to think the absolute but also the rest and again, to think the absolute from the rest, and so forth. The circle is what there is.

As a result, it is true at the same time: (1) That phenomenology contains everything; (2) That everything is affected by an index of exteriority, since consciousness is there in the process of conquering itself. That consequently there would be, in addition to phenomenology, a system of *Wissenschaft*, especially the *Logic*, which is Hegel's metaphysics where experience as discontinuity is overcome, where truth expands in itself and for itself.—One would say that the *Logic* is "the presentation of God as he is in his eternal essence before the [316] creation of Nature and of the finite spirit" (*Logik*, IV, 31). But Hegel does not admit creation; this is thus a manner of expressing that the logic is abstract, a methodological abstraction. In fact, at first objective (Being, Essence), it is then subjective (Concept); it thus envelops the distinction Self-Being.—"self-certainty is *immanent* in this truth."[99] The phenomenology, which has shown that the

Self and Being are identical, is implied in the logic.[100] As, inversely, it implies the absolute-subject in order to put the genesis of experience into perspective. In 1807, while opening phenomenology onto *Wissenschaft*, Hegel conceives their relationship as circular; in 1802 he said: "the world of philosophy in itself and for itself is a world turned upside down"—"When natural consciousness entrusts itself straight away to Science, it makes an attempt, induced by it knows not what, to walk on its head too, just this once."[101] And inversely, for science, ontic consciousness is the reverse of itself—"Phenomenology" is done in order to transform one into the other, and it is not thus simple reference to an exterior regulation of logic that would walk on its head (no more than Marx, Hegel in 1807 doesn't want "to walk on his head." He sees this better than Marx: the head is also the *Object*). One can say that this solution of circularity is ambiguity (*Vieldeutig*), a conscious ambiguity, which is not lacking in univocity.

The *Phenomenology*: ". . . where consciousness itself dies the death into which it has been torn by the power of the absolute. . . . 'God is dead: This means everything except that there is no God.'"[102]

Is the Hegelian solution stable? Or is there a good ambiguity? Does it not always tend toward equivocation? It was not the case in Hegel. The translated fragment, without a title in the first edition, is then called "Introduction"; it is that Hegel himself no longer sees that there is no Introduction to the phenomenology of Spirit, which *is* the presence of the absolute. In 1817, at the time of the *Encyclopedia* [317], phenomenology becomes a discipline again, a part of science. It would no longer be "the whole of the system under a certain point of view" (Hyppolite). There is a relationship of *Ineinander*, a concentric situation, a reciprocal envelopment, in 1807, which gives way then to the enveloping thought of the "positively rational"—or of the speculative.

It is "the identity of identity and non-identity" that finally subordinates *difference*. This is inevitable as soon as it ceases to be experience and becomes *signification*, thing said (old age), that is to say, as soon as it ceases to reconsider itself, to think itself surrounded by an encompassing, the present, vertical world, and presumes to have totalized, *everything* grasped, *everything* overcome.

The risk: return to skepticism, to dogmatism—or rather to both.

The absolute, considered to be expressed in the same way in all that is, *das Bestehende* [the existing] (because what is, is all that can be), the bourgeois State, established religion, thought as expression of the absolute, what they evidently are, but in [concurrence?] with another future.—The Hegelian conciliation: the worst stupidities are treated like historical walls because they are. The absolute empties itself, becomes indifference, and pure conservation because its link with experience, the vertical world, is loosened. One represses skeptic-dogmatism in the name of a nominal absolute. The absolute is almost the empty *Nichts* of the skeptics and the world is almost the positivity of all that *besteht*, whereas in 1807 the negative was engaged in labor.

I have said: it is inevitable; it is the passage from experience to things said. But this would mean that, in a sense, philosophy is denied in its formulation (what Kierkegaard has said: Phariseeism); at least by converting itself into contemplated significations.—The dissociation: *das Bestehende*—the absolute void, the disjunction of the order of phenomena, were inevitable in a philosophy that remained a philosophy of consciousness, of representation, of the *Subjekt.*—Hegel has admirably deepened these notions, has softened them, showing the paradoxical relationship of consciousness to object and metamorphosis; but conserving the relationship to [318] the Self and to the exterior, he couldn't avoid the double envelopment being equivocal, and the break reappearing that the phenomena had to close. Perhaps it was this that caused him to fail to link philosophy and nonphilosophy.

Will Marx succeed better?—If one accepts this appreciation of Hegel, this putting into perspective, it is to be feared that he will not. Because Marx, like Kierkegaard, revindicates experience, the present against the established State and established religion, reopening the vertical world toward the future, but he does not implicate Hegel in what was in fact bringing about the ruin of his endeavor; what he calls into question is not necessarily responsible for the dislocation, and thanks to this misunderstanding, he resumes certain faults of Hegel's, sometimes remaking Hegel badly.

MARCH 13, 1961

The alternative: enveloping experience or thought does not in principle exist. It is not the case, moreover, that experience receives clarification about itself. It is itself that asks for the reversal that makes it true. Inversely: what does absolute knowledge know? That all *Gestalten des Bewusstseins* are *SelbstBewußtsein?* But it only knows this through experience and through the path: the truth is what has become, "end" and "means" are interdependent; the statement "there is *SelbstBewußtsein*" has no sense other than as the totalization of this movement and the totalization that must also appear.—The truth is thus not *only*: there is *SelbstBewußtsein,*[103] but that there is *SelbstBewußtsein* appearing in the other-than-itself and that this is only the unconcealment of itself.—Submit experience to exterior regulation (to *Sinngebung* through *SelbstBewußtsein für uns*, to a philosopher who would identify himself with God, or—this comes down to the same thing—to process [319] in itself behind experience, *an sich*): this would be to walk on one's head. By definition, the In and For itself, the Hegelian absolute, is neither on the side of the In Itself nor on the side of For Itself as they present themselves at the level of *Bewußtsein* (i.e., both correlative and destructive of each other); it is truly In Itself/For Itself and not the pursuit of the In Itself by the For Itself, the movement of one toward the other; it is only in the milieu of experience: it is the frame, it is the figure, the manifestation of the intimacy of one to the other that *Bewußtsein* never succeeds in achieving. In the movement of the experience which understands itself, we touch the absolute that is not something behind it or under it, that is watermarked [*filigrane*] in it and only exists beneath the surface [*en filigrane*]. The negativity of the *Phenomenology of Spirit*, which will no longer appear again in the same role in later works, negativity at work, which is only negativity by being at work, removes the alternative of immanence-transcendence from philosophy. Philosophy is the rebirth of the negative that is only negativity at work, i.e., in contact with the Being that it works on.

Rigorous solution—but is it necessary to say solution? In other words, [is it] the end of interrogation through a positive answer?

The *Zweideutigkeit* [equivocity] of consciousness is not eliminated in the experience that discloses its *Verkehrtheit* [perversity] and realizes *Umkehrung* [reversibility], because the exterior is ineliminable: the absolute knowledge that I have become remains a "figure of consciousness" and is not reabsorbed as such, thus I never cease to be *Bewußtsein*—to this extent, there is no "definitive recovery [*redressement*]."

The ambiguity is not lacking univocity. It is "good." This is not inconvenient if the *Zweideutigkeit* is present as such: the absolute as this light of truth that appears in the thickness of experience and that embraces relativized subject and object. But if one formulates it in terms of *Bewußtsein*, one has equivocation.

One really has experience of knowledge, knowledge of experience: the two faces of ambiguity, which are abstractions, and the absolute is between the two, the transformation of one into the other. But this can only be maintained in contact with experience, with the "vertical" world (whose absolute is "depth"). The very formulation of this [320] living *Zweideutigkeit* makes it disappear. The formulation transforms into things said, into positivity, makes the negative in the 1807 sense disappear—restores the truth of identity. The Hegelian philosophy of 1807 (like Kierkegaard's Christianity)[104] excludes the statement. Once stated, it returns to identity, speculation is separated from the dialectic, that is to say, the absolute is conceived as absolute negation or as absolute positing (the "positively rational" of the *Encyclopedia*), in any case, as separately thinkable: hence skepticism (the empty *Nichts*)—and dogmatism (the *Bestehende* is entirely positive).—Mixture of indifference and conservatism. The bourgeois State, established religion are thought as the sole expressions of the absolute; experience is localized.—The Hegelian "conciliation"; there is no longer living communication between the absolute and history.

Conclusion: Either (1) if consciousness keeps its rights, [then] relapse into positivism or abstract negativism, disjunction of the order of phenomena (*Phenomenology* becomes again a part of science, our text becomes "Introduction," it is no longer "the whole system under a certain point of view" [Hyppolite]).—Or (2) perhaps an unformulated philosophy; in any case, one which manages to do without the notion of consciousness.

Do others succeed in maintaining the link of philosophy and experience better than Hegel?

Marx? He certainly had the intention (early texts of 1843–1844). He mobilizes the philosophy of right. But did he finally accomplish it? What he criticizes in Hegel: the theoretical attitude, philosophy as exhaustion—return to phenomenology—*praxis* against *theoria*—search for a thought-action which does not have the positivity of all thought, the *profane* character of all action, the exteriority of all action, which thus remains faithful to the negativity of 1807.[105]—Fine.—But also: Nature (impasse)—so [321] come back to the "overthrow" of Hegel's dialectic.—Return to the object.—Now, in order to achieve this, it is necessary to use the Hegelian Concept from Hegel's *Logic*.—At the moment when he believes he is overthrowing Hegel's dialectic, he resumes the Hegelian mode of thought (applied to the analysis of Capital where the self-destruction of all *Bestehende* is written).—Polemic against idealism, accompanied by counter-idealism and the return to Hegel's logic.

[II. Marx]

Marx

Text from the "Introduction" to the *Critique of Hegel's Philosophy of Right* (published in the *Annales Franco-Allemandes*, written in August 1843) + texts from the *Economic and Philosophic Manuscripts of 1844.*

Before translating the text: why we study it, what questions we put to it—in our context, the problem of *Philosophie-Unphilosophie*; why and in what terms this Hegelian problem is then posed to Marx.

Hegelian Marx, "Young Hegelian"—associated with a *reform* movement for Hegelian philosophy, especially Feuerbach. (Feuerbach 1839 article: contribution to the critique of Hegelian philosophy).—*Reform* in what sense? We will see.

Following his separation from Feuerbach ("Theses on Feuerbach," 1845), six months after *The Holy Family* (1844)—perhaps from all philosophy: the "Preface" to the *Contribution to the Critique of Political Economy* (1859) says that with *The German Ideology*, he wants to "liquidate the philosophical consciousness of yesteryear."

But when he writes the postface to the second edition of *Capital* (1875), again [he] praises [*éloge*] Hegel in opposition to his adversaries— has the coquetry to express the first book of *Capital* in Hegelian form.— Writes that one day it would explain how Hegel's *Logic*, in its mystified form, has provided true accounts.

Usual interpretation: pre-Marxist and "philosophical" period (Feuerbach); rupture with philosophy as [322] alienation (critique of other alienations extended to philosophy), passage to science and to "scientific" socialism founded on the scientific analysis of *Capital.*

Difficulty: (1) there are three different views on Feuerbach from the first period mixed in with Feuerbach's ideas: for example, in our text—it is necessary that destruction must be the realization of philosophy and the realization of destruction (philosophy's truth and lies) and not only the turning-around of speculative philosophy.

(2) If socialism were "scientific," how and why would the dialectic of Hegel's *Logic* be valuable? Would it become empirical

truth, fact? (Engels)—This removes everything from the *Begreifen* [understanding]—or else, on the contrary, it is the resumption of Hegelian logic in absolute objectivism.

Marx did not do his own *Logic*. It is, say the Marxists, *Capital*. But *Capital* goes from the essence to the appearance, [and] reconstructing experience from the essence implies a Hegelian logic.

In total: Hegelian from one end to the other.

But at first, very much in the sense of the *Phenomenology*: humanist, Feuerbachian themes of 1843–1844; in the end, very much in the sense of the *Logic* (*Capital* follows the inverse order of the *Phenomenology*: from essence to appearance).

This is not a passage from philosophy to science; it is the passage from "direct" philosophy (man, nature, Feuerbach) to another conception of philosophy (man, nature attained by means of the experience of capitalism; this experience understood, and led toward the concept, discloses the proletarian class that is the historical formulation where capital's intelligibility is realized; identification of that which thinks the functioning of capital with this historical formation: this, thus, reveals the *corresponding point* of absolute Knowledge, is *Erscheinende Wissen*. *Capital* rejoins the institution of the proletariat as Hegel's logic rejoins the *Phenomenology*).

Marx does not say this: is limited to *making use* of Hegel's logic without specifying its relationship with the facts. One wants to ask him in the same way he asks Hegel: is this the *Logik der Sache* [logic of the matter] or *Sache der Logik* [matter for logic]? And if it is *Logik der Sache*, why is there a logic of content?

Moreover, he takes up, until the end, criticisms of Hegel that [323] are Feuerbachian: (overthrow speculative philosophy—materialism in place of idealism) that are not dialectic.

Lukács: "overthrowing" cannot simply consist in reversing the signs.

Materialism opposed to idealism expresses the *Capital* that involves essences-ideas very badly. Besides, for dialectical philosophy, it is the same opposition of thing-idea that is overcome. Hegel in no way withdraws from History its *Eigenbewegung* in order to give it to the Absolute or to Consciousness of Self (he has explicitly said that philosophy comes after history as well as passions and contemplation).

Scope of all this: extends to the question of the Absolute and of philosophy.

If (as said above) philosophy is experience understood and led to the concept; if the absolute is the self-presentation, the apperception of the fact that it is oneself that consciousness grasps in such an exterior form—or, at least, if the absolute is the movement of truth which bears and makes possible this movement of consciousness (Hegel)—when Marx wants to come back to immediate philosophy (nature man, 1844), with Feuerbach, he is deceived about his own path; he falls back under the Hegel who had characterized sense certainty as abstract. And when he believes he has abandoned "philosophy" (with *Capital*) he actually finds it again, as he had felt in defending Hegel.

When he polemicizes with idealism as a "war of the gods" and against the personal union of philosophy and God, this should not be understood as a kind of positivism, according to which the "idealist joke" is deprived of sense, but as the truth of this philosophy "under a mystified form." Not as passage from philosophy to *Unphilosophie*, but as the negation of the philosophy which realizes it. It is certainly no longer necessary that the "world become philosophy," but it is necessary that "philosophy becomes the world."

Marxist praxis is the heiress of *SelbstBewußtsein*. There is a Marxist "sacred" which is the totality, the alienation of alienation or revolutionary action—action that is never solely mine, whereby the problems of the transcendent return. [324]

Hence, the philosophy of Marx's *Capital* still remains to be accomplished—beyond what Marx could say about philosophy—and considering what the human experience of capitalism and of Marxism has revealed after Marx.

Our texts:

Those of 1844 are very Feuerbachian—one has to ask to what extent the idea of nature and of history that they express is pre-Marxist and pre-Hegelian.

That of the "Introduction" (1843), remarkable in its precocity and its permanent value—contains:

–reference to man, not as received directly but as *Welt des Menschens*;

–view of speculative philosophy as ambiguous: false and true, true and false exactly as abstract. And not only, as Feuerbach said: false insofar as abstract.

–derivation of praxis from speculation as denied but realized speculation;

–positive evaluation of philosophy as, in a certain case, the germ of life and the point of departure for the Revolution, head of the Revolution for whom the proletariat is the core.

What is missing is the idea of a concrete-economic analysis; the proletariat is a philosophical god. But this is perhaps the best document of Marxist philosophy: it would be sufficient to link this intuition of praxis and the proletariat to objective structures of Capital and to the *Begreifen* of Capital in order to have the philosophy of *Capital*.

APRIL 10, 1961

"Introduction" to the *Critique of Hegel's Philosophy of Right.*

Thus the question:

Hegel has envisaged (order of "phenomena") the identification of philosophy and nonphilosophy, the Absolute and the *Erscheinung* of the Absolute—then subordinated the dialectic of consciousness to the movement of truth. [325]

Does Marx not follow an analogous path? Hegelian, from one end to the other, even in this.

Especially: the passage of the young Marx to *Capital* would not be so much passage from philosophy to science as passage from the *Phenomenology* to the *Logic.*

What blurs things is the approbation at first given to Feuerbach: Feuerbachian themes in the *Economic-Philosophic Manuscripts*; the role of the idea of nature, which is not Hegelian; polemic against Hegel in the name of sensible man and of *Unphilosophie.* But Marx [is] profoundly Hegelian from the beginning. And, in what follows, it is not that he moves away from Hegel, it is that he moves away from direct philosophy.

Hence, to show, in him as well as in Hegel, the failure to connect philosophy and nonphilosophy: what he wanted at first because of the domination of the philosophy of the concept over the philosophy of *Erfahrung* (*Capital*).

To show first in Marx:—the impregnation of Hegel (at the same time as the attempts of direct philosophy to describe the "here—there is")—the elaboration of the notion of praxis as heir of absolute knowledge: it is unity with a true form of existence (the proletariat) that is the presentation of the true society and true man.

"Introduction" to the *Critique.*[1]

It is a matter of "critiquing" Hegel, of reforming speculative philosophy (Feuerbach—the Hegelians). But in what sense?

I. The Problem

(1) Historical situation of Hegel's philosophy. It is equivocal, true and false.[2]

(2) One has reason to want to deny philosophy. But one can only do so if one overcomes or overcomes it (*aufzuheben*).[3]

(3) And one has reason to want to realize philosophy, but one can only do so if one overcomes it or surmounts it (*aufzuheben*).[4]

(4) The critique of the philosophy of Right is equivocal [326] as

philosophy of Right. It is for and against—For, as critical analysis of the modern State, against, in the sense that this State is a fantasy—Germany, beneath and beyond the modern State.[5]

(5) The problem: to find a praxis (because it cannot be a matter of theorizing: Germany is backward) that expresses the depth of the philosophy of Right and thus the future of humanity—To overcome both the modern State and the splintering of the modern state that is backward Germany—the two are linked.

This praxis will be both the realization of the philosophy of Right *and* its overcoming. Head and heart of the Revolution.

(Inequality of development—idea of the Revolution.—In order to mark this appearance of the revolutionary idea: compare with the text of Marx's thesis, the appendix on the Hegelians).

(1) Philosophy of the historical situation in Germany.

The philosophy of Right: *Traumgeschichte* [dream history] of the Germans.—Philosophy in Germany is lived *Naturgeschichte* [natural history], as in primitive [societies], mythology is lived *Vorgeschichte* [pre-history].

The philosophy of Right is contemporary with the ("official") Principles of the modern state.

It is associated with a backward German historical reality. It is in the "abstract continuation."

This ambiguous situation (de facto backwardness—boldness of thought) means that the future is neither in the immediate negation of historical reality nor in the immediate realization of philosophy already overcome.

(2) One thus has reason to want to deny philosophy—But this negation cannot consist in ignoring it: philosophy is part of German reality. It is even the only living germ in Germany. One cannot overcome it without realizing it. It is necessary that practice realize philosophy.

(3) One has reason, inversely, to want to realize philosophy (the Hegelians, the partisans of the "critique" that measures things according to the idea), but one forgets that philosophy belongs to this German world, that it is the ideal *Ergänzung* [complement]. One realizes it only by denying it *als Philosophie*. [327]

(4) Marx's enterprise: critique of Hegel. This critique is *beides* [both]: destruction *and* realization.—Consciousness of the modern State and of its infrastructure, and negation of this consciousness insofar as it is satisfied with itself and with the "theory" that it is.

The picture of the modern State, its "truth," is possible in Germany *because* Germany is backwards (that the ancien régime is artificial, lacking conviction, that the power of industrialists is not the result of development but its condition).

This "truth" is at the same time a fantasy: the modern State that it describes is fiction.

The philosophy of Right is equivocal—as is its critique.

Idea that the true, as true statement, formula, conceptualization, is itself associated with lies: it is necessarily non-reflective of what exists in the same location but a fantasy—and fantasy even with respect to England and to France—Philosophy is (1) part of a historical whole and (2) content, mask, "abstract sequence"—and truth as fantasy—For example, religion at the beginning of the "Introduction."

(5) What to do in the face of this ambiguity? A critique that will be ambiguous as well: rupture; it requires change; it requires praxis (against philosophy as sleep), but praxis that is above principles (which is not less true than philosophy but more true), that indicates the future and thus is beyond the fantasy of the modern State.

II. The Solution

(1) The Proletariat as *Gestaltung* [shaping] of existence that is the presentation of truth[6]—This before the period of economic and political analysis, which begins in 1844.

(2) The thought that reconnects it realizes the philosophy of Right and does not suppress it.[7] This is Hegelian in the sense of *Erfahrung*.

We will see next time: yet what does he blame Hegel for? What philosophy does he put in place of speculation? [328]

APRIL 17, 1961

We have seen the problem: the eminently dialectical relationship of philosophy-historical reality (*Unphilosophie*)—i.e., not simple parallelism, reflection or mystification.

Hegel's philosophy: (1) is not reflection of a backwards Germany and is not a simple lie or mask of this Germany—it is the theory of the modern State. The living germs are in a Germany on its head—(2) is no longer simple reflection of modern States: nowhere does it happen in the way Hegel says—Nor lies: this philosophy is the spirit of a time without spirit.

Philosophy is *Traumgeschichte*, imaginary history, like religion, but the dream of a historical function, like the myths of *Vorgeschichte* in primitive [societies]: it is *Nachgeschichte* [post-history].

Dream and reality in a dialectical relationship: the dream is part of human reality. Also Philosophy as philosophy.

What happens in order to get out of this equivocation?

If one simply wants to realize the philosophy of the modern State, one maintains German backwardness; because this philosophy is the ideal *Ergänzung* of this backwardness, the radicalism of philosophers remains verbal.—To directly realize is to annul philosophy, and this is also to conserve everything in the state. So, will we turn our backs on philosophy? Rely on pure action (*praktische Partei* [practical party])? But this is still to do the contrary of what we want; it is to still forget that philosophy is part of German reality, is the living part: action without principles.

Instead of this realization that destroys and this destruction that maintains, a realization-overcoming is required. Instead of dialectic that does the contrary of what it wants, a dialectic that achieves *beides* [both] is required (see Plato, "the two").—See Péguy, *Clio*: that the "scandal," the failure of all public life, becomes "mysterious," i.e., paradox well done, "justified scandal." [329]

This is the problem that Marx poses:

Proof by the appendix to the doctoral thesis (written 1839–1841) on the Hegelians.[8]

Already, then, Marx opposes the attitude of Hegel's reformers, of the Hegelians who want (1) to keep Hegel's philosophy as it is, (2) to realize it: Hegel's only wrong would have been to "accommodate"—it would suffice to apply it in order to realize it—"*unphilosophische*" manner of criticizing Hegel; it is not a matter of "moral" fault; the fault had to be in the very principle of philosophy as separate philosophy, as statement, *Begreifen*. Their Hegel was *werdende Wissenschaft* [nascent science], it is what "his own spiritual heart's blood pushed to the last periphery."[9] It is necessary to philosophically criticize Hegel, i.e., (dialectic) (1) more profoundly, more faithfully (2) in remaining more faithful to him by remaining a philosopher.—It is in criticizing Hegel that one accomplishes Hegel (parricide).—The Hegelians inevitably [commit] the error of missed liberations—liberations which are dependence.—The theoretical spirit becomes *praktische Energie* [practical energy], *Wille* [will], but this praxis itself is entirely impregnated by theory: "the *praxis* of philosophy is itself *theoretical*."[10] In what? In that one wants to replace philosophy with "Critique," which "measures the individual existence by the essence, the particular reality by the Idea."[11] Now, this will to immediate realization is bad theoretical spirit: it is theoretical spirit, since it is referred to concepts, but it is theory perverted since the concepts employed immediately lose their value, their truth.

Philosophy is turned against the world that it criticizes (the backward German reality), becomes a "side" of the world, its relationship to it is in *Reflexionsverhältnis* [reflection-relation], tension against another (Hegel is right here, opposed to the Hegelians who want to "apply" him):

> What was inner light becomes an outwardly turning consuming flame. The result is that the philosophical becoming [330] of the world is at the same time a worldly becoming of philosophy,[12] that this realization is at the same time its loss, that what it outwardly fights is its own inner deficiency, that precisely in its struggle it falls into those defects [weaknesses][13] that it fights as the defects of the opposing side. . . . That which opposes it and that which it fights is always the same as itself, only with factors inverted.[14]

(There is a will to realize ends, ideas that destroy them—It is the immediate will—It is empty, hollow; it is its own void that it fights in the world; it is itself that it fights; its action is disagreement with itself; as lack of the world, it is in profound agreement with backwardness; it can carry nothing. On the pretext of realization, it ruins philosophy without profit. There is an engagement that is profoundly theory, precisely because it is the immediate negation of the world—Thus, looking badly on the relationship between philosophy and the thing: it is "inverted in itself."[15] (See the Hegelian analysis of unhappy consciousness.)

On the side of the consciousness of philosophers, this attitude of "Critique" is equivocal; there are two contrary requirements: "one edge turned against the world, the other against philosophy itself. . . . Their liberation of the world from nonphilosophy is at the same time their liberation [331] from philosophy."[16] Lassitude of philosophy that is still philosophy—The replacement of system-philosophy with the *Akt* and with the "immediate energy of development" proves that "in theoretical terms [*sic*], they have not yet emerged from that system."[17]—The Hegelians feel strongly about their opposition "to the plastic self-equality of the system"[18]—and do not realize that in purely and simply denouncing it, they truly change nothing. One only destroys philosophy if one realizes it.

This equivocation of the young Hegelians ultimately results in two opposed philosophical tendencies: (1) liberal party, who want to apply philosophy (the "Critique"), (2) the opposed party, *positive Philosophy*, who posit the *Nichtbegriff* [non-concept] of philosophy as essential, "the moment of reality."[19] "Each of these parties does exactly what the other one wants to do and what it itself does not want to do."[20] The "Critique" ruins philosophy while wanting to "realize" it—"Positive philosophy" (Schelling? Feuerbach? the "practical" political party?) conserves ideologies, masks, because it wants to physically, immediately destroy them.

Difference of this text from ours:

The two unilateral, immediate, non-dialectical attitudes are brought back to a common principle in 1839–1841: it is a false liberation with respect to Hegel; one wants either to apply it or wants to replace the *Begriff* with an act or the immediate energy of development; this is not a dialectical, it is a "reflexive" relationship—Philosophy-world—The true liberation of Hegel is Hegelian, is dialectical, does not turn its back on philosophy or critique the world from the loftiness of philosophy, which are the same—The Hegelian attitude applied to the history of Hegelianism [332] consists in understanding it dialectically: (1) there is at first a *verkehrt* [inverted] relationship philosophy-world which *erscheint*, a tension of abstract opposition between them; (2) this becomes an opposition of philosophical consciousness with itself; (3) finally, a division and a duplication of philosophy, which interiorizes its opposition to the world—Conclusion of the dialectical analysis of 1839: the two tendencies are put in the same bag, both false. Tactical rallying to the "liberal party" insofar as it is *die Partei des Begriffs*, immediately conserves philosophy, while the other is *Verhkehrheit* to the pure state, *Verrücktheit* (derailment [*détraquement*], madness). Position of waiting for a realization that is not destruction.

The diagnosis (each does the contrary of what it wants) remains the same in 1843. But, instead of saying: they are both wrong (and for the same reason, which is false liberation, poor critique of Hegel) Marx added: they are both right; it is necessary to destroy and necessary to realize. And this is what is proposed in making itself a critique of the philosophy of Right.

Why?

The end of 1842, violent reaction: Frederick William IV abolishes journals, especially the *Annales Allemandes* of 1843 directed by Arnold Ruge—the *Gazette Rhénane* of 1843 directed by Marx—Marx to Ruge, September, 1843: "a general anarchy rages among the reformers . . . each is obliged to confess to himself that there is no longer an exact notion of what the future should be."[21] The "liberalism" of the Hegelian State is a myth. It is the illusion of wanting to put the State back on its road, that of freedom—Feuerbach recommended the alliance of German theory and French practice—Marx feels the need to leave the waiting attitude: revolutionary dialectic puts the State back on its road, motor of historical evolution—since the State turns out to be reactionary.

Hence: *no longer*: the philosopher party and the practical party are both wrong (especially the practical party) (non-engaged attitude), *but*: they are both right. It is the same thing, since Marx continues to say that each, unable to do what it wants, does what the other wants. Thus they are right, but one can only extricate their truth by [333] overcoming them— Simply put, the positive formula indicates that a position must be taken.

This position will be both: for philosophy, for practice, cease to be mutually exterior in a *Reflexionsverhältnis*—A practice that is the true realization of philosophy (a theory that is the true destruction of itself as separate theory) where the light of philosophy finds everything, that thus incorporates it entirely, and in this sense, destroys it, truly overcomes it, because it contains it.

Thus: (1) for praxis; (2) for a praxis that keeps the promises of philosophy.

1) "Even as the resolute opponent of the previous form of *German* political consciousness, the criticism of speculative philosophy of Right turns, now toward itself, but toward *problems* which can only be solved by one means: *praxis*."[22]

One goes against German political consciousness as a "point of honor," ideological justification of backwards reality. It is a matter of transforming German reality, of passing into action, into an action that is not hidden theory (as before), but which changes the world.

2) But—difference with the practical political party which, in action, forgot philosophy (and in this remained "theoretical," was an intellectual praxis, anti-philosophy, and thus philosophy)—it must be an action that realizes philosophy. Is it thus giving the State a formal notice to apply Hegel's principles? No: it is impossible in the backward State of Germany. And, moreover, Hegel's principles are not applied anywhere—The realization of Hegel will consist not in *reforming* the real according to its concepts, but in arousing the transformation of this real by itself, to seek in itself the principles of overcoming, negative work, which Hegel's philosophy of right seeks in Spirit. [334]

> The question arises: can Germany achieve a *praxis à la hauteur des principes*,[23] i.e., a *revolution* which will raise it not only to the *official level* of modern nations, but to the *height of humanity* which will be the near future of those nations?[24]

An action worthy of the highest principle, i.e., which realizes not less but more than the principles of the Hegelian State.—This always remains "official," i.e., of masks, and in Germany they cannot even have this official existence. They can only be realized there by overcoming them as principles, i.e., in animating a historical movement that realizes them in concrete human beings and not in bringing about a less advanced society, but one more advanced than English and French society, model for their future.

How is this philosophical action itself possible? Especially in Germany? The Germany that hasn't even practically achieved the degree which it has theoretically overcome, which thus has to pass through, not only the limits of its reality, but even the limits of modern States, and which does not appear to offer the "radical" needs that make this radical revolution possible?[25]

Where is the positive possibility of a German emancipation?[26]

Answer: it is exactly in the formation of an absolutely forgotten class, the proletariat.—Definition of the proletariat.[27]

The work of the negative, at its maximum in the proletariat, wants to accomplish the dialectical union of the proletariat and philosophy.[28]— The proletariat is the *Weltgeist*, [335] the historical figure of the *Weltgeist*— The proletariat's taking power (defined as above) is the advent of negativity and of the universal, since it can only be saved by saving humanity and by overcoming itself as a class, in bringing about a classless society. But this imposes a condition on revolutionary praxis: that it is praxis animated by the negativity of the proletariat, and, in this, philosophical praxis. Not action, in the pragmatist sense of success, or in the relative and "realist" sense of achieving certain particular aims, certain ends by any means, but a praxis that is not *poesis*, that is the complete means—means and ends being in dialectical interdependence—Refusal to choose between Being and Making: one is not to be preferred over the other; they are indivisible in praxis—Refusal to choose between moralism and cynicism. This is why praxis is not empirical action. Strictly speaking, [praxis] does not have an *aim*; it is rather a "manner," action for the sake of nothing (empirical, positive) and for everything (the universal, mankind)—*Todo y nada*—"Mystery of existence" of the proletariat, "Secret of its own existence."[29]—Philosophical function of the proletariat commanding its economic function.

Such is the philosophical-political attitude.

More specifically, what "philosophy," what conceived superstructures, what conceptual preparations make this praxis possible? We will see this in the *1844 Manuscripts*—which offer Marx's phenomenology: the conceptual preparations that go beyond the practical recognition of the proletariat as bearer of the universal. It is a matter of a "philosophy" that is not philosophy of consciousness but of carnal humanity.

As Hegel will make phenomenology part of Knowledge, once he has installed himself in it, Marx will consider these essays as preparatory; once through them he will have installed himself in the becoming of truth, i.e., in *Capital* and its self-overcoming.

The next two lessons:
    April 24: *Manuscripts of 1844*   [336]
    May 2: "Postface" of *Capital*
    May 8: Text of Kierkegaard
          Text of Nietzsche
    April 24, 1961[30]
    Read MEGA I.2, 620–621.[31]

Praxis includes *its* theory—the human being is the supreme being for humanity—theory that overcomes the modern as modernity overcomes the Middle Ages, which is *fondamentale* and universal: what philosophy is in words, the proletariat is in act—It expresses "the secret of its own existence."[32]—The "secret" or speculative mystery (negativity) is passed on to the proletariat. See *Capital*: the mystery of *Verdinglichung* [reification]— the proletariat and praxis that it is (as negativity) and that it defines: philosophy realized—Praxis: non-fabrication of a certain result, e.g., of an apparatus of technical Power, but practical, a (universal and fundamental) historical mode of existence. Praxis not defined by deliberate ends but by the movement of history (the industry that creates the proletariat) extended into the re-creation of human society—Obviously a political technology is needed to enlighten the de facto proletariat, but the final measurement will always be the mystery of negativity and the negation of negation that the proletariat is in idea—i.e., an action that is action for all (the universal, humanity), because it is in a sense action for nothing and for no *particular* interest.

Philosophy: conceptual preparation for this historical adhesion.

Concepts like: positive and negative, universal, *grund* (fundamental), history, humanity, nature, mind, are the science of the experience of history—This is why Marx deals with it in 1844.

One finds his concept of the proletariat as *Selbstaufhebung* [self-overcoming] anterior to the experience of "advanced" countries and to an extensive reading of Hegel's sources—This is not an argument against—But only to show that Marx [337] is a philosopher. He will remain so: *Capital* was interrupted before it arrived at classes and at the proletariat, but the analysis of the structure of *Capital* reveals the same metaphysical mechanism: Capital, as a reality that "overcomes" itself, contradicts itself—Here, one goes from the reality (Capital) to the appearance (the proletariat); it is the "becoming of truth" substituted for the "becoming of consciousness," as with Hegel's *Logic*, but it is always philosophy and always Hegel—it is the most audacious philosophy under the appearance of abandoning philosophy: is hidden in "things," masked by apparent positivism—philosophy even insofar as it doesn't want to be. And, inversely, the philosophy declared in 1844 is not far from the concrete.

Why this change now, these declarations about abandoning philosophical consciousness? Because: (1) a more acute sense of the weight of things—these are what must be understood, especially after 1848—*their* movement; (hence) *Capital*, which in reality founds proletarian philosophy; (2) sense of political practice stirring up a consciousness of the difference [*écart*] between the de facto proletariat and its philosophical and historical function. Action is the strategy and the technique of overturning capitalism (hence) objective analysis. The sketches of 1844, from this point of view, appear too "immediate"—schematics. One cannot half "realize"—But what is to be realized through the analyses of Capital and action is always the game of the positive and the negative.

APRIL 24, 1961

The *Economic-Philosophic Manuscripts of 1844*.[33]

(1) Critique of Hegel—leaving aside for the moment the Feuerbachian critiques (overturning, subject-object), superficial critiques ("idealism" which *aufhebt* history and takes away its *Eigenbewegung* [proper movement]). [338]

(a) Critique of philosophical exhaustion in the name of *Dasein*.

See MEGA, book I, vol. 3, p. 165.[34]

Negation and confirmation philosophy equivocates real modes of existence with philosophical existence.

(b) Critique of the pretension of *SelbstBewußtsein* to be other than itself—pretention of pure *Wissen* that allows for the identification of objectivation and alienation—This is linked to the very essence of Hegel's philosophy (negativity) and not to "accommodation."

See MEGA, book I, vol. 3, pp. 163–164.[35]

(c) Critique of the negation of negation and of the equivocal *Aufheben* that it realizes.

See MEGA, book I, vol. 3, p. 164.[36]

This (the text cited) is in agreement with Feuerbach.

See MEGA, book I, vol. 3, p. 152.[37]

However, the negation of the negation is a good description of human pre-history (ibid.). Positivist Marx for the sake of a distant future beyond communism—communism: negation of the negation supported by a future positivism.

See MEGA, book I, vol. 3, p. 125.[38]

(d) In parallel, Marx accepts the idea of the alienation of the subject in the object but not as a definition of *Gegenständlichkeit* [objectivity]; as an episode which will succeed non-alienation objectivation (positivist perspective).

Critique of Hegelian alienation: the alienation of alienation must be added, in short, a negation that absolutely gets carried away into the positive.

(e) Critique of nature according to Hegel.

It resumes everything that has preceded it: the critique of *Wissen*, of speculation, of the negation of negation, of alienation.

See MEGA, book I, vol. 3, p. 170–172.[39]

(2) Attempt at a Marxist philosophy.

(a) The *Aufheben*—the negation of negation is to be kept. Only, it is necessary that it is true overcoming and not negation that conserves (i.e., in elevating to thought). Makes an abstraction of abstraction— "Thought" is in *alienated* [339] *language* this negation of the negation that is the reconquest of the object-being of humanity, of its *Wesen* and positive humanism.

See MEGA, book I, vol. 3, p. 166–167.[40]

(b) Thus nature before and after pre-history. Relationship to concept: nature, humanity, history, praxis.

Humanity as sensible-objective being.

See MEGA, book I, vol. 3, p. 160.[41]

Humanity as social historical as soon as it is un-alienated.—It is its *nature* and it is nature that becomes human in it—dialecticalization of the relationship nature-history.

See MEGA, book I, vol. 3, p. 115–116.[42]

See MEGA, book I, vol. 3, p. 160.[43]

This is the critique of Hegelian negativity (Spirit)—its reform (final and primordial positivism) and, consequently, elaboration of the concepts humanity-nature.

It remains to appreciate this:

exact relationship with Hegel, with Feuerbach. Is it overturning Hegel, as Feuerbach says? Or does Marx introduce something else? And as a function of that, relationship with Marx's final thought.

MAY 2, 1961

Marxist critique of Hegel

(1) Philosophical *Denken* as exhaustion, unconditioned thought, identity with the thing itself, is destruction and conservation, this in an equivocal manner:
(human attitudes):

> In their actual existence [*wirklichen Existenz*], this *mobile* nature of theirs is hidden [their history is blind]. It appears and is made manifest [*Offenbarung*] only in thought, in philosophy. Hence my true religious *Dasein* is my *Dasein* in the *philosophy of religion* . . . my true natural *Dasein*, *Dasein* in the philosophy of nature . . . my truly human *Dasein*, *Dasein* in philosophy. Likewise the true existence of religion, the state, nature, art, is the *philosophy* of religion, of nature [340], of the State and of art. . . . So, it is only as a *philosopher of religion* that I am truly religious, and so I deny *real* religious sentiment and really *religious* humanity. But at the same time I *assert* them, in part within my own *Dasein* or within the alien *Dasein* which I oppose to them—for this *is* only their philosophical expression—and in part I assert them in their distinct original shape, since for me they represent merely the *apparent* other being, allegories, forms of their own true *Dasein* (i.e., of my *philosophical Dasein*).[44]

Marx: philosophy is equivocally phenomenology as well as speculation: "to understand," i.e., to seize upon the truth of . . . i.e., (a) deny, in their immediate form, art, nature, religion, the State—destroy them—transform them into their truth, which is not them; (b) but in which all of them are the same, since they are only philosophical expression and only allegories, emblems of this truth, and thus true.

But does Marx not say that it was precisely necessary to destroy and to realize? Yes, but philosophy, at bottom, does neither: neither destruction, nor conservation, nor maintenance—Pseudo-destruction and pseudo-conservation, each only being the alibi for the other's escape— What we blame philosophy for is not ambiguity but bad ambiguity.

And where does it come from, that the ambiguity of philosophy is bad? Because like the *Denken* that soars over [*de survol*], exhaustive, possession of the thing "in thought," philosophy, wanting to be everything, is nothing, does not dwell in the things about which it speaks—and being nothing in particular, is not even against what it criticizes. It is neither yes nor no: not no because it is not yes. It has no enemies but also no friends, and it has no friends because it has no enemies. It lacks everything, the particular and the universal. It should, on the contrary, have both. This thought will not be a soaring over, the pretension to dwell at a distance, to see, to haunt, to contemplate—which is yes on the pretext of no and no on the pretext of yes. It must be, on the contrary, a manner of thinking that is both concrete and universal, hence the yes is [341] no, and the no a yes without equivocation. It is a matter not of coming back beneath Hegel, for example, toward a philosophy that gives up understanding nonphilosophy or toward a nonphilosophy that would take nonphilosophy without criticizing it (art, religion, nature, the State). It is a matter of succeeding where he failed, of making a concrete philosophy: but truly concrete.

(2) More precisely:

Marx criticizes the pretension of philosophical *Denken* to remain itself in what is other than itself, to contain in itself and possess its contradictory—to overcome it from the inside or to understand it from the inside, without experience. The problem is to reconceive philosophical proximity and distance, philosophy's nowhere and everywhere, with this condition: not to give to consciousness, and especially to "consciousness of itself," the power to carry in itself its contradictory, to be itself in what is its inverse. Not to fabricate, in the name of *Wissen*, an illusory power of being everything, a negativity so total that it digests and founds everything and nothing.

> In this discussion all the illusions of speculation are brought together.
>
> *First of all*: consciousness, self-consciousness is *at home* in *its other-being as such*. It is therefore—or if we here abstract from the Hegelian abstraction and put the *self-consciousness of humanity* instead of self-consciousness—it is *at home* in its *other-being as such*. This implies, for one thing, that consciousness (knowing as knowing, thinking as thinking) pretends to be directly the *other* of itself—to be the world of sense, the real world, life—thought surpassing itself in thought [*sich uberbeitende*]: (Feuerbach). This aspect [of the doctrine] is contained herein, inasmuch as consciousness as mere consciousness [*Bewußtsein*] [of the exterior] takes offense not at alienated [*entfremdeten*] objectivity [*Gegenstandlichkeit*] but at *objectivity as such*.
>
> Secondly, this implies that the self-conscious human being, insofar as he has recognized and overcome [*aufgehoben*] the spiritual world (or his world's spiritual, general mode of *Dasein*) as self-alienation [*selbstentäußerung*], nevertheless again confirms it in this alienated shape [342] and passes it off as his true mode of *Dasein*—reestablishes it, and pretends to

be *at home in his other-being as such*. Thus, for instance, after overcoming religion, after recognizing religion to be a product of self-alienation, he yet finds confirmation of himself in *religion as religion*. Here *is* the root of Hegel's *false* positivism, or of his merely *apparent* criticism: this is what Feuerbach designated as the positing, negating, and reestablishing of religion or of theology—but it has to be expressed in more general terms. Thus reason is at home in un-reason as un-reason. The human being who has recognized that he was leading an alienated life in law, politics, etc., is leading his true human life in this alienated life as such. Self-affirmation [*Selbstbejahung*], self-confirmation *in contradiction* with itself—in contradiction with both the knowledge and the essential being of the object—is thus true *knowledge* and *life*.

There can therefore no longer be any question about an act of accommodation [concession] on Hegel's part vis-a-vis religion, the state, etc., since this lie is the lie of his [philosophical] progression itself.[45]

Relationship of the critique of pure *Wissen*, pure *Denken*—enriching themselves, realizing their own overcoming—with the problem of the bearer of the dialectic: sensibility, reality, life, nature, the human being, carrying *SelbstBewußtsein* and are not engendered by *SelbstBewußtsein* "enriching" itself.[46] [343]

In other words, *SelbstBewußtsein* in the midst of things and not producing things, negativity among things already there and not extracting them from itself.

Problem of alienation (passage from self into the other who deprives the self of its ipseity)—This passage is, for Hegel, coextensive with objectivity, *SelbstBewußtsein* being pure subject. It would be necessary to think a relationship of *SelbstBewußtsein*-object that is not necessarily contradictory, genesis of an antagonist.

Problem of *Aufheben* (already named)—Hegel's progress (the thought of the negative) is responsible for the equivocation of *Aufheben*: because for thought this can only consist in increasing the critique, to critique the critique, i.e., in "false positivism," reestablishing, on the pretext of drawing out the truth, what has been critiqued.

(3) Critiques of Hegel: Marx and Feuerbach

Through this text, therefore, the problem of *negation* appears as central in the Marxist critique of Hegel—this problem, and not that of "materialism" or "idealism," or of "returned" or "redressed" dialectic, which are subordinated to it—It is a matter of arriving at a conception of negation (and of the positive-negative relationship, of alienation, of the *Aufhebung*) that is not, like Hegelian negation [344], this pseudo-destruction and pseudo-conservation that one obtains by replacing the thing with the thought of the thing.

Not one word in all of this is opposed to the idea of negativity. This is very different from the Feuerbachian critique of Hegel. In his provisionary theses, Feuerbach says: "the method of the reformist critique of speculative philosophy, in a general manner, is not different from the method already applied in the *Philosophy of Religion*. In order to obtain the naked truth, the pure and simple truth (*die blanke Wahrheit*), it is enough for us to transform the predicate into a subject, and, once a subject, into an object and into a principle, thus reversing speculative philosophy." For Marx, whenever he has occasionally taken up these formulations, they do not express his thought or no longer do so. "Direct thought (*die Direchtheit*), the conscious elimination of all mediation, eliminates the dialectic by means of Hegelian idealism."[47]

One sees this temptation on the part of Feuerbach, of Feuerbachian return, and Marx's reaction in his appreciation of Feuerbach:

> [When he opposes] the negation of the negation, which claims to be the absolute positive, the self-supporting positive, positively based on itself . . . Feuerbach thus conceives the negation of the negation *only* as a contradiction of philosophy with itself—as the philosophy which affirms theology (the transcendent, etc.) after having denied it, and which it therefore affirms in opposition to itself
>
> The positive position or self-affirmation and self-confirmation contained in the negation of the negation is taken [by Feuerbach] to be a position which is not yet sure of itself, which is therefore burdened with its opposite, which is doubtful of itself and therefore in need of proof, and which, therefore, is not a position of demonstrating itself by its *Dasein*—not an acknowledged position; hence it is directly and immediately confronted by the position of sense-certainty based on itself.[48]

This is the temptation of positivism opposed to negativity—of a therefore non-dialectical philosophy.

> But because Hegel has conceived the negation of the negation, [345] from the point of view of the positive relation inherent in it, as the true and only positive, and from the point of view of the negative relation inherent in it as the only true act and spontaneous activity of all being [*Selbstbestätigung alles Seins*], he has only found the *abstract, logical, speculative* expression for the movement of history, which is not yet the *real* history of humanity as a given subject, but only the *act of creation*, the *history of the origin* of humanity.[49]

Feuerbach and his positivism, or a humanist-immediate philosophy, didn't account for history or the human being as being made across history, producing itself as subject, becoming *SelbstBewußtsein.*

Yes, Hegel was wrong to draw out the nature of thought, or the human being of thought (or religion, or art, or right), but this is not a reason to simply overturn Hegel by making nature or the human being into the subject and consciousness into the predicate. (One could also just as well make right or religion into the subject and Spirit into the predicate, [make] of the positive the subject and of the negative an attribute.) This would misunderstand the problem—The problem is to have a conception of the negative that does not transform nature, the human being, and history into abstractions, of a negative that is in their tissue, and especially in that of history. Marx will say that Feuerbach, when he affirms the material, is not a historian, and when he recognizes history he is not a materialist. A historical materialism is, for Marx, a concrete conception of negativity and of the negation of the negation, a just but algebraic formula for the *movement* of history.

It is in this spirit that Marx tries, in the *1844 Manuscripts,* to elaborate his philosophy, his dialectic, to redefine the concepts of nature, humanity, history, and of "realizing" the *Aufhebung* and Hegelian negativity—A dialectic that would no longer be the history of consciousness, no longer even be the history of humanity (Feuerbach), but *Seinsgeschichte* [the history of being].

Sketch for a Marxist *Seinsgeschichte.*

One no longer starts from *Denken,* from pure *Wissen,* i.e., from the equivocal relationship of consciousness (*Bewußtsein*)-object, finally becoming consciousness of itself and absolute self.

Where do we start? From nature or from the human being? No [346] more than from pure nature: which for itself is not the human being. And the human being, taken positively, will not be a valid philosophical principle: it itself is not two natures but double nature: "both the material of labor and that of the human being as the subject, are the point of departure as well as the result of historical movement."[50]

The philosophy sketched by Marx is essentially dialectic, i.e., nature, humanity, and nature are understood not as substances definable through a principal attribute, but as movements without locatable discontinuity where the other is always involved—No cleavage of material-idea, object-subject, nature-humanity, in itself-for itself, but a single Being where negativity is at work—Thus: nature will not be defined as pure object, exteriority, but as "sensible," carnal, nature as we see it. Natural beings have internally preordained relationships to each other. The human being will be defined neither as pure subject nor as a fragment of nature but through a kind of two-sided *Subjekt-Objekt* coupling, relative to an object or active object, and thereby as essentially related to the other human being, generic being (*Gattungswesen*), *Gesellschaft* [society], this relationship being transformation and continuation of the natural relationship of the living being to exterior beings. History is, in this sense, the very flesh of humanity.

> The *human being* is directly [= superficially] a *natural being* [*Naturwesen*]. As a natural being and as a living natural being he is on the one hand endowed with *natural powers, vital powers*—he is an *active* natural being. . . . [A]s a natural corporeal, sensuous, objective [*gegenstandliches*] being he is a *suffering* [*leidendes*], conditioned and limited creature, like animals and plants. . . . To say that the human being is a *corporeal*, living, real [*wirklich*], sensuous, objective being full of natural vigor is to say that he has *real, sensuous objects* as the object of his being [*Wesens*] or of his life, or that he can only *express* his life [*Lebensausserung*] in real, sensuous objects. *To be* objective, natural and sensuous, and at the same time to have object, nature and sense [*Sinn*] [347] outside oneself,[51] or oneself to be object, nature and sense for a third (being),[52] is one and the same thing [*ist identisch*]. *Hunger* is a natural *need*; it therefore needs a *nature* outside itself, an *object* outside itself. . . . The sun is the *object* of the plant—an indispensable object to it, confirming its life [*bestatigend*]— just as the plant is an object of the sun, being an *expression* [*Ausserung*] of the life-awakening power of the sun, of the sun's *objective* essential power. A being which does not have its nature outside of itself is not a *natural* being. . . . An object-less being [*ungegenstandliches*] would be a non-being [*Unwesen*].
>
> Suppose a being which is neither an object itself, nor has an object. Such a being, in the first place, would be the *unique* being [*das einzige Wesen*]: there would exist no being outside it. . . . For as soon as there are objects outside me, as soon as I am not *alone*, I am *another*—a reality other than the object outside of me. For this third object I am thus a *different reality* than itself; that is, I am *its* object.[53]

The human being is in this way suffering (*leidend*) and because it feels its suffering, a passionate being (*leidendschaftliches Wesen*).

> But the human being is not merely a natural being: he is a *human* natural being. That is to say, he is a being for himself [*für sich selbst seiendes Wesen*]. Therefore he is a species-being [*Gattungswesen*[54]]. . . . Therefore, *human* objects are not natural objects as they immediately present themselves, [348] and neither is *human sense* [*der menschliche Sinn*] as it immediately

is—as it is objectively—*human* sensibility. . . . Neither nature objectively nor nature subjectively is directly given in a form adequate to the *human* being. And as everything natural has to *come into being*, the *human being* too has its act of origin [*Entstehungsakt*]—history—which, however, is for him a known history, and hence as an act of origin it is a conscious self-overcoming act of origin [*als Entstehungsakt mit Bewusstsein sich aufhe-bender Entstehungsakt ist*]. History is the true natural history of the human being.[55]

The sensible-practical human being is the transformation of nature into history—nature that wants to be for itself and thus is realized in its destruction, is conserved in its overcoming—and carnal, "material" history that shifts onto natural forces and onto an always "objective" movement that serves as its "steering wheel [*volant*]."

It is Feuerbach, but with the supplementary dimension of history as producing the human being and produced by it. It is thus Hegel and his negativity descended into the flesh of the world.

But the philosophical problem was, then, the exact status of this negativity floating above nature and one that is no longer absolute Self.

If we stop there, it is after all of Hegel: an act of origination which "overcomes itself" as act of origination because it is "for itself." Is it not access to *knowledge*, to *Wissen*?

But in introducing the concept of nature, Marx refrained from leaving negativity floating in the air. He maintains, against Feuerbach, the negation of the Hegelian negation as abstract formula of history before the birth of the human being. But this negation of the negation is the installation of a positive Being of the human or of a second nature, and it is why Marx praised Feuerbach for having taken the positive resting in itself as a principle; he only blamed him for not having considered the mediations that precede it. Marx considers the *Aufheben* of history as itself the *Selbstaufhebung*, as the blossoming of a "*wahre Wesen*" of humanity:

If I *know* religion [349] as *alienated* human self-consciousness, then what I know in it as religion is not my self-consciousness, but my alienated self-consciousness confirmed in it. I therefore know my self-consciousness that belongs to itself, to its very nature, confirmed not in *religion* but rather in religion *annihilated* and *overcome*.

In Hegel, therefore, the negation of the negation is not the confirmation [*Bestätigung*] of the true essence, effected precisely through the negation of the pseudo-essence. With him the negation of the negation is the confirmation of the pseudo-essence, or the self-alienated essence in its denial; or it is the denial of this pseudo-essence as an objective being dwelling outside the human being and independent of him, and its transformation into the subject.[56]

In reference to the problem of the relationship to the exterior, this means that this relationship can no longer be that of the negative to the positive, as in Hegel, an alienation of the negative in the positive, but that the two terms are relativized: the establishment of a relationship without contradiction with the positive, and in reference to the problem of *Aufheben*, that it is the establishment of a human being who "appropriated" its essence, the production of a new state of humanity where it is in equilibrium with itself.

Thus: (1) the negation of the Hegelian negation pulled in its positive direction [*sens*]:

> Thus, by grasping the *positive* meaning of self-referred negation (although again in an alienated fashion) Hegel grasps humanity's self-alienation, the alienation of essence, the loss of objectivity, of essence, objectification, realization. In short, with the sphere of abstraction, Hegel conceives labor as man's act of *self-genesis*.[57]

> Positive moments of the Hegelian dialectic. . . . (a) the *Aufheben* as objective movement of *retracting* the alienation *into* [350] *self*. This is the insight, expressed within the very heart of alienation, concerning the *appropriation* of the objective essence through the overcoming of its alienation; it is an alienated insight into the *real objectivation* of humanity.[58]

Hence negativity (and especially negation of the negation) is only the inverse of a "true essence" of humanity who has never been but who will be. Simple, positive nature, not only at the origin but at the end:

> In the same way atheism, being the overcoming of God, is the advent of theoretical humanism, and communism, as the overcoming of private property, is the vindication of real human life as humanity's possession and thus the advent of practical humanism, or atheism is humanism mediated with itself through the overcoming of religion, whilst communism is humanism mediated with itself through the overcoming of private property. Only through overcoming this mediation [overcoming of overcoming]—which is itself, however, a necessary premise—does positively self-deriving humanism, *positive* humanism, come into being.[59]

More clearly, description of a future of true self-possession by humanity (implied by the concept of nature) which supports the prerequisite phase of the negation of the negative negation.

> Since the *real existence* of humanity and nature has become evident in
> practice [*praktisch sinnlich*] . . . the question about an *alien* being, about a
> being above nature and humanity . . . has become impossible in practice.
> *Atheism*, as the denial of this unreality, no longer has any sense. . . . But
> socialism as socialism no longer stands in any need of such a mediation.
> It proceeds from the *theoretically and practically sensuous consciousness* of
> humanity and of nature as the *essence* [*als des Wesens*]. Socialism is hu-
> manity's *positive self-consciousness*, no longer mediated by the overcoming
> of religion, just as *real life* is the positive reality for humanity, no longer
> mediated by the overcoming of private property, by communism. Com-
> munism is the position as [only] the negation of the negation, and hence
> the *actual* moment necessary for the next [*nächste*] stage of historical
> development in the process of human emancipation and rehabilitation.
> *Communism* is the necessary form and the dynamic principle of [351] the
> immediate [*nächste*] future, but communism as such is not the goal of
> human development, the form of human society.[60]

The face that communism turns toward a beyond (its negation of the
negation side as positive): the "positive development" of private property,
the veritable appropriation of human being—

> The *genuine* resolution of the conflict between humanity and nature and
> between human beings—the true resolution of the strife between exis-
> tence and essence, between objectification and self-confirmation [*Selbst-
> bestätigung*], between freedom and necessity, between the individual and
> the species. Communism is the riddle of history solved, and it knows itself
> to be this solution [*er ist das aufgelöste Rätsel der Geschichte und weiss sich als
> diese Lösung*].[61]

So Marx [is different from] Feuerbach, (is different from) immediate positivity. But the domain of negativity is enclosed on two sides by
Nature and Equality with itself.—Resolution of the historical enigma (or
pre-historical . . . is Marx's hesitation).

Now, as Lukács has put it, is this "direct thought" (even if it is rejected in the distant future, it colors the entire dialectic which leans on it;
it gives its style to the *Aufheben* and to labor as the possibility of *anything
whatsoever*, as absolute re-creation of the world and of humanity) not the
elimination, with Hegelian idealism, of the dialectic as well?[62]

> It would be dangerous to understand Engels's sentence as if the material-
> ist reestablishment of Hegel's philosophy should only consist in a reversal
> of philosophical signs [*als so das materialistische auf die Fusse Stellen der Hege-*

lische Philosophie bloss in einen Umkehren der philosophischen Vorzeichen bestehen wurde].[63]

Hyppolite, *Logic and Existence*:

> Marx adds this historical dimension to Feuerbach. He rediscovers then, more or less, Hegelian dialectic in the concrete conflicts of history, but he refuses to reduce the positive to the negation of the negation. . . . Human objectification is not for him an alienation, because the determined object is not a negation; it is first. History then has created the conflicts and will put an end to them.[64]

> For the negation of the negation, it is necessary to substitute the first positivity [352] of nature; it is necessary to understand man objectifying himself on the basis of this positivity.[65]

> Human nature will then present itself after the resolution of historical conflicts. Positivity is first, positivity will be last, and this positivity must have no fissures in it, nothing negative.[66]

From that moment on: praxis ceases to be openness, action that does everything, because it is not particular and is animated by the class that is its self-overcoming. Praxis becomes the technology of power for this class—Return to the positive through the Party and the dictator. It is certainly efficient, but is it the realization of negativity?

Positivism, in a sense—ironically—produces the same result as absolute negation or Hegel's absolute negative: i.e., hidden sense of history, battle of the gods—Stalinism and Hegelianism—One could even say that Hegel maintains more of the sense of negativity, of the tension.

Awareness today? Oppositions, not antagonists, recognized in Soviet society, which are no longer presented as marching toward nature.

Philosophy and nonphilosophy: separate philosophy always reappears in disguise—That one doesn't freeze in negativism or positivism would require the negation of the negation.

Texts from *Capital* (and from the introduction to the *Critique of Political Economy*)—The renunciation of philosophy must be consciousness of the difficulties with nature/history.

Appendixes

Draft of a Chapter from
The Visible and the Invisible[1]

[103] October 1960.[2]
The visible and the invisible.

I. Being and World
    1st Part: Reflection and interrogation
    2nd Part: The vertical world and wild Being
    3rd Part: Wild being and classical ontology

2nd Part: The visible and wild Being
[or perhaps relate paragraphs 1 and 2 to the 1st part: Reflection and Interrogation].

§1. The *Ineinander*

Of all the questions that we ask ourselves, there is only one that does not imply any other, which is radical or philosophical, and this is not even "What do I know?" since that could be a simple call to enumerate the things that we know. One can even, without any examination of the idea of knowledge, put forward that all experience is knowledge as an ultimate question only by implying it as a matter of course. "What do I know" is then only a question of knowledge [*connaissance*]—like "where [356] am I?" or "what time is it?"[3, 4]—where one hesitates only on the application to the case of particular entities—time, space, knowledge—in themselves unconstituted. These questions are only the provisional absence of a positive statement, lacunae in a tissue of indicatives of which we are assured that it is in principle continuous, since there is a time, a space where everything is, a knowledge where everything lived has its place. But when we say "What do I know?" in the course of a sentence, it is another question entirely as to what we do to ourselves: it does not expect an answer that abolishes **[104]** it; it does not imply "where am I?" or "what time is it?," an order of identical Being beyond our perplexities: it indicates, lacking more precision, a certain intelligible place where, should we find facts, examples, find what we miss, like the *je ne sais quoi*, it is the invocation of a knowledge that is more ample, more precise than ours, and which is not a dream that we have almost in hand. Here, the interrogation is no longer a mode derived from the simple inversion of the indicative. It is an original manner of aiming at Being, "Expression ready made"; it is a rhetorical figure: it doesn't wait for an answer; it doesn't formulate a problem: it indicates a little mystery.

In this "What do I know?" or in that of Montaigne, in any case, it is the same idea of knowledge that is called into question, the question going so far as to concern the terms it uses to express itself. In this way, it is fully a question—neither affirmation nor veiled negation, and it insinuates the idea that perhaps ultimate knowledge is a knowledge-question, the interrogative mode proper to Being; that Being, in other words, is the mute interlocutor of our questions, that which makes way for our interrogation and which our answers do not contain since they take the enigma away from it. In this profound sense, where "What do I know?" wants to mean as well and finally "What is it?,"[5] the philosophical question is—and this is where this question is, as one sees it—not one to which any [357] knowledge [*connaissance*] whatsoever can put to an end, since it holds itself in suspense as a formulated question, since Being is perhaps only accessible through the question, since the function of this question is not to efface itself before something positively stated, but perhaps to disclose [*dévoiler*] what motivates it from behind and calls to it from ahead, like the interrogation of the gaze discloses the things that arouse and attract it.

Now, this question of questions cannot end as they [105] do through some positive answer. This is impossible in principle. Any statement would always be something said. Even if by a miracle it could never be faulted, even if there were no conceivable term to which it did not apply, and even if it threw some light on [106] everything, it would only have the predicative truth of taking a position, of a judgment, and would leave out what carries it above chaos, which thus has a position in being before taking one—thinking thought [*pensée pensante*] before thought [already] thought [*pensée pensée*], and with it, the world and the savage Being that it frequents. Now, it is all of this that philosophical interrogation precisely aims at, all that goes without saying, everything that is before the problems of knowledge and leads there.

It demands full elucidation; it also wants to know why, from what it is itself born. And this demand is reiterated to each "answer" as it begins. It takes nothing at face value. The same views that it gets from our pre-reflexive life, the tatters of our profound history that it brings to the surface, it does not immediately include them among the number of acquired truths; it does not peacefully accumulate them: to do this, it would be necessary, at the moment of interrogation, to coincide with what we want to know and have the power to communicate this contact with the self we will have tomorrow. Now, without speaking here of the mediators that interpose themselves between ourselves and others, and even between ourselves and ourselves, to consider philosophical interrogation only at the moment where I exercise it, outside of any effort of notation or of expression, even then it is not indistinct from what it interrogates; it is a practice, an attitude that has its history, its genealogy, in me (and outside of me). And even if I [358] reinvent it in an instant, the fact that it endures, however short, places it among instituted things; it does not begin—it has begun; it works upon an acquired inactual—it is given to itself. So it comes **[107]** too late to know the naive world that was before it and too early to know everything precisely as initiative, optional operation, critical enterprise, and cultural second that it includes in its circumstances, emerging habits, conventions of self to self. What it interrogates is already behind it and defies any effort of ideal genesis. And, in order to equalize this mass, to overcome its frail power and its wise limits, it turns its curiosity upon itself in order to perceive that it doesn't even actually seize upon, that it must await from the future, the revelation of motives which carry it and that render it only partially: it is this premature time.

[108] But if this is so, if the philosophical question is in principle inextinguishable—if it is not the explication of the world and of ourselves which makes it and makes us "completely naked" [*tout naturels*]—not reflection that installs us in some unique source from where we would see it and would see it proceed, not even coincidence with ourselves and with it, then is philosophy not the mute face-to-face with the opaque world and ourselves, different from but no less obscure than it; [is it not] the overwhelming confrontation with what *is there*, pure anxiety that leaves us forbidden, speechless, and without an answer before the incomprehensible proliferation of the world, of our life, of our speech, of our actions? And therefore is it not the question mark [*point d'interrogation*] that one places in order to form it upon all being and all experience, and from which there is nothing to draw forth? Fine, the world and ourselves are unthinkable—after that, the serious things begin, if in its radicalism, philosophy rejects any system, any reflection, and everything immediate, which places everything in suspense, and deprives itself of any light, any language, any logic, [then] in what name would it challenge positive statements as obscure, naive, or derivative? Is it not like nothing, an old dream to liquidate or a nightmare to forget? And is not itself that decreed its own end?

This is the case only if philosophy has no choice between [359] two impasses: reflective coincidence and intuitive coincidence. If one wants philosophy to be absolute overview [*survol*] of things and of ourselves (one sees that so-called constituting consciousness is always poorer than psychological, ethnological, historical experiences and that left to itself, the all-powerful reflection would hardly go beyond the categories that the philosopher already had in hand and the signification of her words). But if one must open consciousness, this will not be through fusion with the thing itself. Because we are no longer the pebble or the lobster as soon as we think about it, as soon as we speak: in order to remain faithful to the things themselves, it would be necessary to say nothing: the things themselves are chaos.

But is this dilemma foundational? Are these the only two possibilities for philosophical interrogation? In reality, thought does not have to choose between the reassessment of its favorite significations and the impossible fusion with the things, as if it is closed thought, [or] let's say more generally, proximal thought. We mean by this a thought which is haunted by the ideal of an absolute proximity, whether it is ideal significations pierced all the way down by the mind or that of existing things which we see at the very point and very instant where they are. This thought, which wants to be as close as possible to things, which believes neither in distance nor in appearance, cruel thought, which **[109]** takes away and denudes, fear of error more than love of truth; it is what, in accordance with language and the sensible, closes us in ours significations, in the garden of things said. When it seeks the outside, the world itself, it can only conceive them as an opaque Being with which we would have to confuse ourselves. But the two attempts are equally vain; the two failures are avoidable if the requirement for an absolute proximity to being is a prejudice, if the internal adequation of the idea as well as the thing's self-identity is a myth, if it is essential to the idea, as well as to the thing, that it present itself in a distance that is not an impediment to knowledge, that is, on the contrary, its guarantee, the idea itself, the thing itself, not being something that clogs the mind and puts an end to its movement, but that which fulfills its expectations without suffocating it. [360]

[6] [Proximal thought is also: negativist thought (I am nothing) [and] positivist thought (being is), and between them, the myth of a *Weltlichkeit* of the mind modeled on that of Nature. Proximal thought in short: thought of idealization. Philosophy: Reduction to operating upon all idealizations (the form itself of the double tendency: constitution *zu der Sache selbst*). What does it leave? Not chaos or the immediate but the *Ineinander*.]

At bottom, under the postulate of proximal thought, there is ignorance of philosophical interrogation understood as an uncertainty or even as a negation that could only make way for the positivity of the idea or the thing itself—while [philosophical interrogation] does not break with Being, while it does not destroy it, does not even disengage from it in order to see it emerge from nothing, but only places it in suspense,[7] establishes between it and us a divergence where its relief is visible, and where it discloses its silent presence, which goes without saying, before any thesis.

We say the same thing in a third way: what condemns philosophy to death is this entirely negative (I am nothing) and entirely positive (Being is) thought which believes it can fix nothingness in its nothingness, Being in its being, while precisely if nothingness is not and if Being is, one can speak neither about nothingness nor identical Being: they are like the place and the reverse of each other, and to the extent that a scrupulous examination excludes from me **[110]** all the properties of things (I am neither a breath nor a smoke . . .), I must rely on them in order to come into the world. It is necessary to believe that one does not easily enter into this thought of the negative: it had hardly appeared when it was rejected as thought of nothing, since nothingness has no properties. In its place appeared *mens sive anima*, a being that doubts as if no being could challenge it. So begins the confused history of the *psyche*, from which we have not yet emerged. Between the mind that is defined through negation of all the characteristics of things, and things purely as things, naked things, without any attribute of value or of quality, a mixture must be made [361] if they belong to the same world. Things form a world because they are in relationships of contiguity and edge-to-edge action. Minds would float, here and there, upon this full world, like islands of negativity, if the notion of the objective world did not contaminate them: is it not necessary for it to embrace them and to reunite them since it crosses and reunites their bodies? So the laborious mythology of the psyche is created. One follows the paths of physical causality to the brain, and we extend them beyond, up to the thought to which they must be joined if it is true that they belong to the world, that it sees the things of the world or at least that it sees depending on the world. A whole ensemble of entities is introduced that the following four [?] will inherit: sensation, image, attention, memory, between which relationships are of the same type as those of physical causality. For a philosophy that did not take great care in elucidating the concept of the world, and which immediately identified it with all content of things purely as things united by causal relationships in order to connect the I think to the world, there must be an interior world, the double and phantom of the other. Psychology is not finished by populating it: because finally it is clear that we live more among things than in thinking: to the infrastructure of sensations and images one adds that of unconscious sensations and images. So much so that finally each moment of our lives is so simple that living appears to us as carried by a swarming of psychic elements, and we can no longer look at[8] an object before us without dreaming **[111]** of obscure operations that sustain this vision "deep inside us." This common idea of consciousness as a series or a system of psychic beings linked by coordination functions would no doubt have been maintained for a long time if the social sciences had not come to question it: because how could consciousnesses made in this way exist for each other as they exist for themselves? How could the traits, the characteristics, the dimensions of the human world that [362] has no physical existence, come to play as precociously as the first qualities, the role of stimuli? Our notion of the *psyche* is thus in crisis and can no longer be maintained. But in order to surmount the crisis, it is necessary to understand the origin, and the origin is in this thought that defines the mind through the pure negation of the body and body as absolute positivity and which, having thus disjoined the world into two orders, can regain unity only through the bastard mythology of the *psyche*. The crisis will only be surmounted when we have defeated the pure idea of the understanding as pure positivity and the counter-abstraction of the mind as pure negativity, and of course the bastard mythology of the *psyche*. We must tear these veils apart, whose tradition has enveloped our relationships with others, with our bodies, with nature, with Being, find contact with them again, remake, tailor-made, all of our concepts of the *psyche*—that, for example, of memory, of sensation stimulus that has led psychology to the dead end where it is. It is no longer a question of populating the mind with a swarm of phantoms, with positive entities that understand nothing, not even our relationship with the past. It is necessary to reconceive the *Weltlichkeit* of the mind without being constrained by principles of the physical world, moreover recently upset. Philosophy is this destruction of idealizations, of idols; it is reborn, not as a return to a chimerical immediate that no one has ever seen, but to the indivision of Being and nothingness that we are, and which we know in some manner since we live it.

The *Ineinander.*

[112] So when one thus worries about philosophical interrogation, which places everything in suspense and is not satisfied with any answer; when one asks in the name of what it is done; when one demands that it be justified first by designating some immediate—that of significations themselves or that of things themselves—which supports its critique of appearances—and when, finally, in failing to find any (how convincing would an immediate be since it is by definition laboriously recovered only to be immediately lost, that therefore there are intermediaries [363] from it to us, that it is not, in any case, our origin, and that finally it is false immediate), one declares the debate closed and terminates the philosophical age, it is necessary to answer that in a sense it begins or recommences with the end of proximal thought—of this homeless[9] thought that arrogated to itself a universal power of overview, forgetting that, precisely if it is nothing, it is never weightless or pure—which was looking for everything in the concept or in the existing world or in "psychological life," forgetting about us in this fundamental solidity, all the thicknesses crossed, which transferred its path from its results, its approaches, itself, and which got lost in its idealizations.

Philosophy lives again precisely in this failure because it is not a simple failure to think, an inexplicable catastrophe, and hence there is nothing to conclude; [in] unlearning explication, reflective coincidence and intuitive coincidence, philosophy learns: it learns why its attempts have been unsuccessful—what prejudices restricted its field, it learns this field in all its magnitude . . . And what is this field, what is the secret science that makes all knowledge, all experience appear at its tribunal? This last instance, to which it submits as naive all of our propositions? No longer an order of absolute coincidence, an entirely immediate positive, an experience (whether it is that of the adequate idea or sensible acceity [*accéité*] or that of duration in us) that would get as close as possible to Being, relative to which everything else should be considered second, derivative, abstract—not, therefore, to a single plane of reference, a univocal Being always put in default by subjectivity—object-being, [put in default] by the thing—as if it is a matter of a metaphysics of the subject, but the passage through us, the encounter, the overlap, the intersection, the confrontation of these multiple references in us, because they are all on the horizon of our life: and since we live them together, there must be the means to think them together. We have natural things around us, [113] and this means that they rest in themselves, that the perception we have seems to be in them. No constant effort of ours will make us pass into them: by the time it would succeed, there would be neither [364] seer nor visible. *What is there*, thus, is not things identical to themselves that we would have to blend ourselves into: these are things that become transparent through a subjective form, that we palpitate through the tissue of our life, to which we would not be closer if, by the impossible, they were given to us entirely naked. It is up to us to understand this first paradox. And also this one: that the same things can appear through several lives. Each is nonetheless sealed within itself, and all representation of the other that I give to myself always has the major fault of being mine. As long as I conceive myself as representation, synthetic activity, consciousness, in short, as a spiritual being, I can see in others only a not-me, and there is no coordination function, no perception of others, no synopsis, no reasoning by analogy that can transfer to another being the ipseity that I feel as mine.

And yet, if he is never himself to my eyes in the same sense that I am myself to myself, he is not only the absolute Other, an absence, a fissure in my sufficiency: he is also, he is precisely, this very particular other whom I lack [*qui me fait défaut*], that I should be or who should be me. Not that a certain place is reserved in myself: this means that there is a terrain that is mine and which he claims, and upon which we meet to compete, something undivided between us, a Being from which we are both taken: however, this Being with several entryways, which I cannot see without it decentering me and driving me beyond myself, which reaches to my most secret self and carries it to the public domain, which is very close to me and infinitely far from me, is still the horizon of sensible things, and it is in understanding how we are there, in them, that we understand how others can be others for us. My relationship to things finally clarifies this relationship to myself that is myself, this relationship to itself that is, in general, subjectivity: I am in a strange situation of "partial coincidence" towards myself, and in particular my duration, as towards the things: surely I am myself; if someone knows themselves from within, it is myself; I am my duration; it is only in myself that I can [365] attend to the impulse [*poussée*] of time. And yet this me that I am, this duration that I am, there is no question of approaching or even of contemplating it face to face: this would be to kill it, to interrupt its continuous birth, to break its identity, which is that of a being that is always new and in this precisely always the same. Even myself, I see myself only at a distance because I am not in the sense of identical being **[114],** because I am noncoincidence, tearing-off, and which like the thing itself, is always behind the appearance that I see: my cohesion is always behind my changing, my unity behind my multiplicity, a horizon, without anyone being able to imagine a view closer to me than this one since it is mine. Being itself is thus not coincidence, not even with noncoincidence; I have only the light before me; I see only a certain place, a certain kind of life and knowledge, and before me as behind everything, there is a latency.

If such is our relationship to natural things, to other human bodies and to our own involuntary duration, then what happens to them when one passes to cultural relationships that are carried by language and significations? Here still, one cannot force one's experiences down onto the other's plane. There is a double reference of my life to the mute world of passivity and to the voluntary universe resumed by speech, action, and knowledge, duplicity that is not dualism since it is the same human being who sees and speaks and who we have to understand: how the two orders appear in the same world. It is a fact that we speak of sensible things as sensible; they are thus not unspeakable; it is another fact that the universe of culture descends into the visible: since vision of a single picture can change my idea of the world, the mind is thus not only in the invisible.

The two orders, once more, are less superimposed than intertwined; each relies on the other and supports it; they carry each other above nothing. The entire world of knowledge lives by implication; the discourses that are made are only supported from time to time by some positive vision. Our thought about time, for example, is taken from the time from which it emerges. It does not rest on itself; it is artificial, fragile. Our significations are [366] less positive entities than divergences of signification, figures on a background that is inactive and that must be in order for something to be profiled in it. The whole only fits onto this base. However, when one examines it, one still finds many unfinished, incomplete, partial thoughts there, and in order to arrive at the aim, it would be necessary to descend beneath knowledge to this irrefutable visible, which I don't really know what it is but which I know is there. But moreover, obvious like everything, the visible is in each case a contestable particular, and it is the usage and the discipline of significations that teach me to see better. So the world of passivity is neither model, nor copy of the other. The impalpable significations and the greyness of words both prolong and rectify it.

[115] What philosophy seeks are these crossroads older than paths, these echoes, each of which claims be the course of the murmur [*rumeur*]. It is not analysis, as if it were sufficient to unmake: the action of unmaking itself attests that the order of our reasons is not the order of things. It is not synthesis, as if one could compose or recompose what encompasses all of our operations, what is in solidarity before them. It is not fusion or immediation or coincidence, since by pretending to do so it would at least forget its project for fusion, immediation, coincidence, privileged orientation upon bygone Being, and would generally ignore the praxis that always supports our views on the world.

Philosophy is, as method, knowledge of the *Ineinander*, of the paradoxical implications that make the actual world [367] emerge fully armed when one pulls the wire of significations, others or Nature, when we explain the self, and these relationships are reversed when one begins from the other end.[10] And the only "solution" to these paradoxes, the only "answer" for philosophy to its fundamental interrogation, is to turn the weapons we took from it back on it, to point the finger and make us present through (all the concepts—"subject," "object," "mind," "consciousness," "act of consciousness," "matter," "form," "image," "memory," "perception," "sensation," "thought"—that mask) our discourse, the Being that our eyes, our hands, our speech aim at—since finally I know what it is to see, to touch, and to speak, and how all of this is arranged, being that in which all the traffic of Nature and the mind are accomplished.

[116] §2. The voices of silence or the philosophical question

We are trying to situate philosophical interrogation more precisely. Any question is suspension, hiatus, but our ordinary questions are only hesitations: one cannot know whether it is yes or no, but it is one of the two. One cannot know the cause of an event, but one can classify the possible answers, and the true answer has its place within the picture in advance. Philosophy appears to ask the same kind of question: whether the world, movement, the multiple are, or whether Being is outside of them; but the true philosophical question appears under these formulations, which is to know first what it is to Be.

Now, this question of the *What*[11] is also that of science. Even if only to fill in the lacunae of knowledge, it involves received categories; it sometimes invents new kinds of being.

[12] With science, any question touching upon the *That*[13] is enveloped in a context of questions touching upon the *What*, [117] and the two kinds of questions constantly overlap each other. Since the theoretical ensemble can always [368] be called into question by the very experiences that it has suggested, one cannot hope that the back-and-forth ceases at any moment, or that the world will one day become the simple consequence of a definitive theoretical ensemble under the gaze of the scientist, and to this extent, scientific knowledge is always on borrowed time [*en sursis*]. One can dream of completing it by reiterating to it the question [*interrogation*] that it addresses to things—to undertake an integral elucidation of our experiences and operations or the constructions by which knowledge develops it in its sense. Philosophy would be this universal putting in suspense that discloses a sphere of absolute certainty, since it is necessary that I find in myself a coherent ensemble of operations, a system of fundamental structures, an inner sense of Being, if I must have experience and if I must be able to represent it to myself. Philosophy would be more exact (the only exact) science, that which masters both our experiences and the [constructive?][14] operations of knowledge and its own operation, and philosophical interrogation would obtain what science cannot obtain for lack of being sufficiently radical: the conversion of the world, including

we who see and think it, into a "signification world," the exact correlate of an absolutely free gaze, the disinterestedness of a *Kosmos* [118] *theoros*, of an *unbeteiligte Zuschauer.* When it asks what the world and Being are, it would be, in an unlimited universality, the same question as the *What* that science has opposed to the massive fact of the world.

Finally, philosophy [would be] the inventory of concepts, principles, spiritual acts, that ensure the unity of consciousness and the unity of the world.

It is certainly no coincidence that science and philosophy were born and raised together in the history of the West. But do we really express their true relationship if we consider them as two degrees of consciousness, two answers to the question of essence, one imperfect and the other complete? In the very effort that it makes to link knowledge [*connaissance*] and philosophy, transcendental idealism (whether that of Kant or Husserl) discloses the radical originality of philosophical interrogation: the ensemble [369] of operations of science or of knowledge is justified as ontogenesis, as explication of conditions of *Erfahrung*, what is measured by this measuring. However, this reference to *Erfahrung* = reference to a contact with Being, to an ontology which is revealed only to an interrogation that is more than eidetic. For example, in Husserl, the theory of imaginary variation is inflected toward a recognition of the *Wesen* as a manner of *ester* [being]—and the theory of transcendental reduction toward a recognition of a *vor aller Thesis.*

[119] The critical justification of knowledge shows within itself the deployment of an ontological function, of an originary contact with being and with itself that calls itself experience. And doubtless experience is dealt with through the analysis, the reflection, the explication that makes an implicit understanding appear within it. But from the moment that it is placed at the center of philosophy, a question is asked: is there a contact with Being before reflection? How can one understand their relationship? Is it necessary to say that it coincides with a constituting dynamism? But then why are we ourselves constituted? And if we are given to ourselves in a global and blind apprehension, if reflection can only enumerate and discursively project, beneath our experience, the conditions without which its appearance to us would be impossible, without ever coinciding with the functioning of the ensemble, then what is this reverse side of reflection where reflection is prepared, and what is the hyper-reflection[15] that will reveal it to us?

In any case, the philosophical question no longer simply asks what being is and what the world is, and what knowledge of the world and being is, like one asks what a circle or a triangle is: we know in advance that philosophy is not an immediate reading of essences, that they appear in an experience of the actual world, actual being, against an ontological background. Philosophical interrogation demands restitution.

This is the profound sense of the modern search for the genealogy of essence and signification when they wonder what being or the self [*moi*] or consciousness signify. [The novelty [is not] recourse to the *sinnvoll* of [370] language, no longer recourse to essences presupposed as positively given. The novelty is that signification is prospective, i.e., oriented on a contact with being in advance of us.][16]

[125] This is why these formulations have appeared insufficient to us. Philosophical interrogation is truly radical only if the hollow of non-being where it pronounces itself is neither the pure absence nor the pure presence of Being and truth, if the answer is neither given with the question nor absolutely outside of it, if the question opens a field or a horizon in such a manner that one knows what it wants to say and on which side to seek, without in principle any of the beings of this field or horizon exterminating the interrogation that has opened it—if thus this interrogation remains interrogation, remains as an intention that has not been fulfilled, adds to positive beings a dimension of which they do not take account and without which, [126] however, they would not be seen and would not be, and which questions itself no less than them, questions itself insofar as it questions them, of a kind that finally the question and the ensemble of beings are like the reverse or the other side of each other, it is implied in them no less than they are in it—this means that it did not come to question them from elsewhere, that it was born in their heart as through the invagination or folding of their mass, that what questions is truly of the world that it questions, fold in this fabric, like my body is part of this visible that it sees, yet [371] sees it from within, is something like that which it sees, sees a world which is something for it, which is flesh like it—and like myself, speaking subject, at the moment where I call out to the others, I hear myself, I speak to myself as well, I call out to myself, I institute myself as allocutionary by making myself locutionary, making myself an other by making them into others for me, so that I do not have speech as an attribute or a product of mine, either a construction or a thought of mine; I speak from within and from the milieu of Speech; it is what takes me and what has me at the very moment where I strive with all my strength to make myself understood—and as finally myself, thinking subject, I never have the feeling of producing my thoughts: who has never seen his best ideas born, who has constituted them, who has produced them: it is rather a ray of sunlight which pierces a breaking fog, an axis of our life that is disclosed and denuded. When I actively think in a productive manner, I do not have my thought before me like a hypothesis or like a vision; it thinks itself in me; I am thought [by it] as much as I think, and

the voice, in the grammatical sense, of my thought is neither the active nor, of course, the passive; it would be rather what the Greeks called the middle voice: this action that one makes upon oneself, and thus where one is indivisibly active and passive. In total, any question being the opening of a field is segregation, delimitation within a domain to which that which questions is already initiated, which is already the territory to which it belongs, which circumscribes or encompasses it—and the question of questions, philosophy, being openness to Being, cannot be content with the thought that we envelop in our judgments, in our statements which are before us, that we manipulate, a sphere cut by our acts, our operations in a wider being and which does not cease to belong to it, just as the visible world is far from being reduced to the thin and narrow pellicule of *visibilia*. Philosophy's interrogation, therefore, is not created by us; it is pronounced through us by the crossing-over of the visible and the seer, of speaking and understanding, of thinking and being thought, which makes it such that there is someone, in other words, as Homer magnificently put it, nobody, οὔτις,[17] the contrary even of a monad, this space full of air, this **[127]** [372] crossroads where all things begin to exist for each other. The philosopher is this, like everyone, the X where Being comes to itself, is lived or is lived again.[18]

[129] Not that philosophy seeks adequation without speaking to an immediate lived experience: it realizes it only by speaking to itself, and it would be its part of the last inconsistency to treat language like a screen between itself and being; it would be no less inconsistent if it were content to develop definitions, syntactic operations, the immanent laws of the universe of speech once established, as if language spoke of nothing, opened onto nothing. She who is language is also philosophy of language, and (in the Kantian sense) critique of language; she is no more the mistress of language than she is its servant; she does not condemn it, does not give it a monopoly over sense because she **[130]** seizes it (and is herself seized) at work in the process of making silence cease, of opening up, thus, onto one side of the horizon of configurations, articulations, mute gestures that prolong and transform it, and onto the other, onto the new order of evidences that it is in the process of instituting and of which there is no question of disqualifying but of putting in place and reintegrating into its context.[19] The critique of spoken essence and existence is not done in the name of and to the profit of an unspeakable immediate before them but in the name of speaking essence and existence, that is, of silent experience, and of that which in it arouses the speech of that which wants to say and of what speech makes it say; all of this, one in the other, in discordance and in concordance, as we live it. Because, as much as it is necessary not to stick to the immanent sense of words, to the inner rule of the game, as much as it is sure that speech, at the moment where it emerges, has evidence as convincing as that of any mute thing, and actually of the same order, since one learns to speak, since it is necessary that at a certain moment speech is justified and imposes itself like a mute thing, pierces the child's silence by insinuating [373] itself in silence, but silence this time private, that is, immanent speech. The speech that is no longer a screen between philosophy and being is not even a restriction of its power and its freedom for it, a prison, because born in Being, born from Being, proffered at the request of Being, it could neither mask it, provided account is taken of its emergence and the silent being from which it arises, nor disclose it in its entirety if it is taken ready-made. There is no alternative between lived experience and the spoken unless one omits the articulation of lived experience, organization around a tacit sense, the sensorial fields where every individual is already a variant of a dimension, an exemplar of an alogical essence, what Hermes Trismegistus has called "the scream of light" in order to reduce lived experience to pure muteness and contiguity, and if one omits, moreover, the presuppositions of speech, the establishment, for example, of a linguistic field that envelops every possible being in the order of the nameable and expressible. If, on the contrary, one knows how to find in both orders these institutions of the same type, and thus not only the wild sensible but wild speech and thought, then there is no longer a choice between them: from lived experience to the spoken there is agreement through reversal, chiasm, and one can say, with Husserl, that philosophy is "still mute experience, that it is a matter of bringing to pure expression its proper sense," that is, that philosophy speaks and that its speech leans against silence, that it speaks from the inside of being and not from on high or from afar, that it speaks especially of itself, that is to say, of speech, that it speaks like the trees grow, like time passes and like human beings speak.[20]

[131] It is thus a matter, where philosophy is concerned, neither of reflection (we have already said enough) nor of a return to the immediate (of which Bergson would say, with good reason, that it "is reflection": because it shares with reflective philosophies the supralapsarian prejudice), that of an original integrity, of a lost secret to be found again which would annul the questions. Coming after the world, after nature, after life, after thought, finding them [374] constituted before it, philosophy indeed interrogates this preliminary being, and interrogates itself and its relationship with it. It evidently returns to itself and to all things: but [this is] not a return to an immediate, to an original, that of things or that of significations, to a buried truth of which we would be the fallen heirs,

to a system of operations, to a thrust of duration of which we would be the products. The re-commencement, the re-conquest of being from forgetfulness, distraction, and habit, the re- of philosophy, if it includes the restitution of the true past, not limiting itself to this retrospection and (even with respect to the past) not making an appeal to a lost coincidence that it would be a matter of reestablishing: if it is lost, it is lost forever, since we are neither trees nor things; to have a past is to open onto an abyss that is not only unfathomable: which has no ground where one can get a foothold and where the past would be given in person precisely as absolute distance, pure memory. It is one or the other: if we really get back to what it was as present, it is no longer past; at the moment when it is accomplished, the coincidence ceases through the disappearance of its present witness; and if memory has distance, it is not pure: it borrows from the flesh of the present. In fact, past and present are not given in the same sense, and neither is [given] in the sense of coincidence. What is given to us—but this time continually and without restriction—is their differentiation in our massive belonging to the world, to Being, and to the space and time of Being, and this belonging itself is signified to us through our eyes, our hands, through the visible, the sensible of which they are also a part, that they therefore see and touch from the inside, through our words, our thoughts, the Being that they see and where they are inscribed as well, in their place, at their date, with their tenor of truth. Because the visible that we see, of which we speak, is the same one, *numerically* the same one that Plato and Aristotle spoke about and saw: behind each landscape of my point of view, even if it is not the Hymettus, the Ilisos, or the plane trees of Delphi, since it is a landscape, not a flock of ephemeral sensations or of judgments, homeless spiritual acts, but a segment of the durable flesh of the world, behind these are the hidden landscapes of all [375] human beings, of all those who will be, of all those who could have been or could still be, undivided between themselves and myself, like the object that I hold between my right hand and my left hand. Greek humanity has faded between Plato and us; another humanity is made who brings his own flavor with him, his own odor in everything that he undertakes; but when he reads Plato, when he follows Plato into the ancient Greek "there" and finds the vein [*nervure*] of the dialogues, then at the center of himself and synchronically, something moves and comes alive again that was and is Plato's thought. Nature and Speech, the visible and writing, otherwise and similarly, re-create at each instant a universal simultaneity.

Philosophy thus does not seek an abolished immediate behind us in order to meld into it: what it wants is to be transported onto the visible's ring of fire, [**132**] the nameable, the thinkable, where actual seeing, speaking, thinking reconnect with all visions, all speech, all thoughts that could be or could never be—crisscrossing between them and with them, re-creating one another and re-creating them in the immobile winding of Nature upon Nature, and in this, similar to the folds of the sea that merge into a single wave—of history over history . . . The source of sense is no more behind us than it is before us, no more a lost immediate than an omega point to be attained, to be done; it is in vision, speech, thought, with their interlockings, their horizons, backwards and forwards references with which they swarm, their openings, their overcomings that go without saying, because they do not add to each other and are, on the contrary, circumscription, carving-out [*découpage*], segregation in the flesh of the world and of Being; philosophical return is also a departure, and philosophy is actually neither one nor the other, neither solely retrospection nor prospection. It is the invitation to see the visible again, to speak speech again, to rethink thinking.

[The sleeping power of all horizons—sleeping because they are acquired, sedimented—and, however, visible to the wild state at each instant in them, that is, in ourselves at each instant—power that [376] is not thesis and that is inaccessible to all thetic thought.][21]

Not in order to seek before or behind them a foundation that is more certain than them, but in order to awaken the ontological power in them that crosses them, and which in the same movement they continue and ignore because sense only spreads or is transmitted by making its origin forgotten, by installing itself as an acquired dimension that no longer needs to be thought about and upon which subsequent experiences themselves are raised at a distance . . . to see the world again, to speak speech again, to rethink thought will not, therefore, undo them, remake them like a tissue, or stick to them like an immediate, but will again find the hollow mold that fashions them, to which they owe their form and cohesion, to turn them over like a glove whose reverse side is shown, exposing adherence in the body, the circuit of the seer and the visible: in speech, [133] that of the locutionary and the allocutionary, in thinking, that of the act of thinking and of its trace, its wake or its inscription, discerning, therefore, behind all these thoughts the anti-thought that is their truth. This operation assumes that one does not simply adhere to each visible, to each nameable, to each thinkable—which would not be to philosophize but to live—that to this extent, one pushes them away, one puts them in suspense in order to see how they make themselves seen, named, and thought, what they want to say, what their own way of pronouncing themselves, announcing themselves is, their being, and finally that all of this is fixed in words. This operation is thus circular, since it is necessary that vision sees itself, that speech speaks itself, that thought thinks itself—since whoever accomplishes this uses the same power to accomplish it that he undertakes in order to disclose it, and which he keeps gathered behind him at the moment when he wants to give it to the spectacle. But this circle is not a fault and has no inconsistencies since neither vision, nor speech, nor thinking are immanent operations, since they are openness, since there is no longer any possible coincidence with them, and since to coincide with them would be precisely to destroy them. Between vision and the philosophy of vision, between speech and the philosophy of speech, thinking and the [377] philosophy of thinking, there is an exchange, chiasm, recovery, not coincidence; and philosophical speech in particular speaks of silent vision without contradiction, speaks of the same speech without a vicious circle because, like all new speech, it demarcates [*jalonne*], but does not contain or close or even carry its sense: it is sufficient that it makes a sign and that, like a gesture, it manifests both the style of human being and of the thing, or that, like the movement of a branch, it attests at the same time to the wind and to the resistance of the deep chord. Provided, therefore, that philosophical speech is born close enough to the heart of things and to the heart of speech, [it] will bear the mark, it will speak to us about its birth only on the condition that we allow it to speak in us instead of silencing it by first asking it for its titles and definitions. Philosophy, which is speech, speaks *of* speech without difficulty because speech is always aimed at by all speech, just as the seeing body is also visible. And philosophy that is speech speaks about the world of silence without difficulty because all speech lends itself to the things of which it speaks and allows them to say what they themselves [134] want to say:

> Now a Wisdom makes utterance,
> And rings out in the sovereign voice
> Which when it rings can only know
> It is no longer anyone's
> So much as the wood's and water's voice![22]

From the world of silence to the universe of speech, and to that of thought, there is a passage, back and forth, not that there are three parallel orders among which there would be the search for coincidence and a point-by-point recovery, but because they are three dimensions of the same Being. Their problematic unity, when one considers the products, the discrete acts of the three domains—the perceptions, the statements, and the thoughts, obviously, on the contrary, if one considers the horizons that encompass them and from which they are [378], so to speak, taken: the horizon of the visible, the horizon of the nameable, and the horizon of the thinkable. But in order to conquer this thought of horizons, it is necessary to make oneself sensitive to a relationship with Being that precedes acts of circumscription, of knowledge, that supports them all and persists after all knowledge. Let us attempt to do this with respect to the visible.

§3. Rediscovery of the visible [or perhaps §1 of part II]

Supplementary Materials for the 1959 Course

[**37**[i]] So: motivated by the *Crisis,* Husserl retrieves his problem with philosophy and his relationship with intersubjectivity, history, the world. The crisis of rationalism = *Sinnentleerung* [emptying of meaning] of a philosophy that only surmounts this crisis by becoming a philosophy of the *Lebenswelt* = of operative Nature and history as foundations for idealizations, wild being and wild mind—"mute" experience that must itself *speak.*

Husserl still says sometimes: the *Lebenswelt* is not entirely phenomenology—it is accessible through the natural attitude; the historian knows the *Lebenswelt.* He still needs to pass into transcendental philosophy.

But this transcendental philosophy is no longer immanent consciousness of *Auffassungen* [apprehensions] as limpid constituents—The history within us—"In this way, a one-sided rationality can certainly become an evil . . . it belongs to the essence of reason that the philosophers at first understand and labor at their task in an absolutely necessary one-sided way"[1] (already in the "Vienna Conference"). In order to remake reason, [380] it is necessary to rediscover the *fundierend* [founding] history within us. This task remains transcendental insofar as there is no process history here, history of a causal chain of determined events, but history as ambiguous *Stiftung,* resumption that is forgetting, forgetting that is tradition, interiority in exteriority, *Ineinander* of monads ("vertical" history and not "horizontal")—Entering into this domain requires "alogical" thought, i.e., refusing to make use of the sedimented, questioning the sediments, reactivating. . . .

Therefore: rediscovering the *paradoxes* at which the *Cartesian Medita-*

tions arrive, but this time not as obstacles to the new philosophy so much as its themes:

Paradox of intersubjectivity: identity of my empirical ego and my transcendental ego; the *Ichheit überhaupt* of Fichte can only be the man, Fichte.[2] This paradox ceases to be a contradiction because there is no longer a subject-object philosophy where the empirical ego is an object for the transcendental I. *Sinngebung* as openness [38[ii]] to a field, *Urstiftung* (and not immanent consciousness) always includes *Sinnverschiebung* [shifts in sense], transgressions, whether it is a matter of myself or the other. Therefore: it is indeed a centrifugal operation but not pure production; therefore it does not exclude composition. To maintain both (1) the *Einsamheit* of the indeclinable subject, solipsism, (2) the plurality of transcendental subjects. There is no opposition because my intentional system is not positive and full; it is incomplete, and this centrifugal vortex that I am specifies itself in particular vortexes who are alter egos. Their link is precisely this refused imperfection that they have in common. *Ineinander* of Egos. The reduction, in this way, has repercussions in all the others: it is neither in one alone nor gradually; it is simultaneous. There is no *Auseinander* but the *Vergemeinschaftung* [co-belonging] of their thoughts. This is because inherent history and the *Lebenswelt* reunite subjectivities through their pre-theoretical origin, making up their *Ichlichkeit* and their "spiritual generativity."

What is philosophy? More than "positive" or "objective" philosophy—Reconquest of the *Lebenswelt*—*Wissenschaftlichkeit* of a new type, overcoming all given [381] *Wissenschaftlichkeit* since it is a matter of entering into the domain of the *fungierende*, overcoming all constituted philosophy—doubting itself as *Gebilde* and forgetting—circling in on itself.

See 37[i] (with citation p. **38**).

[37[i]] If this is the case, what is philosophy?

It is always "the transcendental," i.e., *Selbstbesinnung*—but the Kantian transcendental does not call the possibility of the world into question ("If a world must be possible"). It is not necessary to give this possibility along with its indications: that would be to resort to the *selbstverstandlich* ("self-evidence") that is precisely a matter of scrutinizing.

Why the *Selbstverstandlichkeit* of a world? *Welträtsel* in Hume's or Descartes's sense. *Fundamentalbetrachtung* of Descartes ignored by Kant, ignored by Descartes, who keeps a piece of the world (*anima*)—one intention: justify science. To see the initial emergence of a world and of science—i.e., something that is behind us as products, as parts of being, as "attitudes," as having "*Absicht*." One finds here "constituting life" which is not that of a possessor of a *Gebilde*, of the theoretical I, of the *Zuschauer*—return to the "mothers of consciousness."

Patent *Flächenleben* and latent *Tiefenleben*.

Ideal identity and unity that bears it—idealized sense, pre-ideal sense—*Selbigkeit* of the idea, *Selbigkeit der Welt*—unity of the horizon, of the *Offenheit*, of the *Umwelt*—Temporality: Heraclitean flux and sense (citation p. **38**)—Reference to pre-Socratic philosophy and to the Sophists as astonishment before the *Gegenbenheitwire*-subjective-world correlation (cited p. **38**).

Thus, this correlation is no longer in immanence; the transcendental is no longer consciousness and *its* objects in transparency—impossible to describe in the language of "subject" and "object." It must be "mute," "wild," pre- and post-cultural being ([*Boden?*] and praxis) that expresses itself—"teleology" as non-chance, exclusion of non-sense.[3]

> for the emergence of a set of world-enigmas which were unknown in earlier times . . .[4]

> new dimensions . . . questions never before asked . . .[5]

> the essential strangeness and precariousness of the ideas which will necessarily become involved . . .[6]

> Since we seek in vain in world literature for investigations that could serve as preparatory studies for us . . .[7]

Audacious simplicity: the reduction is the greatest revolution of European culture.

Philosophy, thus, is *Tat*, construction, *Gebilde* of what is *von selbst*. It is without *Boden* and it must create this *Boden*, but I have taken this path and it is doable. Without any support from "logic" (*Genealogie der Logik*).

There are only philosophies and nonphilosophy—failure—but in this failure, this isolation, there is a link: one resumes the other in this vain attempt, constitutes a *Vorhabe* that has its evidence; success in this failure; link through solitude: "The point of 'it' ultimately was, in the hidden unity of intentional inwardness . . . in all these philosophers"[8] provided that it is resumed in a solitude that is present, lived, in a *Gegenwart* (cited p. **37**).

Philosophy as a problem for itself, interrogation that is sufficient: philosophy does not cease to be uncertain that it is Philosophy "as serious, rigorous, indeed apodictically rigorous science—*the dream is over.*"[9]

Our definitions do not exhaust our *Wissen*—in our definitions and our obscure *Wissen* "the historical is concealed"[10]—how to *befragen* it? We haven't read Plato. We read him, and this transforms us. It should be necessary to read it again. The other [383] is *"Dichtung."* And it is in this *Dichtung*, however, as well as in the others, that this universal, which "philosophy" is, is understood, common to all.

Translation and Commentary on Beilage XXIII of Husserl's *Crisis of the European Sciences*[1]

[Text of *Beilage XXIII*]

[1] 1—For the human being biology is essentially guided by its humanity, which is experienceable in a truly original manner; there alone life is given in an original way and in the most authentic manner through the self-understanding of the biological dimension. Such is the guiding thread for all biology, and for all the variant forms of *Einfühlung* [empathy], only through which the animal can have sense [*sens*]. But this subjective element also guides everything in the world that we call organic life, and which however does not receive its life from an "*anima*" that is analogically understandable, thus it does not receive it from *egoity* [*Ichlichkeit*]. But what are those variant forms [*Abwandlungsformen*] that ultimately lead back to an ego and to myself, the inquirer here, as an originary mode [*Urmodus*]? Only from here does the concept of organism draw its ultimate sense, and similarly the construction of organisms out of partial organisms, which do not function freely and independently for themselves, but rather as simple and necessary elements of construction.

2[2]—Naturally one always has a biological a-priori starting point from the human being: here we have the a priori of the body's instincts, originary drives [*Urtriebe*], which bring to fruition (eating, mating, etc.) the a priori [384] itself. Of course, this holds for animals, to the extent that animality is actually experienced through *Einfühlung* [empathy]. Thus we have a generative a priori.

Beyond the structure of animal "milieu" [*Umwelt*], in which every animal has the "social" horizon of its species—in the world of dogs, the horizon is an open multiplicity of dogs in the interconnections possible for dogs [*im möglichem Hunde-Konnex*]. This a priori is anticipated as a hypothesis within the hypothesis "other animal," while it is not directly experienceable as animal, and even more so in the case of plants. Of course, one has with animals the structure of the world of other animals [*tierische*

Mitwelt]—not only the species, but instead the understanding of other animals and of the sociality of their species—and the counter-structure [*Gegenstruktur*] of the non-animal world, things [*Dinge*], etc. Thus one already has the beginnings of a real, and not altogether paltry, [2] animal ontology from the inside and the outside. Yet what one has lies within an infinite horizon as of an unknown ontology [*unbekannte Ontologie*] prefigured in its infinity. See Teleology.

3—In its naive, technicist method [*Kunstmäßig*], biology mirrors the intentional intermingling [*das intentionale Ineinander*] behind the externality of biological research according to ontogenesis and phylogenesis and behind the research concerning specific classes and species of animals. In their great generalities eidetic laws [*lois d'essence*] [or verbal "*Wesen*"][3] announce themselves, biology hides an ontology in itself, an ontology which is not based on intuitive givenness and which is even less analogous to the ontology of nature; that is, of the mathematics of nature: as an ontology that is completed in advance and which can be known in its completion.

Indeed biology—like any positive science—is also a naive science and "artwork" [*Kunstwerk*], the latter understood as a superior analogue to craftwork. Its superiority [385] lies in the fact that it carries within itself a hidden sense [*verschlossenen Sinn*], the true and authentic sense of being, which biology believes it can develop thanks to the art [*kunstmäßig*] of elaborating it as knowledge [*travail d'art d'élaborer comme connaissance*], while in fact never being able to attain it. However, unlike mathematics, biology, in particular, could never become, as a concrete theory in the *Lebenswelt*, as a descriptive science, such a pure work of art, so completely rootless, entirely freed from naive evidence, from the sources of intuition [*Quellen der Anschauung*]. Its admirable constructions are not constructions that rise up dizzily to the sky—through countless stages and levels—like those of mathematics, though the totality of this science is a massive accomplishment of scientific operations [*Ein gewaltiges Sein wissenschaftlicher Leistung*].

4—Biology's proximity to the sources of evidence [*Quellen der Evidenz*] grants it such a proximity to the depths of the things themselves [*Tiefen der Sachen*] that its access to transcendental philosophy should be the easiest, and with it the access to the true a priori to which the world of living beings refers, in its greatest and most constant generalities which cannot be captured without question in their a priori nature (as unconditionally universal and necessary). What it discovers, through the universal and systematic opening of outwardly [3] visible generalities, which are systematically connected in their sense, always produces new transcendental questions. Hence, it seems to me that biology, which is apparently inferior to mathematics and physics and which for so long has been considered almost pityingly by physicalism as a preliminary phase, incomplete and purely descriptive with regard to the subsequent physicalistic explanation, has always been able to remain closer to philosophy and to true knowledge. This is mainly because it has never been threatened by the wonderful symbolic arts [*Künste*] of the "logical" construction of its truth and its theories. These arts made physics and mathematics into an astonishing miracle of actual accomplishment [*einer Wunder . . . an tatsächlicher Leistung*], but also, as with all miracles—into something incomprehensible. . . .[4]

[The description must retain the *Leistung*.][5] [386]

. . . Therefore, it has no explanatory task other than that demanded by the transcendental or, if you will, the transcendental-psychological approach to the lifeworld and its constitution. . . .[6] The centuries following Descartes were blinded by the miraculous work of mathematics. It is here that a genuine method of reduction to the sources of understanding [*Verständnisquellen*] is required. The very nature of mathematics and physics makes it much harder for them, incomparably more difficult, to break free from the principles of the symbolic and technical *kunstnäßig* (artificial) method [*de la méthode kunstnäßig (artificieuse) symbolique et technique*] with which they conduct their experiments, an art that connects intuition and symbolic practice, and to see the need to return[7] to the transcendental acts that found signification [*actes transcendantaux qui fondent la signification*] [*transzendentehen Sinngebungen*].

5—Biology is concrete and genuine psycho-physics. It has everywhere and necessarily a universal task, and is only apparently at a disadvantage when compared to physics, which extends to astronomical infinity and reaches laws that aim to arrive (even though hypothetically) at a sense [*den Sinn*] of unconditional generality. Biology only appears to be limited to our small and insignificant world, and as anthropology, to this negligible creature called the human being. In [4] returning to the ultimate sources of evidence, from which the world in general draws its sense and being as meaningful for us, what it signifies, and to all the imaginable essential necessities that emerge, it seems that biology is not a contingent science for the insignificant world, like Germany's zoology, the botany of the Baden plant world. Rather, a general biology has the same worldly generality [*Weltallgemeinheit*] as physics. Every sense that a biology of Venus could have, which we ought to speak of as a possibility [*von der wirs als Möglichkeit sprechen sollten*], is thanks to the original sense-formation of our lifeworld [*der ursprunglichen Sinnbildung unserer Lebenswelt*] and moreover to the theoretical elaboration of this sense-formation through biology. Admittedly, this universal task gives it an infinite horizon, which, articulated into farther horizons, does not assign it, as a conceivable aim, comprehensive knowledge of laws [387], reaching from here to all [horizons] in the world, to infinity, [*depuis ici jusqu'à tous les [horizons] à l'infini*] in the same sense [as in physics].

Yet on the other hand, biology is not purely formal like mathematics and physics; it does not refer to the merely abstract structure of the world. In fact, biology, as genuinely universal biology, embraces the entire concrete world, and thus implicitly physics too, and in the examination of (subjective) correlations it becomes a completely universal philosophy.

[Merleau-Ponty's Commentary on Beilage XXIII]

Text from Beilage XXIII.

Show the idea of the *Ineinander,* of intentional implication, elaborated apropos the *Einfühlung* of others, becoming coextensive with being, and substitute [for] the idea of transcendental immanence.

Philosophy of the *Ineinander.*

In particular:

Text 1: organism: *Ineinander of subjectivity,* I (and finally meditation I) and of corporeal machines. The organism [as] variant of *Einfühlung.* I know the organism because I am it. Relationship of human Being see Heidegger (All things within humanity—but because humanity is all things). READ.

2: The animal [as] variant of *Einfühlung;* our work [is] an ontology. Its "world," its "*Mitwelt*"—"unknown ontology": we do not know everything through our *Einfühlung* with the world, but we have its style, its arrangement, its "teleology" founded on the fact that it could not otherwise enter into our experience. READ.

3: Biology, two pages:

A contact of *Einfühlung* with the organism, intentional implication of the organism within us and of the parts of the organism with each other. In this way, biology is a theory of the *Lebenswelt,* borrows from our contact before idealization (*anima*).

A "technical" or "artificial" knowing (physical determinations in the organism) that expresses the being of [388] the organism in the physico-mathematical language of the in-itself.

But, closer to the "sources of evidence," i.e., to the philosophical world of the *Ineinander,* biology cannot pretend to occupy itself only with *bloße Sachen.*

4: The world of the *Ineinander,* of philosophy, of *Einfühlung* is very

close to the generalities of biology. They lead there—and must be rectified upon contact. Dialectical relationship of philosophy-science: science
winkt [signals].

5: Through its contact with the depth of things, biology is almost
philosophy. Life ≠ local fact; it has its worldly signification [*Weltallgemeinig-
keit*]; it has its *Weltlichkeit,* its value as revealing Being. Not only because
its factual domain may be more extensive than one thinks (Venus), but
again because its structures, not being abstract like dependent physico-
mathematical structures, envelop them (physics as a product of the
human *Umwelt*) and are closer to being universal, i.e., philosophy.

So sense of the *Lebenswelt* as originary "source" of evidence = the
world of the *Ineinander.*

Question: Can this world of the *Ineinander* be spoken about beyond
object-being and Being-subject?

Psychoanalysis[8]

Psychoanalysis
We have seen Positivism, artificialist thought, responsible technician
of certain decadent facts = abstract thought, aimed at manipulation.

Similarly in psychoanalysis: there is a symptom of decadence in
psychoanalysis insofar as it posits a separate unconscious or opposes the
unconscious to conscious control; there is a psychoanalysis that discovers
a more profound unity on the occasion of disintegration: unconscious
thought as nonconventional [389], ego as deeply related: its repression
is blind.

Dig beneath the antithesis—Sexuality, aggression, and competition—
overestimation of the visible.

Dig beneath the antithesis—pathological aggression has archaeo-
logical roots.

Similarly for integration or reintegration: it is not subordination of
one element to another for this simple reason: that there are no elements,
but that each person carries his enemy within and is linked to the other.
The cure—psychoanalysis as therapeutic.

Our nonphilosophy that is perhaps more profound philosophy:
Destruction of our historical *Boden*: unconscious ethnocentrism:
our history as law of the world—unconscious as egocentrism—(as well
as transitivism)—ethnocentrism = to ignore other historicities—and not
to repress them. Importance of this interpretation: if one believes that

there has been repression, decolonization: return to normal; one does not see the problem, which is of knowing whether the developments are compossible—one remains within a classical framework (either natural harmonies—or (Marxism) harmony of the domination of nature-agreement between human beings)—if ethnocentrism is ignorance, awakening of the underdeveloped = new problem of co-development;

Destruction of our *Boden* in nature: ordered Nature, superficial concretion, chained energy—do not take it for granted—this destruction of *Selbstverstandlich* results in a science that was from the beginning founded upon the necessity of Nature (laws of creation = laws of conservation—the figure of this world would have been the same in all cases)—implemented, this idea is overcome. [390]

Supplementary Materials for the 1960–1961 Course

Ontology (interspersed pages)[1]

Ontology—Course of the 23rd II

The moderns rediscover a Renaissance through the magical idea of visibility:

It is the thing that allows one to see (without and within), over there and over here; what it gives is not this opaque, but also "not-unsealed" [*non-decachetée*] form which, through the body, passes into the picture; this mute, non-free signification alogically orders the articulations of the visible: "phantom"-beings—reflections, specular images, illuminations—which have only to be visible and yet make it the case that there is Being without restriction—Between the in-itself and thought—*L'oeil du miroir* (Claudel); the alogical essence, "picture"—absolute visible to which things co-appear, pictures and even the painter (the painter within the picture).

What does Cartesian thought tell us about all of this?

Course on ontology.

(1) This is not history of philosophy in the current sense: what one has thought is what one has thought within the framework and horizon of what one thinks—invoked in order to make what one thinks understood—Aim: contemporary ontology—from there, go to Descartes and the Cartesians [391], then return to what philosophy today can be—outside of the history of philosophy, whose position is uncertain (Gueroult); outside of more or less positive disciplines (sociology, psychology, Physics, mathematics, and *their* "philosophy") (Lupasco).

(2) Official philosophy is in crisis—and yet there is a whole spontaneous philosophy, fundamental thought, especially in literature (January *NRF*: Saint-John Perse—The inferno, time (Claude Simon)—the

most profound question (Blanchot)—in the arts (painting-cinema)—Wahl, *Claudel et la simultanéité*—Valéry, "defense and broadening of philosophy"—André Bazin, ontology of the cinema—

See above: Proust (essences and the night of the soul) (essences are also the sensible); Claudel (according to Wahl); Valéry (from the pseudo-Leonardo to "Mon Faust";[2] evolution that has been Leonardo's); Today, St. J. Perse, Claude Simon.

Philosophy that is inseparable from literary expression, i.e., from *indirect* expression (two kinds of indirect) that does not attain adequation—intellectual possession—but which makes a sign [*winkt*].

Philosophy that is a question (and not yes or no) (Blanchot, the most profound question, I. 10–84). Interrogation makes what is appear, what gives itself only to interrogation (e.g., stars). The human being is a question for God himself (ibid., II, p. 85). We are not masters of this question. The dialectical movements of our time are more profound questions than their abstract formulation (86): the *overall* question of dialectic or circularity believes that it can resolve the profound question in the question as search for an indispensible totality (87), the going beyond of which (88) does not interfere in any way with fundamental thought, which is the perception that does not arise, the *Ungedachte* [unthought], emerging from a backward step toward the dialectic's *Wesen*. Fundamental thought, which seems to be confused with this historical question with each revolution, then reappears (89) (Sartre's book).

(3) In the arts

Cinema: ontology of cinema—Ex. the question of cinematic movement. [392]

Painting: dialectic of the visible and of the invisible—See the article in *Art de France*—the part on painting.[3]

In sum

Proust: carnal essences; Valéry: consciousness is not in immanence but in life; Claudel: simultaneity, the most real is *beneath* us; St. J. Perse: Poetry as awakening to Being; Claude Simon: the zone of credulity and the zone of sensible being.

[There is] a reversal of the relationships between the visible and the invisible, between the flesh and the mind; discovery of signification as the vein of full Being; overcoming of the insularity of minds.

Painting: communication, not through thought but behind thought—discovery of the figures of the visible.

All of this is ontology in the sense of overcoming beings as interior to the world, partial, against a background, all facts, hierarchized, objects, toward horizons, dimensionality, Inscription, epochal Memory, which is only manifest through them and nevertheless constitutes an order of the vertical and of the wild that is more than ontic. Philosophy that is nonphilosophy = non-Theology, non-anthropology, non-positivism. In order to see this better through a contrast, we move on to Descartes and the Cartesians, regarding them as ethnologists.

From there, we will return to a more precise philosophical formulation of our ontology.

Notes

Translator's Preface

1. See Lefort's editorial note to Merleau-Ponty, *L'Oeil et l'esprit*, 1.

2. The earliest working notes for *The Visible and the Invisible* date from January 1959, which would have coincided more or less with the inception of "The Possibility of Philosophy Today."

3. Merleau-Ponty's courses "Study of the Variations of the Concept of Nature," "Modern Science and Nature," and "Animality, the Human Body, and the Passage to Culture," as well as "Nature and Logos: The Human Body," are published together in *La Nature* (1995); translated into English as *Nature: Course Notes from the Collège de France* (2003).

4. See Maurice Merleau-Ponty, *Notes de cours sur "L'Origine de la géometrie de Husserl" suivi de "Recherches sur la phénoménologie de Merleau-Ponty"* (Paris: Presses Universitaires de France, 1998); translated into English by Leonard Lawlor and Bettina Bergo as *Husserl at the Limits of Phenomenology* (Evanston, IL: Northwestern University Press, 2002).

Foreword

1. [Trans.]: Published in Maurice Merleau-Ponty, *In Praise of Philosophy and Other Essays*, translated by John Wild, James Edie, and John O'Neill (Evanston, IL: Northwestern University Press, 1970).

2. [Ed]: Republished as "Everywhere and Nowhere," in *Signs*, translated into English by Richard C. McCleary (Evanston, IL: Northwestern University Press, 1964), 157.

3. Martin Heidegger, "Only a God Can Save Us," in *Heidegger: The Man and the Thinker*, edited by Thomas Sheehan (New York: Precedent, 1981), 219.

4. [Ed]: See Maurice Merleau-Ponty, *Phénoménologie de la perception* (Paris: Gallimard, 1945), 450; translated into English by Donald Landes as *Phenomenology of Perception* (London: Routledge, 2012), 454.

5. Maurice Merleau-Ponty, *Le Visible et l'invisible*, ed. Claude Lefort (Paris: Gallimard, 1964), 219; translated into English by Alphonso Lingis as *The Visible and the Invisible* (Evanston, IL: Northwestern University Press, 1968), 165. Henceforth cited as *Le Visible et l'invisible* and *The Visible and the Invisible*, with their respective paginations.

6. Merleau-Ponty, *Le Visible et l'invisible*, 326; *The Visible and the Invisible*, 272–73.

7. Maurice Merleau-Ponty, *L'Oeil et l'esprit* (Paris: Gallimard, 1961), 42; translated into English as "Eye and Mind," in *The Merleau-Ponty Reader*, ed. Ted Toadvine and Leonard Lawlor (Evanston, IL: Northwestern University Press, 2007), 362. Henceforth cited as *OE* and "EM," with their respective paginations.

8. Merleau-Ponty, *Le Visible et l'invisible*, 263; *The Visible and the Invisible*, 210; note dated September 1959.

9. Merleau-Ponty, *Le Visible et l'invisible*, 263; *The Visible and the Invisible*, 210.

10. Merleau-Ponty, *Le Visible et l'invisible*, 196; *The Visible and the Invisible*, 149.

11. [C.L.]: These notes were published separately, at the initiative of Jacques Neefs, in *Genesis* 6 (1994): 133–65.

12. Merleau-Ponty, *Le Visible et l'invisible*, 251; *The Visible and the Invisible*, 197. Note dated June 1959.

13. Merleau-Ponty, *Le Visible et l'invisible*, 251; *The Visible and the Invisible*, 197.

14. Martin Heidegger, "Hegel's Concept of Experience," in *Off the Beaten Track*, translated into English by Julian Young and Kenneth Haynes (Cambridge: Cambridge University Press, 2002), 86–156.

15. Lefort's emphasis.

16. Lefort's emphasis.

Editor's Note

1. Maurice Merleau-Ponty, "Le Possibilité de la philosophie," in *Résumés de cours: Collège de France (1952–1960)* (Paris: Gallimard, 1968), 141–56; Merleau-Ponty, "Philosophy as Interrogation," in *In Praise of Philosophy and Other Essays*, 167–80. The title of the course is translated as "Philosophy as Interrogation," apparently a liberty of the translator.

2. The course of 1959–60, "Nature and Logos: The Human Body," is included in the study of the concept of Nature. It was published in Maurice Merleau-Ponty, *La Nature*, ed. D. Séglard (Paris: Seuil, 1995); translated into English by Robert Vallier as *Nature: Course Notes from the Collège de France* (Evanston, IL: Northwestern University Press, 2003), 201–84. Henceforth cited as *La Nature* and *Nature*, with their respective paginations.

3. The 1960–61 courses also began in January.

4. The notes of March–May 1961 were published in *Textures* 8–9 (1974): 88–129 and *Textures* 10–11 (1975): 147–73.

5. See "Draft of a Chapter from *The Visible and the Invisible*" later in this book.

The Possibility of Philosophy Today

[Overview]

1. [Ed.]: Bibliothèque Nationale mark: Merleau-Ponty, Box VII, volume 4. This text corresponds with "Le Possibilité de la philosophie," in *Résumés de cours: Collège de France (1952–1960)* (Paris: Gallimard, 1968), 141–56. [Trans.]: The English translation of these, which is included in *In Praise of Philosophy and Other Essays*, lists this course as "Philosophy as Interrogation," which is apparently a liberty taken by the translator. As mentioned in a translator's note of *In Praise of Philosophy*, this course was originally listed as "Symbolism and the Human Body."

2. [Trans.]: This course was offered over the academic year 1958–59, starting in January 1959, after the first two courses on nature: "The Concept of Nature, 1956–1957," and "The Concept of Nature, 1957–1958: Animality, the Human Body, and the Passage to Culture." In this sense, "The Possibility of Philosophy Today" can be read as part of this series.

3. Jean-François Revel, *Pourquoi des philosophes?* (Paris: Julliard, 1957). [Trans.]: Revel was a journalist and philosopher, as well as a member of the Resistance during the Second World War. The pamphlet mentioned is a polemic against many of the philosophical signs on the horizon of Merleau-Ponty's thought, including Marx, Heidegger, and Lacan.

4. [Trans.]: The third course on nature took place the following academic year, "The Concept of Nature, 1959–1960: Nature and Logos: The Human Body."

5. [M.-P.]: Philosophical "void" after Hegel. Something ended with him. After him, philosophy is called into question by philosophy, and called into question confusedly. Destiny of metaphysics and anticipations of our nonphilosophy (thought: Nietzsche, Mallarmé *has advanced* over history). For that matter, begin from our experience.

I. Our State of Nonphilosophy

1. [M.-P.]: Moreover, this characterization of our time is not an explanation of the crisis of philosophy: there is a project of being (phase of *Seinsgeschichte*) at the origin that our time only discloses.

2. Edmund Husserl, *Die Krisis der europäischen Wissenschaft und die transzendentale Phänomenologie (1935–1936)* (The Hague: Nijhoff, 1954), 348; translated into English by David Carr as *The Crisis of the European Sciences and Transcendental Phenomenology* (Evanston, IL: Northwestern University Press, 1970), 299. Henceforth cited as *Krisis* and *Crisis*, with their respective paginations.

3. [Ed]: "Institution."

4. [Ed.]: See the second part of the 1956–57 course in Merleau-Ponty, *La Nature*, 177ff.; *Nature*, 132ff.

5. [Trans.]: In English.

6. [Trans.]: In English.

7. [Ed.]: This is possibly a text by Agnes Arber, from whom Merleau-Ponty

cites some titles: "The Interpretation of the Flower: A Study of Aspects of Morphological Thought," *Biological Review* 12: 157–84, or *The Natural Philosophy of Plant Form* (Cambridge: Cambridge University Press, 1950). [Trans.]: These texts appear in English in the text, though in a garbled form. I've amended the grammar as necessary.

8. Husserl, "Science of nature," *Krisis*, 42ff.; *Crisis*, 43ff.

9. [Ed.]: See the second course on nature, 1957–58, *La Nature*, 182; *Nature*, 136.

10. [M.-P.]: This is no longer the limited absurdism of the nineteenth century ("Reason" criticizing the senses). The science that discloses our relativities has nothing further with which to replace them.

11. [Ed.]: Connected by an arrow passing a few lines: "anxiety, as mixture of desire and fear before the other."

12. [Ed.]: Added in a revision.

13. [Ed.]: See Edmund Husserl, *Logical Investigations*, vol. 1, translated into English by J. N. Findlay (London: Routledge, 1970), §7.

14. [M.-P.]: Husserl: if I were a bird—See *Logical Investigations*: if we were to meet an angel. See again *Ideas II*. If we imagine truth as the correlate of an absolute mind.

15. [Ed.]: Edmund Husserl, "Umsturz der kopernikanischen Lehre: Die Erde als Ur-Arche bewegt sich nicht." Merleau-Ponty had access to this work in 1939 through Aaron Gurwitsch. See *Phenomenology of Perception*; [Trans.]: Translated into English as "Foundational Investigations of the Phenomenological Origin of the Spatiality of Nature: The Originary Ark, the Earth, Does Not Move," by Fred Kersten and revised by Leonard Lawlor, in Merleau-Ponty, *Husserl at the Limits of Phenomenology*, 117–31.

16. [Trans.]: "*à couleur 'fin de siècle,'*" where "end of the century" refers to French culture at the turn of the nineteenth and twentieth centuries, i.e., the historical and cultural backdrop of Mallarmé, Rimbaud, and Proust.

17. [M.-P., marginal note]: Future of the primordial—this burning and freezing primordial, gift and curse.

18. Arthur Rimbaud, "Barbarian," in *Rimbaud Complete*, English translation by Wyatt Mason (New York: Random House, 2002), 256. These are Merleau-Ponty's excerpts. The French text reads:

> Bien après les jours et les saisons, et les êtres et les pays . . . .
>
> Remis des vieilles fanfares d'héroïsme—qui nous attaquent encore le coeur et la tête—loin des anciens assassins— . . .
>
> Les brasiers, pleurant aux rafales de givres—douceurs!—Les feux à la pluie du vent de diamants jetés par le coeur terrestre étternellement carbonisé pour nous—Ô monde! . . .
>
> O Douceurs, o monde, o musique! Et là, les formes, les suers, les chevelures et les yeux, flottant. Et les larmes blanches, bouillantes—o douceurs!—et la voix féminine arrivée au fond des volcans et des grottes arctiques.

19. [M.-P., marginal note]: Destruction and veneration of language.

20. André Breton, *Pas perdus* (1924; Paris: Gallimard, 1949), 171: "*Les mots*

du reste ont fini de jouer. Les mots font l'amour." "The words of the rest have stopped playing. The words make love."

21. Breton, *Pas perdus*, 167.

22. Breton, *Pas perdus*, 151.

23. [M.-P.]: In relation with a certain signified.

24. Marcel Proust, *La Prisonniere* (Paris: Gallimard, Nouvelle Revue Française, VI, 1923), 69ff.; translated into English by C. K. Scott Moncrieff and Terence Kilmartin and revised by D. J. Enright as *The Captive* (New York: Modern Library, 2003), 84–85.

25. [M.-P., marginal note]: Relativization of the signifier and signified: search for a speech of things (Martinville—the book writes itself in us), one is no longer satisfied with their parallel.

26. Bernard Berenson, *Esthétique et histoire des arts visuels* (Paris: Albin Michel, 1953).

27. [M.-P.]: See page [**11**].

Henri Bergson, *La Pensée et le mouvant* (Paris: Presses Universitaires de France, 1934), 264–65; translated into English by Mabelle L. Andison as *The Creative Mind* (Mineola, NY: Dover, 2007), 195–96. [Trans.]: Merleau-Ponty quotes the following texts from *The Creative Mind*:

Da Vinci's Treatise on Painting: "the living being is characterized by the undulous or serpentine [*serpentine*] line, which each being has its own manner of undulating [*serpenter*] and the object of art is to render this undulation [*serpentement*] distinctive."

Ravaisson: "Discover in each object the particular way in which a certain flexious line which is, so to speak, its generating axis, is directed through its whole extent . . ."

Bergson: "It is possible, moreover, that this line is not any one of the visible lines of the figure. It is not in one place any more than in another, but it gives the key to the whole." Certainly! However, *are there* lines? Contour is not one. "Objective" lines are not to be rendered by lines—more strongly rendered by many lines or interrupted and repeated lines."

[Ed]: See Merleau-Ponty, *OE*, 72–73; and Bergson, "La Vie et l'oeuvre de Ravaisson," in *La Pensée et le mouvant* (1934).

28. [M.-P.]: Henri Michaux on Klee's lines:

Michaux, "Adventures of Lines" (Preface to W. Grohmann, *Paul Klee*).
Lines:
"Lines walking around. The first the West had ever seen walking around
   in this way.
Travelers, lines that don't so much make objects as trajectories, paths . . .
And penetrators: contrary to the possessors—eager to envelop, to
   surround, makers of shapes (and then what?)—they're lines for what is
   underneath . . .
Allusive ones . . .
The ones that are mad about enumeration, about endless juxtaposition . . .
A line meets a line. A line avoids a line. Adventures of lines.

> A line for the pleasure of being a line, of going ahead, as a line. Points. Dust of points. A line is dreaming. Before then, no one had ever let a line dream.
>
> A line is waiting. A line is hoping. A line is rethinking a face . . .
>
> Here's a line thinking. Another is fulfilling a thought. Lines at stake. Line of decision . . .
>
> A line gives up. A line rests. Stop. A stop with three clinging roots: a habitat.
>
> A line closes itself in. Meditation. Threads are still sprouting from it, slowly . . ." etc.

[Ed]: See Henri Michaux, "Aventures de lignes," in *Passages* (Paris: Gallimard, 1954), 175–78; translated into English by David Ball as "Adventures of Lines," in *Darkness Moves: An Henri Michaux Anthology, 1927–1984* (Berkeley: University of California Press, 1994), 317–18.

29. [In the margin and highlighted by M.-P.]: A line arouses the field that gives it sense by deforming the field given—For example, the writer and language are given provided that the error is not arbitrary.

30. See Will Grohmann, *Paul Klee* (New York: Abrams, 1954), 375; French translation cited by Merleau-Ponty, *Paul Klee* (Paris: Filkner, 1954), 376.

31. Michel Leiris and Georges Limbour, *André Masson et son univers* (Geneva: Des Trois Collines, 1947).

32. Leiris and Limbour, *André Masson et son univers*, 152; reference to Masson's *Massacre au soleil* (1934), 170.

33. [Ed.]: Article added by M.-P.

34. Hubert Juin and Jean-Clarence Lambert, *Sixteen Painters of the Young School of Paris* (Paris: Arts, Inc., 1958), 34.

35. [Ed.]: This passage on the Paris school was added during a different period of work.

36. Juin and Lambert, *The Young School of Paris*, 56.

37. [Ed]: Reference to Robert Lapoujade, *L'Enfer et la mine*; see *The Young School of Paris*, 50. On Lapoujade, see Sartre's article in *Meditations* 2 (1961), "Le Peinture sans privilege"; translated into English as "The Unprivileged Painter," in *Essays on Aesthetics*, edited and translated by Wade Baskin (New York: Philosophical Library, 1966).

38. [Ed.]: The reference to Klee's study and the references to the texts that follow are a collection of citations and notes from January 1959—after the date on the first sheet—which Merleau-Ponty takes from Grohmann, *Paul Klee*. Rather than presenting these reading notes in an appendix, it seemed preferable to extract the passages to which Merleau-Ponty returns and place them in endnotes, with the numbering corresponding to the lecture notes. [Trans.]: All the Klee texts are from the English edition of Grohmann.

39. [M.-P.]: This is to put what we have said about Klee's "lines" in context. The art of lines is the variant of the art of colors [*taches*] "exhaled in the right spot"; trace and realization of color: that which is always already there, Being

older than everything. [Trans.]: The text cited is from Michaux, "Adventures of Lines," in *Darkness Moves*, 316.

40. Grohmann, *Paul Klee*, Klee text 1: April 7, 1914, at Tunis; April 15, at Kairouan: "I shall stop working now. I can feel everything sinking deep inside me of its own accord, and this gives me great confidence because I do not have to do anything. Color has taken hold of me; no longer do I have to chase after it. I know that it has hold of me forever. That is the significance of this blessed moment. Color and I are one. I am a painter" (57).

"I must not hurry when I want to do so much. This evening has sunk deep inside me and will remain forever. Many a blonde northern moonrise will incite me softly like a muted reflection of this, again and again. It shall be my beloved: my other 'self'! An incentive to find my 'self.' But I myself am the southern moonrise" (56).

September 1914: "Now, I dally in that shattered world only in occasional memories—the way one recollects things now and again. Thus I deal abstractly with memories" (57).

41. Klee text 2: 1915: "The more horrifying this world becomes (as it is these days), the more art becomes abstract; while a world at peace produces realistic art" (57).

42. Klee text 3: "Everything transient is only comparative. What we see before us is but a suggestion, a possibility, a makeshift. True reality is at first buried and invisible" (60).

43. Grohmann, *Paul Klee*, 183.

44. [M.-P., marginal note]: "The work of art, too, is experienced by us first of all as a product of creation, rather than as its passive product. The creative impulse suddenly springs to life, like a flame, passes through the hand on to the canvas, where it spreads further until, like the spark that closes an electric circuit, it returns to its source: the eye and the mind" (Grohmann, *Paul Klee*, 99).

45. Klee text 4: "Pictorial art springs from movement, is itself fixed movement, and is perceived through movement" (181). "Subjects": "An apple tree in bloom, its roots, the rising sap, its trunk, the cross section with the annual rings, the blossom, its structure, its sexual functions, the fruit, the core with the seeds. A complex of states of growth" (181)—or just as well: "a sleeping person, the circulation of the blood, the measured breathing of the lungs, the delicate function of the kidneys, in the head a world of dreams related to the powers of fate. And complex functions united in repose" (Grohmann, *Paul Klee*, 181).

46. [Trans.]: We could also render this "nature naturing," which is effectively the same as Spinoza's Latin expression.

47. Klee text 5: ". . . From prototype to archetype! . . .

What artist does not yearn to dwell near the mind, or heart, of creation itself, that prime mover of events in time and space?

In nature's own womb, the soil whence all creation springs, which holds the key to every riddle?

But not all of us are destined to go there. Each must obey the command within him, wherever it may lead.

Thus the Impressionists, our adversaries of yesteryear, were quite right, in their time, to dwell among the underbrush of everyday appearances.

Our own heart, however, urges us to go deeper, down to bedrock. . . .

Only then do these oddments become realities—artistic realities that widen the horizon of our life beyond its ordinary limits.

Because they don't simply reproduce, more or less idiosyncratically, what our eye has seen, but cast into visible form our secret visions and insights."

[From Klee's 1924 Jena Lecture (Grohmann, *Paul Klee*, 367).]

48. Klee text 6: "I seek a place for myself only with God . . . I am a cosmic point of reference, not a species . . . I cannot be understood in purely earthly terms [Trans.: rendered in French as *Je suis insaisissable dans l'immanence*, "I cannot be grasped in immanence"]. For I can live as well with the dead as with the unborn. Somewhat nearer to the heart of all Creation than is usual. But still far from being near enough" (Grohmann, *Paul Klee*, 182). Merleau-Ponty adds: "Written 24 years before his death (at 37 years old)—it would become his epitaph."

49. Klee text 7: "Art is a likeness of the Creation. It is sometimes an example, just as the terrestrial is an example of the cosmic" (181).

Klee text 8: "Symbols reassure the spirit that it need not depend exclusively on terrestrial experience with its possible enhancements . . . Art plays an unwitting game with the ultimate things and achieves them nevertheless" (181). "It helps us to rejoice in the sacred vigils when the soul sits down to supper" (182).

Klee text 9: Klee: "Art does not render the visible, but makes visible" (181).

"We used to represent things visible on earth which we enjoyed seeing or would have liked to see. Now we reveal the reality of visible things, and thereby express the belief that visible reality is merely an isolated phenomenon latently outnumbered by other realities. Things take on a broader and more varied meaning, often in seeming contradiction to the rational experience of yesterday. There is a tendency to stress the essential in the random" (181).

50. Klee text 10: "The work of art is concerned with the need for deformation due to the penetration into the specific dimensions of the painterly medium. For there the rebirth of nature takes place" (184–89). "'Now it looks at me,' Klee used to say of a work" (189).

51. Klee text 11: Grohmann cites Klee: "the artist is 'a philosopher without really wanting to be one' . . . 'instead of a finished image of nature' he sees 'its genesis, the only essential thing' and 'thus extends the creative act from the back forward, endowing genesis with duration" (189).

52. Grohmann, *Paul Klee*, 192.

53. Grohmann, *Paul Klee*, 205.

54. Grohmann, *Paul Klee*, 214.

55. Grohmann, *Paul Klee*, 191.

56. Merleau-Ponty's emphasis.

57. [Ed.]: In the margin, Merleau-Ponty returns to the following statements by Klee: "The artist is man, nature himself and a piece of nature in nature's space" (Grohmann, *Paul Klee*, 183).

Exterior and interior vision where "pictures which 'differ complexly from the optical image of an object and yet, from the standpoint of the totality, do not contradict it" are born (183).

"Behind the ambiguity lies an ultimate mystery, and the light of the intellect is miserably extinguished" (214).

"The truth that reveals itself to us in Klee's work is a 'founded truth,' as in Heidegger, where 'to found' means 'to give,' 'to establish,' 'to begin.'" "Leap" of the painting (G), "the end is already latent in the beginning" (214).

58. Grohmann, *Paul Klee*, 191.

59. Michaux, *Passages*, 175; *Darkness Moves*, 317.

60. [Ed.]: Merleau-Ponty refers to these statements by Klee from Grohmann in the margins: Epitaph extracted from the *Journal.*

"I cannot be understood in purely earthly terms [Trans.: rendered in French as *Je suis insaisissable dans l'immanence*, "I cannot be grasped in immanence"]. For I can live as happily with the dead as with the unborn. Somewhat nearer to the heart of creation than is usual. But still far from being near enough" (95).

Cézanne: "idea of color as the 'place where our spirit and the universe meet'" (143).

Klee refers to that Goethean reason "of which nature consists and in accordance with which she acts" (152).

"All art is a memory of age old things, dark things, whose fragments live on in the artist" (381). "some layman onlooker will devastate him with the remark 'But this still doesn't look like uncle!' . . . yet sooner or later he himself may come to associate his structure with something like 'uncle,' with or without the layman's help . . . Once he affirms the representational aspect of his design, he is apt to add some things, or shapes, that further identify the subject he has fixed in his mind. If he is lucky, he will manage to place these representational elements in such a way that they look as if they had always been part of the basic structure, rather than mere appendages to it. . . . When it comes to subjects in painting, we know only our own private enthusiasms. And, of course, once in a while it may give us great pleasure to see a familiar face suddenly emerege from a picture" (Grohmann, *Paul Klee*, 366–67).

61. Grohmann, *Paul Klee*, 198.

62. [M.-P.]: The drawing is rigously monumental (or charactural) because it must show human beings in the register not of the familiar, not of the *selbstverstandlich*, but in that of the originary.

63. [M.-P.]: a fortiori evidence: it happens that the title is abstract and that the drawing is concrete.

64. Klee, *Fir Tree* (1940), in Grohmann, *Paul Klee*, 1.

65. [M.-P.]: Also from there, "subjects":

66. [M.-P.]: possible cities, "place of election."

67. [Trans.]: Apparently the drawing referred to here dates to 1920. Not included in the English edition of Grohmann; French pagination, 1.

68. Klee, *Bird Drama* (1920), in Grohmann, *Paul Klee*, 151.

69. [M.-P.]: It makes you think: we are before X as they are before us—in

relation to the Silence of the abyss [*Sige l'abime*],* our dramas, our "senses" are derisory and touching—Our obscurity.

    * [Ed]: See *Le Visible et l'invisible*, 233; *La Prose du monde*, 157; *Signes*, 395.

    70. Klee, *The Tear* (1933), in Grohmann, *Paul Klee*, 83.

    71. [M.-P.]: the appearance of the human being, spectacle and the one who is thereby "darkness stuffed with organs." Infrastructure.

    72. Klee, *Family Matters (among Fruit)* (1927), in Grohmann, *Paul Klee*, 257.

    73. Klee, *Group with the Fleeing Scold* (1940), in Grohmann, *Paul Klee*, 343.

    74. Klee, *Brotherhood* (1939) (not included in the English edition of Grohmann; French pagination, 344).

    75. Klee, *Forgetful Angel* (1939), in Grohmann, *Paul Klee*, 348.

    76. Klee, *Angelus Militans* (1939), in Grohmann, *Paul Klee*, 350.

    77. Klee, *Poor Angel* (1939), in Grohmann, *Paul Klee*, 304.

    78. [M.-P.]: Schoenberg.

    79. Henri Michaux, "A Certain Phenomenon One Calls Music" (*Passages*, 181); this text first appeared as the "Preface" to the *Encyclopédie de la musique* (Paris: Fasquelle, 1958). [Trans.]: The text was reprinted in *Passages* in 1963 and is not included in *Darkness Moves*, and as far as I know, has not been translated into English other than what appears here.

    80. Michaux, "A Certain Phenomenon One Calls Music," 182–86.

    81. Michaux, "A Certain Phenomenon One Calls Music," 182–86.

    82. [M.-P.]: 1959 Course.

    Hegel, *Aesthetics: Aber mit der Kunst haben wir es mit keinem bloss angenehmen oder nutzlichen Spielwerk, sondern . . . mit einer Entfaltung der Wahrheit zu tun.*

    Entfaltung: deployment—and not explication-thematization. Truth deploys itself. *Wahrheit*: yet the painting does not speak of the empirical world, nor does music (program music) speak of things, of feelings, especially generalized music. No—but [it speaks] of the seeds of things, of figures of feeling like contemporary painting speaks of the *welten*, of the *dingen*.

    Michaux: night comes upon the *object*—the flood that covers objects and even beings—no distance between ourselves and music. And yet is it feeling [*sentir*] sensory pleasure or pain? No—it is a discourse—a mute eloquence—It takes place and it tells itself something. There is a quasi-world with its contours, levels, gaps [*écarts*].

    See Klee: music is archaic axis, addresses itself to and reveals, in us, articulation before articulation; is "divinely" taking place; [does not] know (subject-object relation) but yet [has] sense, i.e., organization around musical beings which are monograms of a whole series of empirical realities, made readily available, without obstacle, without anything troublesome [*genant*].

    Danger and truth: (see **19**): truth which is only *Entfaltet* [unfolded]—But this *Entfaltung* [unfolding] (*Ineinander* myself-world) awakens [the] vertical world (we have to know the objectal, profane world, already constituted by this origin—others resistant in this originarity—See Klee: in principle it is necessary to recover immanence in this way). This consciousness of music is forever (Kant, *Critique of Judgment*, beneath subject-object, universal without concept).

    What is new is the idea that the universe of knowledge is derived by way of a relationship to this regulating usage; it is the idea (generalized music) that each music creates its proper *Boden* (Boulez, says Rostand, does not even take the scalic conception for *Boden*), presupposes only sensorial means of communication and no diacritical system, no culturally given *Boden*.

83. [Ed.]: On the back of this page, Merleau-Ponty strikes out the comment "**20** Psychoanalysis—See 20 again": he has clearly given up on further development of psychoanalysis, probably thinking that it was moving him away from the subject of the possibility of philosophy. We have recovered this text, which corresponds to the missing pages, **20** to **25** in the dossier for the course of 1959–60; Merleau-Ponty would have placed it following the course "Nature and Logos." We have included a transcription on 80–85 at the end of the course of 1958–59.

[II. Philosophy in the Face of This Nonphilosophy]

Husserl: Philosophy as a Problem

1. [Ed.]: See 85, "Philosophy in the Face of This Nonphilosophy," the title given to this part by Merleau-Ponty when it was first written.

2. [M.-P.]: Husserl seems to have ignored Nietzsche and all irrationalism.

3. [Trans.]: Merleau-Ponty refers to the first-edition German text, *Logische Untersuchungen*, vol. 2 (The Hague: Nijhoff, 1900–1901); translated into English by J. N. Findlay as *Logical Investigations*, vols. 1–2 (London: Routledge, 2001).

4. [Trans.]: See Edmund Husserl, *Philosophie der Arithmetik: Psychologische und logische untersuchungen*, HUA XII (The Hague: Nijhoff, 1970); translated into English by Dallas Willard as *Philosophy of Arithmetic: Psychological and Logical Investigations with Supplementary Texts from 1887–1901* (Dordrecht: Kluwer Academic, 2003). See also Husserl's "Philosophie als strenge Wissenschaft," *Logos* 1 (1910–11): 289–34; translated into English by Quentin Lauer as "Philosophy as Rigorous Science," in *Phenomenology and the Crisis of Philosophy* (New York: Harper Torchbooks, 1965), 69–147.

5. [Trans.]: Merleau-Ponty contests the typical translation of *Wesen* as "essence" or even as "Being." In order to underline this ambiguity, I leave the term in German.

6. [Trans.]: Merleau-Ponty seems to have in mind a passage that appears in paragraph 36 of the "Prolegomena" to the *Logical Investigations*: "What is true is absolutely, intrinsically true: truth is one and the same, whether men or non-men, angels or gods apprehend and judge it. Logical laws speak of truth in this ideal unity, set over against the real multiplicity of races, individuals and experiences, and it is of this ideal unity that we all speak when we are not confused by relativism" (Husserl, *Logical Investigations*, vol. 1, 79).

7. Edmund Husserl, *Ideen I* (1911), *Ideen zu einer Reinen Phanomenologie und Phanomenologischen Philosophie* (The Hague: Niemeyer, 1922); translated into English by Fred Kersten as *Ideas Pertaining to a Pure Phenomenology and to a Phenomenological Philosophy, First Book: General Introduction to a Pure Phenomenology* (The Hague: Martinus Nijhoff, 1982).

8. Edmund Husserl, *Cartesianische Meditationen*, 1929, HUA I. [Ed.]: Merleau-Ponty had read the 1933 French translation of this work by Emmanuel

Levinas and G. Peiffer, a translation with which he did not seem to be satisfied; the work was translated into English by Dorion Cairns as *Cartesian Meditations* (The Hague: Martinus Nijhoff, 1960).

9. [Ed.]: Merleau-Ponty has not written "givenness" [*donation*].

10. Edmund Husserl, "Vorlesungen zur Phänomenologie des inneren Zeit-bewusstseins," ed. Martin Heidegger, in *Jahrbuch für Philosophie und phänomenolo-gische Forschung* 9 (Halle: Max Niemeyer, 1928), 367–498; translated into English by John Barnett Brough as *On the Phenomenology of the Consciousness of Internal Time (1893–1917)* (The Hague: Kluwer Academic, 1991).

11. [M.-P.]: To reflect is to disclose a *Boden*, a *selbstverständliches*. Astonish-ment before nonphilosophy.

12. [Trans.]: *Ideen II* would not appear until 1952, fourteen years after Hus-serl's death. Apparently this text was a source of perpetual dissatisfaction and revision for Husserl, perhaps, as Merleau-Ponty seems to suggest, because of the unresolved paradoxes that transcendental phenomenology seems to produce.

13. [M.-P.]: and the autonomy of the *unbeteiligte Zuschauer* which appears as an "I."

14. [M.-P.]: Two attitudes exclude: (1) Indifference of the philosophy that would eliminate all responsibility—it is at issue—it has to be understood; (2) There is no more philosophy, the proof is there. On the contrary: it is neces-sary to understand the crisis of philosophy as *Sinnentleerung* [emptying of sense] and make it regain its hold. It is what makes us understand the crisis of European humanity. It is at issue because history is the history of philosophy. Total respon-sibility because of total right [*droit*].

15. [M.-P., in the margin]: Philosophy tussles with the world—precisely as philosophy in its own right.

16. [Ed.]: At the bottom of the page Merleau-Ponty writes "III. Final works," but this title is not followed by any text on this page.

17. [Trans.]: A public lecture held in Vienna on May 7 and 10, 1935, en-titled "Die Philosophie in der Krisis europäischen Menschheit"; translated into English by David Carr as "The Vienna Lecture," in *The Crisis of European Sciences and Transcendental Phenomenology* (Evanston, IL: Northwestern University Press, 1970), 269–99.

18. [M.-P.]: Passage from an "organic" history, without infinite idea-goal, to a *Geschichtlichkeit* [historicity] that would be an indefinite approximation of truth and growing power and re-creation of humanity.

19. [M.-P.]: Husserl, *Krisis*, 314; *Crisis*, 269.

20. [Trans.]: A reference to the French translation of the Vienna Confer-ence, "La Crise de l'humanité européenne et la philosophie," *Revue de Métaphy-sique et de Morale* 55, no. 3 (July–September 1950): 225–58. The reference to the English translation in *The Crisis of European Sciences* is 285–86.

21. [Trans]: The reference to the English translation in *Crisis* is 297.

22. [Ed.]: Husserl published these texts in 1936 in Belgrade in the journal *Philosophia*.

23. [Ed.]: *Husserliana VI* was published in 1954 by Martinus Nijhoff.

24. [M.-P.]: The Vienna Conference has already said: "*So kann einseitige*

Rationalitat . . . zum Ubel warden . . . : Es gehort zum Wesen der Vernunft, dass di Philosophen ihre unendliche Aufgabe zunachst nur in einer absolut notwendigen Einseitigkeit verstehen und bearbeiten konnen"; "In this way, a one-sided rationality can certainly become an evil . . . it belongs to the essence of reason that the philosophers at first understand and labor at their task in an absolutely necessary one-sided way" (*Krisis*, 338; *Crisis*, 291).

25. [Ed]: See Husserl, *Krisis*, 176; *Crisis*, 173.

26. [M.-P.]: Idea of approximation, of the *in infinitum*, of the method for perfecting the method, ideas which make no sense with respect to qualities, *Krisis*, 33; *Crisis*, 35, which are always "at a distance."

27. [Ed]: "*Geistiges Sein ist fragmentarisch*"; "Spiritual being is fragmentary" (Husserl, *Krisis*, 342; *Crisis*, 294).

28. Husserl, *Krisis*, 53; *Crisis*, 53.

29. [M.-P.]: Forgetting that is characteristic of *all* tradition, sedimentation. The evidence of the *Erwerbe* [acquisitions] is forgetting—i.e., the certainty of memories. The certainty of what one has done or of what one anticipates (*Vorhabe* [intending]) is prepossession or postpossession without actual presence, at a distance. This founds the "pure thinking" that as such is technicization (Husserl, *Krisis*, 23; *Crisis*, 26). Recovering the *Lebenswelt* [lifeworld] is here to recover the sedimented history which *Strecke* [distances] within us. It is language, *niedergeschlagene* [dejected] *Logos*. A spiritual generativity that is not forgetting: this would be adequacy to the *Lebenswelt*.

"Pure thinking," pure *theoria*, uses of *Boden*, of *Lebenswelt*, is secretly praxis, and has only *Vorhabe* as evidence—*Krisis*, Beilage V, 401. [Trans.]: Beilage V is not included in the English edition of the *Krisis*.

30. Husserl, *Krisis*, 45; *Crisis*, 48. [Trans.]: The page 121 is given for the German text, but this must be a mistake.

31. [M.-P.]: Problem of *verborgenen Vernunft* [concealed reason] (or teleology) (or dialectical sense, mediation: Descartes refuting his own rationalism by producing his idea of eternal truths). Galileo *entdeckender und verdeckender Genius* [discovering and concealing genius] (Husserl, *Krisis*, 53; *Crisis*, 53). To disclose is to hide.

32. Husserl, *Krisis*, 23; *Crisis*, 26.

33. Husserl, *Krisis*, 4; *Crisis*, 6.

34. [M.-P.]: Opening of the *horizon* through opposition to knowledge of the *infinite*. The three states: finite (organic); infinite (in itself); horizon.

35. [M.-P.]: *allumspannende Seinsweise* [all-encompassing manner of Being], Husserl, *Krisis*, 134; *Crisis*, 131.

36. [M.-P.]: In the *Beilagen* of the *Krisis*, the *Selbigkeit* of philosophy (of ideality) is the expression of the *Selbigkeit* of the world.

37. [M.-P.]: The *Ich überhaupt* of Fichte can only be Fichte.

38. [M.-P.]: If transcendental subjectivity is intersubjectivity, this means that *Sinngebung* is *Urstiftung*, the opening of a field and not immanence, *Krisis*, 45–46; *Crisis*, 46–47, that all *Sinngebung* entails *Sinnverschiebungen*. "Intentional transgression" if there were to be one.

39. [M.-P.]: Husserl insists: the reduction is simultaneous in all—there is an

internal bond = not *Auseinander* but *Ineinander*—but this is only possible through co-idealization founded on pre-theoretical *Einfühlung*.

40. *Krisis*, 482. [Trans.]: The reference is to Beilage XXIII, included in this volume. See 255–58.

41. [M.-P.]: "*Einer Art von Welträtseln, die den früheren Zeiten fremd waren*"; "for the emergence of a set of world-enigmas which were unknown in earlier times" (Husserl, *Krisis* 3; *Crisis*, 5); "*neue Dimensionen . . . nie gefragte Fragen*"; "new dimensions . . . questions never before asked" (*Krisis*, 16; *Crisis*, 18); the difficulty of prior reflections justified by "*die Fremdheit und Gefährlichkeit der dabei in Funktion tretenden notwendigen Gedanken*"; "the essential strangeness and precariousness of the ideas which will necessarily become involved" (*Krisis*, 137; *Crisis*, 134). The *Lebenswelt* is ignored; there is no literature on it, *Krisis*, 114; *Crisis*, 112. "*Wir uns in der Weltliteratur vergeblich nach Untersuchungen umsehen, die uns als Vorarbeiten dienen könnten*"; "Since we seek in vain in world literature for investigations that could serve as preparatory studies for us" (*Krisis*, 158; *Crisis*, 155).

42. [Ed]: See Merleau-Ponty's commentary on this *Beilage* in the appendix "Translation and Commentary on Beilage XXIII of Hussel's *Crisis of the European Sciences*," later in this volume, 258–59.

43. [M.-P.]: See **37**. See the appendix "Translation and Commentary on Beilage XXIII of Hussel's *Crisis of the European Sciences*," later in this volume, 255–59.

44. [Ed.]: See Husserl, *Krisis* §25, 100; *Crisis*, 96.

45. [Ed.]: Husserl, *Krisis*, 91; *Crisis*, 89.

46. [Ed.]: Husserl, *Krisis*, 512; *Crisis*, 394.

47. [Trans.]: The words "*ça*" in French and "*es*" in German both translate to "it." Here, "*es*" is a reference to what is commonly referred to in English as the "id"; the word "id" is from Strachey, who used the Latin to render Freud's use of "*das es*" in English in the *Standard Edition*.

48. Husserl, *Krisis*, 159; *Crisis*, 156.

49. *Krisis*, 173; *Crisis*, 170. Merleau-Ponty provides his own translation of this passage. The text is from the English edition.

50. [M.-P., marginal note]: The true transcendental, the *Fundamentalbetrachtung*: positive or immanent evidence responding to *attitude*, to purpose, cannot provide it. It must be adequate to all, to that which precedes the *Gebilde* as to what is beyond—"constituting life" across the *Je Zuschauer* [I-observer]—the "mothers."

Patent and latent = (ideal) identity and unity—idea and concept—the organization of nature and history as *field*. *Offenheit* [openness] of *Umwelt* [environment]—Temporality—Heraclitus, the pre-Socratics = the unity of the horizon.

Philosophy: is *Tat* [deed], construction, *Gebilde* of what is its *Selbst*—but I have taken this path.

Philosophical intersubjectivity: there is a link that I grasp only by being myself, alone.

51. [Trans.]: Beilage V is not included in the English translation of the *Krisis*.

52. [Trans.]: Beilage X is not included in the English translation of the *Krisis*.

53. [Trans.]: Beilagen XVI and XIX are not included in the English translation of the *Krisis*.

54. [Trans.]: For Beilage XXIII, see the appendix "Translation and Commentary on Beilage XXIII of Husserl's *Crisis of the European Sciences*" later in this book. Beilage XXV is not included in the English translation of the *Krisis*.

55. Husserl, *Krisis*, 173; *Crisis*, 170.

56. Husserl, *Krisis*, 508; *Crisis*, 389, Beilage XXVIII, "Denial of Scientific Philosophy. Necessity of Reflection. The Reflection [Must Be] Historical. How Is History Required?"

57. [Ed.]: This page is not numbered by Merleau-Ponty and is presented as a separate note.

58. [Trans.]: This text appears in the English translation of the *Crisis* as Appendix IX: "Denial of Scientific Philosophy. The Reflection [Must Be] Historical. How Is History Required?" 389–95.

59. [Ed.]: Husserl, *Krisis*, 508; *Crisis*, 389.

60. Husserl, *Krisis*, 512–14; *Crisis*, 394–95.

61. Husserl, *Krisis*, 512; *Crisis*, 394.

62. Husserl, *Krisis*, 510; *Crisis*, 391.

63. Husserl, *Krisis*, 513; *Crisis*, 395.

64. Husserl, *Krisis*, 512; *Crisis*, 394.

65. Husserl, *Krisis*, 59; *Crisis*, 58.

66. Husserl, *Krisis*, 512; *Crisis*, 394.

67. [Trans.]: In English in the text. A "connex" is a mathematical relationship in which all the parts are interrelated.

68. Husserl, *Krisis*, 512; *Crisis*, 394.

69. [Ed.]: See Merleau-Ponty, *Le Visible et l'invisible*, 142; *The Visible and the Invisible*, 107ff.

70. Husserl, *Krisis*, 513; *Crisis*, 395.

71. Husserl, *Krisis*, 74; *Crisis*, 73.

72. J. Paulhan, *Les Fleurs de Tarbes* (Paris: Gallimard, 1941), 138.

73. Husserl, *Krisis*, 73; *Crisis*, 71.

74. Husserl, *Krisis*, Beilage XXIII, § 65. [Trans.]: The German text is quoted in the body: "*da allein is überhaupt Leben original und in eigentlichster Weise im Selbstverstandnis des Biologischen selbt gegeben.*" See later in this volume, 255.

75. Martin Heidegger, *Sein und Zeit* (Tubingen: Niemeyer, 1957), 49–50; translated into English by John Macquarrie and Edward Robinson as *Being and Time* (New York: Harper Perennial, 1962), 75. Henceforth cited as *SZ* and *BT*, with their respective paginations.

76. [Ed.]: It seemed appropriate to publish the translation of Husserl's text as an appendix—Beilage XXIII, June 1936—to which Merleau-Ponty refers because he adds, as we shall see, a commentary, and he reports that he will read these texts in public. See "Translation and Commentary on Beilage XXIII of Husserl's *Crisis of the European Sciences*" later in this book.

Heidegger: Philosophy as a Problem

1. [Ed.]: The outline (below) is a summary and redefinition of the composition for the part on Heidegger, from page **39**. In the outline, Merleau-Ponty refers to the pagination of his own text. This outline confirms his rearrangement of the succession of his arguments.

Heidegger:

Turn: from the analytic of *Dasein* (anthropology) to the *Seinsfrage* (mysticism); but a turn that is rather clarification: the *Seinsfrage* is the goal from the beginning; the change in signs which intervene respond to the opening of the field of being.

The negativity of *Dasein* is an exterior view, relative to being, the ontic, on this plane it remains what it was; but precisely once one finds this abyss, one perceives that it *doesn't* open onto *anything*—elimination of *nichtiges Nichts*. It no longer opens onto a full positivity; it opens onto *Nichts-Seiend* which is Being, and which, and relative to Being-been, rests on not-Being—third stage.

In this way, a change of signs {*Sein* includes *Welt, Dasein, Zeitigung* change in the sign of *Zeit*, **41**, n.1 [*note 1, **41** says "*Sein aus der Zeit begriffen wundern soll*" (*SZ*, 18)]

Freedom; truth; man} **40**; *Dasein; Welt*} **46**.

The negative turns out to be openness onto Being, but this new being is not the one which had passed (object-being).

From *Dasein* to *Da-Sein* (from noun to verb).

Dasein **45** (against "consciousness")—

Text from *Vorträge und Aufsätze* insisting on openness (**45**).

Truth and idea of openness: intrinsic relationship and not immanent—prepossession of a "measuring" (**42–43**).

Hence: the freed "we have" (**43**), see Sartre.

Difference: the relationship is not immanent, i.e., the unconcealment *is* concealment, not evidence (**43**), *Da-sein*, being-the-there.

To clarify: relationship with Sartre (**48–49**), relationship with Bergson (**48**).

Hence elimination of anthropology, of objective or subjective metaphysics—reconquest of the *Seinserfahrung* [experience of Being] (**44**)—because "there is" something other than the subject and its objects, man and his creations, **57**.

Heideggerian notion of Being.

(1) Best way to clarify: the Being-beings [*Être-étant*] relationship (new notion of *Wesen*) **49–51**, and following from **51**.

2. [Trans.]: Merleau-Ponty is referring to *die* Kehre, the "turn" in Heidegger's thinking. I render changement as "turn" when it refers specifically to this.

3. Martin Heidegger, "What Is Metaphysics?" in *Pathmarks*, ed. William McNeill (Cambridge: Cambridge University Press, 1998), 82–96. [Trans.]: Merleau-Ponty references the original publications of texts that were later collected in *Wegmarken* (*Pathmarks*) in 1967, six years after his death. I will refer to the German text cited by Merleau-Ponty, followed by the English translations of these texts found in *Pathmarks*, henceforth abbreviated as *PM*.

4. Heidegger, *SZ* 8; *BT* 27–28.

5. Heidegger, *SZ* 15; *BT* 36.

6. [Ed.]: In the margin, Merleau-Ponty refers to the question: "What happened?" See in this volume, 94.

7. Martin Heidegger, *Vom Wesen des Grundes* (Frankfurt: Klostermann, 1929), 44; "On the Essence of Ground," in *PM*, 127.

8. Heidegger, *Vom Wesen des Grundes*, 53; *PM* 134.

9. [Trans.]: The editor of the French edition has this word marked with a question mark.

10. Martin Heidegger, *Der Satz vom Grund* (Pfullingen: G. Neske, 1957); translated into English by Reginald Lilly as *The Principle of Reason* (Bloomington: Indiana University Press, 1991). Henceforth cited as *SG* and *PR*, with their respective paginations.

11. Martin Heidegger, *Wesen der Wahrheit* (Frankfurt: Klostermann, 1954), 14; "On the Essence of Truth," in *PM*, 144.

12. Heidegger, *PM* 288. [Trans.]: Perhaps more accurately rendered as "placeholder for the nothing."

13. Martin Heidegger, *Über den Humanismus* (Berne, 1946); "Letter on Humanism," in *PM*, 252.

14. Heidegger, *SZ* 227; *BT* 270.

15. Heidegger, *SZ* 18; *BT* 40: "Being is to be understood in terms of time." Martin Heidegger, "Einleitung" ["Introduction"] of 1949, in *Was ist Metaphysik?* (Frankfurt: Klostermann, 1949), 17: "Time becomes the preliminary name [*Vorname*] . . . for the truth of Being" (Eng. trans., "Introduction to 'What Is Metaphysics?'" in *PM*, 286). [M.-P. notes]: "preliminary name or first name?" [*nom préalable ou prénom?*] [Trans.]: The translator's choice of "preliminary name" for *Vorname* in the English translation of Heidegger's "Introduction" to *What Is Metaphysics?* is problematic because this simply means "first name" in German. Merleau-Ponty's note here underlines the ambiguity in what Heidegger intends by saying "Time is the first name of the truth of Being." The note in the text here also includes the following quote from the "Introduction" to *What Is Metaphysics*: "In *Being and Time*, Being is not something other than time: 'Time' is a preliminary name [*Vorname*] for the truth of Being, and this truth is what prevails as essential in Being and thus is Being itself" (*Was ist Metaphysik?* 16; *PM* 285).

16. [M.-P.]: The *Jemeinigkeit* of *Dasein* was like a participable essence for the other *Daseins*: Heidegger, *SZ* 42; *BT* 67–68: it signifies that there is always *mitsagen*, a personal pronoun.

17. Heidegger, *SZ* 25; *BT* 47, translation modified.

18. Heidegger, *SZ* 64–65; *BT* 92–93.

19. [Ed.]: The manuscript provides a clear indication of placing "From *Dasein* to *Sein*" here, situated at **45** and **46**. Merleau-Ponty employs two different orthographies for *Sein*.

20. Heidegger, *SZ* 116; *BT* 151–52.

21. Martin Heidegger, "Bauen, Wohnen, Denken," in *Vorträge und Aufsätze* (Pfullingen: G. Neske, 1954), 157; translated into English by Albert Hofstadter as "Building, Dwelling, Thinking," in *Poetry, Language, Thought* (New York: Harper Perennial, 1971), 141–60, 154. *Vorträge und Aufsätze* is henceforth abbreviated as *VA*. [Trans.]: This text is translated into French by André Préau as *Essais et*

conférences (Paris: Gallimard, 1958). The French translation includes all of the essays originally published in *Vorträge und Aufsätze,* and even though Merleau-Ponty refers to the German edition, it's clear that he was familiar with the French translation. There is no single volume in English corresponding with *Vorträge und Aufsätze,* as the essays are disparately translated in various other texts. English translations of these essays are referenced as necessary.

22. Heidegger, *SZ* 64–65; *BT* 92.

23. Heidegger, *SZ* 227; *BT* 270.

24. Martin Heidegger, "Einleitung" ["Introduction"] of 1949, in *Was ist Metaphysik?* 13; *PM* 283.

25. [M.-P.]: Come back to **42**: analysis of truth.

26. Heidegger, *Wesen der Wahrheit,* 14; *PM* 146.

27. Heidegger, *Wesen der Wahrheit,* 15; *PM* 147.

28. Heidegger, *Wesen der Wahrheit,* 16; *PM* 147.

29. Jean-Paul Sartre, *Les Mouches* (Paris: Gallimard, 1943); translated into English by Stuart Gilbert in *No Exit and Three Other Plays* (New York: Vintage, 1989), 47–124.

30. See Merleau-Ponty, *Le Visible et l'invisible,* 236 and 307; *The Visible and the Invisible,* 185 and 259.

31. Heidegger, *Wesen der Wahrheit,* 19; *PM* 148.

32. Heidegger, *Wesen der Wahrheit,* 20; *PM* 147.

33. Heidegger, *Wesen der Wahrheit* 17; *PM* 146.

34. Heidegger, *Wesen der Wahrheit* 17; *PM* 146.

35. Heidegger, *SG* 113; *PR* 64.

36. Heidegger, *SG* 114; *PR* 65.

37. Martin Heidegger, *Zur Seinsfrage* (Frankfurt: Klostermann, 1956), 36; *PM* 315.

38. Heidegger, *Zur Seinsfrage,* 36; *PM* 315.

39. Martin Heidegger, *Einführung in die Metaphysik* (Tubingen: Niemeyer, 1952), 64; translated into English by Gregory Fried and Richard Polt as *Introduction to Metaphysics* (New Haven, CT: Yale University Press, 2000), 93. Henceforth abbreviated as *EM* and *IM,* with their respective paginations.

40. Heidegger, *SG* 27; *PR* 11.

41. Heidegger, *Zur Seinsfrage,* 23; *PM* 304.

42. Heidegger, *SG* 17; *PR* 5.

43. [Trans.]: I've left this section title untranslated since the object is to establish an equivalency between the French and German terms, which have no correlate in English. We could translate it as "Being, being, essence: Being, being essence," but this seems cumbersome, not to mention useless.

44. Heidegger, *EM* 23; *IM* 34.

45. Heidegger, *EM* 23; *IM* 34.

46. Heidegger, *EM* 23–24; *IM* 33–34.

47. Heidegger, *EM* 26; *IM* 37.

48. [Trans.]: Merleau-Ponty's interpolation.

49. Heidegger, *EM* 26; *IM* 37.

50. Heidegger, *EM* 26; *IM* 37.

51. [Ed.]: These examples are drawn from *Introduction to Metaphysics, EM* 27; *IM* 39.

52. [Trans.]: The editor indicates that Merleau-Ponty emphasizes *"ist,"* but the same emphasis is found in the English translation.

53. Heidegger, *EM* 27; *IM* 39.

54. [Trans.]: A reference to Stendhal's novel *La Chartreuse de Parme.*

55. Heidegger, *EM* 27; *IM* 39.

56. [M.-P.]: See **41.**

57. Heidegger, *SG* 67–68; *PR* 35. [Trans]: In German in the text: *Die Ros ist ohn warum; sie blühet, weil sie blühet, Sie acht nicht ihrer selbst, fragt nicht, ob man sie siehet;* in French: *"La rose est sans pourquoi, fleurit parce qu'elle fleurit, / N'a souci d'elle-même, ne désire être vue."*

58. Heidegger, *SG* 72; *PR* 37.

59. Heidegger, *SG* 73; *PR* 38.

60. Heidegger, *SG* 78; *PR* 42.

61. Heidegger, *SG* 93; *PR* 51, translation modified. [Trans.]: I substitute the German *Grund* for the translator's use of "ground/reason" in order to conform the quotations to Merleau-Ponty's analysis.

62. Heidegger, *SG* 185; *PR* 111.

63. Heidegger, *SG* 93; *PR* 52.

64. Heidegger, *SG* 93; *PR* 52.

65. Heidegger, *SG* 93; *PR* 51. [Trans.]: I include Merleau-Ponty's interpolations of the German text in square brackets.

66. Heidegger, *EM* 67; *IM* 96.

67. Heidegger, *EM* 69; *IM* 99.

68. Heidegger, *EM* 131; *IM* 191.

69. Heidegger, *EM* 62; *IM* 89.

70. Heidegger, *EM* 55; *IM* 80.

71. See within this volume, "II. *Seyn* or ~~*Sein*~~" **[47]**, 48.

72. Heidegger, *SG* 111; *PR* 63. [Trans.]: I've included Merleau-Ponty's interpolations.

73. [Trans]: The French translation is referenced. *PM* 276.

74. [Trans.]: Merleau-Ponty provides his own translation of this passage, which I render here. The English translation in "Poetically Man Dwells . . . ," in *Poetry, Language, Thought,* 218, reads: "The between is measured out for the dwelling of man. We now call the span thus meted out the dimension," which is at variance with both the German and Merleau-Ponty. The German text is: *"Wir nennen jetzt die zugemessene Durchmessung, durch die das Zwischen von Himmel und Erde offen ist, die Dimension"* (Heidegger, *VA* 195).

75. Heidegger, *Humanismus Brief,* 80; *PM* 254. [Ed.]: It is Heidegger's *Über den Humanismus* (Frankfurt: Klostermann, 1947) that Merleau-Ponty notes as *"Humanismus Brief."* Merleau-Ponty modified the translation, and always cites the pages of the German text of this bilingual edition. [Trans.]: I give the English translation of this work as found in *Pathmarks,* modified to suit Merleau-Ponty's changes.

76. Jean-Paul Sartre, *L'Existentialisme est un humanisme* (Geneva: Nagel,

1946), 36; translated into English by Carol Macomber as *Existentialism Is a Humanism* (New Haven, CT: Yale University Press, 2007), 28.

77. Heidegger, *Humanismus Brief*, 82; *PM* 254–55. [Trans.]: Heidegger's text switches back and forth between French and German, and Merleau-Ponty likewise switches back and forth between French and German. I give the English translation of the passage Merleau-Ponty references from *Pathmarks* and have included Merleau-Ponty's German interpolations.

78. [Ed.]: Merleau-Ponty thus indicates that he does not follow Munier's translation, which translates "*gibt*" as "*donne.*"

79. [Trans.]: The title of a poem by Guillaume Apollinaire, 1915.

80. [Trans.]: From Goethe's "Wandrers Nachtlied," quoted by Heidegger in *EM* 68; *IM* 98. Giving the translation from *IM*. In German in the text: "*Uber allen Gipfeln ist Ruh.*" Apparently Merleau-Ponty is transcribing the question marks from Heidegger, where they appear in the first reference to Goethe on the page cited: "'Over all the peaks / is peace': i.e.—???" (*EM* 68; *IM* 98).

81. [M.-P., marginal note]: "already said."

82. Heidegger, *EM* 156; *IM* 228.

83. Heidegger, *EM* 84; *IM* 121.

84. Heidegger, *EM* 156; *IM* 228.

85. [Ed.]: "*Lien*" is feminine in German.

86. Charles Péguy, *Notre conjointe* (Paris: Gallimard, 1935), 230–31.

87. [M.-P., marginal note]: Resume: it is not the human being who has freedom, it is freedom who has humanity. See *On the Essence of Truth.*

88. [Trans]: The French translation is cited. Heidegger, *PM*, 239.

89. [Ed]: Lecture—"Was ist Metaphysik?" July 24, 1929, University of Freiburg; Heidegger, "What Is Metaphysics?" in *PM*, 82–96; "Postcript to 'What Is Metaphysics?'" (1931), in *PM*, 231–38.

90. [Trans.]: Merleau-Ponty does not cite this remark, but it is from Heidegger's "Letter on Humanism," in *PM*, 243;

91. Heidegger, *Was ist Metaphysik?* 49.

92. Heidegger, "Nachwort" ["Postscript"], in *Was ist Metaphysik?* 77; "Postscript to 'What Is Metaphysics?'" in *PM*, 233.

93. Heidegger, *Was ist Metaphysik?* 46.

94. Heidegger, *EM* 22; *IM* 32.

95. Heidegger, *EM* 22; *IM* 32. See *SZ* 64.

96. Heidegger, *EM* 65; *IM* 93, translation modified.

97. Heidegger, *Zur Seinsfrage*, 25; *PM* 307.

98. Heidegger, *Zur Seinsfrage*, 30; *PM* 310.

99. Heidegger, *EM* 22; *IM* 32.

100. Heidegger, *SG* 183; *PR* 110.

101. Heidegger, *SG* 183–84; *PR* 110.

102. Heidegger, *Zur Seinsfrage*, 34; *PM* 313.

103. Heidegger, *EM* 77; *IM* 111.

104. Heidegger, *EM* 77; *IM* 111.

105. Heidegger, *EM* 78; *IM* 112.

106. Heidegger, *SZ* 35; *BT* 59.

107. Heidegger, *SZ* 36; *BT* 60.

108. [M.-P.]: Try to find a text on praxis and φύσις here.

109. Martin Heidegger, *Identität und Differenz* (Pfullingen: G. Neske, 1957); translated into English by Joan Stambaugh as *Identity and Difference*, edited by J. Glenn Gray (New York: Harper and Row, 1969).

110. [Ed]: The brackets are Merleau-Ponty's.

111. Heidegger, *EM* 64; *IM*, 92.

112. Heidegger, *VA* 136; Martin Heidegger, *What Is Called Thinking?* translated into English by J. Glenn Gray (New York: Harper Perennial, 1968), 10, translation modified.

113. Jean Giraudoux, *Eglantine* (Paris: Grasset, 1927), 230.

114. Heidegger, *EM* 124; *IM* 181.

115. Heidegger, *EM* 136; *IM* 198.

116. Heidegger, *EM* 136; *IM* 198.

117. Heidegger, *EM* 136; *IM* 198.

118. [Ed]: See Maurice Merleau-Ponty, "On Humanism," in *La Nature*, 182; *Nature*, 136.

119. [Ed.]: The following notes a title under which nothing is written: II. The theme of *Sage Sein und Sprache*.

120. [Ed.]: [Merleau-Ponty's outline for the third part on Heidegger]:
Speech and Being

(1) a: "essential intertwining [*entrelacement*]" of Being and Speech.

b: notion of "image" or "metaphor," or "*analogon*," or "symbol"—the "house"—the "bridge" = node of *Geviert*.

(2) Similarly, the "sign" is not an added index to be made.

a: Sign and "sense" (*Sinnveleibung objekte* [sense-objects]) phonic, semantic.

Problem of *Sinngebung*: how to account for [acquisition?]? His solution: not latency, not "conventional" sense, but history, myth.

b: Wild meaning "upholstering" the words (= sense made from differences, open). We use our language like we use our bodies. Not from the "intelligible world."

c: True signification of the etymological method: historical agreement with phonologists (employer and employee) in order to relativize "signifier" and "signified."

d: Interrogation, incomprehensible for Plato, becomes on the contrary the essence of thought-speech as made of *differences* of signification.

e: There are no statements about being because it is being that speaks in human speech—"parataxic" language—true speech introduces the other to a "site," not to significations.

(3) Definition of *sense*: it is made through the relationship of being [*l'être*] to beings [*l'étant*] that founds the "*es selbst*" and that *is* speech itself.

(4) a: Hence, it is language that speaks, that has *us*, and not we who have it (see freedom in *Wesen der Wahrheit* (Heidegger, *Vom Wesen der Wahrheit* [Klostermann, 1943], 14).

b: Our more expressive words, speaking in us, are not deliberate. For example, the word of the spirit [*l'esprit*] and the spirit of the word—game of language, ambiguity that comes from being, not from us. *Gedachte* [thought] and *Ungedachte* [unthought]—language and the All-Powerful.

Time and Being

The *Seinsgeschichte.*

(1) a: Why Heidegger otherwise no longer speaks about *Zeitigung, Zeit*: anthropological equivocation, cosmic time, Time of *Dasein* with the quasi-intuition of being, time becomes the *Seinsgeschichte.*

b: *Seinsgeschichte* that is not "creative evolution" nor "*causa sui,*" continuous creation.

Thus a new point of view on the operation of being's withdrawal.

(2) The *Seinsgeschichte* and the "philosophy of history."

(3) The *Seinsgeschichte* and the history of philosophy.

Philosophy as product of Being and not "conception" of being.

(4) Conclusion a: What is absolute knowledge for Heidegger? It is not "philosophy"; b: But it is not nihilism; c: *Denken* and *Besinnung*; d: Possibility of philosophy as indirect philosophy, non-positive philosophy, non-objective philosophy.

121. Heidegger, *EM* 41; *IM* 59.

122. Heidegger, *PM* 272. [Trans.]: Only the French translation is cited.

123. [M.-P., marginal note]: "One finds in the image only that which was already there: the same mystery of Being again which inhabits the image as the 'direct' expression."

124. Heidegger, *VA* 153ff.; "Building, Dwelling, Thinking," 151. [Trans.]: I have added Merleau-Ponty's interpolations.

125. Heidegger, *SG* 156; *PR* 92.

126. Heidegger, *EM* 131; *IM* 191. [Trans.]: I have added Merleau-Ponty's interpolations.

127. [M.-P.]: and the exercise of speech (hearing a sentence or pronouncing it to the letter) is something other than employing knowledge of representation; it is making use of an organ; and the intelligibility of speech (understanding the sense of this sentence) is something other than the reactivation of *Sinnverleibend Akte.*

128. [M.-P.]: Heidegger: all "origin" is *myth.*

129. Heidegger, *VA* 48; translated into English by William Lovitt as "Science and Reflection," in *The Question Concerning Technology and Other Essays* (New York: Harper Perennial, 1977) 159; the German terms are added by Merleau-Ponty.

130. Heidegger, *VA* 172; translated into English as "The Thing," in *The Question Concerning Technology and Other Essays*, 171–72.

131. Martin Heidegger, *Was heisst Denken?* (Tubingen: Niemeyer, 1954); translated into English by J. Glenn Gray as *What Is Called Thinking?* (New York: Harper Perennial, 1976). Henceforth cited as *WD* and *WT*, with their respective paginations.

132. *WD* 89–90; *WT* 131.

133. Heidegger, *WD* 90; *WT* 132.

134. Heidegger, *SG* 161; *PR* 96. [M.-P., marginal note]: see further: *Was heisst Denken?* 13–14, the words *sprachen und ungesprochene*, a *Sache zum Sprache kommt*, disclose a symbolic matrix.

135. [M.-P.]: *Erlebnis: besinnung* [?] (text about it).

136. [M.-P.]: text (that I did not find) where Heidegger says that the question is not the statement of an *Erlebnis*.

137. [M.-P., marginal note]: See Heidegger: The *cogito* presupposes that we know what it is that questions and what it is that answers. For the nature of the *Fragen* depends on the nature of philosophy.

138. Heidegger, *VA* 88; translated into English as "Overcoming Metaphysics" by Joan Stambaugh in *The End of Philosophy* (New York: Harper and Row, 1973), 100.

139. Heidegger, *WD* 83; *WT* 118–19.

140. Heidegger, *WD* 163; *WT* 162.

141. Heidegger, *WD* 113 n.; *WT* 185.

142. Heidegger, *WD* 110; *WT* 178.

143. Heidegger, *WD* 113; *WT* 185.

144. Heidegger, *WD* 100; *WT* 154.

145. [Trans.]: "noncontradiction," ἀντίφασις being the word Aristotle uses in his logical treatises. It's worth noting here that φάσις is a variant of φαίνω, "to show, to appear."

146. Heidegger, *EM* 143; *IM* 209.

147. Heidegger, *SZ* 151; *BT* 192–93.

148. Heidegger, *SZ* 151; *BT* 193.

149. Heidegger, "Einleitung," in *Was ist Metaphysik?* 18; "Introduction to 'What Is Metaphysics?'" in *PM*, 286.

150. Heidegger, "Einleitung," in *Was ist Metaphysik?* 17; "Introduction to 'What Is Metaphysics?'" in *PM*, 286.

151. [M.-P.]: Self in difference, as withdrawal.

152. Heidegger, *EM* 62; *IM* 89, translation modified.

153. Heidegger, *EM* 63; *IM* 90.

154. Heidegger, *SG* 161; *PR* 96.

155. Heidegger, *VA* 190; translated into English as "Poetically Man Dwells . . ." in *Poetry, Language, Thought*, 213–14.

156. Heidegger, *WD* 83; *WT* 118. [Trans.]: The English translation renders *Wesen* as "nature." I leave it untranslated since the sense of this term is at stake in Merleau-Ponty's analysis.

157. Heidegger, *WD* 83; *WT* 118.

158. Heidegger, *WD* 68; *WT* 71.

159. Heidegger, *WD* 72; *WT* 76.

160. Heidegger, *SG* 161; *PR* 96.

161. [Trans]: Merleau-Ponty's interpolation.

162. Heidegger, *EM* 119; *IM* 173.

163. Heidegger, *EM* 119; *IM* 173. Merleau-Ponty's interpolations.

164. Heidegger, *EM* 131; *IM* 191.

165. [Trans.]: "We are a sign, without meaning," from Hölderlin's poem "Mnemosyne," second version (1800–1804). [Ed.]: See the same citation above, 285, note 112, *VA* 136; Martin Heidegger, *What Is Called Thinking?* translated into English by J. Glenn Gray (New York: Harper Perennial, 1968), 10, translation

modified. At the bottom of the page Merleau-Ponty notes a title for the following: IV. *Zeit et Sein*: the *Seinsgeschichte*.

166. Heidegger, *VA* 92; "Overcoming Metaphysics," 104.

167. The text in brackets is Merleau-Ponty's interpolation.

168. Heidegger, *VA* 95; "Overcoming Metaphysics," 107.

169. Heidegger, *VA* 36; translated into English as "The Question Concerning Technology," in *The Question Concerning Technology and Other Essays*, 28. [Trans.]: The German terms are Merleau-Ponty's interpolations.

170. Heidegger, *VA* 41; "The Question Concerning Technology," 33.

171. Heidegger, *VA* 69; "Science and Reflection," 181.

172. Heidegger, *EM* 136; *IM* 182.

173. Heidegger, *EM* 35; *IM* 51.

174. Heidegger, *EM* 139; *IM* 202.

175. Heidegger, *EM* 139; *IM* 202.

176. Heidegger, *EM* 137; *IM* 200.

177. Heidegger, *EM* 141; *IM* 206. [M.-P., marginal note]: It was necessary that Plato be *wieder-holt* [repeated], Hegel: end of a first period, there will be another. All philosophies as the *Geschick* of Being are true. Philosophy is the history of being and not the history of conceptualizations of Being.

But then: all this (relative) justification of history presupposes an absolute knowledge or non-knowledge, access to Being, in the light of which all the rest are destroyed and realized (dialectic for which H. only reproaches himself for keeping it in the order of ἀντίφασις). What is this absolute knowledge in which all philosophy dies and is transfigured?

Conclusion: the *Denken* (silence, [*Altsein?*], the said, poetry) as nonphilosophy, it could only be a-philosophy.

178. [M.-P.]: "*Der reinste Denker des Abendlandes. Deshalb hat er nichts geschrieben*" [The purest thinker of the West—that's why he didn't write anything] (*Was heisst Denken?* 52). The Greeks have created the prototype for all things, the *Geschick* of all things, they only knew how to make "*Geschichlich*": they have traced the *Geschick* of the death of Being.

179. [Trans]: This text is bracketed in the English translation of *Introduction to Metaphysics*. A note indicates that it was in parentheses in the 1953 edition.

180. Heidegger, *EM* 145–46; *IM* 213. The German terms are Merleau-Ponty's interpolations.

181. Heidegger, *EM* 138; *IM* 200.

182. Heidegger, *EM* 150; *IM* 220.

183. Heidegger, *EM* 65; *IM* 93.

184. [Ed.]: See Merleau-Ponty, *OE* 48; "EM" 363, reference to Leibniz.

185. Heidegger, *EM* 154; *IM* 226.

186. Heidegger, *EM* 155; *IM* 227. [Trans.]: I've interpolated Gilbert Kahn's translation of *ester* for *Wesen*, since Merleau-Ponty uses this in his own translation. Otherwise this follows the English.

187. Heidegger, *WD* 108; *WT* 174.

188. Heidegger, *EM* 135; *IM* 197. [Trans.]: Heidegger renders this (in En-

glish translation) as "Never to have stepped into Dasein triumphs over the gatheredness of beings as a whole," whereas the more conventional translation (found in a footnote) is "not to be born surpasses all speech."

189. Heidegger, *EM* 135; *IM* 197.

190. Heidegger, *PM* 243.

191. [Trans]: The bracketed text is Merleau-Ponty's interpolation.

192. Heidegger, *EM* 74; *IM* 106.

193. Heidegger, *Zur Seinsfrage* 25; *PM* 306.

194. Heidegger, *EM* 155; *IM* 226.

195. Heidegger, *EM* 155; *IM* 226.

196. Heidegger, *VA* 58; "Science and Reflection," 180.

197. [Trans]: *Essais et conferences* is the French translation of *Vorträge und Aufsätze*, translated by André Préau (Paris: Gallimard, 1958). See Jean Beaufret's "Preface," viii.

198. Heidegger, *WD* 165; *WT* 170.

199. [Trans]: Merleau-Ponty provides his own translation of the text: "Être vieux, c'est s'arrêter opportunément là ou / l'unique pensée / d'un chemin de pensée/ vibre sur elle-même, / dans tout son appareillage." The English translation, given above, is found in Heidegger, "The Thinker as Poet," in *Poetry, Language, Thought*, 10; the German is from *Aus der Erfahrung des Denkens* (1947; Pfullingen: G. Neske, 1954), 19: *Alt sein heißt: rechtzeitig dort innehalten, wo der einzige Gedanke eines Denkweges in sein Gefüge eingeschwungen ist.*

200. Martin Heidegger, *Was ist das—die Philosophie?* (Pfullingen: G. Neske 1956); translated into English by William Kluback and Jean T. Wilde as *What Is Philosophy?* (New Haven, CT: Yale University Press, 1956). [Trans]: Merleau-Ponty must be referring to the German text, the title of which appears in French in his lecture.

201. Heidegger, *PM* 262.

202. Heidegger, *Humanismus Brief,* 58; *PM* 248.

203. Heidegger, *Humansimus Brief,* 60; *PM* 248.

Supplements

1. [Ed.]: This text provides a link between the first and second parts of the course of 1958–59. Merleau-Ponty had placed this development at pages **20** to **25**, which he removed and placed at the end of the 1959–60 course, "Nature and Logos." We therefore don't reinstate it in this course.

2. [Trans.]: Freud speaks of *das es,* the "it," which Merleau-Ponty renders as "*le ca*" rather than the Latin "id." Because referring to the "it" would probably be confusing to most readers familiar with the typical translation, I've chosen to render "*ca*" as "id," following the usual vernacular. I've rendered "*moi*" as "ego."

3. [M.-P.]: It is ignored as nonconventional thought that has no name.

4. [M.-P.]: Empirical relations ego-purely descriptive [*événementiels*], visible ego.

5. [M.-P.]: As matrices of relations with others.

6. [M.-P.]: The problem is not one of the passage from myself to an external adjustment, but of connecting the oneiric-narcissistic other to the existent other (reality principle).

7. [M.-P., marginal note]: Error: belief that analysis is knowledge; Error: belief that analysis is influence.

8. [M.-P.]: or leads to thinking.

9. [M.-P.]: influence that makes known and a making known that influences—Socrates's love transmuted into love of truth.

10. [Ed.]: Two notes are inserted by Merleau-Ponty. They do not belong to the same sequence of writing as these pages continuously numbered by Merleau-Ponty. See "Psychoanalysis," in the appendixes, 259–60.

11. [M.-P.]: remedy then of the same kind as the disease.

12. [M.-P.]: See **page 25**: Psychoanalysis: mythical time—enclosed in "subjectivity"? The fact is that blood ties are brought back to the ties of choice.

However, the psychoanalytic "choice" (choice of neurosis, choice of health) is something other than decision and dizziness. It is motive, i.e., it precedes itself—Sartre: choice of the intelligible character: myth expressing freedom *in* conformity to itself—The choice is resumed—Not, consequently, a film of *Erlebnisse* and separate life, but egoity more profound than that of the ego. Egoity of the libido where there is everything (superego, the other, the negation of myself, etc.).

Psychoanalysis: Freud, disintegration of the ground of the ego, of censure, etc., but neither perversion nor "adjustment." It is a matter of recovering the lost secret of unity, of recovering the limbs of intersubjectivity or rather of coexistence, the secret solidity that has gone [*a disparue*] (social life—worldly life), style.

13. [Ed.]: The title only is written on **26**.

Cartesian Ontology and Ontology Today

[Our Questions Today]

1. [Ed.]: Bibliothèque Nationale mark: Merleau-Ponty, Box V, volume 1.

2. [Ed.]: Merleau-Ponty numbers the first part of the text "Fundamental Thought in Art," **1** to **42**. The editorial state of the second part ("Descartes") is less complete, and the pagination does not continue.

3. [M.-P.]: That even rejects it, wants to be nonphilosophy and yet is not extra-philosophical.

4. André Gide, *Dostoievsky* (Paris: Plon, 1923); translated into English by Arnold Bennett as *Dostoevsky* (London: Secker and Warburg, 1952). [Trans.]: Merleau-Ponty is making reference to the narrator of Dostoevsky's *Notes from the Underground*.

5. [Ed.]: See *Les Philosophes célèbres* (Paris: Éditions d'Art, Lucien Mazenod, 1956), published under the direction of Merleau-Ponty, notably "Existence and Dialectic," 288 [reprinted in *Signes* (Paris: Gallimard, 1960), 194; translated into English as *Signs* by Richard C. McCleary (Evanston, IL: Northwestern University Press, 1964), 154ff.], and the articles on Bergson 292, Brunschvicg 148, Alain 308,

Blondel 300, Russell 316, Croce 304, and Schopenhauer 394. [Trans.]: "Existence and Dialectic" is published as part 6 of Merleau-Ponty's essay "Everywhere and Nowhere." The pagination to the other texts refers to *Les Philosophes célèbres*.

6. [Ed.]: Cited by Gide, *Dostoievsky*, 218–19. Merleau-Ponty's reading notes on Gide's book. [Trans.]: The text cited is from Schopenhauer, *The World as Will and Idea*, translated into English by Jill Berman (London: Everyman, 1995), 219–20, though Merleau-Ponty apparently pulls it from Gide's *Dostoievsky*, 127–28.

7. Martin Heidegger, *Nietzsche* (Pfullingen: Neske, 1961); translated into English by David Farrell Krell (New York: Harper Collins, 1991).

8. Jean-François Revel, *Pourquoi des philosophes?* (Paris: Julliard, 1957). See the 1959 course "The Possibility of Philosophy Today," 7.

9. Martial Gueroult, *Descartes selon l'ordre des raisons, I: L'Âme et Dieu* (Paris: Aubier, 1953), 11.

10. Martial Gueroult, *Malebranche, I: La Vision en Dieu* (Paris: Aubier-Montaigne, 1955), 23.

11. Gueroult, *Malebranche, I: La Vision en Dieu*, 25–26.

I. Fundamental Thought in Art

1. Interview with Alberto Giacometti in Georges Charbonnier, *Le Monologue du peintre* (Paris: Julliard, 1959), 176; [Ed.]: See Merleau-Ponty, *OE* 24; "EM" 369.

2. Robert Delaunay, *Du cubisme à l'art abstrait*, unpublished notebooks (Paris: SEVPEN, 1957). *Documents inedits*, published by P. Francastel (Bibliothèque Générale of the École Pratique des Hautes Études).

3. Delaunay, *Du cubisme à l'art abstrait*, 109.

4. [Trans.]: In English in the original. [Ed.]: "*empiètement*"; see Rudolf Arnheim, *Art and Visual Perception: A Psychology of the Creative Eye* (London: Faber and Faber, 1956), notably 16, 25, 82–83.

5. [Ed]: See Heidegger, *Identity and Difference*.

6. Plato, *Sophist* 254d; Heidegger, *Identität und Differenz*, 16; *Identity and Difference*, 24: "itself the same for itself."

7. Heidegger, *Identität und Differenz*, 16; *Identity and Difference*, 26.

8. Heidegger, *Identität und Differenz*, 17; *Identity and Difference*, 27.

9. [Ed.]: The passage that follows is very close to Merleau-Ponty, *OE* 65–69; "EM" 369ff.

10. [Ed.]: Merleau-Ponty, *OE* 67; "EM" 370. See Grohmann, *Paul Klee*, 143.

11. Delaunay, *Du cubisme à l'art abstrait*, 118. See Merleau-Ponty, *OE* 67; "EM" 370.

12. [M.-P., marginal note]: No hierarchy of means, concentric means.

13. Georges Schmidt, *Les Aquarelles de Cézanne*, French translation by G. Meister (Basel: Holbein, 1952), 21.

14. [Ed.]: Merleau-Ponty, *OE* 68–69; "EM" 370: "It is no longer a matter of adding one dimension to the two of the canvas, of organizing an illusion or an objectless perception whose perfection consists in resembling as much as possible empirical vision. Pictorial depth (as well as painted height and width) come 'I know not whence' to germinate upon the support. . . . The world no longer stands

before him through representation; rather, it is the painter who is born in the things as by the concentration and the coming-to-itself of the visible."

15. [Ed.]: Merleau-Ponty, *OE* 29; "EM" 358.

16. [M.-P., marginal note]: The natural language of the particular case "resembles" it: silent speech through which the thing *dengt* and the world *Weltet*.

17. Michaux, "Adventures of Lines," in *Darkness Moves*, 317. This text originally constituted the "Preface" to the book by Will Grohmann, *Paul Klee* (1954).

18. Paul Valéry, cited in Merleau-Ponty, *OE* 16; "EM" 353: the relation seer-visible.

19. Charles Bru, *Esthetique de l'abstraction* (Paris: Presses Universitaires de France, 1955), 86 and 99; [Ed.]: Merleau-Ponty, *OE* 69; "EM" 370.

20. [Ed.]: Merleau-Ponty, *OE* 27; "EM" 357. Against Berenson, Merleau-Ponty writes: "painting evokes nothing, least of all the tactile. . . . Painting gives visible existence to what profane vision believes to be invisible."

21. [Ed.]: For this passage, see Merleau-Ponty, *OE* 69–70; "EM" 370.

22. Michaux, *Darkness Moves*, 316.

23. Georges Charbonnier, "Interview with Max Ernst," in *Le Monologue du peintre*, 34. [Ed.]: See *OE* 30; "EM" 358.

24. Georges Charbonnier, "Interview with André Marchand," in *Le Monologue du peintre*, 143–45.

25. [Ed.]: For this passage, see Merleau-Ponty, *OE* 73–74; "EM" 371–72.

26. [Ed.]: Merleau-Ponty, *OE* 73; "EM" 371. See Bergson, *La Pensée et le mouvant*, 264–65; *The Creative Mind*, 196. See "The Possibility of Philosophy Today," **11**, 17, note 27, p. 269.

27. Michaux, *Darkness Moves*, 317. [Ed.]: Merleau-Ponty, *OE* 74; "EM" 372.

28. [Ed.]: Merleau-Ponty, *OE* 74; "EM" 372.

29. [Ed.]: Merleau-Ponty, *OE* 75; "EM" 372. He writes: "[Matisse] decides to put into a single line both the prosaic, identifying characteristics of the being and the hidden operation that composes in the being the indolence or inertia."

30. [Ed.]: See Merleau-Ponty, *OE* 76–77; "EM" 372.

31. [Ed.]: Merleau-Ponty, *OE* 80–81; "EM" 374.

32. Michaux, *Darkness Moves*, 317.

33. [Trans.]: *Verflachtung* appears in the French text, and must be a misprinting of *Verflechtung*.

34. Leonardo da Vinci, *Traite sur la peinture*, ed. André Chastel (Paris: Club de Libraires de France, 1960), 148.

35. [Trans.]: In Italian in the text.

36. [M.-P.]: to the stars as to things near—Coexistence of St. Petersburg and Paris (R. Delaunay*). "The railroad is the image of succession that approximates the parallel."**—R. Delaunay. Simultaneity is the coexistence of incompossibles, non-perspectivism.

[*Delaunay, *Du cubisme à l'art abstrait*, 115: "The world is not our representation re-created through reasoning (Cubism), the world is our craftsmanship [*métier*]."]

[**Delaunay, *Du cubisme à l'art abstrait*, 110: "Simultaneity: my eyes see up to the stars."]

37. Delaunay, *Du cubisme à l'art abstrait*, 171: "[Da Vinci] seeks to prove the intellectual superiority of what is given through simultaneity, through our eyes, windows of the soul, over the auditory function and succession of hearing."

38. [Trans.]: In Italian in the text.

39. Rainer Maria Rilke, *Auguste Rodin*, translated into French by Maurice Betz (Paris: Emile-Paul, 1928), 150. [Ed.]: See Merleau-Ponty, *OE* 82; "EM" 374.

40. Paul Valéry, "Introduction à la méthode de Leonard de Vinci," *Note et digression* (1919), in *Variété* (Paris: Gallimard, 1926), 171.

41. [Trans.]: In Italian in the text.

42. Da Vinci, *Traite sur la peinture*, 76.

43. [Ed.]: We have included a long note by Merleau-Ponty placed between between the development of painting and the part on Descartes. See "Ontology: Interspersed Pages," 261–63.

44. [Ed.]: Merleau-Ponty refers to the Adam and Tannery edition of the work of Descartes in this study. [Trans.]: I give the references to the AT edition, following Merleau-Ponty, in addition to references to the English translation, *The Philosophical Writings of Descartes*, vols. I–III, translated into English by Cottingham, Stoothoff, and Murdoch (Cambridge: Cambridge University Press, 1985). References to this text are abbreviated "Cambridge," followed by the volume and page number. Merleau-Ponty cites the texts in Latin.

45. René Descartes, "Discourse VII," in *Optics*, AT VI, 165; the Cambridge edition omits the last four discourses of the *Optics*.

46. Descartes, AT VI, 83; Cambridge I, 152–53.

47. [M.-P.]: Cartesian operationalism nonetheless limited by the condition of the *intuitus mentis*.

48. Paul Schilder, *The Image and Appearance of the Human Body* (London: Kegan Paul, 1955). [Ed]: See *Le visible et l'invisible*, 274; *The Visible and the Invisible*, 253.

49. Descartes, AT VI, 112–14; Cambridge I, 165–66.

50. [Ed.]: We reproduce a note interposed at this location in the manuscript: Sign = *occasion of thought*.

In reality: signs, in lived experience, are not givens (14) this measuring body of things.

Descartes: what feeling is [*sentiment*], is original but does not change anything with respect to our thinking nature. Because it is the effect of God's thought that validates through us—the duality transported into God: understanding and volition in us: the analysis will consist of showing that it is as if God were thinking in us: through divine signs (not ideas of culture, poetry, creation of equivalences). One deciphers, one reads space in itself through *partes extra partes* projections of *overlapping*. [Trans.]: The word "overlapping" is in English.

Perspectivism and mechanism: there is no more a relationship to a true other with respect to the thing than with respect to automata—It is not the world that one sees—great lie—natural magic that is God's blessing.

Cartesian ontology: truth of immanence that opens onto Being only through divine validation.

Ontology of painting: communication with Being through vision—

opening onto being completed, being made—seen—natural light and scream of light.

51. [Trans.]: This is in English in the text.

52. [Ed.]: Merleau-Ponty returns to his own text.

53. Cambridge I, 101. Cited by Jurgis Baltrusaitis, *Anamorphoses ou perspectives curieuses* (Paris: O. Perrin, 1955), 36.

54. [Trans.]: This could be rendered as "seeing," in the sense of "clairvoyance," seeing through or beyond what is merely present. Because the typical English translations will invariably misconstrue what is at stake for Merleau-Ponty, I leave this untranslated.

55. Descartes, AT I, 80–82; Cambridge III, 12–13.

56. [Ed.]: See Maurice Merleau-Ponty, "L'Algorithme et le mystère du langage," in *La Prose du monde* (Paris: Gallimard, 1969), 161; translated into English by John O'Neill as "The Algorithm and the Mystery of Language," in *The Prose of the World* (Evanston, IL: Northwestern University Press, 1973), 155ff.

57. René Descartes, *Olympica* or *Cogitationes Privatae*, November 1620, AT X, 217; Cambridge I, 4–5.

58. Descartes, AT X, 218; Cambridge I, 4.

59. Descartes, AT X, 217; Cambridge I, 4.

60. [M.-P.]: Visual images of thought, imagination of corporeal things.

61. [Trans.]: The passages referred to are mostly from the "Letter to George Izambard (Charleville, May 13th, 1871)." See *Rimbaud Complete*, 365.

62. Paul Valéry, "La Pythie," in *Poesies* (Paris: Gallimard, Nouvelle Revue Française, 1932), 158–59; English translation by James R. Lawler in *Poems: The Collected Works of Paul Valéry, Vol. 1* (Princeton, NJ: Princeton University Press, 1971), 177. In French:

> Honneur des Hommes, Saint LANGAGE,
> Discours prophétique et paré,
> Belles chaines en qui s'engage
> Le dieu dans la chair égaré,
> Illumination, largesse!
> Voice parler une Sagesse
> Et sonner cette auguste Voix
> Qui se connait quand elle sonne
> N'être plus la voix de personne
> Tant que des ondes et des bois!

63. [Trans]: Jacques Rivière was a French writer and critic, and editor of the *Nouvelle Revue Française* in the period immediately after World War I, who brought Proust under the intellectual eye of the period.

64. [18ⁱ] [M.-P.]: *La Crise du concept de littérature* (Jacques Rivière). [Ed.]: [Only the title of this work by Rivière is written on this page.]

65. Jacques Rivière, *Nouvelles Études* (Paris: Gallimard, 1947), 300; translated into English by Whitmoyer.

66. [Ed.]: See Merleau-Ponty's reference to Malraux in "L'Homme et l'adversité," in *Signes*, notably 294–98; *Signs*, "Man and Adversity," 234.

67. See Albert Thibaudet, *Gustave Flaubert* (Paris: Plon-Nourrit, 1922).

68. Thibaudet, *Gustave Flaubert*, 302.

69. [Ed.]: The text that follows corresponds to a note on 302 of *Nouvelles Études* by Rivière.

70. Rivière, *Nouvelles Études*, 303.

71. Rivière, *Nouvelles Études*, 308.

72. Rivière, *Nouvelles Études*, 313.

73. [Ed.]: Merleau-Ponty notes "above" because these pages were written after the text of p. **19**; in order to restore the order indicated by his annotation, we have followed the directive "above."

74. Marcel Proust, *Du coté de chez Swann*, II (Paris: Gallimard, Nouvelle Revue Française, 1924), 189–91; translated into English by C. K. Scott Moncrieff and Terence Kilmartin and revised by D. J. Enright as *Swann's Way* (New York: Modern Library, 2003), 496–98, translation modified. [Ed.]: Merleau-Ponty underlined the italicized words.

75. [Trans.]: *touches*, as in the keys of a piano.

76. [M.-P.]: or whose intellectual equivalents are only "description."

77. [M.-P.]: against perspectivism.

78. [Ed.]: Merleau-Ponty has written at the top of this page: "Ontology—Lecture of March 9th"; he continues his exposition of Proust.

79. [Trans.]: The French text continues on to p. **24** without mentioning **22** and **23**.

80. [M.-P.]: Find the "little furrow" that the view of a church has hewn within us (Proust, *Les Temps retrouvé*, 39). Signs in "relief."

81. Marcel Proust, *Les Temps retrouvé*, XV (Paris: Gallimard, Nouvelle Revue Française, 1927), 43–44; translated into English by C. K. Scott Moncrieff and Terence Kilmartin and revised by D. J. Enright as *Time Regained* (New York: Modern Library, 2003), 299, translation modified.

82. [Ed.]: At the bottom of the page, Merleau-Ponty notes a title for part "II. Claudel," but nothing is written under this title. Claudel is proposed for what follows, but Merleau-Ponty resumes this only further on.

83. [Ed.]: [A note is inserted here]: Paul Claudel [* *L'Oeil écoute* (Paris: Gallimard, 1946); translated into English by Elsie Pell as *The Eye Listens* (Port Washington, NY: Kennikat, 1969).] [Henceforth cited as *LOE* and *EL*, with the respective pagination of the French and English editions.] Description of Time as *Ekstase*—i.e., that which calls the things to be "that and to be no more." To be no more is not to be nothing; it is to "have been"; it is to be inscribed within the "indestructible archives." In coming to the visible, things inscribe a shadow of themselves that is ineffaceable—The past is not immateriality, "pure remembrance"; it is, on the contrary, what has been seen or visible, indestructible like [the] shadow or [the] double of the visible.

The same subversion of relationships of the "interior" and the "exterior" (Dutch painting*): Dutch "interiors" "invite us more effectively than a treatise on asceticism . . . to the consciousness of our inner being, the contact with our ontological secret" [*Paul Claudel, *L'Oeil écoute*, 136; *EL* 157]. It is not a matter of comparison. With respect to this painting, "we are immediately inside of it;

we live in it. . . . It contains us. We feel its form all about us like raiment. We are impregnated by the atmosphere it encloses. We absorb it through all our pores, all our sensibilities, all the fissures of our soul" (*LOE* 20–21; *EL* 16–17). Where is the "exterior world" (to which the picture belongs)? And the interior world? They are exchanged—one can speak of the interior in showing the visible and one can speak of the visible world without mentioning the figure, the contour, if one succeeds in rendering the fiber.

84. Jean Wahl, "Simultanéité, peinture et nature," in Paul Claudel, *Cahiers Paul Claudel*, vol. 1 (Paris: Gallimard, 1959), 221–49, extract from a course given in 1959 at the Sorbonne, "Defense and Broadening of Philosophy."

85. [M.-P.]: The most object of objects; intellectual Nature without limits.

86. [M.-P.]: i.e., before the separation of intellectual Nature and the body.

87. Henri Bergson, *Matière et mémoire: Essai sur la relation du corps à l'esprit* (Paris: Alcan, 1896).

88. Paul Claudel, *Présence et prophétie* (Freiburg: Freiburg University Library, 1942), 305.

89. Paul Claudel, *Art poétique* (1903; Paris: Mercure de France, 1935), 53; translated into English by Renée Spodheim as *Poetic Art* (New York: Philosophical Library, 1948), 36.

90. Claudel, *LOE* 9–10; *EL* 3–5; and *LOE* 11–12; *EL* 6–7, the rising water.

91. [Ed.]: See Merleau-Ponty, *OE* 32; "EM" 359.

92. Claudel, *LOE* 33; *EL* 31.

93. Claudel, *LOE* 20–21; *EL* 17.

94. Claudel, *LOE* 20–21; *EL* 17.

95. Claudel, *LOE* 23; *EL* 20. [Trans]: The square brackets appear in the French edition.

96. Paul Claudel, *La Pain dur* (Paris: Gallimard, 1928), 158. In French:
Nous sommes seuls tous les deux dans cet horrible désert.

Deux âmes humaines dans le néant qui sont capables de se donner l'une à l'autre,

Et en une seule seconde, pareille à la detonation de tout le temps aui s'anéantit, de remplacer toutes choses l'une par l'autre!

Cited by Wahl, "Simultanéité, peinture et nature," 226.

97. Paul Claudel, *Le Soulier de satin* (Paris: Gallimard, 1929), 195; translated into English by Rev. John O'Connor with the collaboration of the author as *The Satin Slipper* (New Haven, CT: Yale University Press, 1931), 148.

98. Claudel, *Le Soulier de satin*, 198; *The Satin Slipper*, 150.

99. Claudel, *Le Soulier de satin*, 197; *The Satin Slipper*, 149.

100. Claudel, *Le Soulier de satin*, 196; *The Satin Slipper*, 148.

101. [Ed.]: Claudel, see the same reference to Claudel in Merleau-Ponty, "L'Homme et l'adversité," in *Signes*, 297; "Man and Adversity," in *Signs*, 234.

102. [Trans.]: This is presumably a reference to the first line of the *Discourse*: "'good sense' or 'reason'—is naturally equal in all men . . . [but] it is not enough to have a good mind; the main thing is to apply it well" (Descartes, Cambridge I, 111). [Ed.]: In Merleau-Ponty's reading notes on Laporte, called "*Rationalisme de Descartes: Connaissance et sense*," one can read: "*Bonna mens*, or vision is the same in

all—but not the *ingenium* (application, method). Everyone is able to understand the truth. Once disclosed—but not the disclosure . . . Perspicacity and sagacity (for inferences) are confused when the mind becomes less slow, having amplified its capacity." Merleau-Ponty quotes the *Regulae* VII, AT X, 388, and comments: "This capacity, intellectual grasp, is by no means defined logically but only as a variant of *seeing*—and sedimentation is only 'conservation.'" Merleau-Ponty pursues his commentary: "Analogue *intuitius-visio*: Is it not legitimate since vision is thought? Response: certainly, but at least vision should be well understood. Now is it? No, Descartes has no idea of the *field*, of the chiasm, of the *Umfang* [expanse] of transcendence. And it's both his idea of vision as well as his idea of thought that must be rectified. The intuitionism of simple natures and of 'details' . . . completely missing in the theory of vision." [Trans]: These are notes made by Merleau-Ponty on Laporte's text, *Le Rationalisme de Descartes*. See above, note 11.

103. See Maurice Merleau-Ponty, "Cinq notes sur Claude Simon," *Meditations*, no. 4 (Winter 1961–62): 5–10; translated into English by Hugh Silverman as "Five Notes on Claude Simon," in *Texts and Dialogues* (Amherst, NY: Humanities Books, 1992), 140–43.

104. Joseph Conrad, *The Nigger of the "Narcissus"* (London: New Review, 1897); Merleau-Ponty refers to the French edition, *Le Nègre du Narcisse*, translated into French by R. d'Humieres (Paris: Mercure de France, 1910).

105. Jean-Paul Sartre, "Le Peintre sans privilege," *Meditations*, no. 2 (1961): 29–44; translated into English by Wade Baskin as "The Unprivileged Painter," in Sartre, *Essays on Aesthetics* (New York: Philosophical Library, 1966), 132–59. (Merleau-Ponty writes this on March 16, 1961.)

106. Sartre, "Le Peintre sans privilege," 29; "An Unprivileged Painter," 132.

107. Sartre, "Le Peintre sans privilege," 29; "An Unprivileged Painter," 132.

108. Sartre, "Le Peintre sans privilege," 40; "An Unprivileged Painter," 151.

109. Interview, Madeleine Chapsal with Claude Simon, November 1960, in *Les écrivains en personne* (Paris: Julliard, 1960).

110. [Ed.]: See Merleau-Ponty, *OE* 60; "EM" 368. Bertrand Dorival, *Paul Cézanne: Cézanne par ses lettres et ses temoins* (Paris: P. Tisne, 1948), 103ff. See Maurice Merleau-Ponty, "Le Doute de Cézanne," in *Sens et non-sens* (Geneva: Nagel, 1966); translated into English by Hubert L. Dreyfus and Patricia A. Dreyfus as "Cezanne's Doubt," in *Sense and Non-Sense* (Evanston, IL: Northwestern University Press, 1964).

111. [Ed.]: See the treatment of time and space in the 1956–57 course, *La Nature*, 139–52; *Nature*, 101–22.

112. [M.-P., marginal note]: (b) Not something in time, not something within contained space. It is time itself or space itself as rain, as night. "Encompassing" time, element. Not time of "figures."

113. Claude Simon, *La Route des Flandres* (Paris: Minuit, 1960), 29–32; translated into English by Richard Howard as *The Flanders Road* (Richmond, UK: John Calder, 1985), 17–18.

114. Simon, *La Route des Flandres* 29–32; *The Flanders Road*, 17–18.

115. [M.-P., marginal note]: (a) "interior;" in every case opposed to thread-like time.

116. Claude Simon, *Le Vent: Tentative de restitution d'un retable baroque* (Paris: Minuit, 1957), 163; translated into English by Richard Howard as *The Wind* (New York: George Braziller, 1959), 171.

117. Simon, *Le Vent*, 175; *The Wind*, 182.

118. [M.-P., marginal note]: For a magma-time, i.e., which mixes its dimensions and is accomplished everywhere at once.

119. [M.-P., marginal note]: (c) Hence notably the sedimentation of time: time space. Time-space not *symbolized* but *contaminated* by space because the two of them are the world.

120. Claude Simon, *L'Herbe* (Paris: Minuit, 1958), 199–220; translated into English by Richard Howard as *The Grass* (New York: George Braziller, 1960), 168–76.

121. Simon, *Le Vent*, 56; *The Wind*, 61.

122. Simon, *L'Herbe*, 119–20; *The Grass*, 108–9.

123. [M.-P., marginal note]: (d).

124. Simon, *L'Herbe*, 104; *The Grass*, 84.

125. Simon, *Le Vent*, 175; *The Wind*, 185.

126. Simon, *Le Vent*, 98; *The Wind*, 104, translation modified.

127. Simon, *L'Herbe*, 181; *The Grass*, 161.

128. Simon, *La Route des Flandres*, 313–14; *The Flanders Road*, 192–93.

129. Georges Blin, *Stendhal et les problèmes du roman* (Paris: Libraire J. Corti, 1954), 127.

130. Simon, *Le Vent*, 186; *The Wind*, 192–93.

131. Simon, *L'Herbe*, 114–15; *The Grass*, 96–97.

132. Simon, *La Route des Flandres*, 59–61; *The Flanders Road*, 13–14.

133. Simon, *Le Vent*, 172; *The Wind*, 181–82.

134. Simon, *Le Vent*, 165; *The Wind*, 173.

135. Simon, *La Route des Flandres*, 118; *The Flanders Road*, 72.

136. Simon, *La Route des Flandres*, 137; *The Flanders Road*, 84.

137. Simon, *L'Herbe*, 129; *The Grass*, 108.

138. Simon, *Le Vent*, 162–63; *The Wind*, 171–72.

139. Claude Simon, *La Corde raide* (Paris: Minuit, 1947), 64. This novel has not been translated into English.

140. Simon, *Le Vent*, 78; *The Wind*, 82.

141. Simon, *Le Vent*, 173–74; *The Wind*, 182–84.

142. Simon, *La Corde raide*, 59–60.

143. Simon, *La Corde raide*, 58; see also 44–46, absolute revolt.

144. [Trans.]: From Boris Pasternak, *Doctor Zhivago*, translated into English by Richard Pevear and Larissa Volokhonsky (New York: Vintage, 2010), 538.

145. Michel Butor, *La Modification* (Paris: Minuit, 1957).

146. [M.-P., marginal note]: Versus: credulity, persuasion; For: vision, sort of call to vision in things, human beings, the most obscure, the most alone. It is art, not thought, that teaches this because it makes one see and not think through words, is addressed to the "fundamental," "durable," "essential" not to our opinions or certainties or statements.

147. [M.-P., marginal note:] φ = "enigmatic" vision solidarity and death.

148. [Ed]: See Merleau-Ponty, *OE* 81; "EM" 364.

II. Descartes

1. [M.-P., marginal note]: The pre-reflexive; the meta-reflexive.

2. [Trans.]: Adrien Baillet, biographer of Descartes known for his *La vie de monsieur Descartes*.

3. Gueroult, *Descartes selon l'ordre des raisons, II: L'Âme et le corps*, 175, 144. [Ed.]: On truth, see Maurice Merleau-Ponty, "Lecture de Montaigne," in *Signes*, 250; translated into English by Richard C. McCleary as "Reading Montaigne," in *Signs*, 204.

4. [Ed.]: See **2–3**.

5. Jean Wahl, *Du role de l'idee de l'instant dans la philosophie de Descartes* (Paris: Alcan, 1920).

6. [Ed.]: Merleau-Ponty referred us to **1** at this passage when he referred to **2–3**.

7. René Descartes, AT X, 495; Cambridge II, 400, translation modified.

8. Descartes, letter to Arnauld, July 29, 1648. AT V, 223; Cambridge III, 358.

9. [M.-P.]: Psychoanalytic interpretation of *wanting to see.*

10. [M.-P.]: to which one could add the facts of his life: Descartes's dream—baptism certificate when leaving for Sweden.

11. [Ed.]: In his working notes on Laporte, Merleau-Ponty notes that, according to Laporte, *Le Rationalisme de Descartes,* (Paris: Presses Universitaires de France, 1946); reissued Paris: Études d'Histoire de la Philosophie, 1951, 21: "knowing for Descartes 'is reduced to seeing.'" He goes further, saying that "having experiences" signifies for Descartes (according to Laporte, 27) "natural light," "natural reason," the "pure light of reason." "It is equal in all since 'it boils down to this indivisible: to see or not to see.'" Farther on, Merleau-Ponty makes the remark that "what Laporte demands from Descartes is his own combinatory art. A common thread to dispense with thinking." [Trans]: This note refers to "reading notes" on Jean Laporte's book, *Le Rationalisme de Descartes*, included in a bundle of documents at the Bibliothèque nationale de France (Vol. XXI, 79–98). The notes are titled "Rationalisme de Descartes: Coinnaissance et sens" and were among the documents found on Merleau-Ponty's desk after his death.

12. [Ed.]: "envelope, coat, clothing."

13. Descartes, AT X, 369; Cambridge I, 14.

14. [M.-P.]: Reading Descartes, AT X, 400–401; Cambridge I, 32–33.

15. [Trans.]: "Singular point," rendered by Merleau-Ponty as "*chaque point.*"

16. René Descartes, *Principles of Philosophy*, I, §45, AT VIII; Cambridge I, 207, "a clear and distinct perception."

17. Descartes, AT VIII, 22; Cambridge I, 207.

18. René Descartes, "First Set of Replies," Cambridge II, 81.

19. [M.-P.]: "visibility."

20. Descartes, AT VIII, 22; Cambridge I, 207–8.

21. Descartes, AT VII, 365; Cambridge II, 252.

22. Descartes, AT III, 434; Cambridge III, 196–97. [Trans.]: "Hyperaspertes" refers to an anonymous critic of the *Meditations*, presumably one of the authors of the "Sixth Objections," since Merleau-Ponty refers us here to the "Sixth Replies."

23. Descartes, AT III, 434–35; Cambridge III, 197.

24. Descartes, AT X 379; Cambridge III, 20.

25. Descartes, AT X, Rule XII, line 23, 425; Cambridge I, 48.

26. [M.-P.]: Reading Descartes's *Regulae*, AT X, 425; Cambridge I, 48.

27. Descartes, AT X, Rule XIII, 433; Cambridge I, 53.

28. Descartes, AT X, 442; Cambridge I, 58–59.

29. [M.-P., marginal note]: The example of Socrates—Birth of the question: when he doubts his doubt. At the time of the *Regulae*, doubt of the doubt is surmounted by positivity of "seeing": *se esse, se cogitare.*

30. Descartes, AT X, 435; Cambridge I, 54. [M.-P., marginal note]: Know what you're looking for. Is it philosophy?

31. Descartes, AT X, Rule XIV, 440; Cambridge I, 57: "We should note that comparisons are said to be simple and straightforward only when the thing sought and the initial data participate equally in a certain nature."

32. [Ed.]: Merleau-Ponty's translation of the Latin title.

33. Descartes, Cambridge I, 43.

34. [Ed.]: At the bottom of the page Merleau-Ponty has indicated the beginning of a second part, but there is nothing written under this second paragraph.

35. [Ed.]: The following pages doubtless constitute a reprise by Merleau-Ponty of his own intention for the argument of the course of the same date.

36. [M.-P.]: Descartes, AT X, Rule X, 400–401.

37. [M.-P.]: Descartes, *Principles* I, AT VIII, 68–70. Passage to what is beneath the spatial *integumentum* (Gueroult, *II: L'Âme et le corps*, 290), Descartes, *Regulae*, AT X, 375.

38. [M.-P.]: Nature method and fruits, Descartes, *Regulae*, AT X, 397.

39. [M.-P.]: Visual model of physical action, Descartes, *Regulae*, AT X, 402, visual model of the body (the feather), *Regulae*, 414. The models, *Regulae*, 402, in the method, 417. The triangle that is seen is *made* of mathematical relationships, *Regulae*, 422. The obvious extension, 443. The "legitimate" questions, Descartes, *Regulae*, 431, 440. The more difficult: learning to recognize the *per se natum*, *The Search for Truth*. Descartes, AT X, 524.

40. [M.-P.]: human being-reason: *lumen lux* (Descartes, AT II, 209); inner consciousness (AT IX, 225, Gueroult, *I: L'Âme et Dieu*, 82). Reflection is vision, passion—Laporte, *Le Rationalisme de Descartes*, 27.

The soul always thinks as the light shines (Gueroult, *I: L'Âme et Dieu*, 19).

Pre-reflexive knowledge, *The Search for Truth*, Descartes, AT X, 524. Intellectual vision is the refusal of effective vision, AT X, 525.

41. [Ed.]: At the bottom of the page, Merleau-Ponty notes: (See below: the *cogito* as accomplished and as instant) (initiate discussion of the pre-reflexive) (moreover because the free doubt [of the] *cogito* is [a] *proposition*) (Malebranchist Descartes, "Letter to Newcastle").

(3) *Cogito*

(4) God as light

(5) Being and nothingness according to the light

[In the margin]: the Cartesian circle and light, Gueroult, *I: L'Âme et Dieu*, 245–46.

The axioms (purity, nothingness, being, etc.) are anticipations of the light of God—Gueroult, *I: L'Âme et Dieu*, 272.

42. [Ed.]: Picking up from the first point developed in the preceding course of April 13.

43. Descartes, AT X, 524; Cambridge II, 418.

44. Descartes, AT X, 524; Cambridge II, 418.

45. [Ed.]: Descartes, *Regulae*, see above, course of April 13, **5**; Descartes, AT X, 417; Cambridge I, 43–44.

46. Descartes, AT X, 413; Cambridge I, 40.

47. Descartes, AT X, Rule XII, 417; Cambridge I, 43–44.

48. Descartes, AT X, Rule XIV, 438; Cambridge I, 56.

49. Descartes, AT X, Rule XIV, 442; Cambridge I, 59.

50. Descartes, AT X, Rule XIII, 433; Cambridge I, 53.

51. Descartes, AT X, Rule XIII, 433; Cambridge I, 53.

52. [Trans]: The brackets appear in the original French text.

53. Descartes, AT X, Rule XIII, 432; Cambridge I, 53.

54. [Ed]: See the working note of *The Visible and the Invisible*, "Descartes," dated March 1961, *Le Visible et l'invisible*, 320; *The Visible and the Invisible*, 272.

55. [Ed.]: It reads *"utilium,"* while the Latin text gives *"veritatum."*

56. Descartes, AT X, Rule IV, 373–76; Cambridge I, 16–18. [Ed.]: Merleau-Ponty notes *"lumen."*

57. [Trans.]: For the *Meditations*, the Cambridge text references the Latin text of AT, vol. VII (as do almost all English translations), while Merleau-Ponty references the French text of AT, vol. IX. Since the Latin and French versions of the *Meditations* are at variance, I have forgone references to the Cambridge edition and simply translated the French directly.

58. [M.-P., marginal note]: Belief-doubt, doubt that is belief and belief that is doubt—Descartes, "Second Responses," AT VII, 145.

59. [M.-P.]: The same problematic of the *Entretien avec Burman* proves it. If the *cogito* were simple nature, there would be no problem of knowing how I can, thinking, think that I think.

60. [Ed.]: Course delivered by Merleau-Ponty. These notes were placed in a pile of pages found on his desk on May 3, 1961.

61. [Ed.]: Development of the third point started in the preceding course of April 20, 1961.

62. Descartes, AT VII, 145; Cambridge II, 104.

63. Descartes, AT VII, 145–46; Cambridge II, 104.

64. Descartes, AT X, 525; Cambridge II, 418.

65. [M.-P., marginal note]: *Nodum vero satis intelligo quisnam sim ego ille, qui jam necessario sum.* (Descartes, AT VII, 25) ["But I do not yet know clearly enough what I am, I who am certain that I am."]—Be careful not to assert anything whatever of the self. The elimination is only for the sake of knowing *that* I am— existence is global.

66. Descartes, AT X, 524; Cambridge II, 417–18.

67. [Trans.]: Merleau-Ponty annotates the Latin AT text, giving French renderings. I've included these annotations in the corresponding locations of

the English translation in the main text and the English translation of Merleau-Ponty's French, as well as the Latin as notes. [M.-P.]: The French translation—Descartes, AT IX, 225—has "*premièrement*"; "first." [The Latin gives *nisi*, "unless."]

68. [M.-P.]: Descartes, AT IX, 225, "*la nature*"; "nature." [The Latin gives *quid sit*, "what."]

69. [M.-P.]: Descartes, AT IX, 225, "*d'une science de cette science*"; "of a science for this science." [The Latin gives *Scientia scientiae reflexae*, "reflexive science of science."]

70. [M.-P.]: Descartes, AT IX, 225, "*il suffit qu'il sache cela par cette force de connaissance intérieure qui précède toujours l'acquise*"; "it is sufficient that he knows this through the force of interior knowledge which always precedes the acquired." [Latin: *Sed omnino sufficit ut id sciat cognition illa interna, quae reflexam semper antecedit.*]

71. [M.-P.]: Descartes, AT IX, 225, "*naturelle*"; "natural." [Latin: *ita innata.*]

72. [M.-P.]: Descartes, AT IX, 225, "*qu'à leur véritable signification*"; "than to their true meaning."

73. Descartes, AT VII, 422; Cambridge II, 285.

74. Descartes, AT X, 422; Cambridge I, 46.

75. Descartes, AT V, 162; Cambridge III, 344.

76. Descartes, AT V, 221; Cambridge III, 357: Letter to Arnauld, July 29, 1648: DXXV.

77. [M.-P.]: *Wesen* (verbal), Heidegger.

78. [M.-P., marginal note]: part of my being.

79. Descartes, AT VII, 25; Cambridge II, 17. [Trans.]: The French edition of the lectures places the reference to the French version of the *Meditations* before the Latin text here. I've interpolated the reference to AT VII for the sake of clarity and consistency.

80. Jean Laporte, *Le Rationalisme de Descartes*. [Ed.]: Merleau-Ponty took many notes on this text. [Trans]: See above, note 11.

81. [Trans.]: *That* and *What* are in English in the text. See an untitled working note from *The Visible and the Invisible* dated 1959, "Every *that* involves a *what* because the *that* is not nothing, hence is *etwas*, hence *west*—" (*Le Visible et l'invisible*, 253; *The Visible and the Invisible*, 203); see also a similar passage from "Reflection and Interrogation": "When along with other philosophers we said that the stimuli of perception are not the causes of the perceived world, that they are rather its developers or its releasers, we do not mean that one could perceive without a body: on the contrary, we mean that it is necessary to reexamine the definition of the body as pure object in order to understand how it can be our living bond with nature; we do not establish ourselves in a universe of essences—on the contrary, we ask that the distinction between the *that* and the *what*, between the essence and the conditions of existence, be reconsidered by referring to the experience of the world that precedes that distinction" (*Le Visible et l'invisible*, 46; *The Visible and the Invisible*, 27).

82. [Trans.]: Descartes, Cambridge II, 6–7.

83. [M.-P., marginal note]: challenges the order of *veritas rei*.

84. Descartes, AT IX, 21; Cambridge II, 18–19.

85. [Ed.]: Merleau-Ponty returns to this in the margin of the course written for May 4, 1961: "preceding course, **7**." See below, the course planned for May 4, 1961, the texts on the "Second Meditation" and the *Cogito*, 164.

86. Descartes, AT VII, 27; Cambridge II, 18.

87. Descartes, AT VII, 28; Cambridge II, 19.

88. [M.-P.]: "the only thing that cannot be separated from me."

89. Descartes, AT VII, 28–29; Cambridge II, 19.

90. Descartes, AT VII, 33; Cambridge II, 22.

91. [Trans.]: a toothing stone is an architectural device where the corner of a building has alternating blocks or "teeth" that create the possibility of adding another building next to it, creating a continuous surface on the façade.

92. [M.-P., marginal note]: to be resumed.

93. [Ed.]: The pages of the course of May 4, 1961 doubtless correspond to the resumption mentioned in the margin of this page.

94. [M.-P., marginal note]: to be resumed.

95. [M.-P.]: The only certain thing is that there is nothing certain—yes, but even this returns, is certain—in a sense it is true again of certainty—the natural light will be purified. The first truth will have offspring of non-being.

96. [Ed.]: See Descartes, *The Search for Truth.*

97. [M.-P.]: "constitute" it.

98. [M.-P.]: Gueroult.

99. [Trans.]: "*indivisibilité de l'entendement entendant et de l'entendement entendu.*"

100. [M.-P.]: Descartes, "Second Responses," AT VII, 145.

101. [M.-P.]: To separate now is to see as inseparable in a tissue of Being, in a Being of superior dimensionality.

102. [M.-P.]: It is the post-reflexive order that attribute and mode, the past and present make alternatives; and not in the order of existing thought in action, of its formal reality. Descartes often says that it is easier to think the triangle than the simple natures it is made of, the attribute coated with its modes.

103. [M.-P.]: There will perhaps be the order of the thing's truth.

104. [Ed.]: "objective reality" appears as a marginal note.

105. [M.-P.]: Without the psychological processes that almost erase memory through uninterrupted movement of thought.

106. [M.-P.]: innate qualities: the question is not: pure or impure understanding but signifying understanding or operative understanding.

107. [Ed.]: The date shown on this page, May 4, 1961, indicates that Merleau-Ponty dated his notes for the day for which the course is prepared. Obviously it will not be given. [Trans.]: Merleau-Ponty died of a heart attack on May 3, 1961, the day before the day for which this course was planned.

108. Resumption of the third point of the preceding course (April 27, 1961).

109. [M.-P.]: Descartes, "Meditation III," AT VII, 38–39: I can oppose nothing to the ostension of truth which is myself, to "objective" being or being "through representation."

110. [M.-P.]: Distinction which has its place only in flat, horizontal thought through distinction and not in the multi-dimensional thought of the *present.*

111. [M.-P.]: Ambiguous Descartes: distinction and *mixture*. Evidence through separation and evidence through inseparability, cohesion. Both are *per se natum*.

112. [M.-P.]: Descartes, "Meditation III," AT VII, 36.

113. [M.-P.]: Descartes, "Meditation III," AT VII, 36.

114. [M.-P.]: It would be necessary to rejoin essential truths such as "the soul always thinks" to the vertical *cogito*.

115. Descartes, AT VII, 28; Cambridge II, 19. [M.-P. in the margin]: See preceding course notes, **7**.

116. [M.-P.]: The two things will be done together: because the very nature of God's evidence excludes his deceptiveness. There is thus a single question: what is this light that illuminates an immense facticity everywhere?

117. [M.-P.]: The "Letter to Newcastle," which makes of the *cogito* a *direct* knowledge *because* [it is] read in the light of God—does it relate to this proof? Yes—but it is not confused with it: it concerns the action of God upon us, which is beyond the bounds of philosophy for Descartes. The second proof still draws its argument from the presence in me of the idea of God, but no longer as the objective reality of the infinite, [but] as *one of my thoughts*.

118. End of the "Third" and "Fifth Meditations."

119. As dialectic of error and truth.

Philosophy and Nonphilosophy since Hegel

[I. Hegel]

1. [Ed.]: Bibliothèque Nationale pressmark: Merleau-Ponty Box V, volume 3. [Trans.]: A previous English translation by Hugh Silverman of the notes for this course can be found in *Philosophy and Non-Philosophy since Merleau-Ponty*, edited by Hugh Silverman (London: Routledge, 1988), 9–83, apparently translated from the text published in *Textures*.

2. [Trans.]: This introduction, written by Claude Lefort, who also prepared the notes for "Philosophy and Nonphilosophy since Hegel," accompanied their original French publication in the journal *Textures*, of which Lefort was also the editor.

3. [Ed.]: Merleau-Ponty gives his own translations of the German text of Nietzsche's *Die fröliche Wissenschaft* (Berlin: Gruyter & Co., 1886); translated into English by Walter Kaufmann as *The Gay Science* (New York: Vintage Books, 1974), henceforth cited as *FW* and *GS*, with their respective paginations. [Trans.]: Rather than translating Merleau-Ponty's translation, I give an amended version of Kaufmann, including Merleau-Ponty's French in brackets where deemed necessary.

4. Nietzsche, *FW* 8: *GS* 34.

5. Nietzsche, *FW* 8; *GS* 34.

6. Nietzsche, *FW* 9–10; *GS* 34.

7. Nietzsche, *FW* 12–15; *GS* 33–38.

8. [M.-P., marginal note]: "God is dead: this means everything except: there is no God." [Trans.]: From *Holzwege*, see below 203.

9. [Ed.]: Merleau-Ponty is referring to the last four pages of Hegel's text cited by Heidegger in *Holzwege*, "Hegels Begriff der Erfahrung" (Frankfurt: Klostermannn, 1949); translated into English by Julian Young and Kenneth Haynes as "Hegel's Concept of Experience," in *Off the Beaten Track* (Cambridge: Cambridge University Press, 2002), 86–156. These works are henceforth cited as *HW* and *OBT*, with their respective paginations.

10. Heidegger, *HW* 105; *OBT* 86.

11. Heidegger, *HW* 106; *OBT* 87.

12. Heidegger, *HW* 106; *OBT* 87.

13. Heidegger, *HW* 106; *OBT* 87.

14. Heidegger, *HW* 106; *OBT* 87.

15. Heidegger, *HW* 106; *OBT* 87.

16. Heidegger, *HW* 106; *OBT* 87. Italics included in the English translation.

17. [M.-P.]: This fear of making a mistake is the error itself: *schon der Irrtum selbst ist* [is the error itself].

18. [M.-P., marginal note]: *Sie setz. . . . voraus . . . einen Unterschied unserer selbst ist* [presupposes a distinction of ourselves from this knowledge]. Heidegger, *HW* 107; *OBT* 87–88.

19. Heidegger, *HW* 106; *OBT* 88.

20. [M.-P., marginal note]: Cartesian conceptualizations give the appearance of a *work* . . . and dispense with real work.

21. [M.-P., marginal note]: highlighting certainty, like Descartes does, is highlighting a truth outside of truth; "another" truth: cloudy distinction—we have a *Bedeutung* of the absolute, of *Erkennen*, which it is a matter of equating.

[Underneath]: *Erkennen* is not to be placed outside of the absolute because the absolute is not to be placed outside of *Erkennen*: "All these ideas of a knowledge which is divided from the absolute and an absolute divided from knowledge" (Heidegger, *HW* 107; *OBT* 88).

22. Heidegger, *HW* 107; *OBT* 88.

23. Heidegger, *HW* 108; *OBT* 88.

24. Heidegger, *HW* 109; *OBT* 89.

25. Heidegger, *HW* 109; *OBT* 89.

26. Heidegger, *HW* 106; *OBT* 87.

27. Heidegger, *HW* 106; *OBT* 87.

28. Heidegger, *HW* 106; *OBT* 87.

29. Heidegger, *HW* 107; *OBT* 88.

30. Heidegger, *HW* 106; *OBT* 87; [Trans.]: Italics in the English translation.

31. Heidegger, *HW* 107; *OBT* 88.

32. Heidegger, *HW* 107; *OBT* 88.

33. Heidegger, *HW* 106; *OBT* 87.

34. Heidegger, *HW* 108; *OBT* 88.

35. Heidegger, *HW* 108; *OBT* 88; [Trans.]: The English translation renders this "science that comes on the scene," whereas Merleau-Ponty cites *die auftretende Wissenschaft*.

36. [Trans.]: In French in the text.

37. Heidegger, *HW* 108; *OBT* 88.

38. Heidegger, *HW* 108; *OBT* 89.

39. Heidegger, *HW* 109; *OBT* 89.

40. Heidegger, *HW* 109; *OBT* 89.

41. Heidegger, *HW* 109; *OBT* 89.

42. [Trans.]: This appears in German in the text with no reference.

43. Heidegger, *HW* 109ff.; *OBT* 89.

44. Heidegger, *HW* 109; *OBT* 89.

45. Heidegger, *HW* 110; *OBT* 91.

46. Heidegger, *HW* 111; *OBT* 91.

47. Heidegger, *HW* 111; *OBT* 91.

48. Heidegger, *HW* 111; *OBT* 91.

49. Heidegger, *HW* 112; *OBT* 92.

50. Heidegger, *HW* 112; *OBT* 92.

51. Heidegger, *HW* 112ff.; *OBT* 92

52. Heidegger, *HW* 112; *OBT* 92.

53. Heidegger, *HW* 113; *OBT* 93.

54. Heidegger, *HW* 114; *OBT* 93. [Trans.]: Merleau-Ponty cites p. 116 of *Holzwege*, but the text actually appears on 114.

55. [Ed.]: Merleau-Ponty follows Heidegger's practice of breaking the text down into paragraphs. [Trans.]: The paragraph numbering follows Heidegger's designations in "Hegel's Concept of Experience." These correspond to paragraphs are 85–89 in Miller's English translation of the "Introduction" to *Phenomenology of Spirit*.

56. [Trans.]: The English translation of *Holzwege* gives "purely to watch" for *reine Zusehen*; however, Merleau-Ponty translates this as "pure vision." I defer to Merleau-Ponty's rendering.

57. Heidegger, *HW* 115; *OBT* 93–94. [Trans.]: Merleau-Ponty provides his own translation of this text. I give an amended version of the text from *Off the Beaten Track*, including Merleau-Ponty's interpolations in square brackets.

58. Heidegger, *HW* 115; *OBT* 95. [Trans.]: Merleau-Ponty provides his own translation of this text. I give an amended version of the text from *Off the Beaten Track*, including Merleau-Ponty's interpolations in square brackets.

59. Heidegger, *HW* 113; *OBT* 93.

60. Heidegger, *HW* 115–16; *OBT* 95–96. [Trans.]: Merleau-Ponty provides his own translation of this text. I give an amended version of the text from *Off the Beaten Track*, including Merleau-Ponty's interpolations in square brackets.

61. Heidegger, *HW* 117; *OBT* 96.

62. Heidegger, *HW* 106; *OBT* 87.

63. Heidegger, *HW* 106; *OBT* 87.

64. [M.-P., marginal note]: see Goethe: "You never go farther than when you no longer know where you are going"—it is in fully being phenomenon that the absolute is fully absolute.

65. Heidegger, *HW* 111; *OBT* 91.

66. Heidegger, *HW* 113; *OBT* 93.

67. Heidegger, *HW* 114; *OBT* 93. [M.-P., marginal note]: a knowledge where subject and object, wild consciousness and reflective consciousness, are reciprocal: both fall into knowledge which thus is not our *Sinngebung* but the deployment of the *Sache* such that it is in and for itself.

68. [M.-P., marginal note]: what is essentially vision and not *Sinngebung*.

69. [M.-P., marginal note]: experience as *reine* [pure] *Zusehen*. Reciprocally, in Marx, (1) the dialectic of consciousness is not illusory as long as the principle of alienation remains (Lukács: *Funktion-Wandel*). After, the dialectic is no longer a reflection of material—capitalism is the concrete phenomenology of spirit— (2) Even before the revolution, no given force completes Reason: human manner, not objective.—Lenin: it requires oblique consciousness, the party (without which trade-unionism).—The dialectic—*Erfahrung* is the philosophy of Marx as it is of Hegel. For both, it cannot be simple *consent* to the mystery of experience; it requires a *Begriff* where the experience of capitalism will understand itself—or where exteriorization will be recognized as necessary, otherwise consciousness (which is its own concept) risks being mistaken.

Certain Marxisms would give the role of capital to experience: reabsorption of the State into society—or, inversely, would make the work of a dictator this praxis itself. Hegel holds it on the edge. Precisely if the truth is experience, it is necessary that this experience is not glaring; that one has a criterion, a philosophy (a logic).

See §15—Show that experience as progress toward truth required *Umkehrung* of *Bewußtsein* (that the thing becomes consciousness), but this means that science is not life—two orders: the idea itself as experience, as truth, outside the control of experience (the idea itself of the proletariat becoming control of the Party over the the proletariat); the very idea of the phenomena as bearers of truth becoming extreme dogmatism—What is the remedy?

70. [M.-P., marginal note]: *March 6*, recall the problem: (1) from the point of view of consciousness, there is nothing that can enter into it from the outside; it is "open," experience, and thus nothing can happen behind its back.—(2) however, there is discontinuous, "empirical," erroneous, blind experience; it is thus necessarily a *Zutat* for philosophy, something behind the back of *Bewußtsein*—(3) solution added by the last paragraph: *Bewußtsein* is the overcoming of *Bewußtsein*, [hence] the Logic.

71. Heidegger, *HW* 155; *OBT* 127. [M.-P., marginal note]: Ambiguity, concept of representation—"this ambiguity is the essence of representation" (*HW* 153; *OBT* 125)—but the philosophy of the *Vorstellen* tends to be overcome to the extent that *Bewußtsein* accomplishes its reversal.

72. [M.-P.]: ὄν ἤ ὄν—"the other side" (*nach der anderen Seite, HW* 144).

73. Heidegger, *HW* 160; *OBT* 131.

74. Heidegger, *HW* 127; *OBT* 104. Heidegger quoting Hegel, *Werke*, vol. 2: *Jenaer Schriften, 1801–1807*, ed. Eva Moldenhauer and Karl Markus Michel (Frankfurt, 1970), 558.

75. Heidegger, *HW* 132; *OBT* 108.

76. Heidegger, *HW* 151; *OBT* 123.

77. Heidegger, *HW* 163; *OBT* 133.

78. Heidegger, *HW* 153; *OBT* 125.

79. Heidegger, *HW* 166; *OBT* 135.

80. Heidegger, *HW* 166; *OBT* 135.

81. [Trans.]: This is in French in the text.

82. Heidegger, *HW* 170; *OBT* 139. [Trans.]: The English translation has "the appearance of the phenomena."

83. Heidegger, *HW* 171; *OBT* 140. [Trans.]: The English translation reads "existence of the absolute," but I leave this untranslated in order to highlight the important invocation of *Dasein*.

84. Heidegger, *HW* 175; *OBT* 143.

85. Heidegger, *HW* 179; *OBT* 146.

86. [M.-P., marginal note]: planned title for *Phenomenology of Spirit* that had been replaced by *Die Phänomenologie des Geistes*, then (1832), *Phänomenologie*.

87. Heidegger, *HW* 182; *OBT* 149.

88. Heidegger, *HW* 187; *OBT* 153. [Trans.]: Merleau-Ponty translates this passage into French: "*ce mode de l'être selon lequel l'absolu en et pour soi est auprès de nous.*"

89. Heidegger, *HW* 189; *OBT* 153.

90. Heidegger, *HW* 190; *OBT* 154.

91. Heidegger, *HW* 190; *OBT* 155.

92. [M.-P.]: for example, the search for recognition by the master is objectivated and in this way overcome.

93. Heidegger, *HW* 164; *OBT* 134.

94. [M.-P.]: One doesn't even allow men consciousness of what they do, their experience—one overwhelms them under the weight of history.

[Ed.:] Below, at the base of the page, separated from what comes before by a dash, these few lines summarize the development that will follow:

[M.-P.]: Hegel's solution (circularity—Hegelian "*equivocation*"): it is more and more skeptico-dogmatism—the void absolute knowledge—the conciliation—what is the Hegelian absolute?

Impossibility of this solution: return to dogmatism in Hegel (Logic-Encyclopedia)—phenomenology under the particular determination of "consciousness" gives way to a metaphysics or logic, which is the dialectic of Being; in his successors: Marx's critique is close insofar as it does not see: (1) that Hegel has seen the problem of the world turned upside down, and that its secret of experience is *opposed to* dogmatism; (2) that Marx himself, with philosophy of the object, falls back into the dogmatism of the absolute subject.

Reason for this failure: consciousness, subject-object, is the philosophy of representation, which necessarily results in ambiguity, i.e., in skeptico-dogmatism, thus lacks philosophy-non philosophy.

The solution would be: it is neither new experience nor recourse to another source (logic-God before the creation) that decides. There is only choice [alternative] for representation. It is necessary that the *unsere Zutat*, the contribution of philosophy, is precisely the abstention from any contribution, "it is the mute experience of which it is a matter of bringing to the pure expression of its own sense." It is necessary to understand that the Being of beings [*l'Être de l'Étant*], the *Erscheinen* of the *Erscheinende*, the "birth" of truth is not passage to another *Seiende*. Certainly, a phenomenology affected by the index of consciousness is not sufficient, but what is beyond is not necessarily without subjectivity.

95. Heidegger, *HW* 174; *OBT* 142.

96. Heidegger, *HW* 117; *OBT* 96. [Trans.]: The bracketed text is inserted by Merleau-Ponty.

97. Jean Hyppolite, *Genèse et structure de la Phenomenologie de l'Esprit de Hegel* (Aubier Montaigne, 1947), 567; translated into English by Samuel Cherniak and John Heckman as *Genesis and Structure of Hegel's Phenomenology of Spirit* (Evanston, IL: Northwestern University Press, 1974), 588.

98. Merleau-Ponty quotes Hyppolite's French translation of the *Phenomenology*, *La phénoménologie de l'esprit*, translated into French by Jean Hyppolite (Paris: Aubier, 1939), 18; translated into English by A. V. Miller as *Phenomenology of Spirit* (Oxford: Oxford University Press, 1977), henceforth cited as *PE* and *PS*, with their respective paginations. The English translation reads: "It is the process of its own becoming, the circle that presupposes its end as its goal, having its end also as its beginning; and only by being worked out to its end, is it actual" (10).

99. Hyppolite, *Genèse et structure*, 586; *Genesis and Structure*, 566.

100. [M.-P.]: The movement of categories is supposed to understand the Self but tacitly assumes the concept.

101. Hegel, *PE* 24; *PS* 15.

102. Heidegger, *HW* 186; *OBT* 152.

103. [M.-P., marginal note]: the Hegelian absolute is the wasting away of the separated absolute, death of God; which does not mean, *es gibt keinen Gott*, end of all fetishization.

104. [M.-P., marginal note]: see Marx's "I am not a Marxist." It requires the self-critique of absolute knowledge, which is the only absolute, the only *Selbst-Bewußtsein*. An (exterior) knowledge of the absolute in the sense of *Bewußtsein* is by definition a liar. Marxist praxis is something like Keirkegaard's decision.

105. [M.-P., marginal note]: history, but as object.

[II. Marx]

1. [Ed.]: All citations of Marx are to the *Marx-Engels-Gesamtausgabe*, book I, vol. 1–2, ed. David Riazanov (Frankfurt: Marx-Engels-Verlag, 1927). [Trans.]: I refer to the English translations in *Karl Marx Frederick Engels: Collected Works* (London: Lawrence and Wishart, 1975). Henceforth cited as *MEGA* and *CW*, with the book (*band*) number of *MEGA* and the volume number of *CW*, and their respective paginations.

2. Marx, *MEGA* I.2, 613; *CW* 3, "Contribution to *Critique of Hegel's Philosophy of Law*: Introduction," 179–80.

3. Marx, *MEGA* I.2, 613; *CW* 3, 180.

4. Marx, *MEGA* I.2, 613; *CW* 3, 181.

5. Marx, *MEGA* I.2, 613; *CW* 3, 181.

6. Marx, *MEGA* I.2, 619; *CW* 3, 186–87.

7. Marx, *MEGA* I.2, 620; *CW* 3, 187.

8. Marx, *MEGA*, I.1, 63ff.; *CW*1, "The Difference between the Democritean and Epicurean Philosophy of Nature," 74ff.

9. Marx, *MEGA* I.1, 63; *CW*1, 84, translation modified.

10. Marx, *MEGA* I.1, 63; *CW*1, 85, translation modified.

11. Marx, *MEGA* I.1, 63; *CW*1, 85.

12. [M.-P.]: A formula for which Marx doesn't give any more information, that is not expressed according to his goal: there is a becoming-philosophy of the world that is reduced to a becoming-world of philosophy, i.e., to its pure and simple destruction (and, without doubt as well, a becoming-world of philosophy that, in truth, is only a becoming-philosophy of the world, i.e., conservation of the system). Marx's aim is not to realize the two slogans as they are: it could be a simple addition of illusions, practice disguised as theory and theory disguised as practice. His aim would be to realize the chiasm of the two movements, the *two in one.*

13. Interpolated by Merleau-Ponty.

14. Marx, *MEGA* I.1, 64–65; *CW*1, 86, translation modified.

15. Marx, *MEGA* I.1, 64–65; *CW*1, 86.

16. Marx, *MEGA* I.1, 65; *CW*1, 86.

17. Marx, *MEGA* I.1, 65; *CW*1, 86.

18. Marx, *MEGA* I.1, 65; *CW*1, 86.

19. Marx, *MEGA* I.1, 65; *CW*1, 86.

20. Marx, *MEGA* I.1, 65; *CW*1, 86.

21. [Trans.]: This is in French in the text, and is apparently Merleau-Ponty's translation. The letter mentioned does not appear in *CW*1.

22. Marx, *MEGA* I.2, 614; *CW*3, 181, translation modified.

23. [Trans.]: This is in French in Marx's text.

24. Marx, *MEGA* I.2, 614; *CW*3, 182.

25. Marx, *MEGA* I.2, 619; *CW*3, 186.

26. Marx, *MEGA* I.2, 619–20; *CW*3, 186.

27. Marx, *MEGA* I.2, 619–20; *CW*3, 186.

28. Marx, *MEGA* I.2, 620; *CW*3, 187.

29. Marx, *MEGA* I.2, 620; *CW*3, 187.

30. [Ed.]: The following notes appear in the margin of the manuscript of the preceding class. Then new notes bear the date of April 24 again.

31. Marx, *CW*3, 187.

32. Marx, *MEGA* I.2, 620; *CW*3, 187.

33. [Ed.]: The texts to which this class refers are translated and commented upon by Merleau-Ponty in what follows.

34. Marx, *CW*3, "Critique of the Hegelian Dialectic and Philosophy as a Whole," in *Economic and Philosophic Manuscripts of 1844*, 340.

35. See Marx, *CW*3, 339.

36. See Marx, *CW*3, 340.

37. See Marx, *CW*3, 328–29.

38. See Marx, *CW*3, 305–306.

39. See Marx, *CW*3, 344–46.

40. See Marx, *CW*3, 341–42.

41. See Marx, *CW* 3, 336.

42. See Marx, *CW* 3, 292–93.

43. See Marx, *CW* 3, 336.

44. Marx, *MEGA* I.3, vol. 3, 165; *CW* 3, "Critique of the Hegelian Dialectic and Philosophy as a Whole," in *Economic and Philosophic Manuscripts of 1844*, 340. [Trans.]: Merleau-Ponty provides his own translation into French. The text here is an amended version of *CW* 3. The bracketed text is interpolated by Merleau-Ponty, who translates *Dasein* as "*être-là*." I have chosen to use the German term *Dasein* to underline Merleau-Ponty's apparent attempt to connect Marx to Heidegger.

45. Marx, *MEGA* I.3, 163–64; *CW* 3, 339. Merleau-Ponty provides his own translation into French. The text here is an amended version of *CW* 3. The bracketed text is interpolated by Merleau-Ponty, with the translation modified to conform to decisions made by him.

46. [M.-P.]: "It goes without saying that the abstract thinker, who has committed himself to intuiting, intuits nature abstractly. Just as nature lay enclosed in the thinker in the form of the absolute idea, in the form of a thought-entity—in a shape which was obscure and enigmatic even to him—so by letting it emerge from himself he has really let emerge only this *abstract nature*, only nature as a *thought entity*—but now with the significance that it is the other-being of thought, it is real, intuited nature—nature distinguished from abstract thought. Or, to talk in human language, the abstract thinker learns in his intuition of nature that the entities which he thought to create from nothing, from pure abstraction—the entities he believed he was producing in the divine dialectic as pure products of the labor of thought, for ever shuttling back and forth in itself and never looking outward into reality—are nothing else but *abstractions* from *charateristics of nature*. To him, therefore, the whole of nature merely repeats the logical abstractions in a sensuous, external form. He once more *resolves* nature into these abstractions. Thus, his intuition of nature is only the act of confirming his abstraction from the intuition of nature—is only the conscious repetition by him of the process of creating his abstraction. Thus, for example, time equals negativity referred to itself. To the becoming overcome as *Dasein* corresponds, in natural form, movement overcome as matter. Light is *reflection-in*-itself, the *natural* form. Body as *moon* and *comet* is the *natural* form of the *antithesis* which according to logic is on the one side the *positive resting on itself*, and on the other side the *negative* resting on itself. The earth is the *natural* form of the logical *ground* [*Grund*], as the negative unity of the antithesis, etc.

Nature as nature—that is to say, insofar as it is still sensuously distinguished from that secret sense hidden within it—nature isolated, distinguished from these abstractions, is *nothing*—a *nothing proving itself to be* nothing—is *devoid of sense*, or has only the sense of being an externality which has to be annulled. . . . *Externality* here is not to be understood as the *world of sense* [*Sinnlichkeit*] which *manifests* itself and is accessible to the light, to a person endowed with senses. It is to be taken here in the sense of alienation [*Entäußerung*], of a mistake, a defect, which ought not to be. Nature is only the *form* of the idea's *other-being*" (Marx, *MEGA* I.3, 170–71; *CW* 3, 345–46. Merleau-Ponty provides his own translation into French. The text here is an amended version of *CW* 3. The bracketed text is interpolated by Merleau-Ponty, with the translation modified to conform to decisions made by him.)

47. György Lukács, *Der Junge Hegel* (Zurich: Europa, 1948), 708. [Trans.]: This is in French in the text, with the German interpolated. Apparently it is Merleau-Ponty's translation.

48. Marx, *MEGA* I.3, 152–53; *CW* 3, 329.

49. Marx, *MEGA* I.3, 152–53; *CW* 3, 329. Merleau-Ponty provides his own translation into French. The text here is an amended version of *CW* 3. The bracketed text is interpolated by Merleau-Ponty, with the translation modified to conform to decisions made by him.

50. Marx, *MEGA* I.3, 115–16, "Private Property and Communism"; *CW* 3, 298. Merleau-Ponty provides his own translation into French. The text here is an amended version of *CW* 3, with the translation modified to conform to decisions made by him.

51. [M.-P., marginal note]: The human being has its sense, its being outside of itself, the relationship of subject-object born in a conscious relationship outside, it is not "pure" activity (*MEGA* I.3, 160) but "objective," heavy.

52. [M.-P., marginal note]: And, at the same time, because it has this instinctive relationship with things, it is "other" for "another" human being.—Crossing relationship to the world-relationship to the other human being.—Intercorporeity.—Chiasm nature-sociality. The human being produces and reproduces society, is produced and reproduced by it, as it produces objects and is produced by objects (Marx, *MEGA* I.3, 115–16).

53. Marx, *MEGA* I.3, 160–61; *CW* 3, 336–37. [Trans]: Merleau-Ponty provides his own translation into French. The text here is an amended version of *CW* 3. The bracketed text is interpolated by Merleau-Ponty, with the translation modified to conform to decisions made by him. [M.-P., marginal note]: "Society is the perfect essential unity of the human being with nature, the true reflection of nature, the naturalism of the human being and the humanization of nature."

54. [M.-P., marginal note]: All of the preceding was still only natural [particularity? (*spécialité?*)], but because the human being is for itself, it is generality, i.e., it interiorizes relationships to the world and to the other, or it projects itself into them, it is the others and they are it.

55. Marx, *MEGA* I.3, 162; *CW* 3, 337. [Trans]: Merleau-Ponty provides his own translation into French. The text here is an amended version of *CW* 3. The bracketed text is interpolated by Merleau-Ponty, with the translation modified to conform to decisions made by him.

56. Marx, *MEGA* I.3, 164; *CW* 3, 339. [Trans]: Merleau-Ponty provides his own translation into French. The text here is an amended version of *CW* 3. The bracketed text is interpolated by Merleau-Ponty, with the translation modified to conform to decisions made by him.

57. The text cited is in German, *MEGA* I.3, 176; *CW* 3, 342, translation modified.

58. Marx, *MEGA* I.3, 166; *CW* 3, 341. [Trans]: Merleau-Ponty provides his own translation into French. The text here is an amended version of *CW* 3.

59. Marx, *MEGA* I.3, 166–67; *CW* 3, 341–42. [Trans]: Merleau-Ponty pro-

vides his own translation into French. The text here is an amended version of *CW* 3.

60. Marx, *MEGA* I.3, 125, "Private Property and Communism"; *CW* 3, 305–306. Merleau-Ponty provides his own translation into French. The text here is an amended version of *CW* III. The bracketed text is interpolated by Merleau-Ponty, with the translation modified to conform to decisions made by him.

61. Marx, *MEGA* I.3, 114; *CW* III, 296–97. Merleau-Ponty provides his own translation into French. The text here is an amended version of *CW* III. The bracketed text is interpolated by Merleau-Ponty, with the translation modified to conform to decisions made by him.

62. Lukács, *Der Junge Hegel*, 708.

63. Lukács, *Der Junge Hegel*, 686.

64. Jean Hyppolite, *Logique et existance* (Paris: Presses Universitaires de France, 1953), 238; translated into English by Leonard Lawlor and Amit Sen as *Logic and Existence* (Albany: SUNY Press, 1997), 182–83.

65. Hyppolite, *Logique et existance*, 238; *Logic and Existence*, 182.

66. Hyppolite, *Logique et existance*, 239; *Logic and Existence*, 183.

Appendixes

Draft of a Chapter from *The Visible and the Invisible*

1. [Ed.]: Bibliothèque Nationale mark: Merleau-Ponty, Box III, 21 pages.

2. [Ed.]: Claude Lefort transcribed the last version (dated November 1960) of this text in *The Visible and the Invisible*. See his "Editorial Note" in that book.

3. [M.-P., marginal note]: Say that there is a second sense to these questions. See *infra*.

4. See Merleau-Ponty, *Le Visible et l'invisible*, 138; *The Visible and the Invisible*, 105, and 121; 159. [Trans.]: The questions refer to a passage from Claudel, *Art-poétique*, 9; *Poetic Art*, 5.

5. [M.-P., marginal note]: "What is knowledge?" and even "what am I?"

6. [Ed.]: The brackets are put there by Merleau-Ponty.

7. [M.-P., marginal note]: all the concepts of consciousness, positives.

8. [M.-P., marginal note]: Critique of psyche to be carried over to §1 of the 2nd Part, in order to introduce the critique of all of our positive conceptions, perception, image, even intentionality.

9. [Trans]: "sans feu ni lieu," literally "without fire or place" but having the sense of "homeless" or "wandering."

10. [M.-P., marginal note]: [Do not keep all this development on Kant. Start immediately from noematic reflection on the pre-constituted, on the reflection of the one who is over the world and Being.]

11. [Trans.]: This is in English in the text.

12. [Trans]: The French text has an opening square bracket here with no corresponding closing bracket.

13. [Trans.]: This is in English in the text.

14. [Ed.]: Merleau-Ponty writes "construct."

15. [Trans.]: Following Alphonso Lingis's rendering of *surréflexion*.

16. [Ed.]: [Pages **120** to **122**, as well as **124** and part of **125**, are crossed out. A note on page **122** is conserved]:

[**122**] To tell the truth, it is already a grave restriction, and the universality of essences already no longer goes without saying. In the *Logische Untersuchungen* ("Prolegomena zur reinen Logik"), if the fiction of an angelic or superhuman thought (limited case of our imaginary variations) does not affect the essential value of our principles of thought, it is that superhuman [beings?], in order to be taken into consideration, should enter into a connection with us, and thus have a language, senses, and a body like we do.

[**123**] It is thus the universal value of essences and their legal basis, intersubjectivity and concrete intercorporeity. However, solitary eidetic vision is this profound intertwining of minds with each other and of all minds with the Nature that is invoked, but the first writings made only allusions.

17. [Trans.]: "*qui fait qu'il y a quelqu'un, en d'autre termes comme Homère le dit magnifiquement, personne, οὔτις*"; "*personne*" can mean either "someone" or "no one," however, the ancient Greek is less ambiguous, and literally means "no one."

18. [Ed.]: The rest of page **127**, page **128**, and part of page **129** are crossed out.

19. [Trans]: The lack of gendered articles in English makes this sentence awkward. Rather than translating "elle" as "it," I've rendered it more literally, translating "elle" as "she."

20. [M.-P., marginal note]: to perceive again: to speak again: to think again, prospection as well as retrospection.

21. [Ed.]: The brackets are Merleau-Ponty's.

22. Paul Valéry, "La Pythie," in *Poesies* (Paris: Gallimard, Nouvelle Revue Française, 1932), 158–59; English translation by James R. Lawler in *Poems: The Collected Works of Paul Valéry, Vol. 1* (Princeton, NJ: Princeton University Press, 1971), 177. See "Cartesian Ontology and Ontology Today," Part I, "Fundamental Thought in Art."

Supplementary Materials for the 1959 Course

1. Husserl, *Krisis*, 338; *Crisis*, 291.

2. [Ed.]: See Merleau-Ponty, *Résumés de cours*, 150; *In Praise of Philosophy*, 175; and Husserl, *Krisis*, 205; *Crisis*, 202.

3. [Trans.]: The French text here follows with a series of quotations, in German, from the *Krisis* cited in the main portion of the lecture (**37**). I substitute the English translation, citing the German pagination followed by the English.

4. Husserl, *Krisis*, 3; *Crisis*, 5.

5. Husserl, *Krisis*, 16; *Crisis*, 18.

6. Husserl, *Krisis*, 137; *Crisis*, 134 (cited on **37**).

7. Husserl, *Krisis*, 114; *Crisis*, 158.

8. Husserl, *Krisis*, 74; *Crisis*, 73.

9. Husserl, *Krisis*, 508; *Crisis*, 389.

10. Husserl, *Krisis*, 512; *Crisis*, 394.

Translation and Commentary on Beilage XXIII of Husserl's
Crisis of the European Sciences

1. [Trans.]: Merleau-Ponty provides his own French translation of Beilage XXIII. This text was included in the version of the *Crisis* published in *Husserliana* but not in the English translation. For the German version, see *Die Krisis der europäischenWissenschaften und die transzendentale Phänomenologie: Eine Einleitung in die phänomenologische Philosophie, Husserliana VI*, ed. Walter Biemel (The Hague: Martinus Nijhoff, 1954), 482–84. This English translation of the text is by Niall Keane, originally published in *Journal of the British Society for Phenomenology* 44, no. 1 (January 2013): 6–9. I have modified the presentation to more closely conform with Merleau-Ponty's own translation by replacing translated German terms with their German original where Merleau-Ponty uses the German and by including Merleau-Ponty's French as needed. I have also inserted Merleau-Ponty's numbering of the paragraphs. I have retained his interpolation of German text in square brackets. The italics and emphasis are found in the French text.

2. [Trans.]: This text is actually presented as a note, though in the French text it appears in the main text with the addition "Note 2." I've followed Merleau-Ponty's presentation.

3. [Trans]: Interpolated by Merleau-Ponty in brackets.

4. [Trans]: Merleau-Ponty omits the following text: "The physicalistic prejudice could only disturb it insofar as the problems and investigations of a physicalist order, which it contains within certain limits, were overestimated and the descriptive element, which is essential to it, was, by many biologists, not given priority. In truth, description is, for biology, the only proper and essential form of work within pure objectivity, and as such it is naively guided by an ontological generality that has not yet been disclosed."

5. [Trans]: The bracketed text is apparently Merleau-Ponty's interpolation.

6. [Trans.]: Merleau-Ponty omits the following text: "It would hence attain the degree of explanation in the sense of an understanding based on ultimate sources of evidence. The 'explanation' of the physicist, on the contrary, 'knows' what it knows of the world in an incomprehensibility that is severed from all true knowledge."

7. [Trans.]: The English translation interpolates the German, *Rückfrage*, "question-back," which Merleau-Ponty renders simply as "*retour aux.*"

8. [Ed.]: See note 10 on page 290.

Supplementary Materials for the 1960–1961 Course

1. These pages are found in the manuscripts between pages **10** (development on painting) and **11** (part on Descartes).

2. Paul Valéry, *"Mon Faust" (Ebauches)* (Paris: Gallimard, 1946).

3. [Trans.]: A reference to "Eye and Mind," which Merleau-Ponty had agreed to write for André Chastel for the first issue of *Art de France.*

Bibliography

Texts Cited by Merleau-Ponty for the
1959 Course and the 1960–1961 Courses

Arnheim, Rudolf. *Art and Visual Perception: A Psychology of the Creative Eye.* London: Faber and Faber, 1956.

Baltrusaitis, Jurgis. *Abberations: Quatres essais sur la sur la légende des forms.* Paris: O. Perrin, 1957.

———. *Anamorphoses ou perspectives curieuses.* Paris: O. Perrin, 1955.

Beaufret, Jean. "Préface" to *Essais et conferences,* by Martin Heidegger. Paris: Gallimard, 1958.

Belaval, Yvon. *Leibniz, initation à sa philosophie.* Paris: Bordas, 1952.

Berenson, Bernard. *Esthétique et histoire des arts visuels.* Paris: Albin Michel, 1953.

Bergson, Henri. *La Pensée et le mouvant.* Paris: Presses Universitaires de France, 1934. Translated into English by Mabelle L. Andison as *The Creative Mind.* Mineola, NY: Dover, 2007.

Bru, Charles. *Esthétique de l'abstraction.* Paris: Presses Universitaires de France, 1955.

Butor, Michel. *La Modification.* Paris: Minuit, 1957.

Chapsal, Madeleine. *Quinze écrivains: Entretiens.* Paris: Julliard, 1963.

———. "Claude Simon." In *Écrivains en personne.* Paris: Union Générale d'Éditions, 1973.

Charbonnier, Georges. *Le Monologue du peintre.* Paris: Julliard, 1959.

Claudel, Paul. *Art poétique.* (1903). Paris: Mercure de France, 1935. Translated into English by Renée Spodheim as *Poetic Art.* New York: Philosophical Library, 1948.

———. *Le Pain dur.* Paris: Gallimard, "Bibliotheque de la Pléiade," vol. II.

———. *Le Soulier de satin.* Paris: Gallimard, 1929. Translated into English by Rev. John O'Connor with the collaboration of the author as *The Satin Slipper.* New Haven, CT: Yale University Press, 1931.

———. *L'Oeil écoute.* Paris: Gallimard, 1946. Translated into English by Elsie Pell as *The Eye Listens.* Port Washington, NY: Kennikat, 1969.

———. *Présence et prophétie.* Freiburg: Freiburg University Library, 1942.

Conrad, Joseph. *Le Nègre du Narcisse.* Translated into French by R. d'Humières. Paris: Mercure de France, 1910. Original English edition, *The Nigger of the "Narcissus."* London: New Review, 1897.

Delaunay, Robert. *Du cubisme à l'art abstrait*. Paris: SEVPEN, 1957. Unpublished documents published by P. Francastel.

Descartes, René. *Oeuvres de Descartes*. Charles Adam and Paul Tannery. Vols. I–V: *Correspondance*; VI: *Discours de la méthode et essais* [*Dioptriques, Météores*, and *Géométrie*]; VII: *Meditationes de prima philosophia*; VIII: *Principia philosophiae, Epistola ad Voetium, Lettre apologétique, Notae in programma*; IX: *Méditations* and *Principes* (French translations); X: *Physico-mathematica, Compendium musicae, Regulae ad directionem ingenii, Recherche de la vérité, Supplément à la correspondence*. Paris: Gallimard, 1953. Translated into English by Cottingham, Stoothoff, and Murdoch as *The Philosophical Writings of Descartes, Vols. I–III*. Cambridge: Cambridge University Press, 1985.

Dorival, Bertrand. "Cézanne par ses lettres et ses témoins." In *Paul Cézanne*. Paris: P. Tisné, 1948.

Gasquet, Joachim. *Cézanne*. Paris: Bernheim-Jeune, 1921.

Giraudoux, Jean. *Églantine*. Paris: Grasset, 1927.

Gueroult, Martial. *Descartes selon l'ordre des raisons. I: L'Âme et Dieu, II: L'Âme et le corps*. Paris: Aubier, 1953.

———. *Malebranche. I: La Vision en Dieu*. Paris: Aubier-Montaigne, 1955.

———. *Principia philosophae cartesianae de Spinoza*. Paris: Archives de Philosophie, 1960.

Gide, André. *Dostoievsky*. Paris: Plon, 1923. Translated into English by Arnold Bennett as *Dostoevsky*. London: Secker and Warburg, 1952.

Grohmann, Will. *Paul Klee*. Translated into French by J. Descoullayes and J. Phillipon. Paris: Flinker, 1954. English edition, *Paul Klee*. New York: Abrams, 1954.

Heidegger, Martin. *Aus der Erfahrung des Denkens*. Pfullingen: G. Neske, 1954. Translated into English by Albert Hofstadter as "The Thinker as Poet," in *Poetry, Language, Thought*, 1–14. New York: Harper Perennial, 1971.

———. "Bauen, Wohnen, Denken." In *Vorträge und Aufsätze*. Pfullingen: G. Neske, 1967. Translated into English by Albert Hofstadter as "Building, Dwelling, Thinking," in *Poetry, Language, Thought*, 141–60. New York: Harper Perennial, 1971.

———. *Der Satz vom Grund*. Pfullingen: G. Neske, 1957. Translated into English by Reginald Lilly as *The Principle of Reason*. Bloomington: Indiana University Press, 1991.

———. *Einführung in die Metaphysik*. Tübingen: Niemeyer, 1952. Translated into English by Gregory Fried and Richard Polt as *Introduction to Metaphysics*. New Haven, CT: Yale University Press, 2000.

———. *Holzwege*. Frankfurt: Klostermann, 1950. Translated into English by Julian Young and Kenneth Haynes as *Off the Beaten Track*. Cambridge: Cambridge University Press, 2002.

———. *Identität und Differenz*. Pfullingen: G. Neske, 1957. Translated into English by Joan Stambaugh as *Identity and Difference*, edited by J. Glenn Gray. New York: Harper and Row, 1969.

———. *Nietzsche*. Pfullingen: G. Neske, 1961. Translated into English by David Farrell Krell as *Nietzsche*. New York: Harper Collins, 1991.

————. *Sein und Zeit*. Tübingen: Niemeyer, 1927. Translated into English by John Macquarrie and Edward Robinson as *Being and Time*. New York: Harper and Row, 1961.

————. *Über den Humanismus*. Frankfurt: Klostermann, 1947. Translated into English by Frank A. Capuzzi as "Letter on Humanism," in *Pathmarks*, edited by William McNeill, 239–76. Cambridge: Cambridge University Press, 1998.

————. *Unterwegs zur Sprache*. Pfullingen: G. Neske, 1959. Translated into English by Peter D. Hertz as *On the Way to Language*. New York: Harper Collins, 1971.

————. *Vom Wesen der Wahrheit*. Frankfurt: Klostermann, 1954. Translated into English by John Sallis as "On the Essence of Truth," in *Pathmarks*, edited by William McNeill, 136–54. Cambridge: Cambridge University Press, 1998.

————. *Vom Wesen des Grundes*. Frankfurt: Klostermann, 1938. Translated into English by William McNeill as "On the Essence of Ground," in *Pathmarks*, edited by William McNeill, 97–135. Cambridge: Cambridge University Press, 1998.

————. *Vorträge und Aufsätze*. Pfullingen: G. Neske, 1954. Translated into French by Jean Beaufret as *Essais et conférences*. Paris: Gallimard, 1958.

————. *Was heißt Denken?* Tübingen: Niemeyer, 1954. Translated into English by J. Glenn Gray as *What Is Called Thinking?* New York: Harper Perennial, 1976.

————. *Was ist Metaphysik?* (1929). Frankfurt: Klostermann, 1949. Translated into English by David Farrell Krell as "What Is Metaphysics?" in *Pathmarks*, edited by William McNeill, 82–96. Cambridge: Cambridge University Press, 1998; "Postcript to 'What Is Metaphysics?'" 231–38; "Introduction to 'What Is Metaphysics?" 277–90.

————. *Zur seinsfrage*. Frankfurt: Klostermann, 1956. Translated into English by William McNeill as "On the Question of Being," in *Pathmarks*, edited by William McNeill, 291–322. Cambridge: Cambridge University Press, 1998.

Husserl, Edmund. *Cartesianische Meditationen* (1929). *Husserliana I*, 1950. Translated into English by Dorion Cairns as *Cartesian Meditations*. The Hague: Martinus Nijhoff, 1960.

————. *Die Krisis der europäischen Wissenschaften und di transzendentale Phänomenologie (1935–1936)*. The Hague: Nijhoff, 1954. Translated into English by David Carr as *The Crisis of the European Sciences and Transcendental Phenomenology*. Evanston, IL: Northwestern University Press, 1970.

————. *Ideen zu einer reinen Phänomenologie und phänomenologischen Philosophie, Ideen I*. The Hague: Nijhoff, 1950. Translated into English by Fred Kersten as *Ideas Pertaining to a Pure Phenomenology and to a Phenomenological Philosophy, First Book: General Introduction to a Pure Phenomenology*. The Hague: Martinus Nijhoff, 1982.

————. *Ideen II*. (1912–28). *Phänomenologische Untersuchungen zur Konstitution*. The Hague: Nijhoff, 1952. Translated into English by Richard Rojcewicz and Andre Shuwer as *Ideas Pertaining to a Pure Phenomenology and to a Phenom-*

enological Philosophy, Second Book: Studies in the Phenomenology of Constitution. Dordrecht: Kluwer, 1989.

———. *Logische Untersuchungen.* Hamburg: Meiner, 1922. Translated into English by J. N. Findlay as *Logical Investigations, vols. I–II.* London: Routledge, 1970.

———. *On the Phenomenology of the Consciousness of Internal Time (1893–1917).* Translated by John Barnett Brough. Dordrecht: Kluwer, 1991.

———. "Umsturz der kopernikanischen Lehre: Die Erde als Ur-Arche bewegt sich nicht." In *Philosophical Essays in Memory of Edmund Husserl,* presented by M. Faber. Cambridge, MA: Harvard University Press, 1940. Translated into English by Leonard Lawlor with Bettina Bergo as "Foundational Investigations of the Phenomenological Origin of the Spatiality of Nature: The Originary Ark, the Earth, Does Not Move," in *Husserl at the Limits of Phenomenology,* 117–31. Evanston, IL: Northwestern University Press, 2002.

———. *Ursprung der Geometrie.* The Hague: Nijhoff, 1954. Translated into English by David Carr as "The Origin of Geometry," in *The Crisis of the European Sciences and Transcendental Phenomenology,* 353–78. Evanston, IL: Northwestern University Press, 1970.

———. "The Vienna Lecture." In *The Crisis of the European Sciences and Transcendental Phenomenology,* translated by David Carr, 269–300. Evanston, IL: Northwestern University Press, 1970.

Hyppolite, Jean. *Genèse et structure de la "Phénoménologie de l'Esprit" de Hegel.* Paris: Aubier-Montaigne, 1947. Translated into English by Samuel Cherniak and John Heckman as *Genesis and Structure of Hegel's Phenomenology of Spirit.* Evanston, IL: Northwestern University Press, 1974.

———. *Logique et existance.* Paris: Presses Universitaires de France, 1953. Translated into English by Leonard Lawlor and Amit Sen as *Logic and Existence.* Albany: SUNY Press, 1997.

Juin, Hubert, and Jean-Clarence Lambert. *Sixteen Painters of the Young School of Paris.* Paris: Arts, Inc., 1958.

Laporte, Jean. *Le Rationalisme de Descartes.* Paris: Presses Universitaires de France, 1945.

Leiris, Michel, and George Limbour. *André Masson et son univers.* Paris: Des Trois Collines, 1947.

Leonardo da Vinci. *Traité sur la peinture.* Edited by André Chastel. Paris: Club de Libraires de France, 1960.

Lukács, György. *Der Junge Hegel.* Zurich: Europa, 1948.

Malraux, André. *La Psychologie de l'art.* Paris: Skira, 1950.

Marx, Karl. *Capital.* Translated into English by Ben Fowkes. New York: Vintage Books, 1977.

———. *The German Ideology.* In *Karl Marx and Frederick Engels: Collected Works,* vol. 5, 19–539. London: Lawrence and Wishart, 1975.

———. *Werke und Schriften bis Anfang 1844.* in *Werke und Schriften bis Anfang 1844,* book I, vol. 3 of *Marx-Engels-Gesamtausgabe,* edited by David Riazanov, 229–346. Berlin: Marx-Engels-Verlag, 1930. Translated into English as *Economic and Philosophic Manuscripts of 1844,* in *Karl Marx and Frederick*

Engels: Collected Works, vol. 3, 229–346. London: Lawrence and Wishart, 1975.

———. *Zur Kritik der Hegelschen Rechtsphilosohie,* in book I, vol. 3 of *Marx-Engels-Gesamtausgabe,* edited by David Riazanov. Frankfurt: Marx-Engels-Verlag, 1930. Translated into English as "Contribution to the Critique of Hegel's *Philosophy of Law*: Introduction," in *Karl Marx and Frederick Engels: Collected Works,* vol. 3, 175–87. London: Lawrence and Wishart, 1975.

Michaux, Henri. "Adventures of Lines," originally the preface to *Paul Klee,* by Will Grohmann (1954). Translated into English by David Ball in *Darkness Moves: An Henri Michaux Anthology, 1927–1984.* Berkeley: University of California Press, 1994.

———. "Un certain phénomène qu'on appelle musique," preface to *Encyclopédie de la musique.* Paris: Fasquelle, 1958.

Nietzsche, Friedrich. *Die fröhliche Wissenschaft.* Berlin: Gruyter & Co., 1886. Translated into English by Walter Kaufmann as *The Gay Science.* New York: Vintage Books, 1974.

Paulhan, Jean. *Les Fleurs de Tarbes.* Paris: Gallimard, 1950.

Proust, Marcel. *Du coté de chez Swann,* II. Paris: Gallimard, Nouvelle Revue Française, 1924. Translated into English by C. K. Scott Moncrieff and Terence Kilmartin and revised by D. J. Enright as *Swann's Way.* New York: Modern Library, 2003.

———. *La Prisonnière.* Paris: Gallimard, Nouvelle Revue Française, 1924. Translated into English by C. K. Scott Moncrieff and Terence Kilmartin and revised by D. J. Enright as *The Captive.* New York: Modern Library, 2003.

———. *Le Temps retrouvé,* XV. Paris: Gallimard, Nouvelle Revue Française, 1924. Translated into English by C. K. Scott Moncrieff and Terence Kilmartin and revised by D. J. Enright as *Time Regained.* New York: Modern Library, 2003.

Revel, Jean-Francois. *Pourquoi des philosophes?* Paris: Julliard, 1957.

Rilke, Rainer-Maria. *Auguste Rodin.* Translated into French by Maurice Betz. Paris: Emile Paul, 1928.

Rimbaud, Arthur. *Oeuvres completes.* Paris: Mercure de France, 1924. Translated into English by Wyatt Mas as *Rimbaud Complete.* New York: Random House, 2002.

Riviére, Jacques. *Nouvelles Études.* Paris: Gallimard, 1947.

Sartre, Jean-Paul. *Critique de la raison dialectique.* Paris: Gallimard, 1960. Translated into English by Alan Sheridan-Smith as *The Critique of Dialectical Reason,* vol 1. New York: Verso, 2004.

———. "Le Peintre sans privileges." *Méditations,* no. 2 (1961). Translated into English by Wade Baskin as "The Unprivileged Painter," in *Essays on Aesthetics,* 132–59. New York: Philosophical Library, 1966.

———. *L'Imaginaire.* Paris: Gallimard, 1948. Translated into English by Jonathan Webber as *The Imaginary.* London: Routledge, 2004.

Schmidt, Georges. *Les Aquarelles de Cézanne.* Translated into French by G. Meister. Basel: Holbein, 1952.

Simon, Claude. *La Corde raide.* Paris: Minuit, 1947.

———. *L'Herbe*. Paris: Minuit, 1958. Translated into English as *The Grass* by Richard Howard. New York: George Braziller, 1960.

———. *La Route des Flandres*. Paris: Minuit, 1960. Translated into English by Richard Howard as *The Flanders Road*. Richmond, UK: John Calder, 1985.

———. *Le Vent: Tentative de restitution d'un retable baroque*. Paris: Minuit, 1957. Translated into English by Richard Howard as *The Wind*. New York: George Braziller, 1959.

Valéry, Paul. *"Mon Faust" (Ebauches)*. Paris: Gallimard, 1946.

———. *Variété*. Paris: Gallimard, 1926.

Wahl, Jean. *Du role de l'idée de l'instant dans la philosophie de Descartes*. Paris: Alcan, 1920.

———. "Simultanéité, peinture et nature." In *Cahiers Paul Claudel, vol. 1*. Paris: Gallimard, 1959.

References from Working Notes to the 1960–1961 Courses

Beaussire, Émile. *Antécédents de l'hégélianisme dans la philosophie française: Dom Deschamps, son systeme et son école d'après un manuscrit et des correspondances inédites du XVIIIth siècle*. Paris: Germer-Baillière, 1865.

Boutroux, Pierre. *L'Imagination et les mathématiques selon Descartes*. Paris: Alcan, 1900.

Chastel, André. *Le Baroque et la mort*. Venice: Actes du Congrès d'Études Humanists, 1954.

Gilson, Étienne. *Index scolastico-cartésien*. Paris: Alcan, 1913.

Gueroult, Martial. *Étendue et psychologie chez Malebranche*. Faculté des Lettres de l'Université de Strasbourg, 1939.

[Ed.]: We found these additional references in the working notes for the 1961 course:

Burger, Jean Daniel. *Saint Augustine*. Neuchatel: La Baconnière, 1948.

Hermès Trismégiste. *Le Pimandre*. Translated into French by G. Gabory. Paris: La Sirène, 1920.

Gilson, Étienne. *Introduction à l'étude de Saint Augustine*. Paris: Vrin, 1929.

Löwith, Karl. "La Conciliation Hégélienne." *Recherches Philosophiques* 5 (1935–36): 101–23.

———. *Von Hegel zu Nietzsche*. Stuttgart: Kohlhammer, 1950.

Marrou, Henri-Irénée. *Saint Augustine et l'augustinisme*. Paris: Seuil, 1955.

———. *Saint Augustine et la fin de la culture antique*. Paris: Bloccard, 1958.

Parrain-Vial, Jeanne. *De l'être musical: Intervention du concept en musique*. Neuchatel: La Baconnière, 1952.

Ronchi, Vasco. *Histoire de la lumière*. Translated into French by J. Taton. Paris: A. Colin, 1956.

Wahl, Jean. *"Diurne et Nocture."* *Deucalion* 4 (1949).

[Ed]: Bibliographical notes for the 1958-1959 course as initially planned and announced in the Collège de France catalogue:

Faber, Marvin. *Philosophical Essays in Memory of Edmund Husserl*. Cambridge, MA: Harvard University Press, 1940. [Trans.]: This text would have included the famous "Ur-Arch" essay.

Festschrift, Edmund Husserl Zum 70, Geburtstag Gewidmet Ergänzungsband zum Jahrbuch Für philosophie und phänomenologische Forschung. The Hague: Niemeyer, 1929.

Heidegger, Martin. *Anteile, Zum 60 Geburstag*. Frankfurt: Klostermann, 1950.

Lavelle, Louis. *Introduction à l'ontologie*. Paris: Presses Universitaires de France, 1951.

Marcel, Gabriel. *Le Mystère de l'être, II: Foi et réalité*. Paris: Aubier, 1951.

Simpson, George Gaylord. *L'Évolution et sa signification*. Translated into French by A. Ungar-Levillain and F. Bourliere. Paris: Payot, 1951.

———. *Rythme et modalités de l'évolution*. Translated into French by P. de Saint-Seine. Paris: Albin Michel, 1950.

Varet, Gilbert. *L'Ontologie de Sartre*. Paris: Presses Universitaires de France, 1948.

Index